CONTENTS

ABBREVIATIONS

ADA	Anti-Dumping Agreement
ADB	Asian Development Bank
AFAS	ASEAN Framework Agreement on Services
AfDB	African Development Bank
AIIB	Asian Infrastructure Investment Bank
ASEAN	Association of Southeast Asian Nations
ATCA	Alien Tort Claims Act
BCE	Before the Common Era
BIT	Bilateral Investment Treaty
BOT	Build Operate Transfer Agreement
BRIC	Brazil, Russia, India and China
CAO	Compliance Advisor Ombudsman
CE	Common Era
CETA	Comprehensive Economic and Trade Agreement
CFF	Compensatory Financing Facility
CFIUS	Committee on Foreign Investment in the US
CIFA	Cooperation and Facilitation Agreement
CJEU	Court of Justice of the European Union
CMI	Chiang Mai Initiative
CORE	Canadian Ombudsman for Responsible Enterprise
CPTPP	Comprehensive Progressive Trans Pacific Partnership
CRP	Compliance Review Panel
CSR	Corporate Social Responsibility
CU	Customs Union
DSB	Dispute Settlement Body
DSU	Dispute Settlement Understanding
EBRD	European Bank for Reconstruction and Development
ECHR	European Convention on Human Rights
ECT	Energy Charter Treaty
ECtHR	European Court of Human Rights
EFF	Extended Fund Facility
EIA	Environmental Impact Assessment
EPG	G20 Eminent Persons Group on Global Financial Governance
ERPD	Economic Review and Policy Dialogue
FCPA	Foreign Corrupt Practices Act
FDI	Foreign Direct Investment
FET	Fair and Equitable Treatment
FIRRMA	Foreign Investment Risk Review Modernization Act
FPS	Full Protection and Security
FTA	Free Trade Agreement

FOUNDATIONS OF INTERNATIONAL ECONOMIC LAW

This book is dedicated to my mother
for helping me with the editing of this book,
and for one or two other things.

FOUNDATIONS OF INTERNATIONAL ECONOMIC LAW

DAVID COLLINS

The City Law School, City, University of London, UK

EE Edward Elgar
PUBLISHING

Cheltenham, UK · Northampton, MA, USA

Published by
Edward Elgar Publishing Limited
The Lypiatts
15 Lansdown Road
Cheltenham
Glos GL50 2JA
UK

Edward Elgar Publishing, Inc.
William Pratt House
9 Dewey Court
Northampton
Massachusetts 01060
USA

A catalogue record for this book
is available from the British Library

Library of Congress Control Number: 2019951633

ISBN 978 1 78897 568 1 (cased)
ISBN 978 1 78897 570 4 (paperback)
ISBN 978 1 78897 569 8 (eBook)

Printed and bound in Great Britain by TJ International Ltd, Padstow

GATS	General Agreement on Trade in Services
GATT	General Agreement on Tariffs and Trade
GDP	Gross Domestic Product
GI	Geographical Indication
GMO	Genetically Modified Organism
GPA	Government Procurement Agreement
GSP	Generalized System of Preferences
HDI	Human Development Index
IADB	Inter-American Development Bank
IBRD	International Bank for Reconstruction and Development
ICJ	International Court of Justice
ICS	Investment Court System
ICSID	International Centre for the Settlement of Investment Disputes
IDA	International Development Association
IED	Independent Evaluation Department
IFC	International Finance Corporation
IFSWF	International Forum of Sovereign Wealth Funds
IIA	International Investment Agreement
IMF	International Monetary Fund
IRM	Independent Review Mechanism
ISDS	Investor State Dispute Settlement
ITA	Information Technology Agreement
JEPA	EU–Japan Economic Partnership Agreement
MERCOSUR	Southern Common Market
MFN	Most Favoured Nation
MIA	Multilateral Investment Agreement
MIC	Multilateral Investment Court
MICI	Independent Consultation and Investigation Mechanism
MIGA	Multilateral Investment Guarantee Agency
MRA	Mutual Recognition Agreement
NAFTA	North American Free Trade Agreement
NCP	National Contact Point
NDB	New Development Bank
OECD	Organization for Economic Cooperation and Development
OVE	Office of Evaluation and Oversight
PEF	Pandemic Emergency Financing Facility
PITAD	PluriCourts Investment Treaty Arbitration Database
PRGF	Poverty Reduction and Growth Facility
PSNR	Permanent Sovereignty over Natural Resources
RCEP	Regional Comprehensive Economic Partnership
ROO	Rules Of Origin
RTA	Regional Trade Agreement

SAF	Structural Adjustment Facility
SCM	Agreement on Subsidies and Countervailing Measures
SDR	Special Drawing Right
SPF	Special Project Facilitator
SRF	Supplemental Reserve Facility
SWF	Sovereign Wealth Funds
TBT	Agreement on Technical Barriers to Trade
TiSA	Trade in Services Agreement
TRIMs	Agreement on Trade Related Investment Measures
TRIPS	Agreement on Trade Related Aspects of Intellectual Property
TTIP	Transatlantic Trade and Investment Partnership
UN	United Nations
UNCTAD	United Nations Conference on Trade and Development
USMCA	United States Mexico Canada Agreement
USSC	United States Supreme Court
VCLT	Vienna Convention on the Law of Treaties
WHO	World Health Organization
WTO	World Trade Organization

1

Introduction: historic context and rationales for international trade, foreign direct investment, monetary relations and development

1. INTRODUCTION: GLOBALIZATION AND INTERNATIONAL LAW

The depth and complexity of the interconnectedness of people and societies around the world today is almost beyond comprehension. It is no understatement that the consequences of globalization are now so well entrenched in the daily lives of most people that it is misguided to frame economic issues in terms of the nation state, much as the boundaries between countries are imaginary lines on maps rather than natural features of topography. In the twenty-first century there is no longer any such thing as a national economy or domestic banking. Likewise, few successful companies, other than highly localized services, have business models focused entirely on serving home markets. Discerning consumers have come to expect coffee from Ethiopia, bananas from Peru, washing machines from Korea and law professors from Canada. While the pace of globalization may have slowed in recent years, it is still continuing, and there is unlikely to be a reversal any time soon.

Since virtually all economic activity has become international, the legal problems which arise in the delivery of once exotic goods and services on demand require internationally focused solutions. With so many aspects of the modern economy dictated by rules drafted from above at the international or supranational level, there are few spheres of economic interactions between people, businesses or states which are governed exclusively by domestically constituted laws. As it expands its reach, international law is no longer what might be considered a niche area. Familiarity with international law has instead become nearly essential to most kinds of business advice. Commercial lawyers are well advised to pursue this field of study in some capacity or else risk being left behind.

With international law growing in tandem with the global economy, the erosion of nationalism in lawmaking inevitably means that some degree of regulatory control is surrendered by the nation state to the international arena. This transformation, lamented by some while praised by others, means that much of the activity of government, as it has been conventionally understood in terms of the legislative, executive and judicial branches of the state, has been taken up by global institutions. This phenomenon may be expressed in the anxieties of national legislators who see their role in the lawmaking process diminishing. What might be termed a new form of global governance demands a delicate balance of international obligations designed to support the functioning of the global economy while retaining a degree of autonomy over matters which can conflict with the objective of satisfying customers' material needs and wants, such as the protection of the environment, human rights, and perhaps even the functioning of democracy itself. The benefits of globalization, in the form of a greater variety of affordable products, services and experiences, cannot be taken for granted because protectionist tendencies, mistakenly aimed at furthering the interests of the nation state or influential elements within it, have a tendency to reappear at the moments when progress either falters generally or is enjoyed unequally. Meanwhile liberalization, responsible for much of the wealth enjoyed by the modern world, is in danger of over-extension, threatening to exacerbate entrenched tension between the world's rich and poor. International economic law is the system of global rules which was designed to attempt to resolve these issues. In order to appreciate the significance of these statements it is useful to consider the history of global commerce, which has brought us to where we are today.

2.   A BRIEF HISTORY OF GLOBAL COMMERCE

Commerce is almost as old as civilization itself. One of the consequences of the Agricultural Revolution of 10,000 years ago was that communities were able to amass a surplus of food which they could store for later consumption; then, as people travelled between early settlements, they were able to exchange these surplus goods for different ones produced by other peoples. With improvements in agriculture and in the fabrication of handmade tools and other artefacts, early people realized that trade was less exhausting than conquest, and in the long run was more dependable. For example, archaeological evidence has revealed that there was already a flourishing jewellery trade in Mesopotamia in 3000 BCE. This process of bartering was facilitated by the creation of money – stores of value which allowed for transactions that could be delayed (selling crops produced the next month) rather than being instantaneous. Serving this purpose, the first coins were believed to have originated in Turkey around 600 BCE. As trade between different peoples became normalized, trading routes were established between the cities of the Ancient World. These later became roads. The most famous of these was the Great Silk Road which crossed Asia, linking the Far East to the Roman Empire, and through which valuable spices found their way into Europe.

The point at which trade became investment is a matter which is of less concern to archaeologists, because in reality they are merely different varieties of the same phenomenon – commercial activity. But for the purposes of modern international economic law the distinction is crucial. Traders became investors when, instead of exchanging goods, they established a permanent base, or outpost, outside their home territory. By this definition the Phoenicians were among the first investors. Having traded goods such as wood and dye on ships around the eastern Mediterranean around 1000 BCE, these peoples established settlements on the coast of Africa and the Middle East, on some occasions causing conflict with indigenous peoples. These outposts, the largest of which was probably Carthage, later became significant cities where goods like tools and weapons could be manufactured and sold. The Phoenicians also brought language with them to these other places. The Phoenician alphabet is the basis of the alphabet still in use today across Western civilization.[1] Cities such as Byzantium (becoming Istanbul in modern Turkey) and Samarkand (of which there are archaeological remains in modern Uzbekistan) grew up as settlements for traders on the Silk Road.

Centuries later, international trade was dominated by sailing ships delivering cargo from around the world across the ocean back to the advancing societies in Europe. The Portuguese explorer Vasco da Gama was a pioneer of the spice trade between Europe and India at the end of the fifteenth century. In addition to human curiosity, commerce of this nature was one of the drivers of the Age of Exploration by seafarers such as Zheng He, Columbus, Magellan and Cook. Sea trade in this period was also a form of international investment. Financing of a ship's expedition overseas, in some cases lasting years, was often a high risk enterprise which was beyond the resources of one individual. Modern banking, which began in Italy during the Renaissance and quickly spread across Europe, allowed investors to pool their resources to finance overseas trading enterprises. Joint stock companies became corporations and, as the known world expanded, so did opportunities for international trade and investment. The Dutch East India Company, thought to be the world's first multinational enterprise that was formally listed on a stock exchange, was established in the early seventeenth century to engage in spice trade in the Far East, travelling around the Horn of Africa. Similar businesses followed, including Hudson's Bay Company, which was established by Royal Charter in England to explore what later became Canada. This multinational engaged in fur trade for more than a century and played a key role in establishing the original British settlements in this part of the world. One group of British settlements on the Atlantic's western shore in the seventeenth century went on to become the most powerful nation in the world, and home to what became the world's largest corporations.[2]

When European traders and investors visited Africa, Asia and other places rich in products which were in demand back home, it was normally held that the local law did not apply to them because they were already subject to the law of their home country. This position was supported by the writings of some of the first scholars of international law.[3] A person's law was treated as if it were any other piece of baggage which they carried. This meant that although they were not bound to observe local customs, they could not rely on these laws for their protection in the event that they were harmed physically, their possessions were taken or a promise to buy or sell something was not honoured. Early treaties from this period between European powers and Asian and African colonies stated that Europeans remained under the jurisdiction of their home states. It is no surprise that eventually foreigners, whether in foreign lands temporarily as traders or semi-permanently as settling investors, sought special treatment, superior to that which was available to

---

[1] D Abulafia, *The Great Sea* (Oxford University Press, 2011).

[2] W Bernstein, A Splendid Exchange: *How Trade Shaped the World* (Atlantic Books, 2009).

[3] E.g. E de Vattel, *The Law of Nations* (ed J Chitty, 1852).

normal citizens back home. This was often enshrined in the laws of their home country to protect themselves and their assets while on dangerous journeys. Offences committed against them, or which they might commit, would be resolved by reference to the courts of the relevant European nation, extending this treatment as needed. It was understood during the Early Modern period that no state could seize the assets of a foreigner, and further, that they could not invoke their own local laws to avoid their international obligations.[4] This rule was backed up by the threat of military intervention, sometimes referred to as 'gunboat diplomacy'. Eventually an international minimum standard of treatment of aliens came into existence, which remains a key aspect of customary international law today, although its precise content is still contested.

As the colonies began to gain independence into the eighteenth and nineteenth centuries, they began to challenge the notion that foreigners were not subject to local laws. Relying on nascent concepts of sovereignty and sovereign equality, these territories claimed that they were entitled to expropriate the assets of foreigners if the situation so required it and that foreigners were not entitled to greater protection under their home laws than was available under local law. This view was tempered by the widely held view that local laws could only be enforceable if they fulfilled the international minimum standard of treatment, and that if they did not, they needed to be brought up to this standard – although the specific content of that standard was unknown. This understanding helped contribute to the continued expansion of international commerce throughout the period.

Indeed, while economic globalization is often thought of as a recent phenomenon, global commerce was quite vibrant until the early twentieth century. Mercantilist theories based on the imposition of protectionist tariffs to restrict imports, especially of manufactured goods, along with the hoarding of gold reserves (rather than spending them on business activities), had generally failed in practice in Britain, France and Germany throughout the sixteenth and eighteenth centuries. Belief in the effectiveness of mercantilist, isolationist policies began to fade as the writings of Adam Smith, who advocated liberalization of the economy rather than protectionism, and David Riccardo (of whom more below) took hold and the Industrial Revolution unlocked the transformative potential of the mass production of goods which could be consumed in larger quantities – raising the standard of living – and also traded overseas. Britain's repeal of the Corn Laws in the mid-nineteenth century, eliminating tariffs on imports of grain, demonstrated the political will behind free trade. The herculean efforts expended on the building of the Suez (1869) and Panama (1914) Canals are perhaps the greatest testimony of the unshaken belief in the benefits of international markets held during this period of history.

Liberalization and economic globalization suffered a series of setbacks in the early twentieth century. Having previously embraced international trade and investment, the European powers went to war in 1914, resulting in 20 million deaths and economic ruin across the continent. Perhaps even more damaging in terms of its lasting impact, the Russian Revolution of 1917 laid the foundations for the widescale embrace of communism as a system of economic governance. Based on the writings of German philosopher Karl Marx, control of all productive resources in Russia was taken over by the state, now under the rule of Vladimir Lenin. The economic ideology premised on the abolishment of private property was directly responsible for mass poverty and famine

---

[4] S Subedi, *International Investment Law: Reconciling Policy and Principle* (Hart, 2016).

across what became the Soviet Union and in other places where free markets were abandoned, notably China under Mao Zedong. The experiment with communism led to decades of economic stagnation across much of the world. In the few places where it retains a foothold today, as in North Korea and Venezuela, it continues to inflict suffering on broad segments of society. While some still cannot accept it, often motivated by some of the failings of unrestrained markets, communism has failed spectacularly as a system of government wherever it has been tried.

On the other side of the Iron Curtain, where free market liberalism and international trade remained popular, the aftermath of the First World War ultimately led to a period of sustained prosperity and wealth. At least in the West, the 'Roaring 20s' are often associated with carefree excess – a golden age of wealth and good living, fuelled in part by international trade and a taste for the exotic just as knowledge of the wider world was spread by photography, the telephone and improvements in sea and rail travel. But it did not last long. Already by the mid-1920s, the US enacted a series of protectionist tariffs on a range of products with the aim of protecting farms and factories from international competition. Unsurprisingly, the country's trade allies retaliated with their own tariffs, raising prices on both sides of the Atlantic. The problem was exacerbated by a drought in the US Midwest, leading to poor crop yields and even higher prices on many commodities. Then finally, in 1929, the US stock market crashed and instantaneously the rich became poor. This sudden development, which had been brewing for months if not years, reflected the reality that much of the wealth that had ostensibly accumulated in the latter part of the decade had been an illusion. By 1932 world gross domestic product (GDP) had fallen by 15 per cent, and employment dropped in some places by as much as 30 per cent. The US, and to a lesser extent Europe, had descended into the Great Depression, a period of prolonged economic stagnation that left millions in poverty.

Desperate to deal with the crisis, the US and Europe sought to stimulate the economy by imposing more tariffs on a range of traded goods. This was the worst strategy that could have been undertaken. The US Smoot–Hawley Tariff Act, enacted in 1930, led to an almost total collapse in global trade. Retaliatory tariffs were imposed by other countries and food became unaffordable or unavailable. The UK abandoned the gold standard under which it had exchanged pound sterling notes for gold because it no longer held sufficient gold reserves. Other countries, who had also spent their gold or had been forced to print more money, followed suit, and widespread inflation soon followed. Currency controls were put in place, making it impossible for businesses to engage in international commercial transactions or to engage in foreign investment. As the 1930s drew to a close the predictions of British economist John Maynard Keynes came true and the punishing conditions placed on Germany after the First World War culminated in the Second World War, with Germany having fought through its recession through military expansion. Leaving 80 million dead and cities across the world in rubble, the Second World War was even worse than its predecessor, but, strangely, it ended the Great Depression by generating economic activity in the form of the widespread military effort – an economic strategy of demand-led recovery that Keynes had also foreseen. Reeling from the devastation of two world wars separated by a period of horrendous poverty, the nascent global community realized that a unified approach was badly needed to prevent these awful events from happening again. Catastrophes, whether war or recession, were no longer thought as British, French or American, but as global issues which required globally minded solutions.

In July 1944, representatives of the world's leading economies met at a hotel resort in Bretton Woods, New Hampshire, US, to create the world's first system of global economic management. In many respects the chief architect of the initiative was Keynes, along with Dexter White of the US Treasury – both envisaged the need for cooperation in trade and monetary relations in particular, as well as in relation to assistance with recovery from wars. The Bretton Woods system, as it is often known, led to the establishment of the three central pillars of global economic governance that exist today and which will be explored throughout this book: the General Agreement on Tariffs and Trade (the GATT), which later became the World Trade Organization; the International Monetary Fund (the IMF); and the International Bank for Reconstruction and Development (the World Bank). The GATT was designed to prevent the imposition of tariffs, which were understood to lead to an escalation of prices as well as tension between countries. The IMF would ensure that there would be a ready supply of money to prevent recessions and that currency would remain freely exchangeable to facilitate global commerce. The World Bank would assist countries damaged by war, or which needed money to enable them to take part in the global economy.

The United Nations (UN), which came into existence a year later in 1945, undertook the primary responsibility for maintaining peace and security as well as peaceful relations among the world's countries. Although an earlier similar initiative, the League of Nations, failed in the 1920s, the UN quickly grew in prominence, securing membership not just across the world's powerful developed countries but also in the developing world. Premised on a one nation, one vote decision-making approach which fulfilled the doctrine of sovereign equality of states, the UN established itself as a staunch defender of the interests of the developing world, which held a numerical majority in its General Assembly. This technique of governance had significant consequences for international investment law in particular. The UN Declaration on Permanent Sovereignty over Natural Resources (PSNR)[5] of 1962 established the principle of international law that states retained the right to do as they wished with the natural resources within their territory. This led to a number of former colonies declaring independence. More importantly for international investment, one of the main purposes of the PSNR was to allow states to negotiate their way out of their old agreements to ensure that their natural resources, such as oil fields or mines, would be used in a manner that served their own needs. Crucially, however, the PSNR still required states to pay full compensation for expropriation of the assets of foreign investors. Through this instrument the UN's General Assembly attempted to strike a balance between the interests of home and host countries of foreign investors, a goal which is still arguably pursued today through the initiatives of bodies such as UNCTAD (United Nations Conference on Trade and Development).

The PSNR is widely believed to have operated as a catalyst for a series of expropriations that took place across the developed world in the ensuing decades. This movement was further prompted by the oil crisis of the 1970s, which led a number of countries in North Africa and the Middle East to regret the terms of their earlier oil concession agreements with Western companies after the value of oil skyrocketed almost overnight. Foreign companies located in the newly independent states that had begun to flex their muscles with the UN's blessing began to become justifiably nervous about sinking their resources into countries which might seize them unexpectedly, even if

---

[5] Resolution 1803 (XVII) (14 December 1962).

compensation was owed by law. This resulted in the conclusion of modern treaties between home and host states designed to underline the importance of safeguarding the interests of foreign investors against arbitrary intrusions by host states, coupled with the promise to pay the genuine full market value of the compensation.

By the late 1980s the world had begun to change again, and this time it was among the most dramatic changes in modern history. Laissez faire economics, espoused originally by Adam Smith centuries earlier, began to take hold once again across the industrialized world, featuring in the policies of many prominent world leaders of the time, notably Ronald Reagan in the US and Margaret Thatcher in the UK. The writings of economists such as Milton Friedman and Friedrich Hayek advocated the embrace of liberalism as a strategy to unleash economic progress and improve standards of living. This could be practised domestically in terms of lower taxes, smaller government and competitive markets, but also internationally in terms of open policies with respect to trade, investment and currency exchange. Small city-states such as Hong Kong and later Singapore demonstrated how this approach worked in practice. Possessing almost no natural resources, these hyperliberalized hubs of trade and investment became among the richest regions of the world in the space of a few short years. The final nail in the coffin of the earlier twentieth century's flirtation with protectionism was as much a political one as an economic one. Beginning in the late 1980s, communism collapsed in the Soviet Union. In November 1989, the Berlin Wall, established to separate the Soviet-controlled communist East Germany and the Western-controlled capitalist West Germany after the Second World War, came thundering down. This moment symbolized not only the reunification of Germany, but also, at least as it appeared at the time, the final triumph of capitalism as a system of governance. Market liberalism, and with it free trade and investment, had taken centre stage as the ordering worldview. With the creation of the WTO a few years later, bringing into its ambit incredibly communist China in 2001 and former communist Russia in 2012, economic globalization continued at a rapid pace. Propelled by the internet, satellite telecommunications and air travel for the masses, international commerce of the early twenty-first century went into overdrive. The economic crisis of 2009–10 was viewed by many as an unmasking of the dangers of unfettered capitalism, where large financial institutions were permitted to operate beyond the scrutiny of weak regulators, putting the financial lives of many millions in jeopardy just as some CEOs became multimillionaires. To others, the economic crisis was a mere setback on the gilded path to continued prosperity that began with the barter-based societies of the ancient world.

Recent years have seen much resistance to this trend, which many, especially in academia, pejoratively term 'neoliberalism'. Neoliberalism itself had become a highly fashionable concept – it described the trends of liberalization discussed above (especially in relation to trade, if not investment, monetary relations or development), but contemptuously, as if these policies had gone too far and the ensuing free-for-all had resulted in economic, not to mention social, devastation. To be sure, there may be some truth to these accusations, both in theory (markets do fail, often because of imperfect information or irrational behaviour) and in reality (inequality has increased in some parts of the world, much as some large corporations have managed to avoid paying what might be considered their fair share of taxes). Neoliberalism, or market fundamentalism, represents what many believe to be an extreme version of the laudable policies originally conceived at Bretton

Woods. It is a perversion of the desire to eliminate unnecessary barriers to trade through which the relentless forces of capitalism have been unleashed on a fragile world, as seen for example in climate change – of which there are evidently unlimited causes – coupled with political transformations in various parts of the world which were founded on the resentment of globalization and the elites who have profited from it. The financial crisis of 2008–9 and its aftermath led many commentators to speak of the end of neoliberalism, if not quite the end of globalization, with thinly disguised pleasure. The bankruptcy of leading financial services companies in the US and elsewhere, along with the collapse of the housing market in many parts of the developed world, were touted as the clearest evidence that unfettered markets do not work. Not only were the IMF (and to a lesser degree the WTO) wrong in principle about the value of economic liberalization, they failed to anticipate their error or to correct it in time.

It is not difficult to be drawn to the logic of this claim – indeed, it made perfect sense to many well-informed people, including voters. If global financial markets and free trade do not work, if they are causing financial crises and mass unemployment, especially in the manufacturing sector, then protectionism must be the correct strategy. Here were laid the foundations for the antiglo-

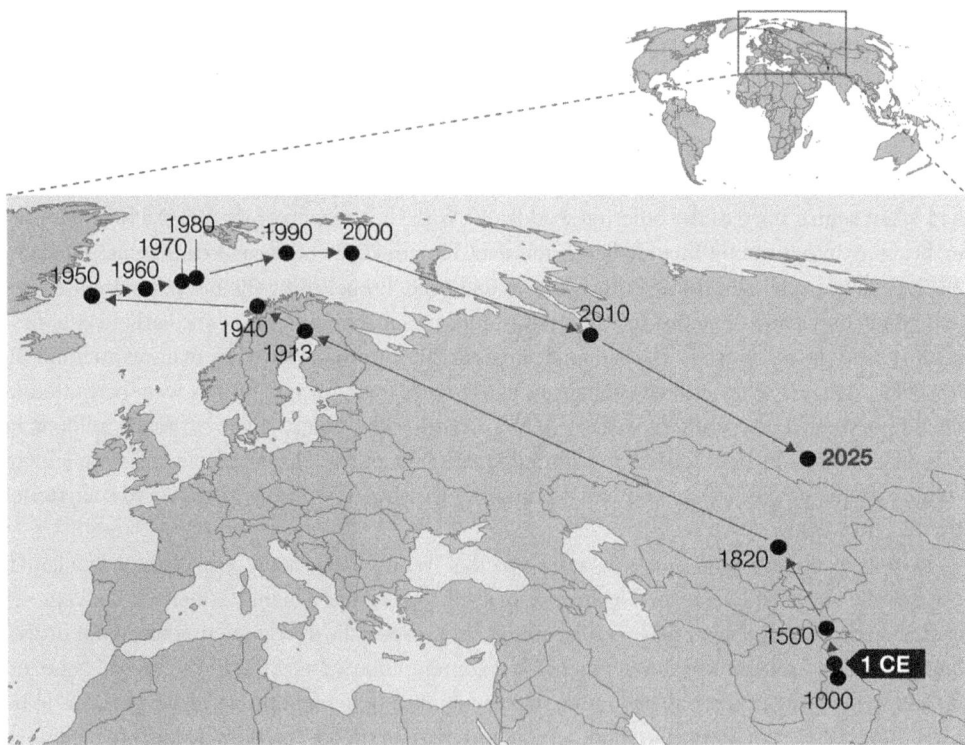

Figure 1.1 The evolution of the Earth's economic centre of gravity (1 CE–2025)

balist political campaigns in the US (resulting in the election of noted free trade sceptic Donald Trump as president) and perhaps relatedly, although perhaps not, the UK electorate's decision in 2016 to leave the EU. Very much embodying a backlash against neoliberalism and/or globalization, recent years have seen a rise of trade protectionism. In 2018 the WTO reported declines in global trade due mostly to an increase in legal barriers around the world.[6] Modern investment treaties are much more cautious than their predecessors, and the IMF has countenanced capital controls as a means of safeguarding against economic crises. Whether these trends in the global economy are actually evidence of protectionism is highly questionable and it is hard to resist the temptation to characterize our age as one which has rejected the globalism which was so warmly embraced at the millennium, even though this is hardly accurate – we have always been wary of too much foreign influence in our lives. Declines in global trade flows are just as likely to be the result of a slowdown in China's domestic economy (the so-called new normal of the Chinese miracle reaching equilibrium). Manufacturing unemployment owes more to automation than to the removal of tariffs.[7] The high price of energy has also hurt manufacturing in many developed countries seeking to reduce carbon emissions. Foreign investors have shown themselves to be as good, if not better, custodians of the environment and of human rights than their domestic equivalents. Climate change is at least in part due to natural cycles.

One of the modern preoccupations with many developed countries is the recognition that, relative to Asia, the West is in decline. Having enjoyed a period of unprecedented growth and wealth generation, the US and Europe have an ever decreasing share of global GDP. This is the consequence of economic globalization, which has seen the rise of China and other emerging markets such as India and Brazil in a surprisingly short timeframe. This view suffers from a short term perspective, however, given that the US, as the world's largest economy, was actually a latecomer to economic progress when set against the history of the world and human civilization. This phenomenon is memorably captured in Figure 1.1, which depicts the evolution of the Earth's 'Economic Centre of Gravity'.

The geographic centre of every country in the modern world (for example, the precise centre of the UK is near Coventry, the centre of the contiguous US is in South Dakota, Australia's is just south of Alice Springs) is mapped against the GDP data for that country. These data points are aggregated to show the point on the surface of the Earth where economic activity is centred at a given time. At 1 CE this point was in what is today northern Pakistan, illustrating the fact that wealth-producing civilization at that time was largely concentrated in the Middle East, with some scattered throughout Asia and the Far East. From that time to 1000 and then 1500 CE, the dot barely moved, demonstrating that there was very little change in the distribution of economic activity for more than a thousand years. As the Industrial Revolution unfolded in Western Europe, the dot crept in a north-westerly direction through Turkmenistan and Uzbekistan and into Kazakhstan. From 1820 to 1913 the Earth's centre of economic gravity moved rapidly across Russia, settling in Northern Sweden. This shift represents the industrialization underway in the UK and Northern Europe, as well as the dramatic growth of the US during the nineteenth century, having escaped

---

[6] World Trade Report 2018, World Trade Organization (Geneva, Switzerland, 2018).

[7] B Lindsey, 'Job Losses and Trade: A Reality Check' Cato (17 March 2004).

from the shackles of colonialism. But it is also due to the relative decline of other regions, including the Middle East, where civilization began, and the Far East, where China was in the midst of its centuries-long period of isolationism. From there the centre of gravity moved slowly but steadily westward across the Atlantic Ocean, in tandem with the rise of the US as the world's preeminent global power. The furthest west the centre of gravity ever reached is a point north of Iceland in the middle of the twentieth century, after which time it began to drift back towards Europe. Veering slightly northward as it slid eastward in response to Japan's ascendency in the 1970s and 1980s, along with the drastic population increase throughout Asia, the dot picked up pace as it passed through the Arctic Ocean on its way back into Russia. It sped up into the twenty-first century and started to drift southward, revealing the remarkable return of China to the global stage, with its unprecedented levels of sustained growth, transforming from a predominately agrarian economy into the world's manufacturing powerhouse. The chart predicts that the centre of gravity will move southward and eastward yet further, as other Asian economies, such as Vietnam and Thailand, undergo similar economic transitions, just as Europe and the US languish in periods of prolonged stagnation.

It may come as a surprise to many in the West to discover that China has already been a major player in the global economy. In the early nineteenth century China accounted for a far larger percentage of global GDP than the US. The same is true of India, which many people living today have always thought of as a place which needs to catch up with the West. However, both of these Asian giants actually shrank in size throughout the second half of the nineteenth century and continued the slide until the very end of the twentieth century. The meteoric rise of the US did not take place until the latter part of the nineteenth century, peaking in terms of its percentage of global GDP in the 1950s, when it literally ran the world. So the Asian miracle of the twenty-first century, especially China and its sustained near double digit GDP growth, more accurately represents Return of the Dragon rather than Enter the Dragon. It is accordingly a cause of some concern to the rest of the world that China, which joined the WTO in 2001, appears to be entering a period of slowed growth. This could have serious repercussions for the volume of both global trade and investment.

Having provided a brief summary of the history of global commerce as context, the main topic of this book will now be introduced.

3. THE DISCIPLINE OF INTERNATIONAL ECONOMIC LAW

As a field of study, international economic law sits at the intersection of public and private international law. It is part of public international law foremost because it deals with the legal relationship between states, meaning nations organized under one government, sometimes composed of subregional political units with autonomy in other aspects of society, as in the 50 US states or the 47 prefectures of Japan. Public international law also covers the interactions between states and non-states, including bodies such as international organizations (such as the IMF) and multinational enterprises such as Google or Toyota. International economic law is also a kind of private international law because it engages with the legal issues facing private entities, mostly multinational enterprises – especially in the sphere of international investment law, where these actors are granted direct rights under treaties which they can contest in international tribunals. International economic law is further private in that it consists of laws which affect commercial issues that have an international dimension – again, trade and investment in their varied forms. International economic law is also, of course, economic law, which means that it is focused on laws which underlie the functioning of international markets, in other words the laws which regulate how goods and services are bought and sold across the world and the money which is used to buy them is supplied. Increasingly, at least as an academic discipline, international economic law concerns global governance, by which is meant the rules which are internal to the global organizations that play a significant role in economic matters, such as the WTO. International economic law tends to serve the interests of liberalization but not, contrary to popular perception, deregulation. It is a field of law governing excessive legal barriers to international economic activity, not the regulation of international economic activity *per se*. Far from eliminating laws, economic relations *rely* on them. Much as money has no value unless it is agreed, you cannot have a functioning market without rule of law to protect property rights and to enforce contractual promises.

It is important also to outline what international economic law does not encompass. First, it does not normally include taxation. While the international rules of taxation are unquestionably critical to global commerce, especially international investment law, there is no global regime governing taxation, nor do free trade agreements cover taxation. Taxation is a highly specialized field which is dealt with by bespoke bilateral treaties. Second, the discipline of international economic law tends not to deal with competition (also known as antitrust) law. Again, since there is no global regime covering competition law – it is resolved by national laws specific to each country – it is difficult to speak of international law in this area. Modern bilateral or regional trade treaties often do contain material on competition policy, but these rules tend merely to require parties to maintain domestic competition laws along with relevant investigation and enforcement agencies; they do not contain substantive principles.

In terms of global governance, other than the three main Bretton Woods institutions (WTO, IMF, World Bank) mentioned earlier, international economic law considers the activities of a number of other international organizations, notably the new development banks such as the largely untested Asian Infrastructure Investment Bank (AIIB). The UN, despite its emblematic status in the sphere of multilateral governance, is not highly influential in international economic law, although it arguably had a larger role in the early days of the discipline before more specialized organizations were established. International economic law has traditionally not covered the work of the various G organizations (G7, G20). While these bodies play an important role in identifying key global economic challenges and illustrating paths forward in tackling these issues collectively, their capacity as generators or enforcers of law is limited, as is the record of compliance with their agreed objectives.[8]

International economic law is primarily oriented towards the promotion of higher living

---

[8] J Wouters and T Carmeliet, 'GX Dynamics and Global Trade Governance' in D Prévost, I Alexovicova, JH Pohl eds *Restoring Trust in Trade* (Hart, 2018).

standards and the creation of wealth. This is premised on the theory that law very often, although not always, operates as an impediment to the generation of wealth in global markets, much as it does in local ones. To that extent, international economic law concerns itself with the removal of laws which restrain this process, and, perhaps more recently, the creation of laws which prevent or mitigate the harmful aspects of it. In addition to this main function, another of the chief purposes behind the pursuit of global market liberalization has been to prevent war. Indeed, this was one of the aims of the Bretton Woods system. The de-escalation or, ideally, the prevention of armed conflict is premised on the assumption, often attributed to Emmanuel Kant, that countries which trade with each other are less likely to go to war with each other. The rationale can be extended to investment as well. The link between economic integration and peace may be subdivided into three composite theories. First, as countries begin to rely on each other for some of the goods (and services) which they need because they can secure these more efficiently from foreign sources, they will develop a kind of dependence. If the only source of a particular commodity is another country, then there is less reason to attack that country – unless of course the purpose of the attack is to seize the facilities of production in that country, including its natural resources. History has told us that this approach tends not to work, as countries are less productive after occupation than when they were free.[9] Second, as countries become interlinked through globalization, sharing tastes and interests in various goods and services, then cultural differences will begin to erode. This is the homogeneity of globalization that is so prized, and perhaps equally resented, by many. The xenophobia or disdain for foreignness that is thought to act as an impetus for much war is therefore eliminated. It may be equally likely, however, that countries which interact with each other more closely may begin to feel bitterness towards each other. In this view, globalization could exacerbate existing tensions, much as some countries bear a grudge against countries which export their values and tastes. This is probably most closely associated with US cultural imperialism. Third, trade increases the volume of goods to be enjoyed by all because it capitalizes on efficiencies developed through specialization, as explored further below. Following from this, with trade between nations, there should be more resources to be enjoyed by all. Throughout human history, including prehistoric times, scarcity has been a source of conflict. As people enjoy higher living standards, they are less likely to want to take up arms against their neighbours.

There are four main topics in international economic law: two large ones and two small ones. All are interrelated to varying degrees. The two large topics are: international trade, comprising chiefly the law of the WTO but also regional trade agreements (RTAs); and international investment law, consisting of several international investment agreements (IIAs). The two lesser topics are: international monetary law (or, more accurately, international monetary 'relations'), which essentially covers the work of the IMF; and international development law, which is found in the rules of the World Bank and a host of regional development banks, as well as some aspects of WTO law.

The sources of international economic law are drawn from the sources of international law generally. These are normally derived from Article 38 of the Statute of the International Court of

---

[9] L Freedman, *Strategy: A History* (Oxford University Press, 2015).

Justice (ICJ)[10] and consist of two primary sources and two subsidiary sources. The primary sources are international conventions, meaning international treaties between states, and customary international law, essentially encompassing the unwritten laws understood to be obligatory by states as members of the international community. The subsidiary sources are general principles of law, referring to rules which are recognized in the national legal systems of countries around the world, and judicial decisions of international tribunals, supplemented by the writings of highly qualified publicists, including academics.

For modern international economic law, which is grounded heavily in treaties, the chief primary sources of law are therefore the laws of the WTO, RTAs and IIAs. Under Article 31 of the Vienna Convention on the Law of Treaties (VCLT),[11] such treaties should be interpreted in good faith in accordance with the ordinary meaning to be given to the terms of the treaty in their context and in the light of its object and purpose. Treaties are accorded varied status in the domestic law of various countries around the world, with many countries, such as the US, requiring additional enabling legislation to give them effect. In international economic law, customary international law tends to occupy a less significant role in modern times. One aspect of customary international law is the minimum standard of treatment of aliens, discussed earlier. Another one is the principle of full compensation for expropriation, also mentioned before. Some domestic legal systems, such as that of Germany, grant customary international law primacy over domestic laws. General principles of law are also marginally important in international economic law due to a lack of consensus among states because of diversity in legal systems. With respect to judicial decisions in international economic law, those of the panels and especially the Appellate Body of the WTO hold much sway, although there is no formal system of precedent. The same is true of investment arbitration tribunals, from which, at least at present, there is normally no right of appeal. The ICJ itself has played a limited role in international economic law and this will most likely remain so for the foreseeable future. The status of academic opinions in international economic law is an interesting one. There is an established community of legal experts in this field (sometimes described as an 'epistemic community') whose work is often cited by international tribunals and in the publications issued by influential international organizations,[12] as well as a range of academic organizations, notably the Society of International Economic Law. There are also several highly respected academic journals, including the *Journal of International Economic Law*. It is a thriving field which should expand further as international economic law remains such a vital aspect of international law and as the open, global economy continues to struggle against the forces of protectionism from time to time. A closer examination of the key principles and rationales for pursuing economic liberalism at the global level will now be undertaken.

---

[10] 33 UNTS 993 (1946).

[11] 1155 UNTS 331 (1969).

[12] D Collins, 'The International Bar Association and Trade in Legal Services: Meta Law-Making in International Economic Law?' 11:3 Indian Journal of International Economic Law (2019).

4. INTERNATIONAL TRADE: PRINCIPLES AND RATIONALE

International trade tends to be regulated domestically but supervised by international rules. It consists of measures both at the border (tariffs and quotas) and behind the border (all other regulations). The principles of international trade are characterized by treaty based rules (mostly WTO but increasingly regional treaties) and case law, primarily that which has been produced by the WTO dispute settlement system. Importantly, the laws governing international trade are rooted in pragmatism, including diplomacy, rather than rigid rules. This is partly the consequence of the need to adapt the regime to suit each country as well as each sector of economic activity. The emphasis on diplomacy is further reflected in the need to grant access to internal markets on a concessionary, reciprocal basis, harmonizing regulations and doing so transparently, with a recognition for noneconomic values.

The purpose of fostering international trade by eliminating unnecessary legal obstacles to it is grounded in the theory of comparative advantage, first identified by the British political economist David Riccardo in the eighteenth century. The essence of the theory is that a country should specialize in the production of a given commodity and, establishing a cost advantage in its production because of the efficiencies engendered by expertise, export it to other countries. That country should import other products where its cost advantage is relatively smaller, meaning products in which it does not have a specialism. Riccardo used the now famous example of England and Portugal producing shirts and bottles of wine. Even if Portugal is relatively better than England at producing both shirts and bottles of wine, it is still in Portugal's interest to produce the commodity where its cost advantage is greater to the exclusion of the other product, and import that other product from England. Portugal should produce wine if it is *more* better (pardon the poor grammar) at producing than it is producing shirts. The demonstration that this strategy of comparative advantage leads to gains in terms of productivity – greater output per unit of cost – is the theoretical basis of international trade. Put simply, it is more efficient to specialize and trade than to produce everything on your own and isolate yourself. Comparative advantage is open to the criticism that not all commodities are readily substitutable, and it can be dangerous to rely on your neighbour for essential goods, such as food and perhaps also commodities like steel and oil. If there is a war, then countries which are not able to source these materials domestically can be vulnerable.

Riccardo's insight into the value of trade, tied to Adam Smith's earlier work on the value of specialization and competition within an economy generally, were instrumental in encouraging politicians to abandon the mercantilist practices of an earlier era, as suggested above. With borders that are open to trade, consumers are able to purchase the best goods and services from all over the world at the lowest prices. This strategy has enabled people to enjoy all kinds of exotic commodities from around the world that would have been unimaginable in an era of protectionism, because these things would have been either too expensive for an ordinary consumer or would have been embargoed entirely. The expansion of international trade should also be credited with declines in global inequality, measured by the Gini coefficient. While the gap in living standards between the rich and poor has increased inside some countries in the past few decades, particularly in the developed world, the gap between people living in advanced and developing countries is narrowing.[13] Many believe that this has led to greater social harmony and a sense of personal wellbeing.

The picture is somewhat different for the suppliers of goods and services. Just as consumers are able to access most things that they want cheaply, producers face ever tougher competition because there are no legal obstacles to the markets in which they once reigned unchallenged. Globalization fostered by trade liberalization has laid bare the inadequacies of many producers who relied on the fact that they were the only option available to their customers, enabling them to charge higher prices for often poor quality goods. The laws of the global free market also apply to the supply of labour. As these firms struggle to survive global competition, they may end up eliminating workers because they cannot afford to keep them or to pay them the high wages they once enjoyed when they were isolated from the pressures of cheap imports. Employees are also consumers and as these people lose their wages, they are no longer able to act as market participants, leading to a downward economic spiral. While Riccardo was correct that trade can lead to efficiency gains, he perhaps did not appreciate, or did not care, that there are losers from international trade as well as winners. The hollowing out of the US working class due to the decline in manufacturing is perhaps the most obvious casualty of trade, although, as suggested above, automation may be the real culprit here. A similar phenomenon has been observed in the UK, where manufacturing employment has also plummeted during the era of global trade. These events have led to unmistakable political developments in recent years premised on the harm inflicted to ordinary people by companies in pursuit of global profits.

Those who lose from international trade are more vocal than those who gain. They are also able to organize themselves into lobby groups which pressure governments to enact protectionist policies. The people who gain from economic globalization tend to be the consumers who enjoy a wider variety of goods and lower prices than they would have done otherwise; however, these consumers do not organize themselves as well and consequently are often underappreciated in the political process.[14] The losers from globalization tend to be workers in companies which produce goods inefficiently and which cannot compete with foreign products, resulting in downward pressure on wages, or, worse, unemployment. Since much of the harm associated with trade is actually caused by automation – which has made many manual jobs redundant – not to mention high energy prices associated with investment in renewables, it is a dangerous misdirection by politicians to point to the declining employment numbers in manufacturing as evidence that globalization has not worked or that it has sidelined the little guy in order to advantage the global elite.

Still, much more work needs to be done to address the harm suffered by those who have seen their wages decline or their employment disappear because of more efficient production in foreign markets, typically in developing countries where labour costs are lower, as are the costs of raw materials. There has been remarkably little attention to this matter from legal academics.[15] Retraining, or reskilling as it is sometimes known, has been explored in a number of contexts with

---

[13] Z Darvas, 'Global Income Inequality Is Declining – Largely Thanks to China and India' Bruegel (19 April 2018).

[14] G Brennan and L Lomasky, *Democracy and Decision: The Pure Theory of Electoral Preference* (Cambridge University Press, 1993).

[15] One useful example is M Trebilcock's *Dealing with Losers* (Oxford University Press, 2015).

varying degrees of success. But labour is often not as mobile as economists think it should be in theory (workers do not move across international borders as easily as the goods they produce), and older workers often struggle to acquire new skills, especially when they are increasingly linked to technology. The important point for trade lawyers to appreciate is that such initiatives are unlikely to transgress WTO disciplines on subsidies – explored further in Chapter 4 – as they are not designed, nor do they operate as, international trade distortions. They are strategies aimed at mitigating the shock of globalization as borne by those which are most vulnerable. In that sense they are squarely within the WTO's objectives, or at least they should be.

In a very real sense, the US had the most to lose from surrendering its right to retaliate against foreign countries through tariffs and other protectionist measures when it joined the GATT and later the WTO. This is because the US has the economic (and military) might to pressure other countries into complying with its wishes, whether in the form of lower tariffs or granting other kinds of market access. It may therefore come as no surprise that in recent years the US has expressed derision for the multilateral trading system, abusing national security provisions to impose tariffs on a wide range of goods and threatening to withdraw from the system if it does not get its way, as will be discussed in Chapter 5. Still, it is preferable for the US to bend its WTO obligations and continue down the path of trade unilateralism, rather than the alternative: military action. It must also be recognized that the US has some genuine criticisms of the world trading system which need to be addressed.

Figure 1.2 shows how, since 1981, the growth in the volume of world trade, as expressed in annual percentage, more or less tracks the growth in world GDP, also expressed in annual percentage. Put another way, generally speaking, the more trade, the greater the economic activity. This is

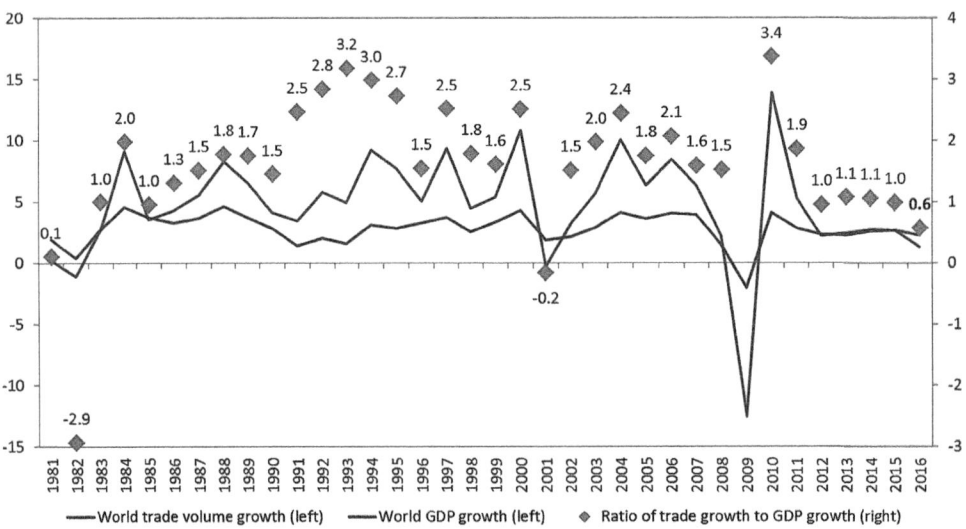

Source: World Trade Organization. Reprinted by permission.

Figure 1.2 Annual world trade and GDP growth over time

why trade tends to decline during a recession and why legal impediments to trade often result in a contraction of the economies of both the importing and exporting state, although there are other factors at play, such as commodity prices and political stability. This chart also reveals the trade growth to GDP growth ratio of the world. Such ratios are indicators of the relative importance of international trade in the economy of a given country, or in this case the world as a whole. It is calculated by dividing the aggregate value of imports and exports over a period by the GDP for the same period. Note that there was a sharp drop in both global trade volume growth and world GDP growth in 2009 as a consequence of the global economic crisis of late 2008. A smaller drop in 2001 represents the bursting of the dotcom or internet bubble caused by overvalued technology equities in the early days of the internet. The past ten years have seen a moderate recovery.

There is much evidence to support Riccardo's theory. Trade has grown remarkably over the past century, in part due to the embrace of liberalization as economic policy, but also partially as a consequence of improvements in technology. These include the advent of containerization and the automation of ports (along with the construction of the Suez and Panama Canals), which increased the quantity and speed at which goods which could be shipped around the world, and, in the past two decades or so, the expansion of telecommunications, which has dramatically expanded the capacity for trade in many kinds of services. While trade and globalization have been experienced at a different pace around the world, today trade is a fundamental aspect of economic activity in every part of the globe.

5. INTERNATIONAL INVESTMENT: PRINCIPLES AND RATIONALE

Foreign direct investment (FDI) refers to the transfer of capital from one country into another for a commercial purpose. This will normally consist of a foreign firm's purchasing of an existing business (known as a merger or acquisition) or establishment of an entirely new one (known as greenfield). FDI must be distinguished from indirect or portfolio investment in that the foreign elements who own the capital maintain a degree of management or control over the enterprise in the host state. If there is no management or control by an entity within the foreign state, then the investment is for all intents and purposes a domestic investment and does not deserve special protection under international investment law. FDI typically also excludes 'round-tripping' investment, consisting of money sent overseas, usually for preferential tax treatment, to be recycled back into the country of origin.

The basis element of international investment, or FDI, is multinational enterprises locating their operations in foreign states as part of their business strategy, choosing locations where they can source inputs at lower cost or where they can access new markets. For their part, foreign states seek to attract these multinational enterprises for the economic growth potential that they represent. Foreign investment offers the possibility of new markets or lower cost production, or in some cases both. Either of these rationales can represent an increase in profits beyond those available to exclusively domestic firms which may have exhausted local markets or face high labour or material costs at home. For the host state, foreign investment is thought to increase economic growth, as defined variously by increases in GDP as well as improvements to the quality of life, as measured potentially by indicia such as literacy and life expectancy. FDI achieves this, at least in theory, by bringing foreign capital, lowering the cost of goods and services and providing employment, training and knowledge transfer for locals, which may be a substitute for aid to development in low income countries. In the case of investment inflows into developed countries, the presence of foreign enterprises can offer added competition, which can improve industry standards and lower prices to the advantage of consumers.[16]

The extent to which FDI flows have assisted in the development of host states and, in so doing, improved the welfare of their citizens is the subject of much controversy. Much like trade, international investment may yield winners and losers. Critics emphasize the overall loss of sovereignty and worsened social conditions tied to foreign investment results from national policies aimed at augmenting FDI.[17] FDI is often thought to prevent the development of local industry and the associated rise of an entrepreneurial class who would otherwise establish industries that do not rely on foreign capital. A dependency problem may be created which is potentially disastrous to host states when a foreign investor suddenly withdraws – the so-called 'capital flight' scenario. New positions created by foreign investors may offer only short term employment at low rates of pay. Foreign firms often crowd out those already present in developing countries. Regarding technology transfer, FDI may have limited capacity to improve local innovative capabilities, particularly in situations where there are insufficient basic skills to adopt technological learning. There are also widely held beliefs that, in pursuit of lower cost production, multinational enterprises are attracted to jurisdictions with comparatively weak regulations, and by engaging in commercial activity in these regions they inflict undue harm on, for example, the local environment and on local workers. This so-called race to the bottom model of foreign investment is associated with many of the worst aspects of economic globalization. The desire to remain attractive to foreign investors could cause a state to pursue pro-market policies which may hamper its ability to provide public services or to fulfil social needs.[18] In that sense, the protection of foreign investors may interfere with a state's sovereignty.

The criticisms of FDI must be contrasted with the more orthodox position, advocated by international organizations such as the Organization for Economic Cooperation and Development (OECD), UNCTAD and the WTO, that foreign investment is a positive force in the global economy, having contributed, along with trade, to growth and the alleviation of poverty throughout the world.[19] This is why most institutions of international economic governance, including the three which are the focus of this book, strongly recommend the removal of barriers to the flow of capital (along with trade in goods and services) to stimulate competition, promote employment, lower prices and in so doing achieve economic stability and growth. Fears of regulatory regression that

---

[16] M Forsgren, *Theories of the Multinational Firm: A Multidimensional Creature in the Global Economy* (Edward Elgar Publishing, 2017).

[17] M Sornarajah, *The International Law on Foreign Investment* (Cambridge University Press, 2010).

[18] S Picciotto, *Regulating Global Corporate Capitalism (International Corporate Law and Financial Market Regulation)* (Cambridge University Press, 2011).

[19] See e.g. OECD Guidelines for Multinational Enterprises – Declaration on International Investment and Multinational Enterprises (7 June 2000) at 5; UNCTAD, World Investment Report 2009 Chapter III: TNCs and Agricultural Production in Developing Countries at 95; see generally the WTO Report on G20 Trade and Investment Measures (8 March 2010).

capture the public's anxiety over globalization have been seriously challenged by empirical studies.[20] It is widely held that FDI, both inward and outward, has lifted millions of people out of poverty throughout the world.

As suggested above, the primary motivation for firms engaging in FDI is profit, not altruistically alleviating poverty in the developing world or anywhere else. With this self-interested motivation in mind, multinational enterprises can be characterized as either cost-oriented or market-oriented. Cost-oriented firms are motivated by a desire to cut costs by establishing a foreign presence. Examples of these investors include those which are in the extractive sector, such oil companies and those which engage in manufacturing, such as automotive companies. Market-oriented investors are motivated to expand the markets in which they can sell their goods and services and increase sales abroad. Automotive companies might also fit into this category, particularly when they locate in countries where there is a large middle class of ready consumers.[21] One implication of the expansion of globalization and the ensuing progress of many developing countries is that enterprises that were once cost-oriented morph into market-oriented ones as the countries in which they have invested transition from developing to developed. Manufacturing companies that once sought out locations because of their low-cost workers may end up selling finished goods to the same people after their wages and living standards have risen.

These two strategies do not necessarily explain why a company would choose to locate abroad rather than engage in trade. The decision to invest rather than trade is a complex one involving a number of concerns which may be particular to the individual company. This could involve the advantages engendered by bringing in local knowhow and expertise, aiding in market penetration in a manner that would be impossible from a remote location. Another reason to move the company overseas may be to 'jump the tariff wall' – this allows the company to evade any trade barriers in place by becoming a local company. Some states still place onerous conditions on foreign investors, as will be explored in Chapter 6, but these are often less burdensome than those faced by traders.

There may be a third motivation for firms to internationalize. This is to break away from the poor regulatory environment at home which has stifled their business.[22] This has been associated with companies from places such as India where the costs of doing business are restrictive. Escaping unfavourable conditions at home also explains why a firm would choose to invest rather than trade: as traders themselves stay put, they are bound by the regulatory environment in which they operate – it is only their inputs and outputs which have to deal with laws imposed in other territories. Internationalization was traditionally viewed as a gradual process, with firms investing abroad typically only after they have already expanded throughout their own country, and then into adjacent regions. Modern telecommunications technology has allowed even small firms to serve global clients, and to purchase supplies internationally, at an early stage. Indeed, many technology companies have been described as having been 'born global'.

---

[20] A Harrison, 'Do Polluters Head Overseas? Testing the Pollution Haven Hypothesis', 6:2 ARE Update (2002).

[21] A Griffiths and S Wall, *Applied Economics* (Prentice Hall, 2007).

[22] K Sauvant, W Maschek and G McAllister, 'Foreign Direct Investment by Emerging Market Multinational Enterprises' in K Sauvant, G McAllister and W Maschek eds *Foreign Direct Investment from Emerging Markets* (Palgrave Macmillan, 2010).

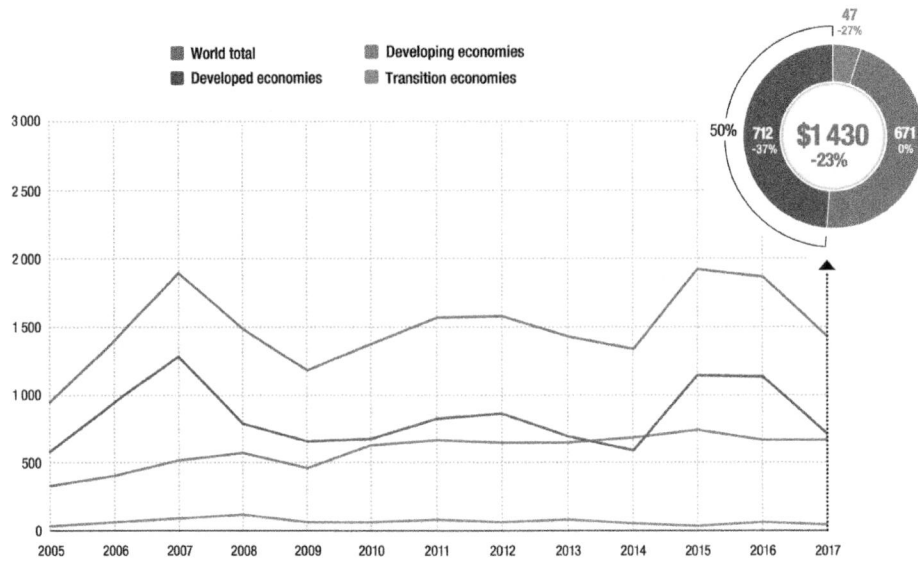

Source: UNCTAD World Investment Report 2018.

Figure 1.3 Annual world FDI inflows over time

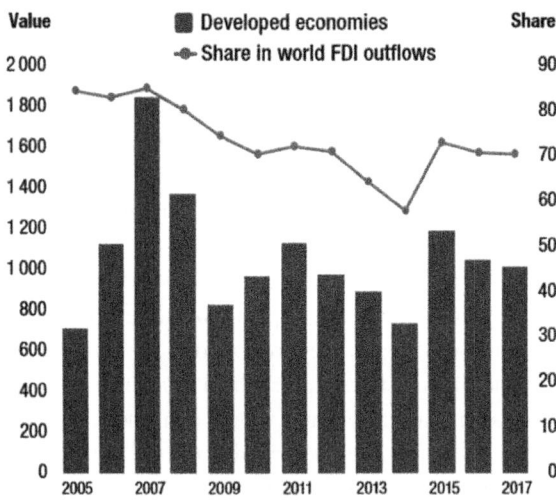

Source: UNCTAD World Investment Report 2018.

Figure 1.4 Annual world FDI outflows over time

Figure 1.3 illustrates annual global FDI inflows from 2005 to 2017 expressed in millions of US dollars. It does so by reference to inflows in three different country groupings: transition economies (essentially former communist countries moving towards market-oriented economies) at the bottom, developing countries and developed countries. World totals (all three categories) are at the top. Across all three categories there was a sharp rise in global FDI flows at the beginning of the period, culminating in 2007, followed by an equally sharp drop due to the global economic crisis of 2008–9 and its aftermath. Global FDI flows have never reached the peak of 2007, although they came close in 2015 only to drop again recently. FDI inflows to the developed world have more or less tracked the global totals; however, an interesting trend is revealed in the data from developing countries – FDI levels have steadily increased throughout the period. Most startling of all, there was a period around 2014 where FDI inflows into the developing world were greater than those to the developed world. The traditional paradigm of foreign investment has been wealthy countries investing in other wealthy countries. But for that short period more investment went into the developing world because these countries felt the effects of the global recession less severely – in fact, some of them continued to grow while the West contracted. At this point many in the West became excited about the so-called BRIC phenomenon – the incredible investment opportunities in Brazil, Russia, India and China, among other places in the emerging world. This phase appears to have been shortlived, as developed countries resumed their status as the dominant destination of foreign investment by 2015 and remain there to this day.

A similar trend can be observed in Figure 1.4, which depicts outflows of FDI over the same period, 2005–17. It is essentially the reverse of Figure 1.3 (one nation's outflow is another's inflow). FDI outflows tend to attract less attention than inflows because it is the inflow of foreign investment that leads to the tensions between states and companies with which international investment law, and all its controversies, are addressed. FDI outflows are also often viewed as something which a state might seek to avoid rather than to encourage, because they are sometimes perceived as indicating a loss of capital or employment, and potentially also taxation revenue, although none of these are strictly true. This bar portion of this chart expresses the annual outward FDI flows from developed countries. The dotted line is the percentage that outflows from these countries make of the world's totals (for simplicity's sake this chart omits transition economies). As with inflows, this chart reveals a peak in 2007, where developed countries' outflows comprised 80 per cent of the world's total. But once again, in 2014 it can be seen that there was a greater outflow of FDI from the developing world than the developed world. This means that there was more international investment being conducted by multinational enterprises from developing countries such as China and India than from the traditional large capital exporting states such as the US and Japan. Again, this period, which at least for now appears to have been temporary, generated much interest in how emerging market investors would behave on the global stage, the types of investment claims they would bring and how international investment law would respond to this role reversal. It may be that many of the changes which have been observed in international investment law in recent years are at least in part due to this phenomenon. As capital importing countries became capital exporting countries and vice versa, the policy objectives they sought to achieve through their international treaty commitments were bound to change, in some respects becoming more balanced than in the past.[23] Some of these trends will be observed in Chapters 6–8.

---

[23] E.g. D Collins, *The BRIC States and Outward Foreign Direct Investment* (Oxford University Press, 2013).

6. INTERNATIONAL MONETARY LAW AND INTERNATIONAL DEVELOPMENT LAW: PRINCIPLES AND RATIONALE

The purpose behind the liberalization of the international flow of money is essentially to facilitate the transactions which underlie international trade and investment. This is achieved through the prevention of currency exchange controls and the maintenance of stable exchange rates. Access to money which holds a stable value allows states to ensure that public services are available and that citizens can buy goods and get paid their wages, generally allowing for the proper functioning of society. The management of a state's access to money is tied to the understanding that states should have a stable balance of payments, which is the summary of all monetary transactions between that state and the rest of the world. If a country imports more than it exports, its balance of payments will be in deficit. This means that the quantity of that country's currency supplied by the domestic market will be greater than the quantity which is demanded in the foreign exchange market, because that state's money is not needed to buy as many of the goods and services which it produces. The currency will therefore likely depreciate in value relative to other currencies. If the country exports more than it imports, then the currency will likely appreciate in value because other countries want to buy that country's goods and services, as denominated in that country's currency. In either situation, if the currency cannot appreciate or depreciate because it is tied to the value of some other currency, problems will arise in terms of the supply of the currency and it will mean that transactions that would have occurred cannot take place. On the other hand, if the currency's value fluctuates too drastically, then buyers and sellers will be cautious about engaging in commerce with that country because predicting the utility of the transaction becomes difficult.[24]

A state's balance of payments may also signal its potential as a business partner for other countries or businesses in the rest of the world. If a state is experiencing significant balance of payments difficulties, it may not be able to increase imports from the rest of the world as required to satisfy its citizens' needs. This might lead it to restrict imports or overinvest in domestic production. It may also discourage capital outflows in order to improve its balance of payments status. A state with a large balance of payments surplus is more likely to expand its imports by buying more goods from abroad. It may also encourage foreign investment because investors will realize that there is more capital in this country which can be used. Such states will also be less likely to impose foreign exchange restrictions. Balance of payments data may indicate the state's overall health including whether its industries are sufficiently internationally competitive – this is precisely why this data should be readily available. If a country is suffering from a shortage of money supply due to balance of payments problems, a short term injection of money can address the problem and allow it to get back on its feet, typically by introducing market-oriented, liberalizing policies and cutting government spending, although such policies may be harmful in some circumstances. While they might be economically beneficial, these conditions represent a major encroachment on the sovereignty of the borrowing state. Once the country has recovered, it may be in a position to repay this loan before

---

[24] H Van den Berg, *International Finance and Open-Economy Macroeconomics: Theory, History, and Policy* (World Scientific, 2015).

the currency crisis leads to recession, which can infect other countries due to the connectedness of the global economy.

The justification for providing resources to poorer countries for the purposes of development on a longer timeframe, addressing systemic rather than short term economic deficiencies, is both a moral and a self-interested one. It is moral because developed countries arguably played a role in the economic suffering of many developing countries when they established exploitative colonies in these places.[25] From the perspective of pure economics, assisting developing countries in improving their economic status can lead to the creation of new markets into which goods and services can be sold, representing new business opportunities for multinational enterprises. Developmental assistance is not always via aid or loans. Foreign investment itself may act as an impetus to development, particularly if it is backed by the protection of the rule of law. Foreign investment brings not only capital but also knowhow and training to underdeveloped countries. Some even believe that it can contribute to the establishment of good governance policies, including democracy, human rights and spread of the rule of law itself.[26]

7. STRUCTURE OF THIS BOOK

This book is structured into ten chapters which roughly correspond to the ten classes that comprise the course in international economic law which I have been teaching at City, University of London for the past ten years or so. There are three main parts to the book, excluding this introductory chapter, corresponding to the general topics of trade, investment and monetary relations/development, as referenced above.

Part I consists of four chapters on international trade law, using the multilateral trading system of the WTO as the basis upon which to describe some of the leading concepts in that field. Chapter 2 introduces the GATT, outlining the main principles of tariffs, quotas, non-discrimination and transparency. It also introduces regionalism as an alternative to multilateralism. Chapter 3 delves into the procedural aspects of the WTO's dispute settlement system, examining the main characteristics of this system, including the panels and Appellate Body process, as well as pervasive problems and potential reforms. Chapter 4 explores the field of trade remedies, focusing on the very pressing issues of dumping and antidumping as well as subsidies and countervailing measures. The second part of this chapter turns to a different field entirely, the GATS, and, flowing from it, some of the nascent rules on digital trade which are derived more from non-WTO instruments. Chapter 5 comprises the remaining agreements of crucial importance within WTO law – the Trade Related Aspects of Intellectual Property (TRIPS) Agreement, and the increasingly important and controversial agreements covering regulatory barriers to trade: the Sanitary and Phytosanitary Agreement (SPS), essentially dealing with foodstuffs, and the Agreement on Technical Barriers to Trade (TBT) – which are poised to become the key battleground for trade protectionism in the twenty-first century. The

---

[25] J Darwin, *After Tamerlane: The Rise and Fall of Global Empires* (Penguin, 2008).

[26] A Anghie, 'Civilization and Commerce: The Concept of Governance in Historical Perspective' 45 Villanova Law Review 887 (2000).

chapter begins with an assessment of the General Exceptions under the GATT which aim to incorporate nontrade concerns into the WTO rulemaking universe. It is important to state here that not every aspect of WTO law will be examined in this book, as this would be impossible for an introductory book on international economic law. Notably, government procurement under the WTO's plurilateral Agreement on Government Procurement will be omitted. Agriculture and agricultural subsidies will also not be discussed.

Part II of the book, on international investment law, begins with Chapter 6, which introduces the chief international legal instruments which are relevant to this important topic, including most importantly the bilateral investment treaty (BIT), RTAs with investment chapters (collectively referred to as international investment agreements or IIAs) and the various multilateral instruments which deal with investment, notably those of the Bretton Woods triumvirate: the World Bank, the WTO and the IMF. Chapter 7 explores the contents of an IIA, beginning with definitions of investment and investor, then turning to the chief standards of protection, ranging from issues such as fair and equitable treatment to non-discrimination, full protection and security and guarantees against expropriation without compensation. Chapter 8, the final chapter on international investment law, examines dispute settlement, specifically the much maligned investor–state dispute settlement (ISDS) and some of the leading reform proposals, notably the European Commission's concept of a multilateral investment court. To be clear in advance, this book is not intended to provide a comprehensive discussion of investment arbitration.

Part III of the book consists of two chapters covering monetary relations and development respectively. Chapter 9 concentrates on the IMF and its vital role in currency exchange as well as sovereign debt relief. There are many other dimensions to monetary law, including a discussion of the role of central banks and rules relating to the functioning of the financial system, which cannot be explored here. Chapter 10 examines the World Bank as the chief multilateral development instrument. This chapter will also consider some of the work of the regional development banks as well as new development initiatives undertaken in the emerging markets, notably the AIIB. Here too, much more could be said on the role of private sector lenders, including a closer look at the contents of aid and loan contracts; however, space does not permit it.

This book adopts an approach in which the four main topics are each explained separately, generally corresponding to the three Bretton Woods institutions (WTO, IMF and World Bank), although the investment topic strays well beyond the confines of any particular institution, with elements of all three organizations applicable in certain contexts as well as various regional regimes. The topic/institution-based structure may be contrasted with one in which the legal principles themselves could have been addressed individually, each time covering a range of topics. For example, the concept of non-discrimination appears in both trade and investment. Transparency is arguably relevant to all four topics. The view of this author, based on my experience teaching international economic law for some time, is that this latter approach is ultimately less coherent and can lead to confusion among students/readers. I believe it is easier to grasp international economic law as an overarching discipline within international law by taking each of its constituent elements in turn. It is very hard to appreciate the significance of national treatment, for example, without first understanding what trade and investment are. Where various principles do overlap with the four core topics, this will be pointed out, hopefully achieving at least some sense of overall coherence in the discipline.

Unlike many other textbooks in the area, this book avoids long excerpts from cases or other articles or books in favour of a running explanatory narrative. Examples are used where necessary as illustrative aids. Finally, as the title of this book is *Foundations of International Economic Law*, it should be made clear from the outset that it does not purport to explore the entirety of this very broad topic comprehensively. Rather, it will provide an overview of the key principles across the discipline, drawing attention to some of the leading debates and current issues.

DISCUSSION QUESTIONS

1. What is international economic law and why is it an important area of study?
2. Why is liberalization in trade and investment thought to be a preferred policy in terms of stimulating economic growth?
3. What are the drawbacks to economic globalization and how might these consequences be mitigated?
4. What role does international law play in maximizing the benefits of economic globalization and has it done so effectively?

FURTHER READING

D Collins, 'Towards a Grand Unified Theory of International Economic Law' 12:2 Manchester Journal of International Economic Law 140–66 (2015).

M Gadbaw, 'The Prevention of Systemic Failure as a Unifying Principle of International Economic Law' 17:4 Journal of International Economic Law 823 (2014).

M Hoffman, 'Principles for Post-War International Economic Cooperation' 52:1 Journal of World Trade 15 (2018).

RL Sakr, 'Beyond History and Boundaries: Rethinking the Past in the Present of International Economic Law' 22:1 Journal of International Economic Law 57 (2019).

PART I
INTERNATIONAL TRADE LAW

2

The World Trade Organization's General Agreement on Tariffs and Trade: quotas, tariffs, non-discrimination, transparency and regionalism in international trade

1. INTRODUCTION

The World Trade Organization (WTO) was introduced in the previous chapter as one of the three members of the Bretton Woods trinity (in the form of the General Agreement on Tariffs and Trade, the GATT) established in the mid-twentieth century to set the world on the path of economic progress, forestalling recessions, promoting international engagement and, by extension, preventing wars. Today the WTO is seen as the standardbearer of multilateralism – a global institution designed to sustain and advance economic globalization as embodied by the trade of goods and services around the world. The WTO is an institution that is not without controversy. Indeed, this agenda has caused it to bear the brunt of the blame for some of the damaging consequences of globalization, such as widespread unemployment in manufacturing in the developed world, persistent poverty in the developing world, climate change and a host of other grievances, in many of which it has actually played little or no role. Protestors regularly appear at WTO ministerial conferences and some world leaders use the WTO as a convenient scapegoat for all kinds of economic and social ills.

This chapter will explore the WTO, first as an institution delivering a specific set of goals, and then as the administrator of a series of international treaties in the sphere of the first major topic in international economic law that will be covered in this book: trade. The chapter will do this through an examination of the main features of the GATT: the prohibition on quotas, the preservation of tariff commitments and guarantees against discrimination. From there, the chapter will examine another major challenge facing the WTO, which in many respects is one which the WTO itself encourages: the rise of regionalism in international trade law. Distinct from the multilateralism embedded in the law of the WTO, the granting of regional preferences among WTO members is allowed, even encouraged, within the WTO's rules provided that these arrangements secure deeper liberalization and therefore further the goal of free trade.

2. THE WORLD TRADE ORGANIZATION

2.1 Objectives

The WTO came into being on 1 January 1995 as a result of international negotiations under the multilateral GATT treaty during the Uruguay Round, named for where the negotiations began. As an international organization, the WTO administers international trade rules as well as interacts with other international bodies, including some which will be explored in this book, specifically the IMF and the World Bank. The WTO's agreements are treaties and, since treaties are one of the primary sources of international law, they are considered to be part of the larger body of international law. Still, there remain quite vibrant disagreements among experts regarding the precise relationship between WTO law and general international law: some argue in favour of a tighter connection in which there is cross-fertilization of ideas and mutual reinforcement,[1] while others advocate for greater separation, with WTO law as a so-called *lex specialis*, meaning that it is apart from the broader universe of customary international law.[2] With regard to the interaction between WTO and domestic law, there is considerable variation among jurisdictions. Some incorporate international law, such as the law of the WTO, into their domestic law, in many cases via enabling legislation. Other countries are more resistant, viewing WTO law as a threat to regulatory sovereignty as well as to democracy because international law is created under very different conditions than most domestic laws. Less controversially, most countries are prepared to grant WTO law indirect effect, which means that it should colour the interpretation of domestic law, preventing conflict between the two systems where possible. Under these systems, such as the US one, legislation which is capable of being interpreted consistently with international obligations, such as those of the WTO, should be interpreted in that way.

The purposes of the WTO are outlined in the preamble to the agreement establishing the WTO Agreement, also known as the Marrakesh Agreement. They are: raising the standards of living of the world; ensuring full employment; ensuring a steady and growing volume of real income; expanding production of trade in goods and services; and optimal use of the world's resources. When evaluating the WTO for its effectiveness or its impacts on society, or levying criticisms for its failures, it is therefore important to be mindful of these aims. The WTO should not be castigated for failing to do something which it never sought to do. It is important to recognize that many of these objectives may also be found in the preamble of regional trade agreements (RTAs), demonstrating the widereaching acceptance of these types of goals as norms within the international community.

It is instructive to pause and reflect on each of the above goals in turn. With respect to raising living standards of the world, this may be assessed by measures such as GDP, ideally on a global

---

[1] J Pauwelyn, 'The Role of Public International Law in the WTO: How Far Can We Go?' 95 American Journal of International Law 535 (2001).

[2] J Trachtman, 'Review of "Conflict of Norms in Public International Law: How WTO Law Relates to Other Rules of International Law" by Joost Pauwelyn' 98 American Journal of International Law 855 (2004).

level. Other measures of living standards could include life expectancy and literacy levels. On most of these metrics, the WTO has performed quite well indeed. World GDP, life expectancy and literacy levels have all risen since the 1990s and even more so since the GATT in the 1940s. While global poverty is far from disappearing entirely, it is not as pervasive as it has been in the past. Of course, the WTO's role in this regard may be minimal as advances in technology and unilateral efforts at market liberalization have brought benefits on their own. Additionally, as noted in the previous chapter, global inequality, measured by the Gini Coefficient (a score of 1 represents maximum inequality and a score of 0 represents perfectly equal distribution), has declined during the WTO era (post 1995). This trend is accelerating, partially thanks to China's accession to the WTO in 2001 and the ensuing expansion of global trade.[3]

Full employment is a more variable measure, prone to fluctuations from year to year. It is also much more closely tied to policies implemented at the domestic level rather than those elements for which the WTO has direct relevance, essentially trade policy. Still, the rise of the emerging markets, especially in Asia, over the past two decades suggests that more people are working than was the case in the past. This indicator is tied to the next one – a steady and growing volume of real income. Again, the expansion of the 'middle class' in China, India and elsewhere in the developing world suggests that more people earn enough money to buy not only the necessities of life, but also things which at one point might have been viewed as luxuries. Improvements in emerging markets may be contrasted with declines in places like America and Europe, particularly for workers in manufacturing, where disposable income is often lower today than in the past. Inequality may be worse in these places too.[4] The metric of expanding production in trade for goods and services is perhaps the one which is most closely tied to the main objectives of the WTO – eliminating barriers to international trade. Here the WTO has performed admirably, as the volume of trade has essentially increased steadily since 1995, with a slight downturn during the period of the financial recession in 2008–9. The final factor, optimal use of the world's resources, is often thought to encapsulate environmental sustainability. This is both difficult to measure and is arguably outside the WTO's core mandate, despite appearing in the preamble. Most would agree that climate change is worsening, although the role played by humanity's industrialization in accelerating this process is controversial. While the WTO aims to address the need to safeguard the environment, it is by no means an environmental agency, nor is there a clear link between increased trade and environmental degradation. Some of these issues will be explored further in Chapter 5.

2.2 Governance and structure

The WTO is best viewed as a negotiating forum rather than an entity which has its own will. The WTO's actions are those of its members. So in that sense it merely provides a place in which members can interact with each other in a formal setting to reach a decision collectively on their own behalf. The governance of the WTO is rooted in the concept of consensus – most decisions require

[3] Z Darvas, 'Global Income Inequality Is Declining – Largely Thanks to China and India' Bruegel (19 April 2018).

[4] For example, inequality has risen in the UK since the 1990s: F McGuinness and D Harari, 'Income Inequality in the UK' House of Commons Library (15 March 2019).

unanimity of the members, with each member having one vote, in keeping with the principle of sovereign equality – meaning that all states are equal to one another.[5]

Crucially for international lawyers, the WTO also comprises a set of rules. These are contained in the agreements which were negotiated by the members, meaning the world's trading nations. These agreements are international treaties, but in another sense they are also contracts containing binding commitments. While the signatories are the member governments, the intended beneficiaries are the exporters of goods and services and the consumers who purchase them. The overall purpose of the WTO's rules is to eliminate unnecessary barriers to trade, allowing goods and services to flow freely across international borders. In many cases the obstacles to international trade will simply be a lack of transparency regarding trade-oriented laws. In many other instances there will be actual types of protectionism, the most common of which has historically been tariffs.

Also of interest to international lawyers is that the WTO additionally incorporates judicial processes. It has a dispute settlement facility which renders binding rulings regarding the meaning of the various agreements. The purpose of this aspect of the WTO is to provide confidence that the rules of the international trading system do indeed carry obligations. The more predictable the system is, the more likely it is that there will be compliance and therefore greater flow of trade around the world. The dispute settlement system will be examined in detail in the next chapter.

The WTO was created by the WTO Agreement, mentioned above. It is a relatively brief document which does not contain any obligations. The substantive commitments are found in four annexes. Annex 1 consists of the Multilateral Trade Agreements, which are mandatory and binding on all members. These include the GATT, the General Agreement on Trade in Services (GATS) and many of the other agreements which will be explored in this book. Annex 2 contains the procedural rules on dispute settlement. Annex 3 establishes the Trade Policy Review Mechanism through which the WTO monitors each member's trade policies as well as their compliance with WTO obligations on a regular basis. Annex 4 comprises the four plurilateral (meaning optional) agreements. This includes the Agreement on Government Procurement, to which a handful of developed countries have accepted.

Figure 2.1 illustrates the organizational structure of the WTO. The highest organ within the WTO is the Ministerial Conference, which must meet at least every two years. This body is composed of representatives of all WTO members and takes decisions on all matters relating to the multilateral trade agreements. Directly under the Ministerial Conference is the General Council. This body also consists of representatives of all WTO members and possesses overall supervisory authority, carrying out many of the functions of the Ministerial Conference between meetings. In practice it meets at least monthly. The General Council also acts as the Dispute Settlement Body, which meets at least monthly to adopt formally the judicial decisions of the panels and the Appellate Body. The General Council's third iteration is as Trade Policy Review Body, which, as noted earlier, carries out monitoring and review of each member's trade policy on a regular basis to ensure compliance. The General Council further directs the activities of the three other councils – the Council for Trade in Goods, the Council for Trade in Services and the Council for Trade-Related Aspects of Intellectual Property Rights. Finally, there is the WTO Secretariat, which

---

[5] Art. 2.1 United Nations Charter, 1 UNTS XVI (24 October 1945).

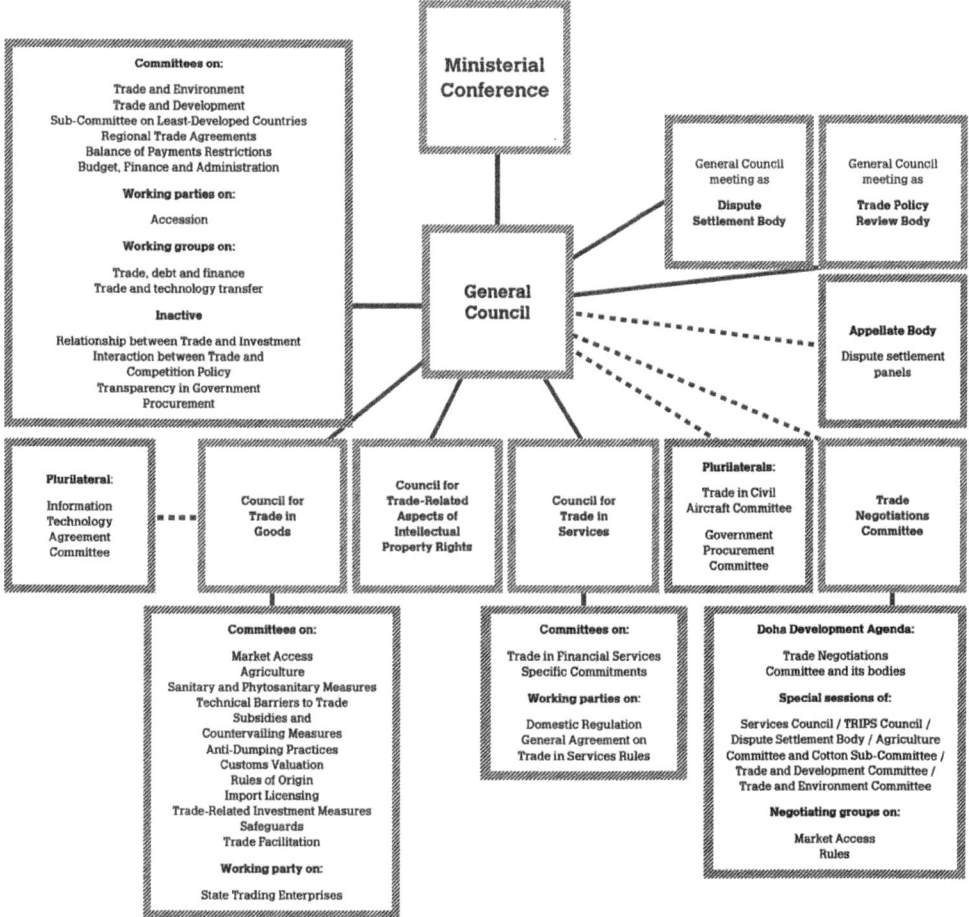

Source: World Trade Organization. Reprinted by permission.

Figure 2.1 WTO organizational structure

is headed by the Director General of the WTO. This is currently Roberto Azevêdo, a Brazilian former trade diplomat who has held the position since 2013. In practice the Secretariat has very limited power. Some feel that the Secretariat should become a true executive, something like the EU Commission.

As noted above, the WTO is a member-driven organization which implements a consensus approach to decision making. This avoids problems associated with majority voting (which might be viewed as an affront to the sovereignty of an individual dissenting member) and weighted voting, as practised by the IMF and the World Bank, which would give preference to larger countries and could also compel a member to act in a manner which is against its own wishes. As of mid-2019, the WTO's membership consists of 164 countries, covering all of the world's major economies and accounting for more than 99 per cent of all trade. Two thirds of the WTO's membership consists of developing countries. It is therefore important to be mindful of the WTO's role in serving the interests of people in these countries, which many believe it has not discharged adequately – an issue which will be revisited in Chapter 10. Recall above the appearance of the word 'world' in several of the WTO's stated goals. The WTO was created not only to make rich countries richer (which it has arguably done) but also to make poor countries less poor. It would appear as though it has succeeded in this goal as well, at least partially, given observed declines in global poverty. Since most of the WTO's members are developing countries, one might imagine that these countries would hold significant clout over the organization's operations. Practically speaking this is not true, as the US and the EU remain the most powerful voices in the WTO, exercising considerable sway in its various committees and pressuring other states to vote for their interests. Traditionally Canada, Japan and Australia have also carried much weight in terms of the WTO's strategic direction. India is often viewed as the most influential of the developing countries, having been a member from the beginning, in contrast to China, which acceded in 2001.

Membership of the WTO requires acceptance of all of the WTO's agreements – it is not an à la carte menu. Still, newly joining members must go through the process of accession, which in some cases requires special treatment consisting of greater or lesser obligations than those of other members, often for a limited time period. These obligations are outlined in accession 'protocols' – legally binding documents which are often interpreted by WTO panels and the Appellate Body to clarify members' individualized obligations towards the rest of the WTO. Russia's Accession Protocol, for example, had phase-in periods for certain tariff and subsidy obligations.[6] These temporary, specialized regimes are designed to cushion the shock of accepting full WTO obligations at once. The time period under which specialized obligations are applied or removed is often controversial, as in the case with the antidumping rules contained in China's Accession Protocol, as will be discussed in Chapter 4.

One of the main problems faced by the WTO today is that it is to an extent crippled by the requirement of consensus decision making, which is increasingly difficult to achieve as WTO membership has grown. Found in Article IX:1 of the WTO Agreement, consensus decision making is often depicted as one of the system's great strengths – if every member does not agree then a change is not implemented. It is the paragon of a democratically engaged institution founded on the fundamental principle of equality among its members, irrespective of size or economic power. But the practical result of the consensus rule is that there is a built-in veto – any member can prevent a decision from being operationalized by resisting. This makes it nearly impossible to effect changes at the WTO, including where reform is badly needed – for example in relation to dispute settlement, of which more will be discussed in Chapter 3. There have been discussions over the years about altering the consensus requirement, perhaps in favour of a supermajority or even a simple majority for decisions, but these have not been forthcoming. It is unlikely that the US or China would surrender their capacity for veto over the world trading system, as these countries have the most at stake when changes work to undermine their economic dominance and clout in negotiations.

Having outlined the essential features of the WTO as an institution, this chapter will now turn to the WTO's main agreement covering trade in goods, the original GATT.

---

[6] WT/MIN (11)/24 (17 December 2011).

3. THE GENERAL AGREEMENT ON TARIFFS AND TRADE

The GATT is the WTO's basic agreement covering trade in goods and is mandatory for all WTO members. Its contents also illustrate some of the central principles of world trade law, which are reiterated in some of the other more specific agreements, in some cases as expansions of more generic provisions of the GATT itself. As discussed in the previous chapter, the GATT of the Bretton Woods conference was originally a standalone agreement and its signatories were referred to as Contracting Parties. These parties later became WTO members when the WTO was created. The GATT remains the most litigated of all of the WTO's 30-odd covered agreements in terms of number of disputes and is the bedrock of the world's trading system for manufactured goods. While in recent years there has been a plethora of bilateral and regional agreements, it is difficult to overstate the importance of the GATT. In a very real sense it may be regarded as one of the twentieth century's great achievements in international law and diplomacy. The agreement's main legal concepts will now be examined.

3.1 Prohibition on quantitative restrictions

One of the GATT's most important functions is establishing the illegality of quotas, or bans on the import and export of goods. This is contained in Article XI:1, which reads as follows:

> No prohibitions or restrictions other than duties, taxes or other charges, whether made effective through quotas, import or export licences or other measures, shall be instituted or maintained by any contracting party on the importation of any product of the territory of any other contracting party or on the exportation or sale for export of any product destined for the territory of any other contracting party.

This provision means that quantitative restrictions on traded goods are prohibited, at least under most circumstances. It is therefore illegal to set a quota, meaning a numerically measurable limit in terms of value, quantity, weight and so on, on imported goods. The most obvious form of a quota is an import ban (a quota of zero) but less extreme forms of quotas are also unlawful. Quotas are correctly described as 'border' measures in that they are imposed at the border – meaning at the point at which the good enters the territory of the importing country. Measures of this nature have been challenged under the WTO dispute settlement system on occasion. For example, the US implemented import quotas in relation to tuna,[7] as well as shrimp,[8] due to concerns about the effect on other marine species (dolphins and turtles respectively) of harvesting these imports, as a result of various types of commercial fishing. Similarly, Brazil imposed an import restriction on recycled tyres out of concern that these tyres contributed to the spread of a disease-carrying mosquito.[9]

---

[7] US – Restrictions on Import of Tuna, Panel Report DS21/R, BISD/39S/155 (3 September 1991).

[8] US – Import Prohibition on Certain Shrimp and Shrimp Products, Appellate Body Report, WT/DS58/AB/R (6 November 1998).

[9] Brazil – Measures Affecting Imports of Retreaded Tyres Appellate Body Report, WT/DS332/AB/R (17 December 2007).

Quotas are prohibited under WTO law because they are significantly more economically harmful than other types of trade barriers, notably tariffs, which – as will be shown below – are allowed, although discouraged. With a quota in place, the availability of the product is reduced, potentially to the point that it is not available at all. Where still available, a quota will artificially raise the price of the good pursuant to the simple rules of supply and demand – things which are scarce tend to cost more. This in turn leads to unsatisfied demand, which may, depending on your view of consumerism and the importance of the product in question, lead to a decline in quality of life. Without this prohibition, the benefits of a free market would be lost and the advantages of competition (better quality and lower price) would be foregone.

There is a parallel export quota provision in GATT Article XI which is often forgotten but which is as important as the prohibition on import tariffs. WTO members are also prohibited from restricting the amount of goods which are exported from their territory into the international stream of commerce. This rule, which so far has had less relevance in terms of WTO disputes, accomplishes the same goal as the import quota prohibition. By curtailing the volume of a good which is available in foreign markets, its price is artificially inflated. China was found to be in breach of this rule when it imposed export quotas on rare earths. Some WTO members viewed this, and other related measures, as indicative of a strategy of hoarding designed to inflate global prices of commodities such as tungsten, vital for use in electronics.[10] GATT Article XI a) does allow temporary quantitative restrictions applied to essential products to relieve critical shortages. For example, Ukraine instituted a lawful export quota on grain shortly after its WTO accession in 2008 because of severe shortages caused by a drought in 2010.

There are additional exceptions to the import and export quota prohibitions in order for members to fulfil their IMF obligations relating to balance of payments.[11] Quotas may also be permitted if they fall within the GATT's General Exceptions, which will be examined further in Chapter 5. They can also be excused if the relevant country is suffering from balance of payments difficulties. In either case, any quotas must be applied in a non-discriminatory fashion, as outlined under Article XIII, meaning that the member cannot impose a restriction on the quantity of goods it imports from or exports to certain countries but not others. The general provision on the elimination of quantitative restrictions found in GATT Article XI is not normally found in RTAs.

3.2 Preservation of tariff commitments

Tariffs, which are often referred to as 'duties' or 'customs duties', are an extra fee imposed on goods when they cross international borders and are sometimes referred to as customs duties or simply duties. In that sense they are also border measures like quotas. As noted in Chapter 1, they are a classic form of protectionism designed to shield domestic goods from foreign competitors by raising prices to consumers in a nontransparent manner. Unlike quotas, however, tariffs are not illegal. The only commitment in the GATT is that members must honour the tariff commitments

---

[10] China – Measures Related to the Exportation of Rare Earths, Tungsten, and Molybdenum, Appellate Body Report WT/DS431/AB/R (29 August 2014).

[11] Art. XII.

which they have made. This is contained in Article II. The operative part of this provision states as follows:

1(*b*) The products described in Part I of the Schedule relating to any contracting party, which are the products of territories of other contracting parties, shall, on their importation into the territory to which the Schedule relates, and subject to the terms, conditions or qualifications set forth in that Schedule, be exempt from ordinary customs duties in excess of those set forth and provided therein. Such products shall also be exempt from all other duties or charges of any kind imposed on or in connection with the importation in excess of those imposed on the date of this Agreement or those directly and mandatorily required to be imposed thereafter by legislation in force in the importing territory on that date.

Departures from these negotiated tariffs (negotiated during various WTO meetings) are illegal. Negotiated tariffs are called 'bound' tariffs, which are set for each individual product in each member's schedule. These are very lengthy documents containing lists of tariffs for thousands of products. Members are free to charge tariffs lower than the bound rate; indeed, they often do. But they cannot go above this level. The tariff which is actually used on incoming goods is known as the 'applied' tariff. Bound tariffs have been agreed on many products, preventing the raising of tariffs in the future. As noted in the previous chapter, the GATT/WTO's success in lowering tariffs on manufactured goods throughout the latter half of the twentieth century has been astounding. Average tariffs dropped from more than 40 per cent in the 1940s to less than 4 per cent today, making a wide range of products from around the world more affordable for consumers and opening up a planet of diverse goods to be enjoyed that were beyond the reach of previous generations. Tariff reductions comprise a significant portion of the negotiations which have occurred through the WTO over the years during the major 'rounds' of negotiation. This process can be quite complex, typically involving the reciprocal exchange of reductions across a range of products. The lowering of tariffs between WTO members was at one point the primary diplomatic activity of international trade representatives of governments at the WTO.

Despite these achievements, tariffs are still the most widely used form of protectionism, granting an artificial advantage to domestic over imported goods and distorting prices. Although tariffs are clearly a cost to consumers, they raise revenue for the governments which apply them and in that sense they may be viewed as an essential policy tool for countries which are unable to secure significant revenue from other sources, such as citizens' income taxes. Developing countries in particular rely on tariffs to raise revenue. Tariffs are preferable to quotas also because the latter are often harder for consumers to identify, creating the potential for corruption. Tariffs are more readily traceable and identifiable to consumers as an added burden, both of which mean that tariffs are conducive to reduction by governments over time. These are the reasons why the WTO does not prohibit them, but rather encourages members to reduce them where possible. The WTO instructs its members who feel the need to protect domestic industry from foreign competition in some sectors to convert their quotas into tariffs – a process called 'tariffication'. Most of the caselaw generated by Article II of the GATT relates to the precise manner in which tariffs are levied by members with respect to certain products, as well as customs classification methodology.[12] Differences in approaches to these issues may lead to disagreements regarding the tariff commitments which have been made.

As with the multilateral GATT, parties to RTAs typically commit to reduce or eliminate customs duties/tariffs on originating goods of the other party in accordance with agreed levels.[13] The focus on tariffs in regional arrangements tends to relate to the conditions under which exporters from each party are able to claim preferential tariff treatment, such as satisfying rules of origin (ROO), which will be explored further below. RTAs also often contain material on the consequences of breaches of preferential tariff treatment which adversely affects the relevant industry, meaning that goods deserving of preferential treatment have not received it, or goods from other countries which were not entitled to it did. Measures to deal with these eventualities may include commitments to cooperate in preventing and detecting breaches and could involve the suspension of preferential tariff treatment where there is evidence that such breaches have been systemic and in relation to certain goods.[14]

3.3 Most favoured nation

Among the most far reaching features of the GATT, and indeed of WTO law in its entirety, are the rules on non-discrimination. The prohibition on discrimination against a product based on its origin is fundamental to the WTO, much as broader types of discrimination are prohibited by other international treaties and in domestic legislation.

Article I of the GATT contains the first of these non-discrimination rules: most favoured nation (MFN), which is perhaps the single most important principle in WTO law. It is found in many of the WTO agreements and has existed in one form or another in international law for centuries, including in international investment law, as will be explained in Chapter 7. GATT Article I reads as follows:

> 1. With respect to customs duties and charges of any kind imposed on or in connection with importation or exportation or imposed on the international transfer of payments for imports or exports, and with respect to the method of levying such duties and charges, and with respect to all rules and formalities in connection with importation and exportation, and with respect to all matters referred to in paragraphs 2 and 4 of Article III, any advantage, favour, privilege or immunity granted by any contracting party to any product originating in or destined for any other country shall be accorded immediately and unconditionally to the like product originating in or destined for the territories of all other contracting parties.

MFN prohibits discrimination in relation to 'like' products originating from (or destined for) different members. The concept of 'likeness' for MFN will be explored further below in the context of national treatment. For now, MFN means that a WTO member cannot treat goods imported or exported from or to one country better than others with respect to laws which impose restrictions

---

[12] Argentina – Measures Affecting Imports of Footwear, Textiles, Apparel and Other Items, Appellate Body Report, WT/DS56/AB/R (22 April 1998).

[13] Art. 2.8 EU–Japan EPA (1 February 2019).

[14] Art. 2.33 EU–Japan EPA (1 February 2019).

on trade. In other words, WTO members cannot pick favourites with respect to the laws which they levy against traded goods. In that sense, the MFN principle prevents alliances, which are not only economically distortive but may also lead to geopolitical tension. Recalling the goal of peace as part of trade, MFN operates as a diffuser of hostilities, embracing the idea of a global community in which all countries regard each other as allies. MFN treatment is offered to all WTO members unconditionally, which means that it is enjoyed regardless of whether any concession has been offered in return. Attempts to impose conditions on the availability of MFN which are unrelated to the relevant product itself will be viewed as unlawful.[15] Article I is very broad in its scope, covering a wide range of governmental action which impacts upon trade, whether at the border in terms of tariff commitments or internally, such as with respect to sales taxes. It is most commonly associated with discriminatory tariffs – meaning that the WTO member in question imposes a higher tariff on a good from one country than it does on the same good from another country.

Since MFN means that benefits are accorded equally to products originating from all countries, it has the practical consequence of distributing the advantages gained by the shrewdest negotiators, perhaps rich countries such as the US, to countries which have the weakest negotiators, such as developing countries. Once something is offered to one WTO member, it must be offered to all, whether it is a tariff or any other kind of trade advantage. Importantly, MFN prevents both *de jure* discrimination (meaning overt discrimination based explicitly on the nationality of the product) as well as *de facto* discrimination (meaning indirect or disguised discrimination which is based superficially on some other factor but actually reflects a product's national origin).

MFN eliminates distortions in patterns of production, allowing firms to choose the most efficient location from which to source their products. Since MFN applies to all WTO members it is a powerful tool of trade liberalization at the multilateral level. It also contributes to more straightforward customs processes precluding the need to investigate complicated ROO of a given good to ascertain whether it deserves to receive the beneficial treatment or not. As a consequence of the MFN provision in the GATT, discrimination among the WTO's 164 members occurs less than it did in the past. Where it does it is often covered by regional agreements, the rules of which will be examined further below. Indeed, the key exception to the MFN obligation is in relation to RTAs.

In the context of RTAs, MFN treatment for goods typically consists of the promise that when a party reduces its MFN applied rate of customs duty (meaning the tariff it imposes to all other WTO members under the GATT), that duty rate shall apply to an originating good of the other party if, and for as long as, it is lower than the customs duty rate on the same good agreed to under the RTA.[16] In other words, parties promise to apply the lower of the tariff in the RTA or the MFN tariff, which in most cases should be higher.

3.4 National treatment

Protectionism in its purest form is the preference for the good produced by domestic suppliers over those which originate from abroad. In theory this gives local firms an advantage, potentially

---

[15] Indonesia – Certain Measures Affecting the Automobile Industry, Panel Report WT/DS54/R (23 July 1998).

[16] Art. 2.82 EU–Japan EPA (1 February 2019).

making their products more attractive to domestic consumers because their price will be artificially lower than they should be because they do not have to bear the a more onerous burden of onerous tariffs or other kinds of laws. Consumers in the relevant country will be disposed to purchase these goods rather than the foreign equivalent, even if the foreign good was of higher quality and should have been less expensive. National treatment, found in Article III of the GATT, was designed to prevent this outcome.

Article III of the GATT is arguably drafted badly and can be challenging to read and interpret because it contains several obligations. The full text of the most important parts of GATT's national treatment obligation are included here:

1. The contracting parties recognize that internal taxes and other internal charges, and laws, regulations and requirements affecting the internal sale, offering for sale, purchase, transportation, distribution or use of products, and internal quantitative regulations requiring the mixture, processing or use of products in specified amounts or proportions, should not be applied to imported or domestic products so as to afford protection to domestic production.

2. The products of the territory of any contracting party imported into the territory of any other contracting party shall not be subject, directly or indirectly, to internal taxes or other internal charges of any kind in excess of those applied, directly or indirectly, to like domestic products. Moreover, no contracting party shall otherwise apply internal taxes or other internal charges to imported or domestic products in a manner contrary to the principles set forth in paragraph 1.

3. With respect to any existing internal tax which is inconsistent with the provisions of paragraph 2, but which is specifically authorized under a trade agreement, in force on April 10, 1947, in which the import duty on the taxed product is bound against increase, the contracting party imposing the tax shall be free to postpone the application of the provisions of paragraph 2 to such tax until such time as it can obtain release from the obligations of such trade agreement in order to permit the increase of such duty to the extent necessary to compensate for the elimination of the protective element of the tax.

4. The products of the territory of any contracting party imported into the territory of any other contracting party shall be accorded treatment no less favourable than that accorded to like products of national origin in respect of all laws, regulations and requirements affecting their internal sale, offering for sale, purchase, transportation, distribution or use. The provisions of this paragraph shall not prevent the application of differential internal transportation charges which are based exclusively on the economic operation of the means of transport and not on the nationality of the product.

Under this provision WTO members must regard all products as equal in terms of how they are affected by the internal legal system both in terms of taxes and all kinds of measures, whether they are domestic or imported. This means that they must treat imported goods the same way that they treat their own equivalent goods, effectively preventing protectionism in favour of domestic producers. The purpose of this provision is to ensure that there will be equality in competitive conditions between suppliers of goods, irrespective of their national origin, allowing for a healthy functioning market where goods compete based on their quality and price. As with MFN, under national treatment, discrimination is prohibited whether it is *de jure* or *de facto*, essentially meaning expressly based on nationality or covertly linked to nationality but superficially disguised to appear to be based on some other factor. The national treatment obligation is seen as being more demanding on WTO members than MFN is because it interferes with a state's own internal regulatory capacity in many ways.

One of the most important issues which must be resolved by lawyers arguing cases based on either of the non-discrimination standards is that of product 'likeness' which was mentioned above in relation to MFN. The guarantee of national treatment or MFN only has meaning if the products in question are worthy of equal treatment. In other words, they must be similar to each other in some fundamental way or else the concept of equal treatment is senseless. Accordingly, the obligations of non-discriminatory treatment rest heavily on the definition of the term 'like', which appears several times in the GATT's provisions on MFN and national treatment (as well as in other WTO agreements). One of the difficulties in coming to terms with national treatment is that the precise meaning of 'likeness' varies according to context – it is wider in some than in others.

In the first sentence of Article II:2 regarding internal taxes, there appears to be a very strict standard where the products are 'like' – even a very small difference in taxes will violate the provision. 'Likeness' here will be ascertained primarily by the products' physical characteristics, but also their end uses by consumers.[17] The second sentence of Article II:2 does not contain all the components of an obligation on its own, but instead refers back to Paragraph 1 of Article III, which requires that internal taxes and charges 'should not be applied to imported or domestic products so as to afford protection to domestic production'. An interpretive note to the second sentence clarifies that this obligation applies where the products are 'directly competitive or substitutable' – a phase which does not appear in the actual text of the agreement, as noted above but was elaborated upon in caselaw. In *Japan – Alcohol* the panel and Appellate Body looked at this phrase in terms of the concept of elasticity of substitution – meaning the extent to which consumers are prepared to switch from one product to satisfy the same need as the other product becomes unavailable or more expensive.[18] Under this sentence the difference in taxes must be greater than in the first sentence in order for there to be a violation. Additionally, the second sentence also requires a demonstration that the objective purpose of the measure was to afford protection to domestic products. In this way there seems to be a harsher level of scrutiny where the products have a higher degree of similarity, possibly because there is a greater chance of protectionism in these circumstances rather than where products are more different from each other.

Article III:4 speaks of regulatory measures generally (rather than just taxes) and is therefore broader in scope. It could cover all kinds of regulations regarding commerce, such as conditions of sale, transport, even packaging. An example of a measure evaluated under Article III:4 was the requirement imposed by Korea that imported and domestic beef be sold in separate areas of the same shop. This *de jure* discrimination required an analysis of whether the differential treatment resulted

---

[17] Japan – Taxes on Alcoholic Beverages, Appellate Body Report, WT/DS8/AB/R (1 November 1996).

[18] Ibid.

in the foreign product being treated less favourably.[19] In Article III:4 the same criteria for likeness is used as in Article II:2, first sentence; however, the Appellate Body emphasized that 'likeness' under III:4 is broader than under III.2 first sentence, involving an examination of the competitiveness between the relevant products.[20] The standard in III:4 is still not as broad as the combined scope of 'like' and 'directly competitive and substitutable' contained in both parts of II:2. A violation of Article III:4 still requires that there is an alteration of the competitive conditions of the products.

It would seem as though Article II:2 first sentence on internal taxes contemplates some kind of effects test, but the precise nature of this test is unclear. It will probably involve a consideration of the overall impact of the measure on the group of imported products compared to the group of domestic products, although individual products tests could also be applied. Intent does not matter here formally, although it may have a pragmatic effect on the outcome of the case in the eyes of the panellist. Under the second sentence of Article II:2 discriminatory effect will be taken into account, along with objective intent. There may be some assessment of subjective intent if this information is available, for example the recorded statement of a politician or other official from the importing state. In the second sentence of II:2 the standard of 'directly competitive or substitutable' is fairly wide, essentially involving an examination of whether the two products are competing for the same consumers as opposed to their physical properties. Under Article III:4, the discriminatory effect of the measure is significant; however, intent does not matter. The standard of 'likeness' contained here is somewhere between 'likeness' under Article II:2 first sentence and 'directly competitive or substitutable' in Article III:2, second sentence. Competition in the market-place is probably relevant here. Clearly, the varied tests can be quite complicated.

Generally speaking, the comparison under national treatment 'likeness' must be drawn between two products not producers. The relevant factors to be considered for unravelling the meaning of 'likeness' have been explored in WTO caselaw and include: the products' end use in a given market; consumers' tastes and habits; the products' properties (physical characteristics); tariff classification and nomenclature; and finally, whether or not national origin is the sole distinguishing criterion in the measure (if the only way to tell them apart is by where they came from). There remains considerable disagreement regarding the scope of the national treatment standard, notably in relation to the differing standards of 'likeness' and the role or nonrole of intent at various stages of the analysis.[21] There is also some controversy regarding the illegality of discriminatory laws which regulate the production process as opposed to the product itself, an issue which appears again in the context of the Technical Barriers to Trade (TBT) Agreement, which will be discussed in Chapter 5. The panel in US – Tuna found that national treatment did not apply to production methods, choosing instead to focus on the ban as a quota under Article XI where production process oriented quotas were held to be unlawful.[22]

---

[19] Korea – Measures Affecting Imports of Fresh, Chilled and Frozen Beef, Panel Report, WT/DS161/R (10 January 2001).

[20] European Communities – Measures Affecting Asbestos and Asbestos-Containing Products, Appellate Body Report, WT/DS135/AB/R (5 April 2001).

[21] E.g. H Horn and P Mavroidis, 'Still Hazy after All These Years: The Interpretation of National Treatment in GATT/WTO Caselaw on Tax Discrimination' 15:1 European Journal of International Law 39 (2004).

[22] GATT Panel Report, US–Tuna above n 7.

From the above it can be seen that national treatment is a sweeping obligation to WTO members with the potential to encroach on all kinds of regulations which have an effect, even an indirect one, on international trade. But it is essential to safeguard the free flow of goods around the world because, even without tariffs, internal regulatory barriers can impose formidable obstacles to goods from other countries wishing to enter and compete effectively in foreign markets.

RTAs typically include national treatment provisions which duplicate that of GATT Article III, which is somewhat surprising given how complex and confusing the provision is. For example, Article 2.4 of the Australia–Indonesia Comprehensive Economic Partnership Agreement covering trade in goods simply incorporates GATT Article III in its entirety. It might seem somewhat of a missed opportunity that modern RTAs do not express national treatment in a more straightforward manner than the GATT.

3.5 Transparency

While it tends to receive less attention than the pivotal issue of non-discrimination based on product origin and tariff commitments, the WTO's devotion to transparency is perhaps equally important in terms of its role in ensuring free trade. Transparency is now well entrenched in many spheres of international and domestic lawmaking to the point that it is arguably an aspect of customary international law and closely aligned with the minimum standard of treatment under international law.[23] It tends to be viewed, at least by lawyers, as an essential pillar of a democratic society governed by rule of law because it guards against the arbitrary imposition of laws without prior notice or explanation. Yet in the modern era of overabundance of information, an obligation of transparency can be burdensome – especially to developing countries – because there is simply so much more data available than in the past, much of which may or may not be relevant. Under certain circumstances the requirement of transparency can be weaponized – raising costs of compliance to the point that the regulatory policy behind a measure may be insufficient to justify the costs involved with implementing it in a manner that is acceptable to civil society.

The GATT's central requirement in relation to transparency is found in Article X:

1. Laws, regulations, judicial decisions and administrative rulings of general application, made effective by any contracting party, pertaining to the classification or the valuation of products for customs purposes, or to rates of duty, taxes or other charges, or to requirements, restrictions or prohibitions on imports or exports or on the transfer of payments therefor, or affecting their sale, distribution, transportation, insurance, warehousing inspection, exhibition, processing, mixing or other use, shall be published promptly in such a manner as to enable governments and traders to become acquainted with them. Agreements affecting international trade policy which are in force between the government or a governmental agency of any contracting party and the government or governmental agency of any other contracting party shall also be published. The provisions of this paragraph shall not require any contracting party to disclose confidential information which

---

[23] A Bianchi and A Peters eds, *Transparency in International Law* (Cambridge University Press, 2013).

would impede law enforcement or otherwise be contrary to the public interest or would prejudice the legitimate commercial interests of particular enterprises, public or private.

2. No measure of general application taken by any contracting party effecting an advance in a rate of duty or other charge on imports under an established and uniform practice, or imposing a new or more burdensome requirement, restriction or prohibition on imports, or on the transfer of payments therefor, shall be enforced before such measure has been officially published.

For most members this obligation should be quite reasonable; however, it could be burdensome to countries at lower stages of development which lack the resources of some of the WTO's larger members. Article X does not require the publication of any confidential information disclosure of which would be contrary to public interests, which may cover matters such as national security, or which is commercially sensitive. It is important to note that Article X states that no laws may be enforceable unless they are published – a very strong incentive to comply with the transparency obligations or risk losing the entitlement to claim violations. The requirement that members must administer their laws in an impartial and reasonable manner with procedures in place for prompt review and correction may work towards improvements in domestic governance where this has been weak in the past – one of the ways in which the WTO can help to reform the functioning of an economy for the benefit of its own citizens. Since transparency is a foundational principle of WTO law, there are many additional notification requirements in other WTO treaties. It also features in international investment law, as will be seen in Chapter 7.

Despite the fact that the WTO has generally been quite strong in terms of its embracing of transparency, as seen most obviously on its exhaustively complete (and in some respects labyrinthine) website, it is often suggested that the WTO needs to improve its transparency. To the extent that this is true, it is less the WTO's external transparency to the world that is needful of improvement, but more its internal transparency in terms of its communications among its members and its committees. Some believe that the notification procedures required by many committees with respect to various measures implemented by members should be more robust.[24] There appears to be a need for more monitoring in terms of members' compliance with their WTO obligations. Members should be more readily able to submit comments with respect to other members' notifications and these should be reviewable by all members, as should replies. The value of this approach would be to pressure noncompliant members to improve their own transparency and, more importantly, to expose the failure to uphold obligations. The reputational effects of public shaming on the WTO website and elsewhere might work towards achieving greater compliance, for example with respect to subsidies and safeguards – topics which will be explored in more detail in Chapter 4.

With regard to the external engagement element of WTO transparency, this has generally been quite good, but there remains a great need for improvement in the WTO's image. Unlike the UN, for example, which enjoys a very strong reputation in most parts of the world, in part due to celebrity endorsement, the WTO is largely unknown, typically mentioned by politicians in the context of re-

---

[24] R Harte, 'Multilateralism in International Trade: Reforming the WTO' European Parliamentary Research Service (October 2018).

vulsion against globalization. This negativity prevails despite the fact that the WTO occupies a position of incredible importance in the global economy. It is noteworthy that in the UK, for example, the public only began to demonstrate an interest in the WTO after the vote to exit the EU, when 'trading on WTO terms' became a distinct practical exigency. Moreover, the WTO's engagement with civil society has been heavily focused on NGOs. This is far too narrow an approach, particularly since many NGOs are themselves large organizations with limited human contact and are often viewed as being unaccountable or politically motivated. The WTO's annual Open Day event in Geneva is a step in the right direction, as are the WTO's many educational programmes for developing countries. More could be done in terms of outreach and responsiveness to the needs of the average person. By coming to terms with the role of the WTO, the general public would be in a better position to appreciate the value of trade liberalization and the need for multilateral solutions to the world's economic problems.

Transparency is a feature of many RTAs as well. For example, the Japan–Australia Economic Partnership Agreement Article 1.3 states as follows:

1. Each Party shall ensure that its laws, regulations, administrative procedures, and administrative rulings of general application as well as international agreements to which the Party is a party, with respect to any matter covered by this Agreement, are promptly published or otherwise made publicly available in such a manner as to enable interested persons and the other Party to become acquainted with them.
2. Each Party shall make easily available to the public the names and addresses of the competent authorities responsible for the laws, regulations, administrative procedures and administrative rulings referred to in paragraph 1.
3. Each Party shall, on request of the other Party, within a reasonable period of time, respond to specific questions from, and provide information to, the other Party with respect to matters referred to in paragraph 1.
4. When introducing or changing its laws, regulations or administrative procedures that significantly affect the implementation of this Agreement, each Party shall endeavour to take appropriate measures to enable interested persons and the other Party to become acquainted with such introduction or change.

This provision goes further than GATT Article X envisioning contact points through which relevant information can be passed. This approach is common to many OECD countries where transparency is highly valued as a principle of global economic integration. With this topic in mind, this chapter will now turn to the very important issue of how the multilateral trade regime under the WTO interacts with regional agreements.

4. REGIONALISM

Even after GATT was concluded in the 1940s and the number of signatory parties to it grew, countries around the world began to sign bilateral trade treaties granting preferential treatment to those signatories beyond that which was available to the GATT signatories at large, seemingly contrary to the principle of MFN. These arrangements became more popular in the 1980s and 1990s and often encompassed international investment provisions. Today purely trade-focused preferential treaties are rare. While regionalism (in other words, preferentialism) is often depicted as a threat to the WTO in many respects both approaches are compatible because they seek the same aim – liberalization through the removal of barriers to trade.

4.1 Benefits of regionalism over multilateralism

The debate regarding the advantages and disadvantages of trade liberalization through regionalism against multilateralism is one of the central issues in international economic law. As multilateralism delivered through the WTO has stalled in recent years, much attention has turned to the more measured advances available through arrangements between smaller groupings of states. There are benefits and drawbacks to both systems.

Multilateralism is often portrayed as the framing of international relations on the basis of universal principles. In contrast, regionalism or (or bilateralism in the case of two parties) is rooted in bargaining and, ultimately, power. This may be why there is sometimes an unfair allocation of rights and responsibilities between larger and smaller trading partners in such arrangements. Regionalism is also thought to emphasize the dominance of the sovereign state and its own domestic interests, whereas multilateralism expands upon the concept of the international community and with it a rules based system of resolving economic issues at the international level. This includes the affirmation of the principle of the equality of states and non-discrimination.[25] The understanding of an international or global community is thought by some to hold more sway today because of the approaching universality of principles such as sustainability and human rights, as well as the recognition that unilateral economic activity often entails global consequences, including those which are noneconomic. At the same time, there is a growing weariness towards globalism, which is perceived by some to represent the entrenched interests of societies' elites.[26]

Regionalism has the obvious advantage of lending itself to easier agreement. With the WTO now at 164 members it is virtually impossible to achieve consensus on any issue, which is why negotiations on issues such as services liberalization and digital trade have faltered. It is simple logic that arrangements among smaller groupings can be concluded with much less difficulty. Similarly, regionalism can facilitate deeper liberalization covering a wider range of topics. This is why RTAs tend to cover more matters than are provided for in the WTO agreements, such as investment and competition law. Such agreement is often built on the foundations of WTO rules and are sometimes known as WTO+ commitments, where groups of states prepared to go beyond the WTO rules can get together. RTAs tend to be more flexible than the WTO 'single undertaking' in which all agreements must be adopted. For example, the incrementalism available in regional arrangements can be seen in the 'ratcheting' approach adopted by some RTAs. A 'ratchet clause' is a provision through which the parties commit that, if they unilaterally decide in the future to further open up their respective markets in one specific sector, this liberalization would be locked

---

[25] S Schill, *The Multilateralization of International Investment Law* (Cambridge University Press, 2009) at 10–11.

[26] I Bremmer, *Us vs Them: The Failure of Globalism* (Penguin, 2018).

in, meaning that there can be no reversal. It must be acknowledged that the WTO has shown willingness to embrace a kind of gradualism as well. For example the Accession Protocol of Russia required that Russia eliminated various subsidies on a staged basis.[27] In some respects accession protocols are bespoke arrangements offered by the WTO for newly acceding countries which might have trouble taking on the full package. Finally, regionalism may be advantageous because it helps assuage geopolitical tensions by encouraging economic integration among former rivals. This is in keeping with the theoretical link between trade and peace noted in the previous chapter. While the diplomatic function of economic engagement may also be present in the multilateral context, it is perhaps less impactful than when nations form these bonds on a one to one basis.

Multilateralism tends to be viewed as more economically efficient than regionalism. The proliferation of hundreds of RTAs (not to mention thousands of bilateral investment treaties) has been memorably referred to as a 'spaghetti bowl', conjuring the image of a confusing mess. The many overlapping obligations contained in these instruments can lead to high compliance costs for trading firms. It may also result in welfare losses from trade diversion linked to preferential treatment, in which less efficient firms supply goods and services simply because they fall within a preferential bilateral or regional arrangement.[28] With multilateral rules, regulatory competition is eliminated through harmonization of rules, creating a situation in which competition is based on natural competitive advantages, meaning the quality and price of products. This should encourage specialization among states as they compete to supply better materials and more skilled labour, just as suppliers compete for foreign consumers. Regionalism has led to problems of compliance for the private sector because of complex, often overlapping rules that each party maintains concurrently on a bilateral level with countries outside the region, especially in relation to ROO, of which more will be discussed below. This has been particularly problematic in Asia where many regional trade and investment agreements are in operation.[29] Consumers are the ultimate losers in these inefficient arrangements. Multilateralism reduces the administrative burdens associated with compliance, allowing greater profits for trading firms coupled with lower prices for consumers – two of the advantages traditionally associated with economic liberalization and globalization generally.

In recent years it was anticipated that megaregionalism involving a large number of parties would capture the most advantageous aspects of both multilateralism and bilateralism. The Comprehensive Progressive Agreement on the Trans Pacific Partnership (CPTPP), which will be referred to throughout this book, is probably the best example of this phenomenon. Larger single markets have the potential to position themselves as hubs in a series of bilateral arrangements, with the economically weaker countries in the area acting as spokes, as envisioned by China's highly anticipated Regional Comprehensive Economic Partnership (RCEP) covering both trade and investment.[30] India and China in particular appear to have adopted this model because of their

---

[27] WT/L/839 (17 December 2011).

[28] J Bhagwati, *Termites in the Trading System* (Oxford University Press, 2008).

[29] J Wang, 'The Role of China and India in Asian Regionalism' in M Sornarajah and J Wang eds, *China, India and the International Economic Order* (Cambridge University Press, 2010) at 343.

[30] H Weng, 'The RCEP Investment Rules and China: Learning from the Malleability of Chinese FTAs' in J Chaisse ed., *China's International Investment Strategy: Bilateral, Regional and Global Law and Policy* (Oxford University Press, 2019).

considerable influence in their regions. However, as 'spoke' nations often receive less advantageous conditions than the hub, these arrangements have been criticized for marginalizing the peripheral countries, much as bilateral relations can be unequal. This situation may be exacerbated when the spoke countries do not liberalize between themselves, leading to multiple layers of discrimination against foreign investors.[31] Inefficiency may result. Progressive regionalism can be problematic because, like bilateralism, negotiation in smaller groups may be impossible in the case of countries that have strained diplomatic relations, as seen for example in the case of India and Pakistan. Multilateral negotiation could mitigate power imbalances between individual states, as suggested above. The emphasis on coordination suggests that multilateralism is seen to be the preferred way of structuring international economic rules.

On the other hand, as modern firms shift their priorities away from cheap labour in favour of automation as well as research and development and as they seek to maximize the speed at which their products reach consumers, global value chains may regionalize. This would tend to fit with the so-called Gravity Model of international trade which suggests that countries will tend to favour trade (in goods) with partners closer to them geographically because of the costs of transportation,[32] although this does not hold true for services. This modern transition in favour of trade with parties closer in space may advantage the most developed countries, where it will be facilitated by an educated workforce coupled with a broad range of RTAs. The global shift towards regional value chains is also being driven by China and other large emerging economies where consumers are buying more of what domestic value chains make and where local firms are capable of supplying more of their needs. This makes them less reliant on imported intermediate goods, meaning those that are sold between businesses as components of more complex, finished goods.[33] Having established some of the benefits associated with regionalism, the next section will outline the legal requirements for such arrangements in terms of their conformity with the laws of the WTO.

4.2 Requirements for RTAs

It is important to clarify that the WTO's multilateralism is compatible with regionalism and RTAs. This is notwithstanding the MFN obligation in GATT Article III which prohibits favouritism. GATT Article XXIV and GATS Article V allow MFN-violating measures to be implemented with an RTA if the formation of the RTA would be impossible without the violation, meaning that the discrimination against members outside the regional grouping is necessary. Some modern RTAs expressly state that they are in conformity with the GATT. This can be seen again in the Japan–Australia Economic Partnership Agreement:[34] 'The Parties hereby establish a free trade area consistent with Article XXIV of the GATT 1994 and Article V of the GATS.' This RTA is illustrative

---

[31] Wang above n 29.

[32] T Chaney, 'The Gravity Equation in International Trade: An Explanation' 126:1 Journal of Political Economy 150 (2018).

[33] S Lund, J Manyika, J Woetzel, J Bughin, M Krishnan, J Seong and Mac Muir 'Globalization in Transition: The Future of Trade and Value Chains', McKinsey Global Institute (January 2019).

[34] Art. 1.1.

because it also sets out principles regarding conflicts between it and WTO disciplines in a segment entitled 'Relation to Other Agreements':

1. The Parties reaffirm their rights and obligations under the WTO Agreement and any other agreements to which both Parties are party.
2. In the event of any inconsistency between this Agreement and the WTO Agreement or any other agreements to which both Parties are party, the Parties shall immediately consult with each other with a view to finding a mutually satisfactory solution.
3. Unless otherwise provided for in this Agreement, if any international agreement, or provision therein, incorporated into or referred to in this Agreement is amended, the Parties shall consult on whether it is necessary to amend this Agreement.
4. This Agreement shall not be construed to derogate from any international legal obligation between the Parties that entitles goods, services, or persons to treatment more favourable than that accorded by this Agreement.[35]

Ensuring that the RTA actually fits with a member's WTO obligations is slightly more difficult than merely stating so. As outlined in GATT Article XXIV, there are three main requirements in order for an RTA to be compatible with WTO law and therefore legal in terms of a signatories' membership to the WTO. First, there is an obligation not to raise the overall level of protection and make access for non-RTA members harder. Second, there is an obligation to liberalize substantially all trade among members of the RTA. Finally, the WTO must be notified of the creation of the RTA. The nature of these obligations will vary depending on whether the RTA being created is a customs union (CU) or a free trade agreement (FTA). CUs differ from FTAs in that CUs have a common external tariff whereas FTAs allow their members to maintain their own, different external tariffs.

With respect to the first obligation, the external trade requirement, for FTAs, members of the FTA may not alter their external protection to affect non-FTA members negatively. This is not problematic – it simply means that the FTA members must each uphold their GATT MTN tariffs with respect to their dealings with countries outside the FTA. For a CU, members of the CU may not raise the overall level of external protection. Since they share a common external tariff level, this means that all CU members must adjust their external protection to the same level. For some members who maintained higher tariffs before, this will involve adjusting downwards; for other members who had lower tariffs before they joined, it may involve an upwards adjustment. In this latter case the member is raising its overall tariff, which is against the WTO's principle of lowering barriers to trade. Therefore, if adjusting external tariffs upwards causes harm to non-CU members, compensation from that particular member of the CU may be required to address the decline in liberalization.

This aspect of FTAs was problematic for Turkey when it was preparing to join the European Community (EC)'s CU for goods. Turkey was required to impose quotas on clothing products so that it was able to comply with the commercial policy imposed by the rest of Europe. The problem for Turkey was that it had never placed clothing quotas on any countries. When Turkey fulfilled this obligation in order to join the EC CU, India, with its vibrant textile industry, initiated a complaint through

---

[35] Art. 1.11.

the WTO dispute settlement system on the basis of a violation of the prohibition of quantitative restrictions found in Article XI.[36] The panel resolved the dispute by looking at the word 'necessary' which appears in Article XXIV of GATT. The panel and later the Appellate Body ruled that a country imposing a trade barrier to join a CU had to show that the requirements to join the union cannot be met without imposing that barrier. Turkey was not able to demonstrate that the quota was essential because there were other ways that it could have upheld the EC's customs requirements for foreign clothes without imposing quotas on Indian clothes. Specifically, the panel and the Appellate Body found that Turkey could have imposed labelling requirements on Indian clothes so that when Turkish exporters sold clothes in Europe, those originating from within the union (including Turkey) would have one label, and those coming from outside (places such as India) would not. Turkey had not done this, so the quotas were unnecessary and had to be removed.

Regarding the second obligation of GATT Article XXIV, the internal trade requirement, there is an obligation for all members of an FTA or a CU to liberalize substantially all trade among its members. 'Substantially all trade' is an ambiguous concept. It might be quantitative – it could be the amount of trade in value per unit of currency, per weight or per unit. Or it might be qualitative – covering all trade in a given industry. It likely precludes RTAs which are sector specific. For example, there could not be an automobile RTA. Generally speaking, it would seem as though there is a high degree of flexibility with this concept. It seems that it refers to 'more than some' of the trade but not necessarily 'all'.

4.3 Regionalism and the 'frontier traffic' exception

Although it is an obscure feature of Article XXIV, some mention of the 'frontier traffic' exception to the MFN obligation is useful because of the recent attention that has been drawn to this provision during the debates surrounding the UK's departure from the EU. Article XXIV.3 states that the GATT 'shall not be construed to prevent: a) Advantages accorded by any contracting party to adjacent countries in order to facilitate frontier traffic.' There has been no caselaw which has interpreted this provision, but a more precise meaning may be inferred. In practice, 'advantages' likely mean customs procedures and formalities at the border which would be made easier for an adjacent country than for other WTO members. With reciprocal trade between the two territories exempted from custom control and other restrictions of trade, other WTO members could not complain that their goods would be subject instead to custom duties when exported to the same territories. Article XXIV sub-paragraph 3(a) on 'frontier traffic' appears to have been based on a US proposal from 1947 which stated that this provision referred to facilities for frontier traffic in cases where a frontier ran through a city. The area affected by this provision was usually limited to a distance of 15 kilometres from the frontier, suggesting that it has limited scope.

4.4 FTAs and ROO

One of the disadvantages with trading under preferential trade agreements is the practical difficulty in complying with ROO, which has been mentioned several times already in this book. ROO

---

[36] Turkey – Restrictions on Imports of Textile and Clothing Products, Panel Report, WT/DS34/R (19 November 1999).

are rules which designate the minimum percentage quantity of a product that may be considered to have originated from a country, entitling that product to benefit from the preferential trade regime. In many RTAs, ROOs are relatively lax, allowing goods to take advantage of the favourable trade terms when only a small portion of the product originates from within the relevant territory. Leniency in ROOs is important because of the modern trading economy, where many goods are composite products, composed of numerous integrated parts, each of which may have been created in a different jurisdiction. An example is the modern automobile, where engines, tyres, seats and so on are manufactured in factories located in a range of different countries – the final assembled product represents the end state of a complex global production chain. Some modern RTAs call for much tighter ROOs, with the new United States Mexico Canada Agreement (USMCA) perhaps the best example. The US had insisted that ROO thresholds needed to be raised to 60 per cent in this treaty, meaning that only products of which 60 per cent originated in one of Canada, Mexico or the US would be entitled to the lower tariff treatment specified under the regime. Higher ROO thresholds underline the benefits available to suppliers within that region and are in many respects defensible on that basis. However, complying with ROOs can be difficult, requiring complicated paperwork and tracking. It is often thought that many suppliers do not even bother claiming benefits to which they are entitled under various RTAs for precisely this reason. In fact some believe it may be cheaper to trade under multilateral WTO tariffs than to go through onerous ROO compliance procedures at the border to secure a modest concession in the form of a preferential tariff. ROO must therefore be crafted with a view to facilitating compliance with a view to accessing the preferential treatment, not to frustrate it.[37] Some have even gone as far as to say that ROO should be omitted entirely from RTAs in favour of MFN-based ROO.[38]

A good example of the complexity of ROO in a modern FTA can be seen in the CPTPP. Article 3.20 on Claims for Preferential Treatment states as follows:

1. Except as otherwise provided in Annex 3-A (Other Arrangements), each Party shall provide that an importer may make a claim for preferential tariff treatment, based on a certification of origin completed by the exporter, producer or importer.

2. An importing Party may:
   (a) require that an importer who completes a certification of origin provide documents or other information to support the certification;
   (b) establish in its law conditions that an importer shall meet to complete a certification of origin;
   (c) if an importer fails to meet or no longer meets the conditions established under subparagraph (b), prohibit that importer from providing its own certification as the basis of a claim for preferential tariff treatment; or
   (d) if a claim for preferential tariff treatment is based on a certification of origin completed by an importer, prohibit that importer from making a subsequent claim for preferen-

---

[37] B Malkawi, M El-Shafie, 'The Design and Operation of Rules of Origin in Greater Arab Free Trade Area: Challenges of Implementation and Reform' 53:2 Journal of World Trade (2019).

[38] P Mavroidis and E Vermulst, 'The Case for Dropping Preferential Rules of Origin' 52:1 Journal of World Trade 1 (2018).

tial tariff treatment for the same importation based on a certification of origin completed by the exporter or producer.

3. Each Party shall provide that a certification of origin:
   (a) need not follow a prescribed format;
   (b) be in writing, including electronic format;
   (c) specifies that the good is both originating and meets the requirements of this Chapter; and
   (d) contains a set of minimum data requirements as set out in Annex 3-B (Minimum Data Requirements).

4. Each Party shall provide that a certification of origin may apply to:
   (a) a single shipment of a good into the territory of a Party; or
   (b) multiple shipments of identical goods within any period specified in the certification of origin, but not exceeding 12 months.

5. Each Party shall provide that a certification of origin is valid for one year after the date that it was issued or for such longer period specified by the laws and regulations of the importing Party.

6. Each Party shall allow an importer to submit a certification of origin in English. If the certification of origin is not in English, the importing Party may require the importer to submit a translation in the language of the importing Party.

The long excerpt is included here to show the level of detail involved in just one part of the chapter on ROO. It is fairly evident, even for a trade lawyer, that ROO can be quite complicated, representing a serious burden for trading firms from within the preferential trade zone, not to mention for the customs authorities in those countries. While the costs of compliance are often thought to be overstated (the WTO estimates that such costs comprise only about 1 per cent of the value of the relevant product[39]), it is perhaps not surprising that some exporters do not bother seeking preferential treatment under the FTA, preferring instead to trade on WTO terms because it is simpler. Greater recognition that ROO costs are often overestimated might change this course of behaviour. It might also help clarify misconceptions regarding the advantages of CUs over FTAs. There is no evidence that CUs outperform FTAs in terms of trade volumes – in fact, there are studies which suggest that FTAs may outperform CUs.[40] This may explain why FTAs, even with their complex ROO, tend to be more popular than CUs around the world.

5. CONCLUSION

This chapter introduced the WTO as the main system of international law governing international trade in goods, as outlined in the original GATT agreement from the 1940s. Since the WTO is a

---

[39] 'New Evidence on Preference Utilization' World Trade Organization Economic Research and Statistics Division, Staff Working Paper ERSD-2012-12 (3 September 2012).

[40] K Head and T Mayer, 'Gravity Equations: Workhorse, Toolkit, and Cookbook' CEPII, No 2013-17 (2013).

member-driven organization, it is not accurate to think in terms of what 'it' does but rather of what the members have decided with a view to their own self-interest, which is normally in line with the collective self-interest of the global trading community. The chapter went on to outline the main components of the GATT. These are the prohibition of quantitative restrictions, the commitment to maintain tariffs no higher than they have been listed for each good and the promise not to discriminate against goods based on their place of origin. The GATT, like many other agreements under international economic law, also places some emphasis on transparency in relation to regulations governing international trade.

The chapter then explored regionalism as an alternative to multilateralism in trade rules, focusing on the rules under the GATT which allow for preferential treatment of goods from designated states, which are somewhat more complicated for CU than for FTAs. The recent shift towards regionalism in trade treaties may be seen less as a failure of the WTO and more as an indication that greater progress in trade liberalization may be achieved when dealing with smaller groupings of countries than it can across the whole world. The next chapter will examine the WTO's special system designed to resolve disagreements which may arise among its many members regarding the rights created under the various WTO treaties.

DISCUSSION QUESTIONS

1. In what sense is the WTO properly described as an instrument of global governance?
2. What are the chief ways in which the GATT eliminates distortions in international trade?
3. Are the tests for assessing violations of national treatment and MFN sufficiently well articulated and what are some of the chief difficulties in terms of their interpretation?
4. To what extent does the GATT accommodate preferential treatment among WTO members and are these arrangements antithetical to the main purpose of the WTO?

FURTHER READING

JB Kim, 'Adaptation of Internal Trade Requirements in RTAs: Substandard Internal Trade Liberalization' 52:3 Journal of World Trade 375 (2018).

PA Lanyi, A Steinbach, 'Promoting Coherence between PTAs and the WTO through Systemic Integration' 20:1 Journal of International Economic Law 61 (2017).

G Marceau, 'WTO and Export Restrictions' 50:4 Journal of World Trade 563 (2016).

G Muller, 'National Treatment and the GATS: Lessons from Jurisprudence' 50:5 Journal of World Trade 819 (2016).

3
Dispute resolution in international trade: the WTO Dispute Settlement Understanding and regional trade agreement dispute resolution

1. INTRODUCTION

One of the central pillars of the WTO is binding dispute settlement among its many members. The WTO contains its own dispute settlement procedure to ensure that its many obligations are enforceable, which means that they have practical significance for the members and, by extension, the suppliers and consumers who are the indirect beneficiaries of the world trading system. The WTO's dispute settlement system also reiterates the organization's commitment to the rule of law, which in some instances may conflict with the relationship building function of diplomacy. Dispute settlement functionality within the WTO is vital because disagreements can arise between WTO members regarding the meaning and implementation of WTO rules, which are often ambiguous and confusing. Some of these were mentioned in Chapter 2.

A special set of procedural rules was developed to facilitate binding resolution of these problems: the Dispute Settlement Understanding (DSU). The DSU comprises a first level of *ad hoc* tribunals to hear and resolve WTO disputes established at members' requests, which might be analogized to trials in the sense that they deal with issues of fact as well as law. These rulings, known as 'recommendations' (most likely because it sounds more diplomatic than 'judgments', the term used by most courts), can be appealed to a standing Appellate Body, which issues binding, final decisions – these are also called 'recommendations'. The WTO dispute settlement system is often considered to be the most successful dispute resolution forum in international law. It is sometimes referred to as the 'jewel in the crown' of the WTO and is held in much regard by trade lawyers and academics around the world. During less than 25 years of existence, the WTO's members (acting as the Dispute Settlement Body or DSB) have adopted more than 300 panel and Appellate Body reports from among more than 550 complaints. By way of comparison, the ICJ has heard less than 150 contentious cases since its creation in 1946.

This chapter will begin by briefly outlining the old system of dispute settlement under the GATT, before turning to an examination of the central features of the current system, including the panels, the Appellate Body, rules of evidence, interpretation, access and confidentiality. The dispute settlement system's unusual approach to remedies will then be explained. It will continue by addressing some of the pressing problems facing the WTO's dispute settlement system today, along with key proposals for reform. The chapter will conclude by briefly considering dispute settlement systems under RTAs.

2. THE OLD REGIME: DISPUTE SETTLEMENT UNDER GATT 1947

The dispute settlement system which has existed in the WTO since 1995 is a considerable improvement on the earlier system that had been used under the original GATT agreement from the 1940s. The GATT used rather imprecise language to cover dispute settlement among its signatory parties. It provided for consultations which were effectively nonbinding negotiations aimed at achieving an agreed outcome which placated both parties. 'Working parties' could be established for this purpose, which were later termed 'panels' – a nomenclature which reflected the growing need for genuine legal, rather than diplomatic, solutions. The problem with the early panels was that their 'recommendations' required consensus of the entire GATT council (all of the signatories) in order to be adopted. Even the losing party could complain that it was not happy with the decision. This meant that blockage was common and consequently the system was not very effective. Recommendations were often crafted to avoid tension rather than to preserve actual legal rights, as the GATT parties needed. Still, the more diplomatic approach worked reasonably well until the 1970s, at which point the increasing number of signatories and the proliferation of nontariff barriers (of which more in the next two chapters) began to place more strain on the dispute settlement features of the system.

A legal office was established in the GATT Secretariat in the mid-1980s. Then, as lawyers became more involved in the dispute settlement process, panel recommendations came to be viewed as rulings. The dominance of US lawyers trained in the common law tradition led to the understanding of these rulings as a system of quasi-precedent. There was also a growing recognition that panels were a kind of international court and accordingly customary rules of international law became incorporated into panel rulings, most likely at the behest of lawyers from civil backgrounds who had experience in other international tribunals, such as the ICJ. The closer involvement of lawyers unsurprisingly led to the codification of procedural rules of dispute settlement with a view to making the system more consistent and predictable. In short, over time there was a distinct shift from a diplomatic dispute settlement system to a rules-based one. The final modifications of the system into the one which exists today took place upon the creation of the WTO and, along with it, the adoption of the DSU.

3. WTO DISPUTE SETTLEMENT UNDERSTANDING

The DSU is a set of procedural rules for the WTO's dispute settlement system that was adopted in 1995 as a result of the Uruguay Round of multilateral negotiations. Article 2.1 of the DSU establishes the DSB to administer the DSU's rules. The DSB consists of all of the WTO members acting together – it has the authority to establish dispute settlement panels, adopt panel and Appellate Body reports, monitor the implementation of rulings and authorize members' suspension of concessions. Under Article 2.3 of the DSU, the DSB meets as often as is necessary to carry out its functions, which in practice is normally every month.

There are no substantive obligations relating to trade in the DSU – it relates only to the process of dispute settlement itself, meaning the procedural rules of the juridical forum in which disputes regarding the main agreements which arise between WTO members are resolved. Its primary objective is to settle disputes through a multilateral process rather than unilateralism, as occurred in the past under the GATT system, especially on the part of the US. There is concern that this may occur again in the future because the US has the economic might to pressure other countries into accepting its stance on trade without the need for the international community's support. In keeping with its diplomatic origins, the DSU requires consultations as a prelude to adjudication. There is also provision for arbitration and mediation with a view to resolving matters before they escalate. The WTO dispute settlement system is used extensively by WTO members, in particular developed countries. With progress stalled under the Doha Round of trade negotiations in terms of achieving deeper liberalization on more trade issues, the dispute settlement system is seen as the most successful feature of the WTO, although in recent times it has faced its own problems and, as of the time of writing, has an uncertain future.

3.1 Consultations

Figure 3.1 illustrates the stages in bringing a claim under the WTO dispute settlement system. WTO dispute settlement begins formally when a member (the complainant) requests consultations with another member concerning its view that there has been a 'nullification or impairment' of its benefits accruing under the WTO agreements. This stage is designed to de-amplify the conflict by giving the parties an opportunity to discuss the dispute and to negotiate an amicable resolution. These meetings are confidential and without prejudice with respect to any further proceedings.[1] Consultations may be bilateral or multilateral if more countries are involved, as the complainant requests. Multilateral consultations are open to any WTO member which has a 'substantial trade interest' in the matter. Members can also request to join consultations. Bilateral consultations are held in private, meaning that only the complaining and responding parties are involved. The DSU itself does not specify how the consultations are conducted – the parties have wide latitude to structure them as they wish. It is believed that a significant number of disputes are resolved at the consultation stage through mutually agreed solutions or discontinuance, taking pressure off the formal adjudicatory stage of panels.

It should be pointed out here that there are other dispute resolution methods available to WTO members in addition to pursuing contentious, adversarial 'litigation' through the panel process. Article 5 of the DSU provides for the nonbinding procedures of good offices, conciliation and mediation, although of the three, only mediation has ever been invoked. Binding arbitration is also available under Article 25. Arbitration requires the parties to agree on the issues which are to

---

[1] Art. 4.6.

Source: World Trade Organization. Reprinted by permission.

Figure 3.1 WTO dispute settlement system process

be resolved and the procedures which are to be used during the proceeding. Awards issued under this process are binding, not subject to appeal and enforceable through the DSU in the manner outlined below. So far there has only been one Article 25 arbitration – it involved the US and the EC and related to the issue of copyright under the TRIPS Agreement.[2]

---

[2] Award of the Arbitrators, US – Copyright, Recourse to Arbitration under Art 25 DSU, WT/DS160/ARB/21/1 (9 November 2001).

3.2 Panels

If consultations fail, the complainant may request that the DSB establish a panel. A panel will be established unless there is negative consensus not to do so (every WTO member would have to vote against it), which means that it is virtually automatic. The panels are *ad hoc*, meaning that they are constituted for each dispute, after which point the individual panellists return to their normal working lives – they are not employed by the WTO. Each panel consists of three members (the phrase 'judge' is not used, probably because it does not sound sufficiently diplomatic). Five members may be chosen if the parties agree. These panellists are not nationals of either party, unless agreed by the parties. They are normally highly regarded experts in international trade law, and in some cases are members of the other state's delegation to the WTO. The complainant and respondent states normally select the panellists. Article 8.4 of the DSU permits the WTO Secretariat to maintain an indicative list of individuals who are suitable to be appointed as panellists, although it is not obligatory to use these people. WTO members are empowered to nominate individuals for the roster, and many often do, listing specific aspects of WTO law in which each person holds expertise. For example, Norway submitted a list of ten individuals in 2019 whereas some countries, such as Canada, have not submitted lists of people at all. If the parties cannot agree on the establishment of the panel, either can request that the Director General of the WTO determine its composition, which occurs approximately half of the time. The DSU further specifies that when a dispute involves a developing country, at least one panellist must be from a developing country, if the developing country so requests.[3]

The panel process begins once the composition of the panel has been established. Article 7 of the DSU outlines the standard terms of reference for a panel, which requires it to examine the complaint as presented in the complainant's request for the establishment of the panel and to make findings which will assist the DSB in making recommendations. As is the case with many international courts, the panel evaluates the factual and legal elements of the dispute based on the written submissions of the parties, additional meetings and expert opinions. Panels make every effort to arrive upon decisions on the basis of consensus of all panellists. Otherwise there is a majority vote. If there is a dissent, it is included in the report, but the identity of the dissenting member is kept secret. The anonymity of the reports, in terms of authorship, is crucial, given that this runs the risk of undermining the impartiality of a panellist who may be nervous about the impact on their reputation in the eyes of their home state government.

According to the DSU, a strict timeframe is observed for panel proceedings – the panel process should last no more than six months and in no case should more than nine months elapse between the point at which the panel is established and the circulation of the panel report. In practice, however, the process normally takes substantially longer. The average length between panel establishment and the issuance of the report is approximately one year, but in some cases it can be much longer. The excessive duration of the panel process, transgressing the periods specified in the DSU, is one of the main criticisms of the system, especially from the US. Delays are becoming more common, in part due to the lack of staff support in the WTO Secretariat and the increasing

---

[3] Art. 8.10.

caseload, in conjunction with the increasing complexity of the cases. This is notwithstanding the fact that the legal staff in the WTO Secretariat has more than doubled since 2000.[4]

Panel reports are adopted by negative consensus. This means that every member of the DSB would have to declare that they are dissatisfied with the ruling for it to be dropped – even if one country is pleased with the ruling it will go ahead, including the party which won the dispute. In this sense panel reports become binding on the parties virtually automatically. This 'reverse consensus' rule was a key innovation of the Uruguay Round, which was essential to address US concerns that the previous panel process had become ineffective. With reverse consensus the blocking problem from the old days of GATT dispute settlement is avoided and the panel recommendations have genuine legal implications. Although panel hearings can be factually complex, they tend to be less fact intensive than many domestic proceedings, especially those relating to commercial matters. There are no witnesses or physical evidence, although the documentary evidence can be voluminous. The focus of panel hearings tends to be on the measures themselves, meaning their wording, how they are applied and their effects. This is in contrast with dispute settlement under international investment law, which will be explored in Chapter 8.

3.3 Appellate Body

A panel decision may be appealed to the Appellate Body before it has been adopted by the DSB. The Appellate Body consists of seven individuals of demonstrated experience in international trade and the WTO agreements, and of high regard in the international trade community. They are standing 'members' (again, not judges) and are not affiliated with any government. Each member is elected for a four-year term which may be renewed once, for a total of eight years' service. The DSU specifies that the Appellate Body should be broadly representative of the membership of the WTO, covering the various legal systems of the world.[5] Each case is heard by three members of the seven member body sitting in 'divisions'. These are assembled randomly on a rotating basis. Decisions relating to each appeal are taken by that division on its own; however, the practice of collegiality has developed, in which the members of the sitting division exchange views with other Appellate Body members before issuing their final decision. This is thought to be effective in achieving consistency.

Approximately 70 per cent of panel decisions are appealed, contributing to a large caseload, especially in recent years. The reason for this high level of frequency is thought to be that appeals achieve delay and help domestic politicians 'save face' by reporting to their constituents that they are doing everything in their power to maintain the measure. As with most courts around the world, appeals are limited to questions of law which are covered in the panel report. The Appellate Body may uphold, modify or reverse a panel decision. Critically, there is no remand power – the Appellate Body cannot send the matter back down to another panel to resolve questions of fact that were not addressed properly, nor can it engage in fact finding or evaluation of the evidence as

---

[4] J Pauwelyn and W Zhang, 'Busier than Ever? A Data-Driven Assessment and Forecast of WTO Caseload' 21:3 Journal of International Economic Law 461 (2018).

[5] Art. 17.3.

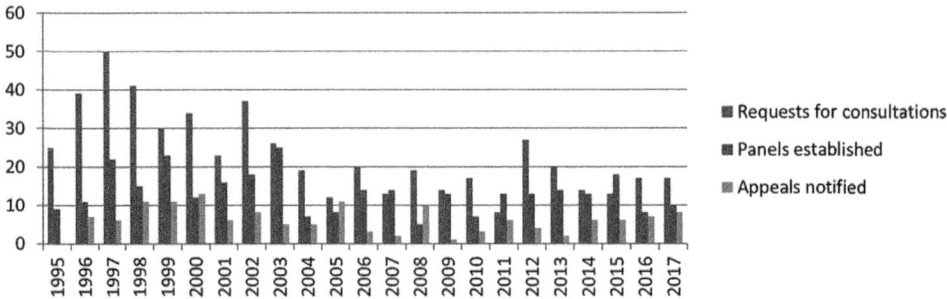

Figure 3.2 WTO dispute settlement system number of disputes per year

presented by the parties. As with panel reports, Appellate Body reports are adopted by the DSB by negative consensus. The number of panel and Appellate Body cases per year since 1995 is shown in Figure 3.2, with the most obvious trend being the decrease in requests for consultations per year, although this may be reversing.

At the time of writing, in mid-2019, the WTO Appellate Body is in crisis. If the US continues to block the appointment of new Appellate Body members as the terms of the old members end, then within a short time this key feature of the system will cease to function, given that at least three members are needed to hear an appeal. Blockage of the appointment of new Appellate Body members is arguably a breach of the obligation to use the WTO dispute settlement system in good faith,[6] not to mention a violation of Article 17 which establishes the Appellate Body in the first place. A number of proposals have been suggested to deal with this issue, including making the appellate mechanism a plurilateral feature of WTO membership, with all members other than the US joining. New members could be appointed without the involvement of the US and these individuals could hear appeals from panel recommendations in disputes involving all other WTO members. Alternatively, it may be possible for the dispute settlement system to continue without an appeal facility. The panel procedure would operate on its own, much as is the case in conventional investment arbitration. This may not resolve the matter, however, because under current DSU rules, the adoption of the panel report must be suspended pending appeal, but without sufficient members (at least three), the Appellate Body would not be in a position to complete its proceedings. This circumstance would signify the *de facto* demise of the negative consensus rule. Any losing party could prevent the adoption of the panel report by appealing it to an Appellate Body which was paralyzed to respond.

The arbitration procedure outlined in Article 25 of the DSU may also provide a recourse in the event that the Appellate Body becomes dysfunctional. Canada and the EU recently agreed to use this feature for appeals in the event that the Appellate Body is no longer able to function. This provision allows for parties to submit their dispute to arbitration should they wish, provided that they

---

[6] Art. 3.

notify the WTO. As noted before, there is only one case of this procedure ever being used.[7] One of the drawbacks to this procedure is that is unclear whether awards issued by these arbitration tribunals would be considered binding, in the sense that they could be considered *res judicata* and not reheard by a WTO panel, or another arbitration tribunal, for that matter. It is conceivable that Article IX of the WTO Agreement covering waivers could be used to break the deadlock over the nonappointment of new Appellate Body members by derogating from the normal consensus-based decision-making requirement. Article IX.3 states: 'In exceptional circumstances, the Ministerial Conference may decide to waive an obligation imposed on a Member by this Agreement or any of the Multilateral Trade Agreements, provided that any such decision shall be taken by three fourths of the Members.'

The dysfunctionality of the Appellate Body would need to constitute an exceptional circumstance for this technique to work. It may well do so, given that lack of the Appellate Body effectively eviscerates the dispute settlement function of the WTO. It is highly likely that four fifths of the WTO members would be able to work towards appointing new Appellate Body members as required. The political implications of this recourse could be severe, however, as it would effectively marginalize the US from the dispute settlement aspect of the WTO, likely leading to the US abandoning the organization in its entirety.

In terms of the excessive workload faced by the Appellate Body, if the blockage problem is resolved it may make sense to increase the number of Appellate Body members. The number seven was decided when WTO membership was much smaller. With 164 members today, it is arguable that nine or more individuals would be more suitable. The inadequacy of the Appellate Body is even more evident when one considers the volume of appeals. It was never expected that such a high number of panel reports would be appealed. This is a significant factor in the long delays now regularly experienced with appeals, which now regularly take years rather than the 90 days envisaged by the DSU. Additionally, some feel that the lack of proper geographical representation on the Appellate Body in terms of the world's legal systems and regional economies undermines the legitimacy of the Appellate Body as the world's trade court. This issue could also be addressed once a way forward with regard to the blocking issue has been achieved.

3.4 Access

The dispute settlement system is exclusive – it is only available to WTO members. It is a state to state dispute settlement system, like the ICJ or the International Tribunal for the Law of the Sea. This is distinct from investor–state dispute settlement (ISDS), which will be examined in Chapter 8 of this book. Crucially, this means that it is only national (or, in the case of CUs, supra-national) governments which can bring or defend disputes. Subregional governments cannot; nor can private individuals, corporations or other organizations, such as NGOs or trade unions. Some view this narrow set of participants as indicative of poor access, particularly for an organization that purports to serve the interests of global trade and which seeks to raise standards of living

---

[7] Award of the Arbitrator, United States – Section 110(5) of the US Copyright Act – Arbitration under Article 21.3(c) of the DSU, WT/DS160/12 (15 January 2001).

worldwide. More tellingly, the WTO's goal of addressing social concerns, such as sustainability and labour rights, is arguably undermined by the WTO's failure to accommodate groups which might represent these interests in a dispute. These issues will be considered again in Chapter 5.

Members which believe that they have a substantial interest in a matter brought before a panel should be able to participate as a third party, although the phrase 'substantial interest' is not defined in the DSU. If granted, these parties may make both oral and written submissions. It is possible for third parties to participate in appeal hearings as a third participant, allowing them to submit oral and written evidence. Third parties are not precluded from later bringing a complaint relating to the same matter.

Panels and the Appellate Body *may* consider *amicus curiae* briefs and have done so on a few occasions, although there has yet to be a case in which either a panel or the Appellate Body has expressly referred to an *amicus* brief in rendering its decision. *Amicus* submissions were not permitted by GATT panels in the pre-WTO days. Early WTO panels also tended to decline *amicus* participation, but this has been definitively overruled and it is now well established that both panels and the Appellate Body can, and sometimes do, accept *amicus* briefs. This change was partly due to the high profile *US–Shrimp* dispute, which attracted the attention of environmental groups and in which the panel declined to accept unsolicited information from nonparties. This dispute will be revisited in Chapter 5. In *US–Shrimp*, the Appellate Body reversed the panel's findings on this matter, deciding that although nonparties have no right under the DSU to have a panel consider their *amicus* briefs, since panels have the authority to seek information under Article 13 of the DSU, they are permitted to consider such briefs if they wish to.[8]

The Appellate Body sought to clarify the rules on the acceptance of *amicus curiae* briefs in a 1998 dispute brought against the EC in relation to its ban on the material asbestos.[9] Canada had challenged the EC's law on the basis that it lacked scientific merit as a risk to health. There were a significant number of nonparties interested in taking part in the appeal because of the health controversies surrounding various forms of asbestos. This led the Appellate Body to establish procedural requirements for any person or entity wishing to file a written brief in the dispute. Under the process, individuals and groups do not have the right to submit documents to the panels or Appellate Body – the decision to accept them rests with the discretion of the Appellate Body members. One of the key requirements stipulated by the Appellate Body in the asbestos dispute was that there was a maximum page limit of 20 pages from each applicant or group. In all, 11 groups ended up submitting applications for *amicus curiae* status in *EC–Asbestos*, and the Appellate Body refused all of them on the basis of their failure to comply with these rules. The *amicus curiae* issue remains quite contentious and there are as yet no clear general rules on the accepting of *amicus* briefs that are applicable to all disputes. To date there have been *amicus curiae* briefs submitted in several dozen Appellate Body proceedings but, as noted above, in none of these instances did the tribunal decide that it was useful to consider the brief in rendering its decision. This may be a

---

[8] United States – Import Prohibition of Certain Shrimp and Shrimp Products, Appellate Body Report, WT/DS58/AB/R (6 November 1998).

[9] European Communities – Measures Affecting Asbestos and Asbestos-Containing Products, Appellate Body Report, WT/DS135/AB/R (5 April 2001).

cause of concern given the WTO's need to cultivate an image of openness and transparency as an institution of global governance.

Historically, among the most controversial features of the WTO dispute settlement system was the fact that the proceedings of the panel and Appellate Body are confidential. There are no transcripts from the hearings, either, and the opinions of panellists and Appellate Body members are anonymous, as mentioned earlier. These features of the system have caused some consternation among the general public (to the extent that it is aware of the WTO and what it does) because the parties to WTO disputes are states, which represent the interests of their citizens, not private companies, which may have a more legitimate need for privacy. Over the years some of the WTO dispute settlement hearings have taken place in public and, as might be expected, there was limited appetite for this among either the public or the media. Hearings are highly technical and lack the glamour of court proceedings which many members of the public may expect from television or films. Final reports of the panel and the Appellate Body become public once they have been circulated to the members. These may be found in full text format on the WTO's website and can be searched based on claimant, respondent, agreement and year. In Chapter 8 it will be shown that the ISDS system of international investment law is grappling with similar issues.

3.5 Causes of action and applicable law

Article XXIII of the GATT establishes the circumstances in which complaints may be brought. First it mentions two kinds of harms. These are: one, any benefits accruing directly or indirectly under the GATT are being nullified or impaired; two, the attainment of any objective of the GATT is being impeded. From there, the GATT outlines three possible causes of that harm. These are three causes of action, or types of complaint, for WTO members seeking to use the dispute settlement system. First, and most important, is a violation complaint. In this category of complaint, the complaining member must demonstrate that a WTO obligation has been breached, meaning that another member has failed to fulfil its obligations. Nullification or impairment of WTO benefits is presumed from the existence of this breach. Second, there is a non-violation complaint. Here there may not be an actual breach of a WTO obligation, requiring the complainant to prove that there has been a nullification or impairment of their benefits as a WTO member regardless of whether the other member's measure conflicts with the GATT. The idea behind this cause of action is that a member may follow the letter of the law, but their actions may still have led to harm suffered by another member. Last, there is an 'any other situation' complaint. In this circumstance, for which there has not yet been an actual complaint, nullification or impairment must be proven. It is uncertain what the 'any other situation' category was intended to address but it is often thought that it provides a degree of flexibility in terms of fulfilling the WTO's objectives on behalf of its members. The non-violation complaints have been explored as a route to address some of the issues in international trade which are not governed directly by WTO law, such as currency manipulation (of which more in Chapter 9) and, more recently, the open-ended language of the National Security exceptions in the GATT and GATS (of which more in Chapter 5).[10] As of the time of writing,

---

[10] US – Measures on Steel and Aluminium, WT/DS551 (5 June 2018).

these disputes have not been resolved through panel reports. The US expressly noted in an earlier decision that GATT national security exceptions might be challenged under the non-violation complaint provision.[11] It is important to mention that the GATS and the TRIPS Agreement (discussed in Chapters 4 and 5 respectively) have similar provisions regarding the kinds of complaints which may be brought through the dispute settlement system. The GATS establishes a violation complaint without any mention of nullification or impairment and it also includes a non-violation nullification or impairment complaint. The TRIPS Agreement provides for violation complaints with a temporary moratorium on non-violation and situation complaints.

GATT Article XXIII explains that a WTO member does not actually challenge the measure of another member directly. The challenge is instead based on the nullification or impairment of the benefits as a result of the measures alleged to cause a violation. This means that it is the concept of nullification or impairment that is the most important. In practice, however, the discussion of nullification or impairment plays a relatively small role in WTO jurisprudence because, as alluded to above, there is a presumption that violations of the GATT will result in a nullification or impairment, essentially meaning a measurable injury to the complainant member. It should be noted further that the DSU requires members to exercise 'judgment as to whether action under these procedures would be fruitful',[12] meaning that they should avoid frivolous claims. This provision has likely had limited effect on policing use of the dispute settlement system. Presumably WTO members will only bring claims if they believe that they are valid, given their expense and the fact that doing so may strain diplomatic relations between the parties, at least in relation to international economic matters.

WTO panels and the Appellate Body use the principles of interpretation outlined in Article 31 of the Vienna Convention on the Law of Treaties (VCLT), which was alluded to in Chapter 1. A closer look at Article 31 shows that it provides:

1. A treaty shall be interpreted in good faith in accordance with the ordinary meaning to be given to the terms of the treaty in their context and in the light of its object and purpose.
2. The context for the purpose of the interpretation of a treaty shall comprise, in addition to the text, including its preamble and annexes:
   (a) any agreement relating to the treaty which was made between all the parties in connection with the conclusion of the treaty;
   (b) any instrument which was made by one or more parties in connection with the conclusion of the treaty and accepted by the other parties as an instrument related to the treaty.

On this basis, the meaning of a term in a covered agreement shall be based on its ordinary meaning in its context in line with the object and purpose of the agreement, which, in the case of the WTO agreements, is essentially to increase trade. The panels and Appellate Body often refer expressly

---

[11] US – Trade Measures Affecting Nicaragua, Report by the Panel (L/6053) (13 October 1986).

[12] Art. 3.7.

to this provision of the VCLT.[13] Crucially, the panels and the Appellate Body must not add to or diminish WTO members' rights and obligations. Panels and the Appellate Body are required to clarify the provisions of the agreement based on the customary rules of public international law. This is often taken to indicate that panellists and Appellate Body members must not engage in judicial activism by adjudicating matters beyond those which were brought to their attention or by making superfluous comments about what provisions mean which are not strictly necessary for resolving the dispute at hand. Paradoxically, the WTO's very attempt to clarify and focus the issues, keeping in mind the need for flexibility, is what may have led to the accusations that it has strayed beyond its appointed mandate.[14]

Article IX:2 of the WTO Agreement sheds light on the interpretive role of the panels and the Appellate Body. It states as follows:

> The Ministerial Conference and the General Council shall have the exclusive authority to adopt interpretations of this Agreement and of the Multilateral Trade Agreements. In the case of an interpretation of a Multilateral Trade Agreement in Annex 1, they shall exercise their authority on the basis of a recommendation by the Council overseeing the functioning of that Agreement. The decision to adopt an interpretation shall be taken by a three-fourths majority of the Members. This paragraph shall not be used in a manner that would undermine the amendment provisions in Article X [regarding amendments to the agreements].

This provision means that the panels and the Appellate Body cannot adopt binding interpretations of the provisions which will affect their meaning and therefore members' rights and obligations on a lasting, forward-looking basis. Official interpretations may only come from the members of the WTO themselves – the highest authority in the WTO. This rule attempts to clarify, in the WTO context, the uneasy tension in many domestic legal orders between the rulemaking power of the legislature and the judiciary. There is some additional controversy regarding the capacity of committees within the WTO, such as the TBT Committee, to render authoritative interpretations of certain WTO agreements. This issue is becoming increasingly important given that the WTO committees issue many more decisions than the General Council.[15]

The applicable law to be examined by WTO panels and the Appellate Body consists of the WTO Agreements, including the DSU itself, international agreements in place between the parties and customary international law. An assessment of customary international law often leads to a consideration of the Law Commission's Articles on State Responsibility. All of the WTO agreements have been the source of complaints under the system, including the DSU itself. GATT is the agreement which has featured the most frequently in cases.

The burden of proof in WTO dispute settlement is a positive one. This means that the onus of proving a fact is on the party asserting it, just as the burden of demonstrating a breach of WTO

---

[13] United States – Measures Affecting the Production and Sale of Clove Cigarettes, Appellate Body Report, WT/DS406/AB/R (24 April 2012).

[14] A Lang, 'The Judicial Sensibility of the WTO Appellate Body', 27:4 European Journal of International Law 1095 (2016).

[15] US – Clove Cigarettes above n 13.

law is on the complaining party. The complainant party must bring forth arguments and evidence sufficient to establish a *prima facie* case for each component of its claim. With the complainant having made its case, the respondent must then rebut that case.[16] The burden shifts at various points, notably in relation to the articulation of a defence under GATT Article XX.

As with most international courts, there is no formal system of precedent in WTO law; however, there is clearly an informal system of precedent, as panels and the Appellate Body regularly cite earlier decisions as support for the statements of law which they make. There is consequently an expectation that prior disputes, where relevant, should be taken into account by the panels and the Appellate Body. Indeed, the Appellate Body noted in *Japan – Alcoholic Beverages* that prior adopted reports are often considered by subsequent panels and therefore create legitimate expectations among members.[17] This contributes to a sense of consistency and predictability within the dispute settlement system, which is thought to be vital to its legitimacy among its members and which is one of the purposes of the DSU. To the extent that there is an informal system of precedent it would appear as though a prior Appellate Body finding holds the highest esteem, with adopted GATT and WTO panel reports in second place. Dissenting opinions of panellists and Appellate Body members, which are becoming increasingly common, would likely occupy the third level of authoritativeness.

It is often thought that the lack of formal precedent prevents the development of jurisprudence upon which future decisions can be based, undermining the predictive capacity of the dispute settlement mechanism and in so doing preventing compliance and raising costs for its users. On the other hand, the freedom of panels and the Appellate Body to depart from previous tribunals' reasoning lends flexibility to the system. This can be incredibly important given the highly disparate economies of the WTO's 164 members, as well as changing patterns of global commerce. Moreover, there is clearly a highly influential informal system of precedent in operation. Panels and Appellate Body tribunals regularly cite earlier decisions – panels are especially prone to citing decisions of the Appellate Body. While they are not obliged to do so, this helps create a body of law from which lawyers, legal academics and adjudicators can draw their reasoning and ground their decisions. It also helps consolidate 'WTO Law' as a discipline of study within international economic law.

3.6 Standards of review

When using the WTO dispute settlement system, complaining members are challenging 'measures' of other members. More than just laws, the category of 'measures' is quite broad in its scope, covering legislation, an implementing regulation, judicial or quasi-judicial decisions of courts and even unwritten policies adopted by governments. The precise degree of governmental involvement in the measure is not always easy to define, often requiring analysis by the panels or the Appellate Body. Typically there must be some official aspect to the governmental action – a passing statement from a Member of Parliament or Congress will most likely not be deemed a measure which can be the subject of a dispute settlement complaint. There is also normally expected to be a compulsory component to a measure which is inconsistent with WTO – legislation which contem-

---

[16] Turkey – Restrictions on Imports of Textile and Clothing Products, Panel Report, WT/DS34/R (19 November 1999).

[17] Japan – Taxes on Alcoholic Beverages, Appellate Body Report, WT/DS8/AB/R (1 November 1996).

plates discretion will probably not result in a violation. In practice, this distinction is often quite difficult to establish and a discretionary aspect to a regulation may not be able to save a measure which has mandatory elements that are in violation of WTO law.[18]

The standard of review adopted by panels requires them to make an 'objective assessment of the facts' by examining the facts of the case and the relevant WTO agreements.[19] The objective assessment standard also applies to the panel's review of a domestic action or measure of a WTO member. This represents the level of deference to be accorded to decisions of domestic authorities. Some of the WTO agreements require assessments based on specific standards, as in the General Exceptions, which will be explored in Chapter 5. There is some evidence of the use of a standard of 'proportionality' or 'balancing' of interests by panels, as well as the Appellate Body. Proportionality is a concept drawn from the jurisprudence of the European Court of Human Rights and is now very much a *cause célèbre* within international economic law academics. As a term, proportionality implies that there is a formulaic methodology for engaging in weighing and balancing divergent interests, such as those contained in the GATT General Exceptions. It is also thought to be instrumental in international investment arbitration,[20] as will be discussed further in Chapter 8. Whether this is actually the case is debatable, but it would appear that most WTO panels adopt a highly flexible approach to their assessment of competing objectives. Domestic decisions relating to SPS measures, safeguards and antidumping can be particularly controversial.

The principle of judicial economy is recognized in WTO law and is often relied upon by panels to decline to examine certain claims made by the complaining party. This is despite Article 7.2 of the DSU, which requires the panels to address all of the agreements cited by the parties. The ability to exercise judicial economy has been expressly acknowledged by the Appellate Body.[21] This strategy may become even more prevalent given the increasing length and complexity of dispute settlement hearings and the pressure to conform to the tight deadlines, although, as suggested above, attempts to focus analysis might end up leading to charges of judicial activism.

The standard of review of a panel decision by the Appellate Body is that the Appellate Body will modify a panel ruling if the panel has made an 'egregious error' in its assessment or if the panel 'exceeded the bounds of its discretion'. In recent years the Appellate Body appears to have adopted a fairly soft approach to its review of the panel's objective assessment of the facts. The panel's 'margin of discretion' has been noted by the Appellate Body in one instance.[22] Generally speaking, the Appellate Body has shown a reasonably high degree of deference to panel decisions. It is important to emphasize that appeals are limited to law – the Appellate Body cannot examine other factual issues.

---

[18] United States – Laws, Regulations and Methodology for Calculating Dumping Margins ('Zeroing'), Appellate Body Report, WT/DS294/AB/R (9 May 2006).

[19] Art. 11.

[20] C Henckels, *Proportionality and Deference in Investor-State Arbitration* (Cambridge University Press, 2015).

[21] United States – Measure Affecting Imports of Woven Wool Shirts and Blouses from India, Appellate Body Report, WT/DS33/AB/R (23 May 1997).

[22] Dominican Republic – Measures Affecting the Importation and Internal Sale of Cigarettes, Appellate Body Report, DS302/AB/R (19 May 2005).

Panels have the authority to seek information and technical advice from any individual or body under Article 13 of the DSU. The Appellate Body has the implied authority to consult experts. These powers are important given the volume of often highly technical information brought by the parties to the dispute settlement process, some of which includes numeric data and economic or financial calculations. As suggested above, the factual complexity of the cases appears to be increasing in tandem with the length of the proceedings, highlighting the importance of this capacity.

3.7 Remedies

Remedies under WTO law are unusual and often the subject of criticism from those used to dealing with domestic legal systems. Under Article 3.7 of the DSU the primary objective of dispute settlement is to secure the modification or withdrawal of the offending measure. When the panels and the Appellate Body make a recommendation under Article 19.1 of the DSU, the member found to be in violation of one of the WTO agreements must bring the measure into conformity with WTO rules. Therefore the primary remedy for breach of WTO law is withdrawal or amendment of the WTO-inconsistent measure, not monetary damages. In one respect this approach to remedies could be viewed as a serious departure from a fundamental principle of customary international law, namely that parties which suffer harm as a consequence of the wrongdoing of states are entitled to full reparation, captured for example in the Articles on State Responsibility.[23] Some have argued that cash compensation may be a more suitable remedy because it allows for 'efficient breach'. The losing party can continue implementing its WTO-illegal measure so long as it is prepared to pay the injured party for the right to do so. As long as the correct measure of damages is ascertained, in theory the injured member should be indifferent between withdrawal of the measure (which might be equated with specific performance in the common law of contract) or suffering the trade barrier but being compensated. One of the problems with a remedy of monetary damages is that the injured party in WTO disputes is not truly the member state, but private individual suppliers as well as consumers. It would be exceedingly difficult to calculate how much compensation each of these parties would be entitled to from a lump sum payment to the winning state.[24]

There are temporary remedies which may be applied by the winning member while the withdrawal or amendment are awaited. These are: compensation, which means additional concessions granted by the losing member to the winning member, often in the form of tariff reductions; and retaliation (although that term is not used), comprising the suspension of concessions by the winning member against the losing member, typically in the form of tariff increases. Both of these alternative remedies must be authorized by the DSB.[25] Requests to suspend concessions tend to be referred to arbitration, during which the responding party may challenge the suspension. This usually involves the original panel, if available, to assess whether the requested suspension amount is equivalent to the level of nullification or impairment suffered by the complainant member.

---

[23] Art. 42.

[24] D Collins, 'Efficient Breach, Reliance, and Contract Remedies at the WTO' 43:2 Journal of World Trade 225 (2009).

[25] Art. 22.6.

If a request is made by the respondent, the parties must enter into consultations to agree on appropriate compensation.[26] This does not refer to cash compensation. In practice, compensation may involve the reduction of tariffs on other products or greater access for certain goods of the complaining member equivalent to the benefit the respondent has nullified or impaired through the application of its illegal measure. Compensation is not retroactive, in that it does not truly address past wrongs (harmful effects of the illegal measure). It is instead prospective in that the respondent 'compensates' the complaining member for harms that may be experienced going forward as the result of its continued breach of WTO rules. Parties must ensure that any compensation in the form of reduced trade barriers must be consistent with the WTO covered agreements. Specifically, the agreement on compensation must conform to the MFN obligation. This means that any benefit granted to the complainant, such as a tariff reduction on certain goods, would also have to be offered to all other WTO members.[27] This may be the reason why compensation tends rarely to be used. One incident was in the *Turkey–Textiles* dispute,[28] where Turkey agreed to tariff reductions on a number of chemicals in order to compensate India for increased barriers on clothing. These reductions were offered to the rest of the WTO membership on an MFN basis. Since this might be an onerous obligation for a WTO member, the suspension of concessions on other obligations tends to be the preferred method.

The problem with retaliation through the suspension of concessions as an alternative remedy to violations of WTO law is that it is antithetical to the purpose of the WTO – namely, to eliminate barriers to trade where possible. Retaliation in the form of a higher tariff is itself a barrier to trade. This approach can lead to an escalation of trade barriers in a tit for tat strategy, worsening trading relations rather than improving them – sometimes referred to as a trade war. It is also often viewed as a kind of self harm, especially for smaller countries which cannot absorb the economic damage caused by higher prices on imports from offending countries. The remedial structure of WTO law has been criticized by a number of commentators on this basis.[29]

It may be that retaliation through the suspension of concessions can induce compliance by the responding members, and indeed all other members who might be tempted to violate WTO law in the future. This is precisely why victorious complainant members target sensitive goods when levying their retaliatory tariffs. For example, in the past the US suspended concessions on various EC originating products such as meat, cheese and clothing in retaliation against measures imposed on bananas.[30] At the time of writing, US tariffs on steel and aluminium from the EU have been met with tariffs on US whiskey, which is produced by a region in the US which currently has a strong measure of political clout. This strategy is despite the fact that Article 22.3 a) of the DSU provides that the complaining party should first seek to suspend concessions or other obligations in the same sector in which the nullification of violation has been found. If the complaining party finds that this is not practical or effective, then it may retaliate in an unrelated sector. Retaliation

---

[26] Art. 22.2.

[27] Art. 22.1.

[28] Turkey – Textiles above n 16.

[29] E.g. J Trachtman, 'The WTO Cathedral', 43 Stanford Journal of International Law 127 (2007).

[30] EC Bananas, Recourse by the US to Article 22.2 of the DSU, WT/DS27/43 (14 January 1999).

under an entirely different WTO agreement, for example by suspending intellectual property pro-tection under the TRIPS Agreement for a breach of the GATS,[31] is known as 'cross-retaliation'. This strategy can be important to small developing countries because their imports in a particular sector or under a certain agreement (e.g. the GATT) may not be large enough to have much of a deleterious impact against the responding member. Smaller countries may also rely on certain key imports from larger states, and imposing barriers against them could increase the price to a point that would be harmful to consumers and possibly to the economy at large. When engaging in cross-retaliation the complainant must demonstrate why it is not practical or effective to suspend concessions under the original agreement, as outlined in Article 22.3 b) and c) of the DSU and articulated in EC–Bananas when this was attempted by Ecuador.[32]

Prompt compliance with WTO panel and Appellate Body recommendations is expected but not always possible.[33] Immediate compliance may not be feasible in situations where the member concerned must initiate and pass legislation, possibly through a bicameral legislature, in order to amend the law which has been determined to be inconsistent with WTO obligations. A reasonable period of time is therefore allowed for implementation. This may be ascertained either by the offending member proposing a schedule which is approved by consensus of the DSB, or more commonly through agreement with the successful complainant member within 45 days of the report. Last, the reasonable period can be established by binding arbitration between the parties, which must be completed within 90 days of adoption of the report.[34] Commentators have drawn attention to the lack of rigour in this arbitration process, which is allowed to drag on longer than is necessary – usually for around 15 months. The losing party may take advantage of the confusion regarding the reasonable period allowance to escape its obligations.[35]

Review of compliance with the recommendations of the panel and Appellate Body is also availa-ble under the DSU Article 21.5. This provision lacks clarity regarding the use of dispute settlement procedures to address compliance issues, but it appears as though this process can involve resorting to the original panel. If the reasonable time to comply has elapsed, the complainant must request determination of compliance before it resorts to retaliation through the suspension of concessions, as discussed further below. Article 21.5 compliance proceedings are similar to the original panel proceedings; however, it is possible that the claims regarding factual circumstances may not be entirely the same. This feature of the process has become contentious. For example, in the *Austral-ia – Salmon* dispute,[36] the respondent claimed that one of the measures at issue was not actually a

---

[31] E.g. United States – Measures Affecting the Cross-Border Supply of Gambling and Betting Services, Appellate Body Report, WT/DS285/AB/R (20 April 2005).

[32] Decision by the Arbitrator, European Communities – Regime for the Importation, Sale and Distribution of Bananas – Recourse to Arbitration by the European Communities under Article 22.6 of the DSU, WT/DS27/ARB/ECU (24 March 2000).

[33] Art. 21.1.

[34] Art. 21.3.

[35] M Qian, '"Reasonable Period of Time" in the WTO Dispute Settlement System' 15:1 Journal of International Economic Law 252 (2012).

[36] Australia – Measures Affecting Importation of Salmon, Appellate Body Report, WT/DS18/AB/R (6 November 1998).

'measure taken to comply' with the ruling of the DSB, but rather an entirely new measure which should accordingly have been beyond the scope of the compliance panel's assessment. The compliance panel ruled that it, rather than the parties, would determine whether a measure was one which was taken to comply or an entirely new one (in this case it was the former). Otherwise a party could avoid scrutiny of its compliance measures simply by designating the measures as outside the scope of compliance review. While the compliance procedure under Article 21.5 is most often invoked by the complaining party, it can also be invoked by the responding party seeking confirmation of consistency with measures it has implemented following the original panel's decision.[37]

Compliance has been observed within a reasonable period of time (usually something around six months from the date of adoption of the relevant report by the DSB) in approximately 85 per cent of cases. This is a tremendously successful outcome for an international court (or any court for that matter) and is testimony to the effectiveness of the WTO dispute settlement system and the high esteem in which it is held by WTO members.

The WTO's system of enforcement for violation of its agreements has, mostly wrongly and often by politicians, been condemned for being ineffectual. Although compliance with WTO panel and Appellate Body rulings is quite good, it is often suggested that there is no truly effective sanction for countries that do not follow through with dispute settlement recommendations and modify their unlawful trade regulations. Retaliation, it is often argued, is only effective when it is used by a country of relatively equal economic power to the losing party; otherwise it is an empty threat that is ultimately self-defeating for the winning country that imposes it. It is thought to be especially unhelpful for developing countries, where the suspension of trade concessions would be barely noticed by a large, developed country against which it has secured a victory in the WTO dispute settlement system. More creative types of retaliation – for example under the intellectual property agreement through the suspension of copyright,[38] or through conventional monetary payments – could offer a solution.[39]

4. WTO DISPUTE SETTLEMENT SYSTEM REFORMS

As the world's trade court, the WTO dispute settlement system has matured since its early days in the 1990s. For example, panels make less use of dictionaries to ascertain the meaning of words, a habit which evinced a distinct lack of sophistication. The Appellate Body is more deferential to panels, which is probably a positive development in that the Appellate Body should not be used simply to rehear cases reflexively. The legal analysis conducted by both panels and the Appellate Body is arguably more teleological than it was in the past. It is more cognizant of the ultimate purpose of clarifying members' rights and obligations with a view to maintaining the stability of the world trading system. At the same time, reliance on the WTO dispute settlement system in-

---

[37] Canada/US – Continued Suspension of Obligations in the EC – Hormones Dispute, WT/DS320/18 (21 November 2008).

[38] E.g. US – Gambling above n 31.

[39] Collins above n 24.

tensified as the negotiation facet of the WTO struggled to achieve progress in terms of improving market access. For example, Brazil originally expected that the US would reduce its cotton subsidies during the Doha Round negotiations, but when it failed to do so Brazil was forced to initiate a complaint through the dispute settlement system.[40] Ironically, as the Appellate Body is currently embroiled in crisis, in the coming years WTO members may attempt to resolve their trade differences through the WTO's negotiating arm once again, breathing new life into an aspect of the WTO that has suffered in previous years.

A number of reforms to the WTO dispute settlement system have been proposed over the years to help keep it useful and relevant. Recently these have dealt with the problem of Appellate Body Member blockage by the US, mentioned above. Access remains one of the WTO dispute settlement system's chief problems, particularly with respect to how it is perceived by the general public. Many feel that the fact that the dispute settlement system can only be used by member states undermines its effectiveness as a world court of trade, since it is often private traders (exporters and importers) who are most harmed by protectionist barriers. If the WTO panels and Appellate Body hearings were open to private parties, like international investment arbitration tribunals, the system would be very different, significantly removed from the domain of public international law where it currently resides. Even if WTO rules were directly enforceable in domestic courts, which they are not under most domestic systems, this could cause problems of enforceability because of potential jurisdictional overlaps, as appears to be occurring within international investment law.

Tied to the problem of access is the question of transparency. The confidentiality of WTO panel and Appellate Body hearings has arguably been a vital contributor to the system's efficiency. Rather than a public trial dealing with facts which may be readily understood by the public, the WTO courts deal heavily with economic data and the interpretation of legal provisions. Although these matters may be of limited interest to nonexperts, the fact remains that courts which are not open to the public suffer from the perception of secretiveness. There is an adverse inference on the part of the public that such hearings are disregarding their concerns and that this is somehow undemocratic, contributing to an overall sense of mystery about how international trade functions behind the theatre of politics. Since WTO hearings involve the interaction of sovereign states, which represent the interest of their taxpaying citizens, this grievance is understandable. But opening up hearings to the public would almost certainly raise costs and lead to delays. Live streaming on the internet, as has been attempted in some investment cases, might be a sensible compromise.

Short timeframes were often depicted as one of the great strengths of the WTO dispute settlement system. Failure to adhere to the strict timeframes has been cited with contempt by the US in particular. Others have contended that the timeframes are already too short and should be extended to reflect the increasing complexity of cases. Compromise in this regard may be very difficult.

Another commonly cited problem with the WTO dispute settlement system is the lack of participation by developing countries, rendered all the more frustrating given that two thirds of WTO membership consists of this category of country. Developing countries may struggle to make use of the dispute settlement system because of its costs, especially those related to the hiring of skilled counsel. The Advisory Centre on WTO Law, which is not affiliated with the WTO

---

[40] S Cho, *The Social Foundations of World Trade* (Cambridge University Press, 2015).

itself, has been able to offer legal assistance to developing countries on a pro bono basis. Additionally, there have also been historically few panel members from developing countries, although the Appellate Body has been reasonably well represented by individuals with this background. It is an entirely legitimate criticism that without further involvement of developing countries, the WTO's dispute settlement system has dubious legitimacy as a genuine world court of international trade.

Remand powers for the panels and the Appellate Body may achieve some progress in addressing the accusation that the Appellate Body engages in judicial activism by considering matters which were beyond its original mandate, notably matters of fact which might be more rightly considered by a newly constituted panel. The veracity of this criticism from certain WTO members has itself been challenged by commentators who hold that what might be viewed as viewed as interventionism in the context of the common law might be seen as normal case management to lawyers from a civil law tradition.[41] Again it seems that satisfying all parties is next to impossible.

As suggested earlier, compliance with panel and Appellate Body recommendations is generally quite good, although this too could be improved. Although losing parties occasionally criticized individual rulings, this has rarely reached the level of a challenge to the overall authority or legitimacy of the WTO dispute settlement system. Decisions are sometimes charged with being too technical and consequently of limited value to nonexpert readers. While this could be said of rulings of almost any domestic appellate courts throughout the world, there is an added problem with WTO cases that they are not only legally complex but often also economically so. Rulings have also been faulted for being too broad in their scope and addressing issues that were not strictly necessary to provide a resolution to the matter at hand.[42] To some this may be viewed as judicial activism; to others it is helpful pragmatism.[43]

The WTO panels and Appellate Body arguably suffer from an excessively burdensome case load, heavy even when the Appellate Body was properly constituted with its seven members. Recently a number of initiatives have been undertaken to simplify the content of Appellate Body reports with this issue in mind. For example, the section in each report on conclusions now summarizes the key points of the reasoning for those who do not wish to go through the entire text. Furthermore, except in some of the very large disputes such as the *Large Civil Aircraft* cases,[44] the length of reports has been greatly decreased, with few now exceeding 70 pages. This is an especially welcome development for students of international economic law.

5. DISPUTE SETTLEMENT UNDER RTAs

The settlement of disputes in the international trade arena is sometimes characterized as fragmented, meaning that there are multiple overlapping fora in which aggrieved parties, usually

---

[41] A Bahri, '"Appellate Body Held Hostage": Is Judicial Activism at Fair Trial?' 53:2 Journal of World Trade 293 (2019).

[42] Comments from US Bhatia, 11th Annual Update on WTO Dispute Settlement (3 May 2018).

[43] Lang, above n 14.

[44] United States – Measures Affecting Trade in Large Civil Aircraft (Second Complaint), Appellate Body Report, WT/DS353/AB/R (23 March 2012).

states, may seek compensation or resolution. This is an embodiment of some of the criticisms of regionalism generally, as discussed in the previous chapter. There are many thousands of RTAs, most of which contain state to state dispute settlement chapters contemplating neutral arbitration panels composed of adjudicators drawn from both state parties. While there has been remarkably limited usage of these systems compared to that of the WTO,[45] a small number of disputes have been brought under RTAs over the years. Bilateral trade remedies panels under Chapter 19 of NAFTA (retained under the new USMCA at the behest of Canada) are among the most high profile of the regional trade dispute settlement mechanisms, having led to several dozen cases over the years. The persistent impasse in multilateral trade negotiations and the ensuing strain on the WTO's dispute settlement system could indicate that RTAs will grow in importance as a means of settling disagreements between trading nations.

Normally consisting of informal committees rather than courts, dispute resolution procedures in RTAs are thought to foster dialogue between disputing parties to deescalate matters, rather than being legally binding determinations.[46] The incremental 'judicialization' of dispute settlement mechanisms under RTAs reflects the ongoing effort to improve the routes available to resolve disputes while achieving balance between state flexibility and the need to delegate dispute resolution to neutral third parties. Dispute settlement systems under RTAs typically contain a common set of core features, with variations capturing the nature of the relationship between the parties, the depth and breadth of the substantive commitments, and regional experiences and preferences. There are several features common to such systems: the initiation of disputes (standing, scope of coverage, choice of forum); methodology of dispute resolution (negotiation, mediation, adjudication); procedures for adjudication (including selection of adjudicators, time limits, appellate review); implementation and enforcement (remedies, surveillance); openness to others (third parties, transparency, *amicus* submissions); and institutional arrangements (political bodies, standing tribunals, secretariats).

Virtually all modern RTAs include some form of compulsory and legally binding adjudication. This usually involves neutral third party determinations based on the adversarial presentation of argument and evidence. Most modern systems resort to *ad hoc* panels of three to five panellists appointed only for the purposes of a specific dispute. Some RTAs, mostly those involving more ambitious regional integration projects which pre-date the WTO, refer disputes to permanent standing tribunals, such as the Court of Justice of the European Union (CJEU), the Court of Justice of the Andean Community, the East Africa Court of Justice and the Caribbean Court of Justice. The most common remedy available under RTAs is the authorization of retaliatory tariffs, as under the WTO DSU.[47]

For the most part, dispute settlement systems under RTAs remain underused relative to their expanding coverage in terms of subject matter and country participation. Several explanations for the lack of recourse to RTA dispute settlement mechanisms have been put forth. Recognition of

---

[45] G Vidigal, 'Why Is There So Little Litigation under Free Trade Agreements? Retaliation and Adjudication in International Dispute Settlement' 20:4 Journal of International Economic Law 1 (2017).

[46] M Melillo, 'Informal Dispute Resolution in Preferential Trade Agreements' 53:1 Journal of World Trade 95 (2019).

[47] D Gantz, 'Assessing the Impact of WTO and Regional Dispute Resolution Mechanisms on the World Trading System' in J Jemielniak, L Nielsen and HP Olsen eds *Establishing Judicial Authority in International Economic Law* (Cambridge University Press, 2016).

the benefits of pursuing dispute settlement through the WTO may be the chief reason. There may simply be incomplete information concerning the actual number of disputes brought before RTA dispute settlement systems. There is, as yet, no central registrar for disputes pursued under RTAs, and most RTAs do not have well-developed institutional support structures to disseminate cases widely. The results of informal settlement mechanisms, such as mediation, are often confidential. This may be due to the fact that many RTAs have a different approach to transparency than the WTO, which has opted to provide a full record of the rulings issued by the panels and the Appellate Body, if not access to the hearings themselves. Additionally, the repeated interactions between states and closer links between trading firms that take place within the framework of an RTA may contribute to avoiding disputes or facilitating their resolution less formally. In this regard it may be that RTA dispute settlement systems were never intended to be used as the main way to resolve disputes, but instead amount to a form of reinsurance against an eventual weakening of the WTO or its dispute settlement system, which may be coming to pass. If this is true, then the effectiveness of dispute settlement mechanisms under RTAs should be assessed in broader terms than outcomes in terms of completed cases. A better understanding of the factors that underlie the low usage of RTA dispute settlement may help improve the design and operation of future RTAs.[48]

Indeed, there could be design constraints or institutional limitations of RTA dispute settlement mechanisms. Ongoing problems associated with the WTO dispute settlement system, especially the weakened Appellate Body, could change this, with more disputes under RTAs forthcoming. In order to make dispute settlement under RTAs more attractive and accessible to parties, policy options could be developed to improve the design and architecture of existing and new RTA dispute settlement systems. Enhanced transparency and information exchange and increased support to the institutions offering the dispute settlement services could be made available, possibly in conjunction with international organizations.[49] Individual RTA dispute settlement mechanisms will rarely justify the establishment of separate institutional structures, such as the NAFTA Secretariat. This has led to a situation in which dispute settlement systems under RTAs suffer from capacity problems. Support for the necessary infrastructure for these processes may be advisable. Such options might include financial assistance from the WTO Secretariat or pooling of resources across many RTAs.[50]

In some cases, trade-oriented disputes have been framed as investment matters so that private companies can access the arbitration panels and the monetary compensation which they may offer, in contrast to WTO panels. Likewise, jurisdictional conflicts between the WTO and RTAs may become more common in the future should regional trade dispute settlement mechanisms gain popularity. While the content of the WTO DSU has largely been replicated in most of the regional adjudicatory bodies, emerging features of some of these RTAs are distinct and potentially incompatible with the WTO DSU. Some RTAs cover matters which are currently outside of the

[48] M Froese, 'Regional Trade Agreements and the Paradox of Dispute Settlement' 11:3 Manchester Journal of International Economic Law 367 (2014).

[49] R McDougall, 'Regional Trade Agreement Dispute Settlement Mechanisms: Modes, Challenges and Options for Effective Dispute Resolution' RTA Exchange (April 2018).

[50] McDougall, ibid.

WTO, again such as investment, and the degree of liberalization in many instruments is substantially deeper than under the WTO. The WTO dispute settlement system would not help with these matters. Some have questioned whether the proliferation of RTAs threatens the existence of the WTO dispute settlement system and, perhaps more profoundly, the extent to which the patchwork of regional trade courts contributes to the development of international law.[51]

One way to resolve them might be through forum choice clauses in RTAs, although this approach is questionable.[52] In a WTO case brought by the US against Mexico as a consequence of the latter's tax regime on soft drinks,[53] Mexico based its defence on the 'forum exclusion' clause in NAFTA. Mexico argued that, since the case constituted part of a broader dispute that had previously been brought against the US under NAFTA, that treaty's forum exclusion clause demanded that the NAFTA arbitration panel should be the only forum to resolve the dispute. The WTO panel disagreed, ruling that enabling a WTO panel to decide its own jurisdiction would diminish a complaining party's rights under the DSU. It would seem therefore that, under WTO jurisprudence, it will be difficult for forum exclusion clauses in RTAs to deny claimants access to the WTO dispute settlement system. The overlapping of multiple dispute settlement procedures for the trade chapters of various RTAs entered into by the same states may lead to situations of forum shopping. Few RTAs offer a clear indication regarding their relationships to other agreements. Such matters may become even more problematic in an era of megaregional trade agreements such as the CPTPP and the RCEP.

6. CONCLUSION

This chapter investigated the WTO dispute settlement system as enshrined in the DSU, among the most comprehensive and successful systems of dispute settlement in international law. It explored the system's main features, including the standing Appellate Body and the remedial structure based on removal of unlawful measures coupled with the threat of retaliation. The chapter also drew attention to the very grave problems currently faced by the system, especially in relation to the nonappointment of members to the Appellate Body, which runs the risk of disabling the DSU altogether, and with it potentially unravelling many of the benefits engendered by WTO membership. Dispute settlement under RTAs has yet to reach a level of maturity but with institutional support these fora could end up lending greater weight to the movement towards regionalism in international trade law as the multilateral dispute settlement system falters. The next chapter will turn back to substantive legal principles under WTO law through a discussion of trade remedies in relation to subsidies, dumping and safeguards, followed by the WTO's regime for liberalization of trade in services.

---

[51] Y Hodu, 'Regional Trade Courts in the Shadow of WTO Dispute Settlement System: The Paradox of Two Courts' 27:4 African Journal of International and Comparative Law (December 2018).

[52] S Yang, 'The Solution for Jurisdictional Conflicts between the WTO and RTAs: The Forum Choice Clause' 23:1 Michigan State International Law Review 107 (2015).

[53] Mexico – Tax Measures on Soft Drinks and Other Beverages, Panel Report, WT/DS308 (7 October 2005).

DISCUSSION QUESTIONS

1. What are the advantages of having dispute settlement based on binding rules in the WTO system? Are there any disadvantages?
2. To what extent may the WTO panels and Appellate Body be considered judicial procedures, and do they have nonjudicial characteristics?
3. What are some of the problems with the WTO dispute settlement system and how might it be improved to deliver its mandate more effectively?
4. Why might a WTO member choose to use a dispute settlement system contained in a regional trade agreement?

FURTHER READING

C Carmody, 'Small Changes in Big Times: The WTO's Informal Mechanism on Procedural Innovation' 2019:1 International Trade Law and Regulation 26 (2019).

Q Kong and S Guo, 'Towards a Mega-Plurilateral Dispute Settlement Mechanism for the WTO?' 53:2 Journal of World Trade 273 (2019).

G Marceau, 'Evolutive Interpretation by the WTO Adjudicator' 21:4 Journal of International Economic Law 791 (2018).

M Melillo, 'Informal Dispute Resolution in Preferential Trade Agreements' 53:1 Journal of World Trade 95 (2019).

4

Subsidies, antidumping, safeguards and trade in services

1. INTRODUCTION

The previous chapter considered the procedural rules contained in the WTO Dispute Settlement Understanding (DSU), designed to resolve disputes between WTO members in relation to the rights and obligations contained in the various covered agreements. This chapter will turn to four of these agreements, each of which deals with specialized kinds of barriers to international trade which can impede global commerce and distort markets, creating waste and inefficiency: subsidies, essentially assistance granted by the producing state, and dumping, a strategy employed by exporting firms to defeat foreign competitors through artificially low prices and safeguards, which is a protective tool available to importing states which cannot cope with an influx of foreign goods. Lastly, this chapter will turn its attention to the field of services, a rapidly growing sector of the global economy which is closely related to emerging discussions concerning the need to regulate digital trade. Together these features of WTO law demonstrate the multilateral system's capacity to adapt to modern trends in trade protectionism, beyond its twentieth century mandate of controlling conventional barriers such as tariffs and quotas. The regional dimension of each of these topics will also be considered briefly.

2. SUBSIDIES

The tremendous success of the GATT in reducing tariffs throughout the twentieth century compelled countries which were eager to continue protectionist policies, under the misguided belief that this would help them, to seek other strategies. Among the most pernicious of these has been subsidies. The logic behind the subsidy is that if you cannot make your foreign competitor suffer because quotas are illegal and tariffs have been lowered, the alternative is to achieve the same outcome by helping the domestic supplier. Put more simply, a benefit to one's own manufacturers is as good as a detriment to foreign ones.

Today subsidies remain one of the most popular forms of protectionism. One of the main problems with controlling subsidies through WTO disciplines is the reality that governments always help their citizens – in fact, this is one of the roles that we expect governments to perform. The level of government support will differ across societies, with those in the West, especially the US, generally embracing a smaller role for government in favour of free markets, and countries like China and Russia having a much stronger tradition of state support, in line with their communist histories. Even in countries governed largely by free market principles, the state tends to maintain a visible presence as a regulator or market mediator, ensuring that certain values such as consumer safety and healthy competition are upheld. Subsidies disciplines seek to ascertain the point at which this support becomes anticompetitive assistance and therefore represents an inefficient distortion of global markets.

2.1 Agreement on Subsidies and Countervailing Measures: scope

One of the great achievements of the WTO negotiations was the Agreement on Subsidies and Countervailing Measures (SCM), the first and only global treaty dealing directly with subsidies. It established a definition of subsidy which is used, often verbatim, in many RTAs. The definition is found in Article 1. It explains that a subsidy is a financial contribution made directly or indirectly by a government body within its own territory which confers a benefit. The Article goes on to provide a list of examples of the types of governmental action which will indicate that a subsidy has taken place. These are: direct transfer of funds (e.g. cash grant); government revenue otherwise due is forgone (e.g. a tax credit); goods or services are made available by the government, or the government purchases goods. Taken together, these examples cover a wide range of circumstances, potentially embracing a range of governmental initiatives which could operate to confer a benefit on the private sector and possibly distort trade. In that sense, the SCM could render a good deal of governmental activity illegal.

However, in order for the measure to count as a subsidy it must be 'specific'. The concept of specificity is one of the key innovations of the SCM – in fact, it is hard to imagine that there could ever have been a WTO agreement on subsidies had this concept not been applied as a screen to legitimize certain types of government programmes, shielding them from legal consequences. Specificity essentially contemplates assistance provided to a certain enterprise or group of enterprises. Article 2.2 outlines the requirements for specificity. First, where the government explicitly limits access to the subsidy to certain enterprises, this subsidy will be deemed specific. Second, where the government establishes objective criteria or conditions governing the eligibility for, and the amount of, a subsidy, then the subsidy will not be specific. Escaping characterization as specific means that these subsidies will not be unlawful under the SCM. Other indicia of specificity include use of a subsidy programme by a limited number of certain enterprises, predominant use by certain enterprises, the granting of disproportionately large amounts of subsidy to certain enterprises and the manner in which discretion has been exercised by the granting authority in the decision to grant a subsidy. Put more plainly, the governmental action may be regarded as a subsidy attracting legal sanction under the SCM where it appears to be designed to favour particular enterprises rather than the economy as a whole. This illustrates the purpose of the specificity requirement in order for a measure to constitute a subsidy worthy of being policed by the WTO regime – only targeted assistance will fall within the discipline of the agreement. Generalized support or relief to large segments of society should not be construed as trade distortive – these are merely the types of projects in which governments should engage as custodians of their own economies and in the best interests of their citizens. In a WTO dispute between the US and China over alleged subsidies to steel and rubber industries, the Appellate Body clarified that the concept of specificity is also a flexible one and its determination will be done on a case by case basis (more discretion to the WTO panels and Appellate Body), but that specificity will be established if there is a clear restriction on the particular enterprise or industry to which the contribution will apply.[1]

The scope of the concept of subsidy was illustrated in a series of disputes between Canada and the US involving softwood lumber. The US brought a claim through the WTO dispute settlement system based on the assertion that the Canadian lumber industry enjoyed a subsidy from the one of the provincial governments of Canada, giving Canadian companies an unfair advantage over US ones. The alleged subsidy took the form of a certain maximum price paid by lumber companies to the provincial government for each tree. The lumber companies were effectively being supplied with trees by the government at set prices that were below the market rate – help which was not available to US lumber companies operating in the US. In determining that this price support received by the Canadian companies should be considered a subsidy, the Appellate Body ruled that the range of governmental measures that can be considered subsidies and therefore fall within the SCM sphere is quite broad.[2]

When assessing whether a subsidy has occurred, the concept of government can be problematic, especially in situations where the state plays a larger role in the economy than is the case in market-based Western countries. This issue is further complicated by the many different levels of government found in many countries, including national, regional and local. This issue was confronted in the US and China dispute mentioned above regarding various attempts by the US to counter Chinese subsidization in Chinese steel and rubber industries. China had argued that contributions made by Chinese state owned enterprises to private companies were not governmental subsidies but effectively intercorporate transfers of capital. The Appellate Body concluded that in order to be considered a public body and therefore be capable of subsidizing, that entity must perform governmental functions and have the authority to give commands to a private body. This determination would need to be done on a case by case basis. In this instance the Chinese state owned enterprises did not have these powers, so the assistance offered could not be deemed a subsidy.[3]

While the concept of 'benefit' under Article 1.1 b) of the SCM is also contentious, it is clear that it encapsulates that which is received by the recipient company and not that which is given

---

[1] United States – Countervailing Duty Measures on Certain Products from China, Appellate Body Report, WT/DS437/AB/R (16 January 2015).

[2] United States – Final Countervailing Duty Determination with Respect to Certain Softwood Lumber from Canada, Appellate Body, WT/DS257/AB/R (17 February 2004).

[3] United States – Countervailing Duty Measures on Certain Products from China, Appellate Body Report, WT/DS437/AB/R (16 January 2015).

by the government. This distinction becomes important when the panels and Appellate Body are required to assess the quantity of the subsidy for the purposes of sanctioning a response from the complaining country. It must be established that the recipient company has been made better off than it would otherwise have been in the absence of that contribution from the government – the so-called counterfactual, or what might have been. One way of identifying this type of situation is where the government provides goods or services to the company but the company either does not pay for them or pays an amount that is below the prevailing market price for those goods or services in the country in question. Under the SCM, proactive assistance to producers is treated the same as the state failing to engage in an action which would be harmful to the producer – both are equally viewed as benefits despite the latter being arguably harder to identify in practice.[4]

In addition to the designation of specificity as a way of controlling the scope of the SCM, the agreement creates categories of subsidy, further providing policy flexibility for WTO member states. The three categories of subsidy in the SCM are often analogized to a 'traffic light', using the colours red, yellow and green. Red subsidies are those which are prohibited. Yellow (or amber) are only prohibited if they cause injury – much as drivers are only allowed to pass through a yellow light if it is unsafe to stop. Green light subsidies were created for subsidies serving research initiatives with no impact on trade, but these have all since expired so no longer have any relevance (although they may have relevance for newly acceding WTO members). It should also be clarified that neither services nor agricultural subsidies are covered by the SCM agreement. Agricultural matters, including members' capacity to assist agricultural producers through subsidies, are covered by their own agreement, the WTO's Agreement on Agriculture, which is not discussed in this book. The subsidization of services is an issue that remains unresolved under WTO law, requiring further multilateral negotiation. The two main categories of subsidy (prohibited and actionable) will now be examined.

2.2 Prohibited subsidies

Prohibited or red light subsidies are those which are never allowed. These are deemed to be the worst or most damaging form of governmental assistance, leading to benefits to certain enterprises which have a clear distortive effect on global trade. In a sense, these types of measures were the precise reason why the SCM was created. The WTO community felt that the provision of support with a view to improving an entity's trade position constituted economically harmful protectionism.

Article 3 of the SCM states that prohibited subsidies are those which are contingent, in law or in fact, whether solely or as one of several other conditions, upon export performance. They are also subsidies which are contingent, whether solely or as one of several other conditions, upon the use of domestic over imported goods, creating another distortion by compelling companies to buy local goods where they may want to buy better or cheaper foreign ones. An Annex to the SCM outlines in greater detail the types of measure which may constitute prohibited export subsidies in the form of an illustrative list, meaning that it is only intended to help clarify the types of measure which will

---

[4] D Collins and TJ Park, 'Deafening Silence or Noisy Whisper: Omission Bias and Foregone Revenue under the WTO Agreement on Subsidies and Countervailing Measures' 51:6 Journal of World Trade 1069 (2017).

be covered.[5] The Annex includes currency retention schemes (essentially cash bonuses from the government due to export performance); favourable transportation charges for exports; exemptions from tax, including special deductions, for exports; and loans below commercial rates. All of these arrangements would place the relevant enterprise in an advantageous position relative to normal market conditions, allowing it to supply goods more effectively than its competitors overseas.

The requirement of 'specificity' noted above does not need to be fulfilled for prohibited subsidies – all prohibited subsidies (meaning those which fit into the definition in Article 3) are deemed to be specific. Precluding the need to establish specificity makes it less difficult for complaining WTO members to bring the case that an export subsidy should be prohibited. This makes sense in that general social programmes aimed at supporting society at large should not have a focused export-oriented agenda. Perhaps more importantly from an evidentiary standpoint, the existence of a prohibited subsidy also precludes the need for the complainant to demonstrate that there has been an injury as the consequence of the subsidy. Injury is presumed if the subsidy is export related in some way. Australia was found to have violated Article 3 of the SCM by subsidizing companies that produced leather for car seats. The financial assistance offered by the government to the leather companies (cash grants) fell into the prohibited category because it was clearly aimed at helping the company increase its exports. The WTO panel inferred this from the fact that the Australian government was aware that its domestic market was too small to absorb all of the automotive leather being produced as a consequence of the grants, indicating that the grants were intended as export assistance.[6]

2.3 Actionable subsidies

The second category of subsidies under the SCM is actionable, or yellow light. These subsidies, outlined in Article 5, are allowed as long as they do not have adverse trade effects on other WTO members. Actionable subsidies are those which do not involve export performance, as outlined in the prohibited category above. As with the concept of specificity, the logic of this provision appears to be that members should retain the autonomy to craft policies which are in their own economic interests insofar as this does not undermine other members' rights and benefits within the world trading system. In order for this kind of subsidy to be prohibited, the complainant must demonstrate that its benefits as a member of the WTO are nullified, impaired or seriously prejudiced. These additional elements to the claim render the establishment of an actionable subsidy (and the remedies for it) somewhat more challenging than that of prohibited subsidies.

Perhaps the most difficult aspect of the actionable subsidy is the concept of 'serious prejudice', which is explained in Article 6. Here the SCM lists the types of circumstances which are indicative of serious prejudice to the industry of a complaining member. This includes displacement or impediment of imports of a like product, severe price undercutting compared to a like product or a large increase in the world market share of the subsidizing member. These are clearly highly fact

---

[5] Annex I.

[6] Australia – Subsidies Provided to Producers and Exporters of Automotive Leather, Panel Report, WT/DS126/R (16 June 1999).

intensive scenarios which will require the submission of detailed evidence by the complainant. Alternative causes of any of these or related harms to the complainant's industry must be discounted. For example, if the displacement or impediment of a like product was caused by a natural disaster or strike or other incident of *force majeure*, then serious prejudice will not be found and there will be no actionable subsidy.[7] This rule captures the element of causality – the industry in the complaining member's territory has to have suffered as a consequence of the defendant member's bestowing of a subsidy on an industry producing a like product. In a dispute regarding Korea's alleged subsidization of computer chips, a WTO panel was required to assess whether the assistance Korea had granted to various companies, which had not been clearly export-motivated, had caused any injury to Japanese firms in the same industry. Finding there was no breach of the SCM, the panel considered other possible causes of the harm to the Japanese computer chip industry, including reduced demand and changed habits of consumption for those products as well as developments in technology, both of which had themselves caused declining sales for Japanese firms.[8]

In ascertaining whether a measure is an actionable subsidy, in *EC – Aircraft*,[9] the Appellate Body stated that panels must consider the design and structure of the measure and relevant factual circumstances. This may further require consideration of a comparison between the ratio of anticipated export and domestic sales of the subsidized product because of the rebate, on the one hand, and on the other hand, the situation that would exist in its absence. Such counterfactuals may possibly be established by reference to existing patterns of trade before the measure was implemented. The WTO Appellate Body, again in *EC –Aircraft*, clarified that in establishing the effects of the subsidy it is not only the actual effects (change in export patterns), but also the anticipated ones, which matter.

2.4 Remedies

The subsidies regime under WTO law is special. It is distinct from tariffs or quotas under the GATT, for example, in that it has its own built-in system of remedies. First, members must withdraw a subsidy if there is determined to be a violation. Prohibited subsidies must be withdrawn without delay. This normally means within about three months, with actionable subsidies having longer timeframes for withdrawal. If the subsidy is not withdrawn the DSB may authorize the injured member to apply countermeasures against the losing respondent. Countermeasures are the retaliatory suspension of concessions for related products, as envisioned by the normal regime for remedies under the DSU. Second, and uniquely for subsidies, there is also the potential to impose unilateral countervailing duties under Article X of the SCM, without the multilateral permission of the DSB.

Whether multilaterally sanctioned or chosen unilaterally by the injured member, the purpose of the countervailing duty is to offset the illegal subsidy. A countervailing duty is a special fee, like

---

[7] Art. 6.7 c).

[8] Japan – Countervailing Duties on Dynamic Random Access Memories from Korea, Appellate Body Report, WT/DS336/AB/R (17 December 2007).

[9] European Communities and Certain Member States – Measures Affecting Trade in Large Civil Aircraft, Appellate Body Report, WT/DS316/AB/R (1 June 2011).

a tariff, imposed by the injured state. In the case of unilateral countervailing duties, this provides instant relief for a subsidy because it precludes the need to go through the dispute settlement process and to achieve a victory by a favourable panel recommendation, in which case a DSB-authorized countervailing duty could be imposed against the losing respondent. In order for a unilateral countervailing duty to be imposed lawfully by the injured member of its own accord there must be subsidized imports, injury to domestic industry and a causal link. The SCM outlines detailed requirements for investigations to be conducted by the injured member before such duties can be imposed against the offending member. Should the member impose the countervailing duty without satisfying these requirements, the allegedly subsidizing member might challenge the duty through the dispute settlement system, acting as the complainant.

As noted above, the concept of subsidy can be problematic for countries that do not have what might be viewed as 'normal' markets. Article 29 of the SCM granted members making the transition to market economy status the ability to support programmes and measures necessary to achieve this end, although such schemes will no longer be able to transgress the rules on prohibited subsidies – this leniency for transition economies is only relevant to actionable subsidies. China's Protocol of Accession to the WTO sheds further light on some of the controversies associated with the application of the concept of subsidy to a nonmarket economy. Article 15 b) of the Protocol refers to 'special difficulties' in applying the rules of the SCM to China, in which case the importing WTO member 'may then use methodologies for identifying and measuring the subsidy benefit which may take into account the possibility that prevailing terms and conditions in China may not always be the appropriate benchmarks'.[10] In other words, the idea of governmental assistance as an unfair trade distortion does not translate very well to an environment where the state naturally maintains a strong influence. In performing this benchmarking to establish whether a benefit has occurred, transparency is key, as with many aspects of WTO law. Western countries, notably the US, have struggled to calibrate their trade remedies to deal with Chinese subsidies (as well as dumping, of which more below). These countries will need to adapt their approach to China if or when it formally graduates to nonmarket economy status.[11]

A more creative remedy was implemented by the WTO in the dispute relating to Australia's subsidy of automotive leather, mentioned above. The Appellate Body reasoned that simply requiring Australia to cease assisting the domestic leather company was insufficient because the company had already been given a significant advantage. The Appellate Body ruled that the beneficiary company had to pay back the subsidy to the government. While the WTO cannot impose conditions on companies directly, because its rules only bind its member states, it insisted that Australia collect the money from the companies it had helped. This backward-looking monetary remedy is highly unusual for the WTO, which is normally focused on prospective remedies. The Appellate Body justified this approach by explaining that the money had already been used by the company to produce new inventory, therefore the harmful effects to its competitors, namely increased exports, were yet to take effect.[12]

---

[10] China Accession Protocol, WT/L/432 (23 November 2001).

[11] J Lee, 'China's Nonmarket Economy Treatment and US Trade Remedy Actions' 51:3 Journal of World Trade 495 (2017).

[12] Australia – Automotive Leather above n 6.

While there are several complicated issues in the sphere of subsidies, the distortive potential of subsidies is fairly straightforward, as is the need to respond to them through properly calibrated duties. A related form of trade protectionism – dumping – raises similar issues but is not as clear cut.

3. DUMPING

For non-economists, dumping is one of the most difficult topics of WTO law to comprehend, because it seems counterintuitive that a state should object to a supplier from another state selling products within its territory at artificially low prices. Surely consumers in the importing state should be more than happy to be able to purchase goods at prices cheaper than those offered to people in the country from which they originated, in some cases at prices below what the item cost to produce? Like subsidies, dumping rose to prominence as a protectionist strategy in the late twentieth century as tariffs began to disappear across the industrialized world. Dumping is often linked to subsidies because if a company is able to offer goods for sale at unrealistically low prices in other countries on a sustained basis, they may be receiving illegal assistance from their home government.

Another important issue to recognize in relation to dumping is that the WTO does not actually prohibit dumping itself. Rather, it controls the injured members' response to it, meaning the imposition of antidumping duties. Such duties can be levied against products in response to dumping only in certain narrow circumstances and must be proportionate to the extent of the dumping, much like unilateral countervailing duties against subsidies, as mentioned above. Antidumping duties cannot punish the dumping nation (or, more accurately, its suppliers). They are intended to normalize the price charged in the importing state to eliminate market distortions resulting from artificially low prices.

Dumping means exporting a product at an artificially low price to drive out competition in the importing country. It may be likened to the strategy of 'predatory pricing' in which aggressive companies undercut their prices to outcompete their competitors with a view to putting them out of business, cornering the market and then raising their prices to gouge consumers.[13] Dumping may take the form of sales below cost, meaning sales of a product at prices below the cost of production. Some sales below cost may be legitimate and not indicative of dumping. For example, there may be very intense competition in a market, as sometimes happens in grocery stores during the holiday season and as is one of the benefits of having a competitive retail sector – if you are a consumer. There may be a decline in demand due to recession, with companies doing everything they can do survive during times of hardship. This happened in department stores during the recession of 2009–10, when prices on a wide range of goods were slashed. Prices may be drastically reduced to the point of being unprofitable in order to increase volume of sales at an early stage in a product's lifecycle, when it is unfamiliar to consumers. Once there is a loyal customer base the price normalizes. It is when sustained artificially low prices affect traders overseas that the WTO becomes involved.

---

[13] A Gillespie, *Foundations of Economics* (Oxford University Press, 2016) chapter 12.

3.1 Anti-Dumping Agreement

The WTO does not control dumping directly; rather, it controls injured members' responses to it through the imposition of antidumping duties designed to normalize the price. These rules are contained in the Anti-Dumping Agreement (ADA). The ADA expands upon material contained in the GATT regarding dumping. Article 2 of the ADA contains rules on the determination of dumping through price comparison. The national antidumping authority of the injured member (for example, in the case of the EU it is the Directorate General for Trade of the European Commission) must determine whether there is a difference between the export price and the 'normal value'. The difference in price must not be small – it must be more than a few percentage points' difference. According to the Appellate Body in *US – Hot Rolled Steel*, a case in which Japan challenged anti-dumping duties which had been imposed by the US, in order to establish 'normal value' the sale must be in the 'ordinary course of trade'. This means that the price comparison must be made at the same point in the transaction. Moreover, differences that would naturally affect prices should be disregarded. For example, prices in bulk sales where there may be discounts should be disregarded, as would sales between affiliated companies where special prices are offered.[14]

Article 3 of the ADA concerns the determination of injury for the purposes of levying antidumping duties. The term 'material injury' is not defined but the standard is lower than the 'serious injury' standard for safeguards, of which more below. Dumping is considered to be a kind of unfair trade so the response to it carries a lower threshold of injury. The determination is based on evidence regarding the quantity of the dumped product and its effect on producers of such domestic products. There must be a significant increase in the quantity of dumped product. In terms of injury, the economic factors to be considered include effects on sales, profits, outputs, market share, productivity, returns on investment, cash flow, inventories, employment and wages. These matters are readily quantifiable and therefore open objective assessment by panels. As with subsidies, there must be a causal link – deleterious effects from dumping must be distinguished from effects of other factors, such as the fact that the company is making a product which consumers do not want at the prices offered, or perhaps that the company is poorly managed. Evidence must be objective, credible and verifiable.[15] It is possible to apply antidumping duties on products where there is a threat of material injury to the domestic industry, without actual damage yet being demonstrated. In the softwood lumber dispute between the US and Canada discussed above, the Appellate Body determined that further dumped imports were imminent and that unless protective action was taken, a material injury would have occurred in the near future.[16]

Since China is often accused of dumping because of its massive exports and efficient productivity,[17] there has been much discussion of China's Accession Protocol to the WTO and its impact on

---

[14] United States – Anti-Dumping Measures on Certain Hot-Rolled Steel Products from Japan, Appellate Body Report, WT/DS184/AB/R (23 August 2001).

[15] Ibid.

[16] Canada – Softwood Lumber above n 2.

[17] E.g. United States — Certain Methodologies and their Application to Anti-Dumping Proceedings involving China DS471 (21 September 2018).

dumping investigations. As mentioned earlier, accession protocols for new members (who joined the WTO after its creation in 1995) typically contain additional special rules for each new member, accommodating their particular concerns usually through phase-in periods during which time strict rules of membership may not apply. China's Accession Protocol also provided for a specialized procedure for the assessment of dumping because of China's nonmarket economy status, allowing a looser methodology for price comparison which effectively made a determination of dumping an easier exercise against Chinese companies.[18] The logic behind this procedure is that it is very difficult to ascertain a normal price for any commodity where prices are not set by market forces but by governmental policy, as in countries with command-style economies, much as is the case with identifying subsidies. This provision was set to expire in late 2016, at which point China was deemed to be a market economy entitled to the normal (harder) method of determination of dumping. Some members, such as the US, have argued that the special nonmarket procedure should still apply. This remains one of the chief points of contention for many WTO members regarding China, given its size and capacity for over-production of goods. Others contend that Asian countries in particular have been unfairly targeted by antidumping duties over the years.[19]

The EU imposed antidumping duties on solar panels imported from China, claiming that the underpriced panels had caused the loss of many thousands of jobs in the EU. In response, the EU raised the tariff rate on solar panels from China by almost 12 per cent, causing many to fear that China, which was denying dumping, would retaliate by imposing increased tariffs on a number of products it imports from Europe. Thankfully, the Chinese solar panel issue never reached the stage of formal WTO dispute settlement, having been resolved through consultations. Still, the solar panel dumping matter placed the EU in a difficult position with respect to two of its key policies – free trade and environmental protection. Antidumping duties would send a clear message that the EU expects China to observe free trade by avoiding the anticompetitive use of dumping in order to corner the European market for a popular new product. But with higher tariffs imposed on Chinese solar panels these important tools for offsetting climate change and reducing fossil fuel dependency would have become significantly more expensive, possibly even out of reach to the average European consumer. These issues will be considered again in the next chapter.

It is important to draw attention to one of the more controversial aspects of enforcement of the ADA through the WTO dispute settlement system. This concerns the manner in which panels should interpret the provisions of the ADA and, by extension, how they should review the factual determinations made by domestic antidumping authorities. Article 17.6 ii) of the ADA reads:

> ii) the panel shall interpret the relevant provisions of the Agreement in accordance with customary rules of interpretation of public international law. Where the panel finds that a relevant provision of the Agreement admits of more than one permissible interpretation, the panel shall find the authorities' measure to be in conformity with the Agreement if it rests upon one of those permissible interpretations.

---

[18] Art. 15 Accession of the People's Republic of China, WT/L/432 (23 November 2001).

[19] R McGee, 'Antidumping Laws as Weapons of Protectionism: Asian Case Studies' 5:1 Manchester Journal of International Economic Law 3 (2008).

The concept of 'permissible interpretation' suggests that the panel should accord broad discretion to national antidumping authorities where possible. Although this may be seen as enshrining a strong degree of autonomy in WTO members, essentially allowing them to use their own judgement when levying antidumping duties against other members, it does run the risk of injecting much uncertainty into the process. It may also transgress what is understood to be the central interpretive aim of the VCLT, namely that words be given an ordinary meaning which conforms to the objective of the agreement in which they are situated.[20] Countries such as the US, which currently exhibit much animus towards the WTO, may rightly view this aspect of the ADA as justifying their expectation that they will be granted deference by panels; when this is not forthcoming, it may lead to dismay and resentment.

4. SAFEGUARDS

Safeguards allow a WTO member to breach its obligations to observe tariff commitments and not to impose quotas in situations where doing otherwise would risk serious harm to its economy. In other words, safeguards are authorized protectionism against goods that have been traded fairly, as distinct from retaliatory measures against unfair trade practices such as subsidies and dumping. Safeguards are dealt with in Article XIX of the GATT, which has been known as the 'escape clause' or 'escape valve' because it allows WTO members to escape from their obligations when it is vital for them to do so. If there had been no Article XIX, then there is a strong probability that there would have been no GATT, because it would have simply been too difficult for states to surrender their domestic trade policy without restriction. The reality is that open trade policies can be harmful to domestic industries – people can lose their jobs and a recession can ensue. Safeguards acknowledge that there needs to be a mechanism to cushion the blow of sudden removal of trade barriers, provided that measures aimed at mitigating these harms are no greater than they need to be and that they are only temporary. The law of safeguards was expanded considerably when the WTO was created through an entire Agreement on Safeguards; however, the essential principles can be understood from a reading of the original GATT.

Article XIX of GATT reads:

1. (a) If, as a result of unforeseen developments and of the effect of the obligations incurred by a contracting party under this Agreement, including tariff concessions, any product is being imported into the territory of that contracting party in such increased quantities and under such conditions as to cause or threaten serious injury to domestic producers in that territory of like or directly competitive products, the contracting party shall be free, in respect of such product, and to the extent and for such time as may be necessary to prevent or remedy such injury, to suspend the obligation in whole or in part or to withdraw or modify the concession.

   (b) If any product, which is the subject of a concession with respect to a preference, is being imported into the territory of a contracting party in the circumstances set forth in

---

[20] Art. 38.

sub-paragraph (a) of this paragraph, so as to cause or threaten serious injury to domestic producers of like or directly competitive products in the territory of a contracting party which receives or received such preference, the importing contracting party shall be free, if that other contracting party so requests, to suspend the relevant obligation in whole or in part or to withdraw or modify the concession in respect of the product, to the extent and for such time as may be necessary to prevent or remedy such injury.

2. Before any contracting party shall take action pursuant to the provisions of paragraph 1 of this Article, it shall give notice in writing to the CONTRACTING PARTIES as far in advance as may be practicable and shall afford the CONTRACTING PARTIES and those contracting parties having a substantial interest as exporters of the product concerned an opportunity to consult with it in respect of the proposed action. When such notice is given in relation to a concession with respect to a preference, the notice shall name the contracting party which has requested the action. In critical circumstances, where delay would cause damage which it would be difficult to repair, action under paragraph 1 of this Article may be taken provisionally without prior consultation, on the condition that consultation shall be effected immediately after taking such action.

Article XIX sets out three conditions which must be fulfilled for safeguards to be applied by WTO members. First, there must be an increase in imports of the product in question; second, the increase must be caused by developments that were unforeseen; third, the increase of imports must cause or threaten to cause serious injury to a domestic industry producing a 'like' or 'directly competitive' product. As will be explored further below, 'serious injury' will not be an easy test to satisfy and will certainly be more difficult than the injury contemplated by subsidies or dumping, mentioned earlier. This higher threshold is a reflection of the fact that safeguards are designed to respond to fair rather than unfair trade.

One of the early safeguards disputes concerned the influx of shoes into Argentina from Europe.[21] Argentina decided to impose safeguard measures in the form of increased duties, beyond the levels they had committed to under their GATT bound tariffs. The EC complained, arguing that under WTO law Argentina's safeguards had to be imposed evenly against injury-causing imports from all countries, including other South American countries with whom Argentina had preferential trading arrangements. The Appellate Body agreed with this assessment, ruling that Argentina's safeguard regime on EC shoes was illegal because it discriminated against EC shoes without justification – the EC imports of shoes were no more damaging than those from other South American countries.

Under the safeguard regime, a WTO member may restrict imports of products temporarily if its domestic industry is injured or threatened with injury that has been caused by a 'surge' in imports. An import surge may be a real or absolute increase in imports of a particular product, or it can be relative – meaning an increase in the imports' share of a shrinking market, even if the import quantity has not increased. Industries or companies can ask their governments to initiate safeguard actions in response to these situations. But in order for this to be done, WTO members

---

[21] Argentina – Safeguard Measures on Imports of Footwear, Appellate Body Report, WT/DS121/AB/R (12 January 2000).

must adhere to the rules set out by the WTO. As with countervailing measures for subsidies and antidumping duties for dumping, safeguard actions require investigations by specialized national authorities, such as the Directorate General for Trade of the EU Commission. These procedures must be transparent and nonarbitrary. The investigating authorities in the country intending to impose the safeguards must announce publicly when hearings are going to take place and provide the opportunity for interested parties, such as the exporters from other countries as well as companies in the importing country, to present evidence about how harmful their imports are or are not.

As noted above, GATT Article XIX establishes criteria for determining whether a serious injury is being caused or is threatened to be caused, including the factors which must be considered in assessing the impact of imports on the domestic industry in question. This could be demonstrated by increases in unemployment, declining profitability, share value or bankruptcies. As with anti-dumping, there is also a causation requirement – it is not enough that the domestic industry is suffering; the suffering must be the result of the import surge. A causal link must be established between the increase in imports and the injury sustained by the industry. The Appellate Body clarified in *US – Wheat Gluten*, concerning a challenge from the EC against safeguards imposed by the US, that the causal link requires the establishment of a 'genuine and substantial relationship of cause and effect', implying a very close connection. Other factors that could have contributed must be discounted, such as poor quality products, high prices or excessive wages, meaning essential poor business management – together known as the 'nonattribution' test.[22] Once allowed, a safeguard measure must only be applied to the extent and duration necessary to prevent or remedy the serious injury and to allow the industry to adjust to the increase in imports.[23]

Safeguard measures as implemented should not reduce the quantity of imports below the annual average for the last three years for which import statistics are available, unless a higher reduction can be clearly justified because of the severity of injury sought to be avoided. In order for safeguards to be lawful, the increase in imports must be recent, sudden and sharp. If these criteria are not satisfied, then there will be no economic emergency, which is the foundation of the safeguard regime. This also requires that the import surge must be unforeseen, the idea being that if the domestic industry had known about it in advance, they would have been able to deal with it by restructuring their commercial activities.

When a WTO member restricts the imports from another WTO member under the safeguards regime in order to shelter the producers in one of its domestic industries, it may be required to compensate the exporting state, which has done nothing wrong. Recall that safeguards are intended to counter fair trade, not unfair trade as in the case of subsidies or dumping. The importing country should enter into consultations with the exporting country to come up with some kind of compensation. There are no recorded incidents of any such compensation having been established. In some cases, members have agreed to voluntarily suspend exports to members experiencing the injury. Importantly, Article 11.1 b) of the Safeguards Agreement prohibits members

---

[22] United States – Definitive Safeguard Measures on Imports of Wheat Gluten from the European Communities, Appellate Body Report, WT/DS166/AB/R (19 January 2001).

[23] United States – Definitive Safeguard Measures on Imports of Circular Welded Carbon Quality Line Pipe from Korea, Appellate Body Report, WT/DS202/AB/R (8 March 2002).

from seeking or taking voluntary export restraints in order to deal with safeguards situations. This is because such arrangements were often thought to be the result of coercion rather than being genuinely voluntary.[24] If no agreement is reached between the two members, then the exporting country can retaliate by taking an equivalent action, such as raising the tariffs on exports from the country that is imposing the safeguard measure. The retaliating country often must wait several years before it is allowed to do this with the WTO's blessing. The process is overseen by the WTO's Committee on Safeguards established under Article 13 of the Agreement on Safeguards, which is essentially an elaboration of GATT Article XIX. There have been several hundred safeguard investigations reported to the WTO, with roughly half resulting in the actual imposition of safeguards.

Given the danger that China posed with respect to import surges in WTO countries because of its vast manufacturing capacity, a special safeguard procedure was established for Chinese exports as part of China's terms of accession to the WTO. This special safeguard mechanism, which expired in 2013 (some would argue prematurely), established a lower threshold for the application of safeguards, including a lower standard of injury, against Chinese imports than against those from all other countries.

5. TRADE REMEDIES AND REGIONAL TRADE AGREEMENTS

Subsidies and dumping, and sometimes safeguards, are often dealt with together in RTAs under the heading Trade Remedies. This is partially because the same national departments are responsible for conducting the relevant investigations prior to the imposition of the associated duties, as noted above. For example, the USMCA contains a special mechanism for dispute settlement in relation to subsidies and antidumping, maintaining a feature which existed in the earlier NAFTA. This system enables the US, Canada and Mexico to challenge each other's antidumping and countervailing duty decisions through an expert panel including members from both countries involved in a dispute. This system was kept in the new agreement despite the objections of the US, in large part because it had lost a number of disputes in the past.

The Comprehensive Economic and Trade Agreement (CETA) between Canada and the EU affirms parties' obligations under the SCM and the ADA.[25] It contains an additional provision regarding the need for sensitivity with respect to public interest issues:

1. Each Party's authorities shall consider information provided in accordance with the Party's law as to whether imposing an anti-dumping or countervailing duty would not be in the public interest.
2. After considering the information referred to in paragraph 1, the Party's authorities may consider whether the amount of the anti-dumping or countervailing duty to be imposed

---

[24] PM Rodriguez, 'Safeguards in the World Trade Organization: Ten Years After: A Dissociated State of the Law?' 41:1 Journal of World Trade 159 (2007).

[25] Art. 3.1.

shall be the full margin of dumping or amount of subsidy or a lesser amount, in accord-ance with the Party's law.[26]

Similarly, Article 10.7 of the US–Korea FTA states as follows:

1. The Parties recognize the right to apply trade remedy measures consistent with Article VI of the GATT 1994, the AD Agreement, and the SCM Agreement, and the importance of promoting transparency in antidumping and countervailing duty proceedings and of ensuring the opportunity of all interested parties to participate meaningfully in such pro-ceedings.
2. Each Party retains its rights and obligations under the WTO Agreement with regard to the application of antidumping and countervailing duties.
3. Except for paragraphs 4 through 7, no provision of this Agreement shall be construed to impose any rights or obligations on a Party with respect to antidumping or countervailing duty measures. Neither Party may have recourse to dispute settlement under this Agree-ment for any matter arising under this Article.

The Korea–US FTA also contains material on safeguards. As with most RTAs, this broadly dupli-cate the procedures available under the WTO. It also clarifies interactions with the WTO safeguard regime. Article 10.5 states:

1. Each Party retains its rights and obligations under Article XIX of GATT 1994 and the Safe-guards Agreement. This Agreement does not confer any additional rights or obligations on the Parties with regard to actions taken under Article XIX of GATT 1994 and the Safeguards Agreement, except that a Party taking a global safeguard measure may exclude imports of an originating good of the other Party if such imports are not a substantial cause of serious injury or threat thereof.
2. Neither Party may apply, with respect to the same good, at the same time: (a) a safeguard measure; and (b) a measure under Article XIX of GATT 1994 and the Safeguards Agreement.

The safeguards chapter of the US–Korea FTA also offers a definition of 'serious injury' and a hand-ful of other concepts which are identical to that found in WTO disciplines. The US–Korea FTA also establishes a Committee on Trade Remedies to oversee the implementation of rules relating to subsidies, dumping and safeguards, encouraging consultation between parties. This committee is composed of official representatives from relevant agencies of each party who have responsibility for trade remedies matters.[27] Since these matters are highly specialized, they often require input from experts which have experience beyond more generic issues of international trade law.

This chapter will now turn to an entirely different aspect of WTO law but one which is equally important to the modern global economy: the regulation of trade in services.

---

[26] Art. 3.3.

[27] Art. 10.8.

6. TRADE IN SERVICES

Services are poorly liberalized relative to goods, possibly reflecting the heavy-handed nature of the way in which they are regulated at the domestic level by most countries around the world – especially developed countries, where services play a greater role in the economy. Today services comprise roughly 60 per cent of world GDP but only 20 per cent of trade, suggesting that the regulation of international services is even more intensive than it within one territory and likely prohibitively so, from the perspective of global commerce. It is anticipated that trade in services is poised to expand in the coming decades due to advances in technology, especially in telecommunications and the associated rise of digital trade, of which more will be discussed below. Efforts to liberalize services are therefore an important aspect of international economic law. Globally, the chief instrument in this regard is the General Agreement on Trade in Services (GATS) of the WTO.

6.1 The General Agreement on Trade in Services

Article I of the GATS fulfils the difficult task of defining 'services', which it does imaginatively and flexibly by reference to four 'modes of supply' of services: Cross Border, Consumption Abroad, Commercial Presence and Presence of Natural Persons. Cross Border covers services which may be supplied across international borders, such as a lawyer in one WTO member's territory providing advice over the telephone to a client in the territory of another WTO member. Consumption Abroad refers to situations where the consumer travels across international borders to consume a service, such as going overseas to receive medical treatment. Commercial Presence is the very wide category of services delivery where a commercial entity from one WTO member establishes itself in another WTO member's territory for the purposes of delivering services. This could be seen, for example, when a US hotel company opens a branch in Dubai. Commercial Presence is also known as Foreign Direct Investment (FDI), which is the second major topic covered in this book, starting in Chapter 6. Finally, Presence of Natural Persons is when the individual supplier moves to another country to supply a service on a temporary basis, such as when a software engineer from the UK goes to work on a project in Australia before returning home. It does not cover immigration in the sense of permanent relocation.

As an important limitation, the definition of Services in Article I does not include services 'normally supplied in the exercise of governmental authority'. This carves out a broad range of services from GATS coverage, including areas such as security, medical services, educational services and some utilities. The breadth of this exception will vary from country to country, being more significant in countries which have a larger public sector. For example, most medical services would not be covered by the definition of services in the GATS in the UK because of the National Health Service; this would not be the case in the US, which favours the private delivery of healthcare.

6.2 GATS general obligations – most favoured nation and transparency

The first part of the GATS consists of general obligations, meaning those which apply to all WTO members on a compulsory basis. Chief of these is the familiar most favoured nation (MFN) provision which was examined in Chapter 2 as contained in Article I of the GATT. In Article II of the GATS, the MFN provision prohibits discrimination between 'like' services or service providers from different countries. Recall that GATT MFN applies only to products, not to their producers. Since the caselaw for 'likeness' under the GATS is much less developed than it is under the GATT, GATT 'likeness' caselaw may be helpful to panels or the Appellate Body interpreting this provision. Under GATS MFN, 'no less favourable' modifies conditions of competition. It also applies both to *de jure* and *de facto* discrimination. Article III of the GATS is the transparency provision. Here members must publish all measures which pertain to services and inform other members of changes. It is broadly similar to the requirement of GATT Article X; however, it could be argued that transparency is even more important in the services context since services tend to be more heavily regulated than goods, suggesting that there will be more relevant regulations needful of disclosure to services suppliers.

6.3 Specific obligations – national treatment and market access

The second part of the GATS consists of Specific Obligations, which is where its structure differs most significantly from that of the GATT. The Specific Obligations are not mandatory – they are only assumed by WTO members to the extent that they wish to do so. In this sense the GATS is a much more flexible agreement than its goods counterpart, although of course under the GATT members can set the levels of tariffs that they want, which is impossible for services as they do not carry tariffs. This built-in optionality reflects the intensity of the regulation of services by many WTO members relative to goods and the associated implications on that country's regulatory autonomy.

Article XVII contains the GATS national treatment commitment. Under this provision, to the extent that members take the proactive step to make this commitment, they must accord to services and suppliers of any other member treatment that is no less favourable than it accords to its own like services or suppliers. Again, it is important to recall that under the GATT, national treatment covered only products, not producers. WTO members can disagree as to whether they have or have not made a national treatment commitment in their GATS schedule. For example, in a dispute relating to China's commitments on the distribution of magazines and audiovisual products, China had argued that 'sound recording distribution services' did not extend to sound recordings that were distributed by electronic means, but only to distribution in physical form, as in CDs.[28] The Appellate Body ruled against China, determining that a reasonable understanding of the phrase did in fact contemplate electronic as well as physical forms of delivery. In making this determination, the Appellate Body relied on the way this phrase had been used by other WTO members in making their services commitments and the fact that the words were sufficiently generic that what they apply to may change over time. A similar controversy was raised in conjunction with the GATS commitments of the US in a dispute brought by Antigua in relation to online gambling.[29]

---

[28] China – Measures Affecting Trading Rights and Distribution Services for Certain Publications and Audiovisual Entertainment Products, Appellate Body Report, WT/DS363/AB/R (19 January 2010).

[29] United States – Measures Affecting the Cross-Border Supply of Gambling and Betting Services, Appellate Body Report, WT/DS285/AB/R (20 April 2005).

As under the GATT, both the MFN and national treatment obligations of the GATS require a 'likeness' test. In order to ascertain whether there has been discrimination, either as between two WTO members or between the member itself and all other members, it must be determined whether the services or services suppliers concerned are 'like services' or 'like services suppliers'. Comparing suppliers, usually companies, is a somewhat different exercise than comparing the service itself. As with the GATT, whether either of these comparisons is satisfied will be decided on a case by case basis. In looking at the suppliers themselves, WTO panels and the Appellate Body have shown that this will also involve a consideration of whether the suppliers are in a competitive relationship with each other (with this phrase appearing in the text of the GATS), although this is not necessarily sufficient to establish likeness. In another GATS dispute involving China relating to electronic payment services, a WTO panel determined that 'likeness' under GATS had a whole range of meanings.[30] Importantly, it did not require that the services be exactly the same, as long as they were 'essentially or generally' the same.

The market access rules in Article XVI of the GATS arguably go much further than the GATT does for goods, penetrating deeply into each member state's capacity for self-government in services, but again only to the extent that each member has made commitments in this area. Under Article XVI, WTO members must not place numeric restrictions on the market entry of service suppliers, regardless of whether they are foreign or local. These rules prohibit quantitative limits on the provision of services, such as the number of service providers in a particular industry, the value of the service transactions in which they can participate, the number of people they can employ or the amount of foreign capital invested in the service supplier. If a market access commitment is made by a WTO member then these types of restrictions on services are prohibited. It must be emphasized that this is so regardless of whether the restriction is discriminatory (only applies to foreign service providers) or non-discriminatory (applies equally to foreign and local service providers). In this sense market access under the GATS concerns liberalization of services generally, not simply internationally. For example, a restriction on the number of foreign banks allowed to set up branches is clearly a discriminatory market access barrier, whereas a licence issued by the government for all new banks based on the minimum amount of capitalization required would be a non-discriminatory market access barrier. Accordingly, in the online gambling dispute against the US brought by Antigua, the US was found to have breached its GATS market access commitment by prohibiting the supply of online gambling services. This was because the panel and later the Appellate Body found that a prohibition was another way of maintaining a quota of zero, which was effectively a numeric limitation that constituted a market access barrier.[31]

Expanding access to markets in more services industries is intended to increase competition, either from local suppliers or from suppliers from other WTO members. More competition should translate to better quality services at lower prices and enhance employment opportunities and innovation. Intensifying competition in services can also lead to some companies going out of business because they cannot withstand new market entrants, much as it can lead to a loss of jobs for service suppliers who are not as good or who have charged their employers or customers too much. Al-

---

[30] China – Certain Measures Affecting Electronic Payment Services, Panel Report, WT/DS413/R (31 August 2012).

[31] US – Gambling above n 29.

though the GATS ensures that foreign suppliers of services in listed sectors do not suffer discrimination and that the sectors in which they operate are not subject to restrictions on market access, it is not intended to compensate foreign companies for any difficulties they might face because they are foreign. This is correctly viewed as a natural feature of a market which does not deserve rebalancing.

Members list their specific commitments (National Treatment and Market Access) in a Schedule of Specific Commitments and may specify certain limitations on these commitments. This is known as a positive list approach, which may be contrasted with a negative list, in which all sectors are committed and only the derogations are listed. The positive list format is thought to be less conducive to liberalization and therefore has been rejected by a number of RTAs in favour of the negative list format. Generally speaking, the level of liberalization achieved through the GATS' positive list approach has been somewhat disappointing, with many members failing to list many sectors or modes of supply.

6.4 Domestic regulation and mutual recognition

These sections of the GATS are tremendously important because they facilitate market access in sectors where GATS commitments relating to national treatment or market access have been made in one or more modes of delivery. Put more plainly, these provisions help smooth access, which might be practically more difficult even if a sector is notionally open to foreign competition. Article VI on Domestic Regulation states as follows:

1. In sectors where specific commitments are undertaken, each Member shall ensure that all measures of general application affecting trade in services are administered in a reasonable, objective and impartial manner.
2. (a) Each Member shall maintain or institute as soon as practicable judicial, arbitral or administrative tribunals or procedures which provide, at the request of an affected service supplier, for the prompt review of, and where justified, appropriate remedies for, administrative decisions affecting trade in services. Where such procedures are not independent of the agency entrusted with the administrative decision concerned, the Member shall ensure that the procedures in fact provide for an objective and impartial review.
   (b) The provisions of subparagraph (a) shall not be construed to require a Member to institute such tribunals or procedures where this would be inconsistent with its constitutional structure or the nature of its legal system.
3. Where authorization is required for the supply of a service on which a specific commitment has been made, the competent authorities of a Member shall, within a reasonable period of time after the submission of an application considered complete under domestic laws and regulations, inform the applicant of the decision concerning the application. At the request of the applicant, the competent authorities of the Member shall provide, without undue delay, information concerning the status of the application.

This provision ensures that practical barriers to trade in services, such as qualifications and licenses for suppliers (e.g. doctors or lawyers), are only applied to the necessary extent and that foreign suppliers in services sectors which have been opened by WTO members have a fair opportunity to obtain those requirements to deliver the service.

These rules are strengthened by Article VII of the GATS, which allows for foreign services suppliers to be recognized as having the competence and authority to provide the service based on their home state qualifications, precluding the need for additional testing or certification. Recognition under Article VII of GATS is an essential feature of modern trade relations both for goods and services. In the case of services, it is not much help to services suppliers, even if a market has been theoretically opened to them, if their home qualifications to supply the service are not recognized in the receiving state. Article VII reads as follows:

1. For the purposes of the fulfilment, in whole or in part, of its standards or criteria for the authorization, licensing or certification of services suppliers, and subject to the requirements of paragraph 3, a Member may recognize the education or experience obtained, requirements met, or licences or certifications granted in a particular country. Such recognition, which may be achieved through harmonization or otherwise, may be based upon an agreement or arrangement with the country concerned or may be accorded autonomously.

2. A Member that is a party to an agreement or arrangement of the type referred to in paragraph 1, whether existing or future, shall afford adequate opportunity for other interested Members to negotiate their accession to such an agreement or arrangement or to negotiate comparable ones with it. Where a Member accords recognition autonomously, it shall afford adequate opportunity for any other Member to demonstrate that education, experience, licenses, or certifications obtained or requirements met in that other Member's territory should be recognized.

3. A Member shall not accord recognition in a manner which would constitute a means of discrimination between countries in the application of its standards or criteria for the authorization, licensing or certification of services suppliers, or a disguised restriction on trade in services.

Recognition is often enshrined formally in mutual recognition agreements (MRAs). The advantage of MRAs is that they are settled and predictable, rather than flexible and prone to change without notice. This allows services suppliers to establish a client base in a target country, secure in the knowledge that their capacity to deliver that service will remain lawful without additional requirements, such as certificates or training periods. Sectoral based mutual recognition initiatives are common, typically pursued at the bilateral level rather than multilaterally.[32]

One of the best known cases in which parties sought WTO dispute settlement under the GATS was in relation to online gambling, as noted above.[33] The US had outlawed internet-based gambling websites operated out of Antigua, in violation of its GATS-specific commitments. The US had attempted to argue that it was legally allowed to prevent these websites from operating in the

---

[32] D Collins, *The Public International Law of Trade in Legal Services* (Cambridge University Press, 2018).

[33] US – Gambling above n 29.

US because they were a risk to its public morals under the GATS General Exceptions of Article XIV, similar to the General Exceptions of the GATT, as will be explored in the next chapter. This defence, although in theory valid under WTO law, was rejected by the panel and Appellate Body because of its arbitrary application, and the US was ordered to change its laws. When the US failed to do this Antigua asked for compensation totalling US$21 million per year. The WTO DSB ultimately allowed Antigua to suspend concessions up to this value under the Trade Related Aspects of Intellectual Property Rights (TRIPS) Agreement.

The GATS is thought to have created a more secure environment for trade in services through the progressive removal of barriers to trade, in part because of the availability of recourse to WTO dispute settlement instead of via unilateral pressure.[34] At the same time, some commentators have criticized the agreement for failing to more fully liberalize trade in services, as suggested earlier.[35] There are also accusations that the GATS has led to the exploitation of developing countries in favour of Western corporate interests, since these countries tend to be the place of origin of most international services suppliers.[36]

6.5 Services and regional trade agreements

Most services chapters of RTAs merely replicate the provisions of GATS, either by incorporating them by reference or simply by repeating the language of GATS verbatim or near verbatim, as in the ASEAN Framework Agreement on Services (AFAS), which was signed in 1995. The aim of AFAS and many other RTAs covering services is to go beyond the commitments made in the GATS, sometimes expressed as GATS+. Going beyond the GATS normally means that the parties to a bilateral or regional arrangement have simply scheduled more sectors under national treatment or market access than they did under the GATS, either under the larger positive list or a smaller negative list. This can be seen, for example, in the schedule of commitments contained in the EU–Singapore Free Trade Agreement, concluded in 2018.

In addition to bilateral and regional initiatives for services liberalization, the Trade in Services Agreement (TiSA) is a planned RTA covering services which was negotiated among 23 WTO member states, including the EU, Canada, the US and many other developed countries, together comprising approximately 70 per cent of world trade in services. As of the time of writing, discussions under the TiSA are moribund. As with services chapters in many RTAs, the TiSA is essentially an expansion of the GATS. Participants are expected to commit to greater liberalization for their services than they did under the GATS, in part because, as developed countries, these parties have more interest in opening services than most WTO members (two thirds of which are developing countries). This is why it is thought that negotiations on the TiSA could proceed more efficiently than would be the case were 164 members involved. Some of the obligations were to be structured as a positive list (as under the GATS) and others as a negative list, as under the services chapters of

---

[34] P Delimatsis, *International Trade in Services and Domestic Regulations* (Oxford University Press, 2007).

[35] R Adlung and M Roy, 'Turning Hills into Mountains? Current Commitments under the General Agreement on Trade in Services and Prospects for Change' 39:6 Journal of World Trade 1161 (2005).

[36] J Kelsey, *Serving Whose Interests? The Political Economy of Trade in Services Agreements* (Routledge Cavendish, 2008).

many RTAs. The plan is eventually to incorporate the TiSA into the WTO, with a view to encouraging other WTO members to join incrementally.

This chapter will now explore the issue of digital trade, which is closely related to that of trade in services.

7. DIGITAL TRADE

Given the size and growth of international services delivered via the internet, the WTO has begun to recognize the benefits offered by establishing rules on digital trade. Digital trade, sometimes known as electronic commerce or e-commerce, can be defined as the use of the internet to conduct business transactions nationally or internationally.[37] Globally, digital trade is thought to be worth several trillion dollars per year, comprising a significant portion of the global economy.

7.1 Multilateral efforts

For the most part, digital trade developed after the creation of the WTO in the mid-1990s. This is why the WTO agreements do not contain specific articles in relation to digital trade. Still, there are several WTO agreements related to digital trade. First, the GATS has some bearing on digital trade because the communication services which underpin digital trade fall into its sphere. The execution of an electronic transaction necessitates infrastructure services, such as distribution and payment, the liberalization of which also falls under the GATS. Due to the acknowledged importance of telecommunication services to services generally, access to public telecommunication networks was incorporated in a separate Telecommunication Annex to the GATS. Whenever unlimited market access commitments are undertaken by a WTO member, as discussed earlier in this chapter, every means of delivery, including remote supply through telecommunications, should be allowed.[38] Additionally, the WTO's Information Technology Agreement (ITA) is relevant to digital trade. Under the ITA, WTO members agreed to a common position with regard to trade in information technology (IT) goods such as computers and computer parts. WTO members committed themselves to reduce their tariffs on such goods in four increments of 25 per cent to reach a tariff-free policy by the year 2000.

Largely at the insistence of the US, WTO members decided to develop a work programme covering digital trade. Four WTO bodies were charged with examining e-commerce issues: the Goods Council, the Services Council, the TRIPS Council and the committee on Trade and Development.[39] According to the WTO Work Programme on Electronic Commerce, digital trade is understood to mean the production, distribution, marketing, sale or delivery of goods and services by electronic means. Although the WTO Work Programme was established in 1998, very little progress has been

[37] 'Study from WTO Secretariat Highlights Potential Trade Gains from Electronic Commerce' World Trade Organization, Geneva (13 March 1998).

[38] US – Gambling above n 29.

[39] WTO Secretariat, 'Development Implications of Electronic Commerce', WT/COMTD/W/51 (23 November 1998).

achieved under it. One of the obstacles has been the issue of categorization. WTO members differ as to whether products which were usually sold as goods due to their ties to a physical supplier, but which can now be delivered online, should be treated as goods under the GATT or as services under the GATS.[40] For example, if a book is ordered online, but is delivered physically in hard copy, for the purposes of WTO trade rules it is a good and is therefore subject to the GATT. If the book is delivered electronically, that is, downloaded onto a device such as a tablet, it is unclear whether this digital product should be treated as a good or a service. If the latter, it falls within the sphere of the GATS. The advent of 3D printing, which could subvert traditional manufacturing methods for high value goods, has only exacerbated this debate. Until the categorization issue is resolved, further progress on the liberalization of digital trade will be difficult. For now, WTO members have agreed not to impose tariffs on imported electronic transmissions. In 2018 a group of WTO members initiated exploratory work towards future WTO negotiations on trade related aspects of e-commerce, possibly with a view to creating a plurilateral agreement on digital trade.[41]

7.2 Regional efforts

Faltering WTO progress on digital trade has led to a number of countries seeking these arrangements under RTAs. For example, the USMCA includes a chapter on digital trade which resembles that of the CPTPP.[42] The USMCA provides a definition for digital products, providing an illustrative list of digitized products, such as electronically traded software, books and music. The USMCA further requires parties not to impose customs duties on electronic transmissions. It also requires that the parties do not establish 'unnecessary' barriers on electronic transmissions.[43] The agreement further contains several principles that deal with technological neutrality, ensuring that basic trade concepts of non-discrimination, national treatment and MFN status apply to digital trade, and regulatory forbearance, meaning avoiding government action that would restrict trade. The USMCA also ensures the validity of electronic signatures,[44] and contains a requirement to maintain antispam rules and online consumer protection laws.[45] Personal information protection requirements in the USMCA call for a legal framework to protect the personal information of users of digital trade; however, a footnote acknowledges that merely enforcing voluntary undertakings of enterprises related to privacy is sufficient to meet the obligation.

The USMCA's chapter on digital trade includes targeted sections on data localization.[46] The purpose of such a provision is to prevent signatory parties from insisting on maintaining con-

---

[40] I Willemyns, 'GATS Classification of Digital Services – Does the Cloud Have a Silver Lining?' 53:1 Journal of World Trade 59 (2019).

[41] World Trade Report 2018, The World Trade Organization (2018).

[42] Y Abe and D Collins, 'The CPTPP and Digital Trade: Embracing E-Commerce Opportunities for SMEs in Japan and Canada' Transnational Dispute Management (December 2018).

[43] USMCA Arts 19.2 and 19.5.

[44] Art. 19.6.

[45] Art. 19.7.

[46] Art. 19.12.

trol over information processing and storage inside their territory, which could act as a market distortion. Parties to the USMCA cannot make it a condition for conducting business that a company from another party must use or locate a computing facility in their territory. The US-MCA further bans restrictions on data transfers across borders.[47] Lastly, the USMCA prevents parties from requiring the disclosure of source code, a vital component of intellectual property for many firms.

The USMCA (and the CPTPP) are often thought of as groundbreaking in terms of their coverage of digital trade, in sharp contrast to the lack of progress at the WTO. For most of the digital trade rules in the USMCA, the parties' approach was based on the premise that digital trade is another variety of traditional trade and that it is only the medium through which the commercial transaction is performed which is innovative. The practical consequence of this recognition may be that RTAs which embrace this understanding may not have to make many changes to their domestic laws.

8. CONCLUSION

The topics explored in this chapter concern adaptations of trade protectionist strategies to the modern era of globalization, in which tariffs on many products have been eliminated and patterns of economic productivity, especially in the developed world, have shifted in favour of services. The chapter examined how WTO rules have attempted to combat subsidization by identifying harmful kinds of governmental assistance to exporters, an enduring problem in part due to the participation of nonmarket economies in global trade. It considered the related problem of dumping and the WTO's efforts to regulate antidumping duties based on deviations from the normal price of goods, again problematic from the standpoint of products which originate from countries that do not operate markets as they are have been understood in the West. The safeguard regime was outlined as an inevitable compromise between sovereignty and WTO membership, allowing states to impose temporary tariffs to relieve the pressures of globalization when potential harms are too much to bear. Finally, this chapter looked at the WTO's flexible, and in some respects underachieving, services agreement which permits members to commit to liberalization only to the extent that they wish, leaving many aspects of the highly regulated services sector closed to foreign competition and illustrating once again how the removal of barriers to some kinds of modern trade may be best pursued at the regional level. The chapter concluded with some thoughts on the WTO's lack of progress in digital trade and the potential for gains in this area in progressive RTAs. Staying with trade and the WTO, the next chapter will explore the WTO's capacity to accommodate nontrade values through its general exceptions and special rules on health and safety regulations. It will also examine the WTO's engagement with the important and controversial field of intellectual property.

---

[47] Art. 19.11.

DISCUSSION QUESTIONS

1. What are some of the problems associated with establishing a definition for subsidy and how does the Agreement on Subsidies and Countervailing Measures address these issues?
2. Why does the WTO concern itself with dumping and is its response to this form of trade protectionism adequate?
3. In what sense do WTO rules on safeguards allow WTO members full discretion to use safeguards as short term protectionism?
4. To what extent is the General Agreement on Trade in Services too flexible in terms of the rights and obligations it imposes on WTO members?

FURTHER READING

D Ahn, K Kwon, J Lee and JH Park, 'An Empirical Analysis on the WTO Safeguard Actions' 52:3 Journal of World Trade 415 (2018).

D Collins and TJ Park, 'Deafening Silence or Noisy Whisper: Omission Bias and Foregone Revenue under the WTO Agreement on Subsidies and Countervailing Measures' 51:6 Journal of World Trade 1069–88 (2017).

K Kim, D Ahn, 'To Be or Not to Be with Targeted Dumping' 21:3 Journal of International Economic Law 567 (2018).

SY Peng, 'The Rule of Law in Times of Technological Uncertainty: Is International Economic Law Ready for Emerging Supervisory Trends?' 22:1 Journal of International Economic Law 1 (2019).

5
General exceptions, health and safety, and intellectual property

1. INTRODUCTION

So far this book has focused on the WTO's trade rules from the perspective of furthering trade liberalization in the sense of creating economic efficiencies through access to lower priced goods and the ensuing beneficial competitive pressures of the global marketplace. Chapter 4 approached this by examining the WTO's disciplines on trade remedies against subsidies and dumping, with a digression into the unrelated field of services. This chapter will turn to a different perspective on international trade, noting that the goals of economic progress through liberalization should be balanced against other, arguably more important, social purposes, such as the protection of the environment and human health. It will explore the WTO's approach to these issues first through a discussion of the general exceptions of Article XX of the GATT, followed by two distinct regimes addressing essentially food health (the SPS Agreement) and product safety regulations (the TBT Agreement) as barriers to trade. WTO disciplines in these important fields may be described as examples of harmonization – rather than mandating specific international rules, WTO law instead aims to achieve consistency among domestic rules to avoid wasteful duplication. In keeping with this approach, the chapter also considers how global trade rules have dealt with intellectual property by attempting to achieve a degree of standardization in the protection of this important aspect of global commerce so that differential protection across the world does not distort trade patterns. As before, the chapter will draw attention to regional initiatives in each of these spheres.

2. GENERAL EXCEPTIONS

The chief embodiment of the WTO's treatment of noneconomic matters is found in the general exceptions provision of the original GATT, which was essentially duplicated in the GATS.

2.1 GATT Article XX

Although the WTO's primary focus is the liberalization of trade for the purposes of economic advancement and increasing prosperity across the globe, it would be a mistake to assume that economic matters are the organization's only concern. GATT drafters were careful to include exceptions which would allow contracting parties to deviate from their commitments where there were sufficiently strong social (or noneconomic) concerns in play, sometimes described by economists as negative externalities. Some have argued that the justifications listed in Article XX allow insufficient regulatory control for members, particularly given that they were drafted more than 70 years ago, during a very different era.[1] This complaint is perhaps even more valid when one considers that it is exceedingly difficult for a WTO member to use one of the Article XX exceptions successfully to defend itself against the accusation of breach of WTO obligations by another member, as will be shown below. GATT Article XX states in relevant part:

> nothing in this Agreement shall be construed to prevent the adoption or enforcement by a contracting party of measures:
> (a) necessary to protect public morals;
> (b) necessary to protect human, animal or plant life or health;
> (c) relating to the importations or exportations of gold or silver;
> (d) necessary to secure compliance with laws or regulations which are not inconsistent with the provisions of this Agreement, including those relating to customs enforcement, the enforcement of monopolies operated under paragraph 4 of Article II and Article XVII, the protection of patents, trade marks and copyrights, and the prevention of deceptive practices;
> (e) relating to the products of prison labour;
> (f) imposed for the protection of national treasures of artistic, historic or archaeological value;
> (g) relating to the conservation of exhaustible natural resources if such measures are made effective in conjunction with restrictions on domestic production or consumption.

Of this list (which is complete rather than indicative), the three most important of the general exceptions are: (a) public morals; (b) human, animal or plant life or health; and (g) the conservation of natural resources. Public morals is significant because it is such an indistinct concept with the potential to cover a wide range of policy measures, including issues relating to cultural values – another amorphous concept. Human, animal or plant life or health is similarly wide and may be taken to cover health generally, including nonhuman health. The conservation of natural resources is often viewed as synonymous with environmental protection, although this is also covered by (b) to a degree. It is worth keeping in mind that there was no public awareness of modern ideas such as global warming or climate change in 1947 when the GATT was drafted. While there has yet to be a WTO dispute in relation to either global warming or climate change (it would be difficult for any court to establish liability because of the tenuous element of causation), if there ever is one it will likely be brought under one of these two sections.

---

[1] E.g. S Cho, *The Social Foundations of World Trade* (Cambridge University Press, 2015).

The specific policy issues noted above are preceded by what is known as the 'chapeau', or hat, to Article XX. It specifies that the enumerated justifications must be '[s]ubject to the requirement that such measures are not applied in a manner which would constitute a means of arbitrary or unjustifiable discrimination between countries where the same conditions prevail, or a disguised restriction on international trade'.

The chapeau appears to embody a principle of good faith: openness and honesty in trade dealings between states. It implies that members will honour the spirit of the law, not just the letter of it. It is designed to ensure that exceptions are not abused. It further ensures that the enumerated exception will be applied even-handedly with a view to minimizing its intrusion into the trading affairs of members of the WTO community. Caselaw has shown that exploitation of Article XX is exceedingly difficult – there are very few cases where members have succeeded in defending trade restrictive measures through Article XX, mostly because of the chapeau.

The procedure for evaluating a measure under the GATT's general exceptions has been explored in WTO caselaw. First, the panel must consider whether the measure fits into one of the enumerated exceptions. Second, the availability of the general exception is limited by the requirement that the exception not be either arbitrary or unjustified discrimination or a disguised restriction on international trade, which the panel must also investigate.[2]

In one of the most famous WTO disputes of all time, India, Malaysia, Pakistan and Thailand brought a joint complaint against the US for a ban it imposed on the importation of shrimp products. The basis of the US ban was the protection of sea turtles, which were allegedly harmed during shrimp harvesting by companies from these Asian countries. The US required all US shrimp trawlers to use 'turtle exclusion devices' to prevent sea turtles from being killed accidentally during shrimp harvesting. Shrimp from countries that did not use these devices was banned. Although an import ban violated the GATT's prohibition on quotas, the general exceptions allow for breach of this rule for purposes relating to 'the conservation of natural resources'. The US tried to use this exception to justify the ban and the four Asian countries complained. The Appellate Body ruled that the laws aimed at protecting sea turtles were a legitimate exception to the GATT prohibition on quotas. This was only permissible as long as the turtle-related ban was applied in a non-discriminatory way, as required by the chapeau, meaning that the ban on turtle-harming shrimp was imposed on some countries but not others. The US lost because it had applied its turtle safety ban on shrimp in a discriminatory fashion, providing countries in the western hemisphere – primarily in the Caribbean – with technical and financial assistance in order to adhere to the turtle safety rules. The US also accorded a longer transition period for fishermen from western hemisphere countries to start using the turtle exclusion devices. These advantages had not been extended to the four Asian countries, which was viewed as arbitrary and unjustified discrimination.

In *US – Tuna*,[3] a WTO panel decided that the US could not ban imports of tuna from Mexico simply because Mexican laws on the way tuna was caught (in a manner that harmed dolphins) did

---

[2] United States – Standards for Reformulated and Conventional Gasoline, Appellate Body Report, WT/DS2/AB/R (20 May 1996).

[3] United States – Measures Concerning the Importation, Marketing and Sale of Tuna and Tuna Products, Panel Report WT/DS381/R (13 June 2012).

not satisfy US requirements. The US could have imposed its rules on the quality of the tuna, but not on the way it was produced. This is the so-called product versus process way of differentiating between products, mentioned earlier in Chapter 2. The panel further decided that the GATT did not allow one country to enact trade laws for the purpose of enforcing its own domestic laws on another country, even where this was done to protect animal health or exhaustible natural resources such as dolphins under Article XX. If a GATT signatory was allowed to do this then any country could ban imports of a product from another country merely because the exporting country has different environmental or health policies of its own. Importantly, the panel did say that the US was allowed to require tuna caught according to its dolphin standards to be labelled 'dolphin safe', leaving it to consumers to choose whether or not to buy it.

China attempted to use environmental protection as a justification for its export ban on rare earths such as tungsten and molybdenum in a dispute brought by the US and the EU.[4] It argued that its export restrictions on these valuable substances, which transgressed the prohibition on quantitative restrictions, were essential because of environmental pollution associated with the mining of these metals. The pollution from mining had to be prevented, so the Chinese argued, because it was harmful to human health, under GATT Article XX b). China also claimed that it had to limit exports of the rare earths because of the need to conserve an exhaustible natural resource under XX g), namely the metals themselves. The WTO panel ruled against China, siding with the US and EU, who had complained because of the restricted market for the rare metals on world markets resulting from China's hoarding. The export ban was not viewed as necessary to fulfil these environmental objectives, in large part because China continued to extract the metals from the ground on an industrial scale for use or storage domestically, which undermined its environmental assertions.

China sought to use the public moral defence found in both GATT Article XX a) and GATS Article XIV a) to support various restrictions on imported films, DVDs and publications including magazines and books. The US initiated a complaint against China arguing that China's laws were unfairly discriminating against US products because they essentially required that their importation and distribution must be done in conjunction with a registered Chinese entity. China claimed that only such an organization would be able to identify whether foreign entertainment could undermine Chinese cultural identity, something that it felt was more important than its free trade commitments under the WTO. The Appellate Body ultimately ruled that the public morals defence could have been used in this way, but that China had failed to demonstrate that the import and distribution controls were necessary for fulfilling the goal of upholding public morals. First, a less trade restrictive way of protecting Chinese culture may plausibly have been available. More importantly, the Appellate Body clarified that the protection of public morals and public order requires some explanation – it cannot simply be asserted. If China had believed strongly that foreign films, music and magazines represented a threat to its cultural identity, then this would have had to be shown convincingly, and it had not been in this instance.

When evaluating the applicability of a general exception to justify a violation of a WTO obligation, it is insufficient to identify a particular nontrade policy that matters to the country enacting

---

[4] China – Measures Related to the Exportation of Rare Earths, Tungsten, and Molybdenum, Appellate Body Report, WT/DS431/AB/R (29 August 2014).

the offending law. The offending country must show that the law was not applied in a discriminatory or arbitrary fashion, meaning that it was applied in the same way to imports from all countries, as required by the chapeau. For public morals and animal health, the country applying the illegal measure also must demonstrate that there was not a less trade restrictive method that could have fulfilled the same objective – this is what is meant by 'necessary'. This will involve a weighing and balancing of various regulatory actions that the government could have taken and the effects that these may or may not have had on international trade in affected products. Some commentators have suggested that this involves a methodical proportionality-based assessment in line with reasoning found in investment arbitration decisions and the jurisprudence of the European Court of Human Rights (ECtHR),[5] although the reality is often less scientific.

The chapeau of the general exception provisions in the GATT and the GATS requires that the WTO member must do so in a manner that is honest and forthright. As suggested above, this is often portrayed as a principle of good faith which is found in a number of domestic legal orders and is arguably a principle of customary international law. A compromise must be struck between the right of a member to invoke an exception and the rights of other members to enjoy the benefits afforded by WTO rules. The panels and Appellate Body are tasked with maintaining this delicate balance, in many ways encapsulating the essential conflict at the heart of the relationship between the WTO as an organization and the sovereign rights of its members. In performing this role, WTO adjudicators are able to guard against the abuse of alleged policy goals as tools of protectionism. In an era of ever intensifying attention to issues such as climate change, health and the importance of cultural identity, this is likely to become an increasingly difficult and critical exercise.

2.2 GATS Article XIV

As mentioned above, the general exception provisions of GATS Article XIV are broadly similar to those of the GATT, and as a consequence tend to receive less attention from commentators. They are mentioned here for the purposes of completeness. Article XIV reads:

> Nothing in this Agreement shall be construed to prevent the adoption or enforcement by any Member of measures:
> (a) necessary to protect public morals or to maintain public order;
> (b) necessary to protect human, animal or plant life or health;
> (c) necessary to secure compliance with laws or regulations which are not inconsistent with the provisions of this Agreement including those relating to:
> (i) the prevention of deceptive and fraudulent practices or to deal with the effects of a default on services contracts;
> (ii) the protection of the privacy of individuals in relation to the processing and dissemination of personal data and the protection of confidentiality of individual records and accounts;
> (iii) safety;

---

[5] C Henckels, *Proportionality and Deference in Investor-State Arbitration* (Cambridge University Press, 2015).

(d) inconsistent with Article XVII, provided that the difference in treatment is aimed at ensuring the equitable or effective imposition or collection of direct taxes in respect of services or service suppliers of other Members;

(e) inconsistent with Article II, provided that the difference in treatment is the result of an agreement on the avoidance of double taxation or provisions on the avoidance of double taxation in any other international agreement or arrangement by which the Member is bound.

Notable differences from the GATT include the reference to public order and the material on privacy, which is typically more relevant to the use of services than to goods. This addition also reflects the fact that the GATS was drafted in the early 1990s rather than the 1940s. Article XIV also includes a chapeau which is virtually identical to that of Article XX of the GATT: 'Subject to the requirement that such measures are not applied in a manner which would constitute a means of arbitrary or unjustifiable discrimination between countries where like conditions prevail, or a disguised restriction on trade in services.'

The general exceptions of the GATS were invoked in a dispute between Antigua and the US over online gambling involved an attempted justification based on upholding public morality, as discussed in Chapter 4.[6] Antigua challenged US laws which prohibited the remote supply of gambling and betting services, including those offered on the internet. While this violated commitments that the US had undertaken under the GATS, the US claimed that these domestic laws were justified because they were necessary to protect public morals and to maintain public order, as specified in GATS Article XIV a). The panel stated that the notions of public morals and public order can vary depending on a range of factors, including prevailing social, cultural, ethical and religious values. The panel resorted to an ordinary dictionary to ascertain the meaning of these terms, concluding that the two concepts (morality and order) overlapped to a degree and, taken together, were generally intended to capture genuine and threats to the fundamental interests of society. The US claimed that internet gambling could lead to organized crime, money laundering and fraud. It also represented a serious risk to children as well as to human health because of the risk of addiction, which can destabilize families and is also very difficult to control, unlike gambling in actual casinos. These concerns were accepted as legitimate by the panel and this was upheld by the Appellate Body, which also ruled that the US ban was necessary to address these harms. The US ended up losing this case anyway because it applied the ban on online gambling unevenly, violating the chapeau. While the US prohibited online card games from Antigua, it inexplicably allowed online betting on domestic horseracing, suggesting a hidden protectionist aim.

2.3 General exceptions in RTAs

In an era of increasing bilateralism and regionalism in international trade, it is important to recognize that some FTAs contain general exceptions which go beyond those contained in the GATT/

---

[6] United States – Measures Affecting the Cross-Border Supply of Gambling and Betting Services, Appellate Body Report, WT/DS285/AB/R (20 April 2005).

GATS. For example, some EU FTAs, which use the GATT general exceptions as a baseline, also contain exceptions for public security.[7] It is, of course, difficult to make comparisons across various treaties regarding the scope of their general exceptions, given that the positive commitments from which they derogate may themselves be different. Article 29.1 of the CPTPP states as follows:

1. For the purposes of Chapter 2 (National Treatment and Market Access for Goods), Chapter 3 (Rules of Origin and Origin Procedures), Chapter 4 (Textile and Apparel Goods), Chapter 5 (Customs Administration and Trade Facilitation), Chapter 7 (Sanitary and Phytosanitary Measures), Chapter 8 (Technical Barriers to Trade) and Chapter 17 (State-Owned Enterprises and Designated Monopolies), Article XX of GATT 1994 and its interpretative notes are incorporated into and made part of this Agreement, mutatis mutandis.
2. The Parties understand that the measures referred to in Article XX(b) of GATT 1994 include environmental measures necessary to protect human, animal or plant life or health, and that Article XX(g) of GATT 1994 applies to measures relating to the conservation of living and non-living exhaustible natural resources.
3. For the purposes of Chapter 10 (Cross-Border Trade in Services), Chapter 12 (Temporary Entry for Business Persons), Chapter 13 (Telecommunications), Chapter 14 (Electronic Commerce) and Chapter 17 (State-Owned Enterprises and Designated Monopolies), paragraphs (a), (b) and (c) of Article XIV of GATS are incorporated into and made part of this Agreement, mutatis mutandis.
4. The Parties understand that the measures referred to in Article XIV(b) of GATS include environmental measures necessary to protect human, animal or plant life or health.

One of the areas of public policy in which some WTO members have gone beyond the general exceptions of the GATT/GATS is in relation to the protection of the environment, now often described in terms of climate change. Again, the CPTPP is illustrative in this regard:

1. The Parties recognise the importance of mutually supportive trade and environmental policies and practices to improve environmental protection in the furtherance of sustainable development.
2. The Parties recognise the sovereign right of each Party to establish its own levels of domestic environmental protection and its own environmental priorities, and to establish, adopt or modify its environmental laws and policies accordingly.
3. Each Party shall strive to ensure that its environmental laws and policies provide for, and encourage, high levels of environmental protection and to continue to improve its respective levels of environmental protection.
4. No Party shall fail to effectively enforce its environmental laws through a sustained or recurring course of action or inaction in a manner affecting trade or investment between the Parties, after the date of entry into force of this Agreement for that Party.
5. The Parties recognise that each Party retains the right to exercise discretion and to make

---

[7] E.g. CETA Art. 28.3(2)a.

decisions regarding: (a) investigatory, prosecutorial, regulatory and compliance matters; and (b) the allocation of environmental enforcement resources with respect to other environmental laws determined to have higher priorities. Accordingly, the Parties understand that with respect to the enforcement of environmental laws a Party is in compliance with paragraph 4 if a course of action or inaction reflects a reasonable exercise of that discretion, or results from a bona fide decision regarding the allocation of those resources in accordance with priorities for enforcement of its environmental laws.

6. Without prejudice to paragraph 2, the Parties recognise that it is inappropriate to encourage trade or investment by weakening or reducing the protection afforded in their respective environmental laws. Accordingly, a Party shall not waive or otherwise derogate from, or offer to waive or otherwise derogate from, its environmental laws in a manner that weakens or reduces the protection afforded in those laws in order to encourage trade or investment between the Parties.

7. Nothing in this Chapter shall be construed to empower a Party's authorities to undertake environmental law enforcement activities in the territory of another Party.[8]

Some of the issues relating to noneconomic matters in RTAs will be revisited in Chapter 7 dealing with exceptions in investment treaties.

3. ESSENTIAL SECURITY

Essential security or national security has emerged as one of the most contentious noneconomic policy issues in international economic law. In the WTO context it appears in both the GATT and the GATS, much as it does in international investment agreements.

3.1 GATT/GATS

A state's safety from attack may be asserted as a justification for breaching any of the WTO's rules, much as it can under international investment law, as will be explored later. The ability of a state to ensure national – or essential, as it is phrased in the GATT and GATS – security is a vital safety valve in the global trading system. It recognizes that a state's capacity to protect itself from an external threat is fundamental to statehood. Of all the elements that are more important than free trade, the safety of a state's citizens is surely the greatest.

These issues are captured in the GATT's provisions on Essential Security, which may be found in Article XXI (which is virtually identical to GATS XIV *bis*):

Nothing in this Agreement shall be construed

(a) to require any contracting party to furnish any information the disclosure of which it considers contrary to its essential security interests; or

---

[8] Art. 20.3.

(b) to prevent any contracting party from taking any action which it considers necessary for the protection of its essential security interests

(i) relating to fissionable materials or the materials from which they are derived;

(ii) relating to the traffic in arms, ammunition and implements of war and to such traffic in other goods and materials as is carried on directly or indirectly for the purpose of supplying a military establishment;

(iii) taken in time of war or other emergency in international relations; or

(c) to prevent any contracting party from taking any action in pursuance of its obligations under the United Nations Charter for the maintenance of international peace and security.

The severity of the essential security exemption is demonstrated by the fact that it is phrased in 'self-judging' language. In the past it was thought that WTO members were therefore able simply to assert that their essential security is under threat and, at least in theory, this could not be challenged through the WTO dispute settlement procedures. However, in a recent panel decision brought by Ukraine against Russia relating to the latter's use of the essential security exception as a restriction on the transit of goods, the panel rejected arguments brought by Russia that Article XXI is truly self-judging and therefore nonjusticiable. The panel upheld Russia's invocation of the provision on the basis that there was an emergency in international relations.[9]

Some have argued that the essential security defence in international economic law is subject to the requirement of good faith, meaning that an international court, such as a WTO panel or the Appellate Body, should be able to investigate whether it has been used illegitimately.[10] Thankfully this provision has been rarely used, although it had something of a renaissance in recent times when it was used by US President Donald Trump to justify steel tariffs against several of its allies, including the EU and Canada. A number of WTO members responded with retaliatory tariffs and others initiated WTO disputes asserting that the steel tariffs had nothing to do with national security and were actually safeguards – a claim which is fairly obviously untrue, given how they were framed by the US government. At the time of writing these matters have not been resolved, although it is worth noting that a domestic US court (the Court of International Trade) ruled that the President's reliance on essential security to justify the imposition of steel tariffs was constitutionally valid under US law.[11] The recent ruling in *Russia – Transit* in favour of Russia's invocation of essential security could embolden countries to use Article XXI.

Where there is clear evidence that WTO-violating measures are not linked to national security, rather than a lack of evidence that they are (which should be assumed if the member so declares), there may be an entitlement to compensation in the form of reduced tariffs elsewhere, as well as the authorization of retaliatory measures. The language of Article XXI contemplates the existence of an extreme circumstance and in that sense it mirrors the customary international law principle of neces-

---

[9] Russia – Measures Concerning Traffic in Transit, Report of the Panel, WT/DS512/R (5 April 2019).

[10] S Schill and R Briese, '"If the State Considers": Self-Judging Clauses in International Dispute Settlement' 13 Max Planck Yearbook of United Nations Law 61 (2009).

[11] American Institute for International Steel v. United States, Court No. 18-00152 (25 March 2019).

sity and *force majeure*,[12] suggesting that it is arguably redundant as a feature of the GATT. Given its importance in international trade law, it is no surprise that essential security provisions appear in RTAs. They are typically worded in the same manner as in the GATT, such as in Article 23.2 of the US–Korea FTA. These provisions have not been formally examined under regional dispute resolution tribunals. Staying on the topic of the need to address noneconomic concerns in international trade law, this chapter will now consider the WTO's treatment of health and safety regulations as trade barriers.

4. HEALTH AND SAFETY REGULATIONS

Another feature of the modern era is that nontariff barriers in the form of health and safety regulations have become far more troublesome than simple tariffs on goods, which were the dominant form of protectionism throughout most of the twentieth century. The notion that certain products may be deemed unsafe for certain markets means that some products will be prohibited entirely from import, whereas many others will only be permitted to cross international borders having undergone costly and time consuming inspection and testing, sometimes referred to as conformity assessment. Such regulatory barriers have grown enormously in the past few decades in step with the rising awareness among governments and the public that many products, especially food, can be hazardous to consumers. While some might view this as the intrusion of the nanny state into our lives, others would see it as the fulfilment of an important duty by the government, safeguarding the interests of its citizens given the risk that foreign products might simply not be good enough to enter the domestic market.

The purpose of WTO law in this regard is to minimize such barriers where they are unnecessary (where risk is minimal) or where different regulations in two member states cover the same risk. At the same time, it is important to recognize that weak regulation, meaning regulation which fails to assess products for their potential to harm people or animals/plants, may itself be viewed as a kind of *de facto* subsidy. Goods produced in countries where health and safety regulations are low avoid many of the costs associated with ensuring that there is no danger to consumers, such as manufacturing/ growing better products or testing more rigorously. Likewise, excessive health and safety regulations are often depicted as a disguised form of protectionism.

The GATT drafters already had many of these issues in mind when they established the Article XX general exceptions. But the GATT general exceptions are fairly thin, at least in terms of their language. When the WTO was created some 45 years later, it was felt that the regulatory complexity of modern nontariff barriers required more comprehensive treatment. Two special agreements were created: the Agreement on Sanitary and Phytosanitary Measures (SPS Agreement) and the Agreement on Technical Barriers to Trade (TBT Agreement). Both will be discussed in turn.

4.1 Sanitary and Phytosanitary Measures Agreement

The importance and complexity of safety standards for food led WTO members to negotiate a special agreement for food safety and animal and plant health standards. This agreement, the SPS Agree-

---

[12] Articles on State Responsibility, Arts 25 and 23.

ment, allows WTO members to set their own regulatory standards in relation to food, animal and plant health as long as they are not excessively burdensome from the perspective of international trade.

Article 1 of the SPS outlines its scope of application: all sanitary and phytosanitary measures which may, directly or indirectly, affect international trade, which effectively means food and food-related products such as beverages, but also toothpaste and soap. The risks intended to be addressed by such measures are those relating to diseases in organic material which may be harmful to human, animal or plant life or health. The central obligation of the agreement is found in Article 2.2, which states: 'Members shall ensure that any sanitary or phytosanitary measure is applied only to the extent necessary to protect human, animal or plant life or health, is based on scientific principles and is not maintained without sufficient scientific evidence.'

In order for such rules to be viewed as legitimate by the WTO from the standpoint of their effect on international trade, they must be justified either through science or through conformity with a recognized international standard setting body such as the Codex Alimentarius Commission or the International Office of Epizootics. Deference to these bodies creates presumptive validity of an SPS measure and in so doing accords significant weight to the decisions of these bodies. It is important to acknowledge that these organizations have their own internal decision making procedures which are susceptible to political influence.[13] This is precisely why the SPS encourages all WTO members to participate in the setting of international standards through these kinds of organizations. WTO members are encouraged to base their SPS regulations on international standards where possible in order to harmonize regulations in order to prevent needless duplication, with such standards presumptively legitimate from the perspective of health protection.[14]

One of the foundational principles of the SPS is that WTO members are permitted to enact laws that result in higher standards than those indicated by international bodies if there is scientific justification. Members may depart from scientific evidence when setting their regulations if scientific evidence is insufficient on the basis of 'available pertinent information'.[15] This means that there must be adequate risk assessment of the risks to human, animal or plant life or health. Adequate risk assessment will likely include having scientists examine the relevant products for various diseases and organisms, testing the likelihood of exposure to citizens under different conditions and what the actual dangers are in terms of health.

Article 2.3 of the SPS goes on to state that members shall ensure that their sanitary and phytosanitary measures do not arbitrarily or unjustifiably discriminate between members where 'identical or similar conditions prevail', and, crucially, that 'sanitary and phytosanitary measures shall not be applied in a manner which would constitute a disguised restriction on international trade'. Furthermore, the SPS Agreement obliges WTO members to recognize each other's standards as equivalent, even where the regulations differ, if the exporting member can objectively demonstrate to the importing member that its measures achieve the importing member's appropriate level of protection.[16]

---

[13] E Vos and S Röttger-Wirtz, 'EU Food Law and the WTO: Trade, Science and Politics' in D Prévost, I Alexovicova, JH Pohl eds *Restoring Trust in Trade* (Hart, 2018).

[14] Art. 3.1 and 3.2.

[15] Art. 5.7.

[16] Art. 4.1.

The SPS strongly emphasizes the process behind risk assessment, essentially deferring to each member state to set its own level of risk provided that it was ascertained on the basis of reasonable evidence. This is seen in Article 5: '1. Members shall ensure that their sanitary or phytosanitary measures are based on an assessment, as appropriate to the circumstances, of the risks to human, animal or plant life or health, taking into account risk assessment techniques developed by the relevant international organizations.'

To this, the SPS adds: 'Members should, when determining the appropriate level of sanitary or phytosanitary protection, take into account the objective of minimizing negative trade effects.'[17] A clear process of risk assessment is key to lawfulness under the SPS. Minority scientific opinions and limited evidence are sufficient, but such measures must not be unnecessarily trade restrictive. Crucially, the same risks must be treated consistently. This captures the WTO's mission to subdue protectionism – health and safety measures must not be used as a cloak to grant favourable treatment to domestic goods or to goods from certain countries because this would operate as an economically harmful market distortion.

It could be said that there are two chief approaches to SPS measures by WTO members. One, which is characteristic of the US, is to focus on the text of the agreement and to enact measures which aim to address only those risks which are genuinely scientifically demonstrable. The other approach is that of the EU, which espouses the 'precautionary principle', in which even small risks, where there is limited scientific evidence of danger, should be eliminated where possible. There is a clear conflict between the 'science-based' approach and the 'hazard-based' one. Science, which tends to be thought of as the paragon of objectivity, is wielded in highly idiosyncratic ways – in fact, the WTO may have precisely intended its members to enjoy this degree of discretion.[18] Despite the fact that it lost the dispute, there are a number of EU member states which still prohibit hormone-treated beef, in clear violation of WTO law. While the manner of addressing food product safety under the SPS Agreement is unquestionably a key aspect of nontariff barriers to international trade, it is also important to recognize that the interests of domestic producers, such as farmers, play an equal if not greater role in dictating these types of barriers.

In keeping with the WTO's overarching aim of transparency as a tool of minimizing trade barriers, the SPS further mandates that members must share information and respond to requests regarding food sanitation regulations, including an explanation for their imposition in various circumstances. As with all of the WTO agreements, breaches of the SPS are actionable through the WTO's dispute settlement system. There have been several such cases.

Canada brought a claim against Australia on the basis of an alleged violation of the SPS in relation to Australia's regulatory approach to imports of salmon.[19] Australia imposed a quarantine on salmon imports from Canada because of dangers the fish could present to the health of its consumers. Canada argued that this violated the SPS because the risk assessment which formed the basis of the quarantine law was arbitrary – it applied only to salmon that was consumer ready (meaning

---

[17] Art. 5.4.

[18] M Du, 'Re-Conceptualizing the Role of Science in International Trade Disputes' 52:5 Journal of World Trade, Issue 697 (2018).

[19] Australia – Measures Affecting Importation of Salmon, Appellate Body Report, WT/DS18/AB/R (6 November 1998).

fresh from the ocean), without any justification for why that particular type of salmon was more dangerous and in what way. The Appellate Body explained that distinctions in the level of protection required (consumer ready and non-consumer ready) may be viewed as arbitrary where the risk is equally high between the two different situations. Essentially, there was no scientific basis for the imposition of different quarantine standards for two different types of the same fish. The quarantine requirement was more trade restrictive than was required to safeguard the health of Australian consumers.

Perhaps most famously of all, the EC imposed a ban on the sale of beef from animals that had been treated with growth hormones.[20] While the ban had almost no effect on European beef producers, it inflicted serious damage on US beef producers, who either could not sell their product in Europe or had to take expensive measures to ensure that it was hormone free. The US argued that the ban was disguised protectionism in favour of European beef suppliers, whereas the EC said that the ban was a legitimate public health measure designed to protect its citizens from the possible health risks linked to hormones in beef. The Appellate Body ruled in favour of the US, holding that the EC's regulatory measures did not conform to international standards – there was no international guideline specifying the dangers of hormones in beef. Further, the European standards were not based on a clear, scientifically based risk assessment; they reflected cultural tastes more than anything else. In reaching this conclusion, the Appellate Body did clarify that there were no minimum procedural requirements for domestic risk assessment in order to satisfy a country's noncompliance with an international standard. In other words, it is not necessary for a member who enacts an SPS-oriented measure to conduct an investigation, engage in formal fact finding or publish a report in which the law is justified scientifically. In this sense, the WTO system accords its members significant freedom to enact the food health laws that they want for the reasons that they want, as long as there is some integrity in the process. The Appellate Body went even further in allowing discretion to members in relation to their SPS rules when it said that the presence of a 'scientific controversy' or disagreement about a particular health danger does not prevent a country from relying upon minority scientific opinion, as opposed to the mainstream. Such minority scientific opinion must come from 'qualified and respected sources'.

The US, as well as Canada and Argentina, challenged the EC's regulatory regime for the approval of genetically modified organisms (GMOs) under the SPS.[21] The EC's approach to these products had resulted in unnecessary delays for genetically modified foods entering the European market. The panel ruled that some of the EC's bans on certain GMO crops did not satisfy the requirements of the SPS. This was because while members are permitted to adopt temporary measures while they are engaging in scientific research to get a more complete picture, some of the studies carried out by the EC up to that point had in fact showed that the GMO foods were safe. The panel saw these as sufficient risk assessments in order to demonstrate that the bans were not

---

[20] European Communities – Measures Concerning Meat and Meat Products (Hormones), Report of the Panel, WT/DS48/R (13 February 1998).

[21] European Communities – Measures Affecting the Approval and Marketing of Biotech Products, Report of the Panel, WT/DS291/R (29 September 2006).

legitimate and therefore had to be removed. The EC complied with this ruling, although to this day some EU member states still maintain some bans on genetically modified maize, in defiance of the WTO. The GMO case demonstrates the emphasis in the SPS on process rather than on results as a way of resolving an incredibly sensitive debate between two superpowers. Panels constituted to resolve disputes relating to the SPS Agreement do not seek to present themselves as the final arbiter of scientific truth in tightly contested disputes, but rather as a judicial body that scrutinizes the way in which any governmental decisions that have effects on trade are reached.

4.2 SPS measures and regional trade agreements

Due to their growing importance as trade barriers and the need to ensure that they are appropriately managed, SPS measures may also be found in some RTAs, typically by reiterating SPS commitments with additional supervisory machinery. For example, Article 5.2 of CETA states:

> The objectives of this Chapter are to:
> (a) protect human, animal and plant life or health while facilitating trade;
> (b) ensure that the Parties' sanitary and phytosanitary ('SPS') measures do not create unjustified barriers to trade; and
> (c) further the implementation of the SPS Agreement

The Article goes on to affirm the parties' rights and obligations under the SPS Agreement. From there, Article 5.6 of CETA speaks of regulatory 'equivalence' in relation to SPS matters.

> 1. The importing Party shall accept the SPS measure of the exporting Party as equivalent to its own if the exporting Party objectively demonstrates to the importing Party that its measure achieves the importing Party's appropriate level of SPS protection.
> 2. Annex 5-D sets out principles and guidelines to determine, recognise, and maintain equivalence.
> 3. Annex 5-E sets out:
>   (a) the area for which the importing Party recognises that an SPS measure of the exporting Party is equivalent to its own; and
>   (b) the area for which the importing Party recognises that the fulfilment of the specified special condition, combined with the exporting Party's SPS measure, achieves the importing Party's appropriate level of SPS protection.
> 4. For the purposes of this Chapter, Article 1.7 (Reference to laws) applies subject to this Article, Annex 5-D and the General Notes under Annex 5-E.

In order to achieve 'equivalence' as noted above, it is often necessary for state parties to engage in collaborative decision making and best practice sharing in relation to specific spheres of regulatory governance. Health and safety in food is a highly specialized field that requires input of experts in setting and calibrating standards across countries. In light of this need, the US–Korea FTA establishes a Committee on Sanitary and Phytosanitary Matters:

1. The Parties hereby agree to establish a Committee on Sanitary and Phytosanitary Matters comprising representatives of each Party who have responsibility for sanitary and phytosanitary matters.
2. The objectives of the Committee shall be to enhance each Party's implementation of the SPS Agreement, protect human, animal, or plant life or health, enhance cooperation and consultation on sanitary and phytosanitary matters, and facilitate trade between the Parties.[22]

While setting up such committees unquestionably represents progress in terms of harmonizing SPS type laws (indeed, this is why an equivalence committee exists within the WTO itself), this kind of arrangement may mask disagreement in relation to the management of risk for food products. In other words, it is an agreement to agree rather than an actual agreement. Since the US–Korea FTA is new, there is no indication that this committee has achieved further integration in these matters.

4.3 TBT Agreement

Regulations relating to product safety, and other technical requirements such as those dealing with environmental protection and consumer welfare laws, can be just as important for safeguarding the citizens of WTO members. Problems arise when there are too many different standards across the world. This is because it is difficult for the producers and exporters of goods not only to comply with these rules, but sometimes even to know what they are in the first place. As with health-related rules, technical regulations of all sorts can become instruments of protectionism – they can be used as obstacles to international trade by imposing entirely unnecessary or overly complicated procedures on exporters. The purpose of the WTO is to ensure that technical regulations are genuine, meaning that they serve a valid purpose in addressing risks to the public.

The TBT Agreement attempts to ensure that regulations, standards as well as testing and certification procedures do not create illegitimate barriers to international trade under the guise of safety or consumer protection. It obliges WTO members not to enact technical regulations that are more trade restrictive than necessary in order to fulfil whatever the legitimate objective is. When assessing this, the member country must consider the risks that nonfulfilment of the goal would impose. This means that the efforts undertaken by each country in achieving a particular product safety or consumer interest objective must be done in a manner that does not restrict international trade. So any such laws must be clearly connected to the risk that is being controlled. The more serious the risk, the greater the permissible imposition on international trade.

The TBT Agreement applies to all technical regulations, which are mandatory and standards, which are optional, that are not covered by SPS. It deals with matters such as product characteristics, labels, packaging, testing and certification.[23] There are non-discrimination requirements for all relevant regulations, designed to prevent unnecessary barriers to trade. Justifications for TBTs

---

[22] Art. 8.3.

[23] Art. 1.

include scientific evidence, as with the SPS, but also consumer preference. WTO members should endeavour to ensure that nongovernmental organizations to apply industry standards in an even-handed, nontrade restrictive way. This can be problematic because the WTO's obligations apply to its members, not to private firms or industry groups. It is thought that some kind of WTO-led procedural guidelines might assist in the standardization of these practices by private standard-setters.[24] As with all WTO agreements, the TBT also contains transparency and notification obligations – these can be especially important in this sphere due to the complexity and volume of relevant measures.

In recent years the TBT has become more widely used by WTO members, in part because of the explosion of safety rules for all sorts of products, many of which could be exploited as potential barriers to trade in an era of declining tariffs. In an early case brought under the TBT, Peru challenged a regulation adopted by the EC that provided that only food products that were prepared from a certain subspecies of sardines found around the coasts of the eastern North Atlantic Ocean as well as the Mediterranean and Black Seas could be marketed and preserved as 'sardines'.[25] This was a problem for Peru as it is on the other side of the world on the Pacific Ocean, and therefore could never produce 'sardines' from its waters. Peru argued that the European regulation violated the TBT because it did not adhere to international standards set by international agencies. The WTO panel and later the Appellate Body agreed with Peru, ruling that the international standard established that the name sardines applied to various species, which included those kinds found in the waters around Peru, and that this international standard was effective in accomplishing all three of the EC's objectives in their tighter regulation: market transparency, consumer protection and fair competition. The EC's attempt to restrict the definition of sardines was nothing more than an attempt to promote the sale of European fish.

Another important instigation of the TBT came about in relation to the French prohibition on the importation or sale of asbestos products. In 2000 this law was challenged through the WTO dispute settlement system by Canada, which has a major asbestos production industry.[26] Asbestos is a material composed of thin fibrous crystals that was widely used throughout the nineteenth and twentieth centuries because of its resistance to heat and its affordability. Many industrial buildings from that period used asbestos insulation inside external walls but the prolonged inhalation of asbestos fibres can cause lung damage and even cancer. In the dispute brought by Canada against the EC, the challenged law was both the ban on Canadian asbestos as well as exceptions to it for certain types of cellulose and glass fibres. Both the panel and the Appellate Body agreed that the French measure was a discriminatory trade barrier because it treated Canadian asbestos differently from French asbestos, but the WTO courts allowed the European law on the basis that it was justified under GATT Article XX's exceptions for human health. The panel and Appellate Body explained what will constitute a technical regulation such that it is captured by

---

[24] E van der Zee, 'Disciplining Private Standards Under the SPS and TBT Agreement: A Plea for Market-State Procedural Guidelines' 52:3 Journal of World Trade 393 (2018).

[25] European Communities – Trade Description of Sardines, Appellate Body Report WT/DS231/AB/R (23 October 2002).

[26] European Communities – Measures Affecting Asbestos and Asbestos-Containing Products, Appellate Body Report, WT/DS135/AB/R (5 April 2001).

the TBT, noting the definition of technical regulations: mandatory requirements relating to a product's characteristics, including physical descriptions as well as functionality. This definition, which the Appellate Body thought fit the EC's asbestos ban, is regularly cited in WTO disputes relating to technical regulations. It means that the TBT Agreement is often engaged whenever the GATT's general exceptions relating to health are used as a justification for an otherwise trade restrictive regime.

The TBT was contested again in Indonesia's 2010 complaint against the US due to its prohibition on clove flavoured cigarettes.[27] The US domestic law banned the production or sale of cigarettes containing the additive clove (as well as other flavourings such as cherry, vanilla and coconut), but expressly allowed the production and sale of cigarettes containing other additives, such as the popular flavouring menthol, almost all of which were produced in the US. The reason for the restriction on these varieties of cigarettes was to ensure that young people, who were seen as being more likely to be attracted by the same types of flavouring found in candy, would not become hooked on cigarettes and become lifetime smokers. Indonesia, which is the world's leading producer of clove cigarettes, argued that this law violated national treatment under the GATT as well as the TBT and the SPS Agreements. The WTO panel found that the ban was a technical regulation, as per the definition established in the asbestos case. It went on to rule that the US ban was also discriminatory, violating the TBT's national treatment guarantee of Article 2.1. This was based on the panel's finding that clove cigarettes are 'like' menthol cigarettes because they appeal to young smokers. The Appellate Body agreed with most of these conclusions, adding that the US law had a severe detrimental impact on the competitive opportunities of Indonesia's clove cigarettes – a critical component of the non-discrimination guarantee in the TBT Agreement.

Australia's plain packaging laws for cigarettes led to a series of disputes brought under the TBT Agreement. Plain packaging laws require that all cigarettes packages must not display any branding, such as colours or logos. Manufacturers may only print the brand name in ordinary, non-stylized letters, in addition to any mandatory health warnings required by local laws. Australia was the first country in the world to implement these laws, with its Tobacco Plain Packaging Act of 2011. The logic behind the scheme was that smokers tend to be highly influenced by the design and presentation of cigarette packaging, and as such it was anticipated that smoking would decline because of the unappealing, nondescript wrapping. Unsurprisingly, the tobacco companies have strongly resisted plain packaging. In fact, the tobacco company Philip Morris brought a claim directly against Australia under the Australia–Hong Kong Bilateral Investment Treaty through the investor–state dispute settlement process outlined in Chapter 8. The WTO panel issued its report in relation to this dispute in the summer of 2018.[28] It held that the complainants, including Indonesia, Cuba and Honduras, had not proven that Australia's tobacco plain packaging measures were inconsistent with Article 2.2 of the TBT Agreement on the basis that they are more trade restrictive than would be necessary to achieve a legitimate objective. In a narrow reading of the

---

[27] United States – Measures Affecting the Production and Sale of Clove Cigarettes, Appellate Body Report, WT/DS406/AB/R (24 April 2012).

[28] Australia – Certain Measures concerning Trademarks, Geographical Indications and other Plain Packaging Requirements applicable to Tobacco Products and Packaging, Panel Report WT/DS441/R (28 June 2018).

text of the TBT, the panel agreed with Australia that a demonstration that the challenged measures may result in some alteration of the overall competitive environment for suppliers on the market did not in itself demonstrate their 'trade restrictiveness' within the meaning of Article 2.2. The ruling in this case has been criticized for departing from the arguments presented by either party, highlighting some of the alleged problems with WTO dispute settlement, especially in relation to the highly sensitive issue of public health.[29]

4.4 TBT measures in regional trade agreements

Many modern RTAs include provisions for technical barriers to trade which are similar or identical to those of the TBT.[30] For example, Article 4.2 of CETA incorporates many provisions of the TBT. CETA goes on to state as follows:

1. The Parties undertake to cooperate to the extent possible, to ensure that their technical regulations are compatible with one another. To this end, if a Party expresses an interest in developing a technical regulation equivalent or similar in scope to one that exists in or is being prepared by the other Party, that other Party shall, on request, provide to the Party, to the extent practicable, the relevant information, studies and data upon which it has relied in the preparation of its technical regulation, whether adopted or being developed. The Parties recognise that it may be necessary to clarify and agree on the scope of a specific request, and that confidential information may be withheld.

2. A Party that has prepared a technical regulation that it considers to be equivalent to a technical regulation of the other Party having compatible objective and product scope may request that the other Party recognise the technical regulation as equivalent. The Party shall make the request in writing and set out detailed reasons why the technical regulation should be considered equivalent, including reasons with respect to product scope. The Party that does not agree that the technical regulation is equivalent shall provide to the other Party, upon request, the reasons for its decision.[31]

It is important to recognize that this provision does not contain a binding obligation, or, to the extent that it does, the obligation is merely for the parties to try their best to ensure that regulations are compatible – this does not mean that they will in fact be compatible. Such provisions may help facilitate trade in manufactured goods, but they by no means eliminate technical barriers to trade. Similar to the creation of a committee for SPS matters noted above in the US–Korea FTA, CETA also establishes that parties will cooperate in terms of conformity assessment procedures: 'The Parties shall observe the Protocol on the mutual acceptance of the results of conformity assess-

---

[29] T Voon, 'Third Strike: The WTO Panel Reports Upholding Australia's Tobacco Plain Packaging Scheme' 20:1 Journal of World Investment and Trade (2019).

[30] D McDaniels, AC Molina, E Wijkstrom, 'A Closer Look at the WTO's Third Pillar: How WTO Committees Influence Regional Trade Agreements' 21:4 Journal of International Economic Law 815 (2018).

[31] Art. 4.4.

ment, and the Protocol on the mutual recognition of the compliance and enforcement programme regarding good manufacturing practices for pharmaceutical products.[32]

Also known as compliance testing, conformity assessment consists of product testing or other activities that determine whether it complies with the requirements of a specification, technical standard, contract or regulation. Put more simply, it is the process component involved in verifying the fulfilment of a substantive legal requirement on a traded good. Such issues can create a significant burden for products as they cross international borders, even where the underlying standard is similar or identical. This chapter will proceed by considering another example of the WTO's agenda of regulatory harmonization, in this case the important and perhaps even more controversial area of intellectual property.

5. INTELLECTUAL PROPERTY

The protection of intellectual property is seen by many as essential to the proper functioning of the global economy, which increasingly comprises trade in high technology sectors such as pharmaceuticals. The rise of big data, artificial intelligence and other features of the knowledge economy has led to significant investment in research and development by multinational firms. Modern technology has facilitated the instantaneous copying of lucrative art forms such as music and movies, much as patents can be reverse engineered, undermining years of effort on the part of those which create these goods. The global market for illegally copied goods and services moving through international trade is thought to be worth more than US$250 billion per year. During the lead up to the creation of the WTO, the US and other major developed countries grew increasingly concerned about the loss of valuable exports in newly industrializing markets due to counterfeiting, which was seen as the consequence of weak, nonexistent or poorly enforced intellectual property laws. Developed countries feared that they were losing their competitive advantage in the production of high value added goods to poorer countries that had acquired the capacity to copy these goods at much lower cost.

There is an economic as well as a moral rationale for protecting intellectual property. Few would argue that it is only right that assiduous and inventive people should be financially rewarded for their skill and effort, perhaps even more so when these activities bring pleasure or improve the lives of others. From an economic perspective, where intellectual property rights are not protected there is a reduction in the incentive to innovate, which in the long term could undermine global welfare because we seek to enjoy new products that will go unproduced.

Critics of strong intellectual property laws argue that it is simply not believable that weak intellectual property protection reduces these incentives, at least in the context of international trade, because poor countries are not significant markets for intellectual property as people in these countries have insufficient disposable income. Furthermore, these countries lack the technological capacity to reproduce many of the most advanced and valuable forms of intellectual property, such as those protected by patents. In this view, strong intellectual property laws have only made

---

[32] Art. 4.5.

it more difficult for people in developing countries to access products they may need, such as vital pharmaceuticals. This is exacerbated by the fact that many kinds of indigenous creations are not covered by Western conceptions of intellectual property and are therefore unprotected. Such claims have led some commentators to suggest that the WTO should never have concerned itself with intellectual property at all.[33]

5.1 Agreement on Trade-Related Aspects of Intellectual Property Rights

The objective of TRIPS is to reduce distortions in international trade while protecting intellectual property rights. In other words, it aims to ensure that intellectual property rights do not become impediments to trade. This is premised on the notion that failure to protect intellectual property is a *de facto* restriction on market access. By this it is meant that few companies would be prepared to trade with countries (or to invest in countries) where intellectual property protections are weak, out of fear that the products which they send there will be copied and undersold. Studies have shown that TRIPS has been successful in pressuring WTO members to strengthen the domestic protection of intellectual property,[34] which has presumably acted as an incentive for firms possessing intellectual property-oriented assets to invest in these countries. Broadly speaking, TRIPS seeks to reward creators of intellectual property but also to serve public interest in terms of disseminating knowledge which is of value to people around the world. In this regard it is important to draw attention to criticisms that TRIPS impairs access to essential goods, most notably medicine. This belies the WTO's own claims that it serves the interests of developing countries, which comprise a significant portion of its membership.

In terms of IP, TRIPS addresses copyright, patents, geographical indicators, undisclosed information, industrial designs and integrated circuits. As with all WTO agreements, the rights and obligations are between member nations, not private individuals or firms. TRIPS does not impose global rules so much as it achieves harmonization along the lines of the SPS and the TBT. It aims to ensure that national laws protecting intellectual property are similar, standardizing the level of protection around the world. TRIPS achieves this harmonization by establishing international minimum standards for intellectual property protection, establishing minimum criteria for enforcement of intellectual property rights, subjecting international IP rights to WTO dispute settlement and setting out common procedural requirements.

5.2 TRIPS obligations

Article 3 contains a national treatment obligation. Each WTO member must accord nationals of other member states treatment that is no less favourable than it accords its own nationals

---

[33] R Wade, 'What Strategies Are Viable for Developing Countries Today? The World Trade Organization and the Shrinking of "Development Space"' 10:4 Review of International Political Economy 621 (2003).

[34] R Cardwell and P Ghazalian, 'The Effect of the TRIPS Agreement on the Protection of Intellectual Property Rights' 26:1 International Trade Journal 19 (2012).

with regard to intellectual property protection. It is important to recognize here that national treatment is extended to the producers of the intellectual property, not to the goods in which they vest or even to the intellectual property rights themselves, much as in the GATS. This is in contrast to national treatment under Article III of the GATT. TRIPS' MFN obligation can be found in Article 4. It states that any advantage granted by a member to the nationals of any other member must be granted unconditionally to all members. Again, the protection is afforded to the 'national', meaning the rights holder, not the object itself. National treatment and MFN apply to both *de jure* and *de facto* discrimination, as they do under the GATT, broadening the practical effect of protection of these provisions. It is also noteworthy that national treatment and MFN are subject to exceptions granted in other international intellectual property treaties, such as the Berne Convention, meaning that TRIPS was designed to fit within international law's existing intellectual property regime.

In the *Indonesia – Autos* dispute,[35] the panel examined the US complaint against Indonesia regarding its national car programme, which required participating vehicles to bear a unique, domestically owned Indonesian trademark. The US argued that the Indonesian law discriminated against nationals of other WTO members with respect to the 'acquisition' and 'maintenance' of trademark rights as specified in footnote 3 to Article 3. This provision defines the type of 'protection' embraced by TRIPS to include matters affecting the availability, acquisition, scope, maintenance and enforcement of intellectual property rights as well as those matters affecting the use of intellectual property rights, including trademarks. The panel denied the US claim regarding an impairment to the acquisition of trademarks, reasoning that the programme merely stipulated that only certain signs could be used as trademarks, and there was no evidence that the right to trademarks excluded from the programme could not be obtained in a non-discriminatory manner under Indonesian law. Regardless of the fact that the measure strongly incentivized firms to undertake expensive foreign registration activities (registering trademarks in Indonesia rather than in their home state), it was not genuinely discriminatory based on national origin. Moreover, as to the maintenance of trademarks, in *Indonesia – Autos* the US had argued that partners in the national car programme would be unlikely to use their global trademarks in Indonesia out of fear of confusing consumers. It would be more likely, it claimed, that the global trademark would be cancelled for non-use in Indonesia.

There is nothing obviously unfair in requiring a firm to register its intellectual property domestically, since this type of system subjects foreign firms to precisely the same rules as domestic firms. Full national treatment would allow every firm to seek intellectual property protection in its home country rather than require it to establish such rights in every host state in which it invests, effectively establishing local brands as well as bringing intellectual property-based claims in the courts of the host state rather than in its own. Article 27.1 of TRIPS states: 'patents shall be available and patent rights enjoyable without discrimination as to the place of invention, the field of technology and whether products are imported or locally produced'. This provision was assessed by a WTO panel in the *Canada – Pharmaceuticals* dispute,[36] which involved a complaint brought by the EC against

---

[35] Indonesia – Certain Measures Affecting the Automobile Industry, Panel Report, WT/DS54/R (23 July 1998).

[36] Report of the Panel, Canada – Patent Protection of Pharmaceutical Products, WT/DS114/R (adopted 7 April 2000).

Canada's patent review regulations which permitted the general manufacturers of pharmaceuticals to produce samples of the patented product for use during the review process. The EC asserted that this law was discriminatory because it was aimed at pharmaceutical products which, in practice, only foreign firms created. Ruling that the EC did not demonstrate that the regulatory review provision was discriminatory either *de jure* or *de facto*, the panel explained that the term 'discrimination' potentially encompasses a wide range of meanings and should be construed on a case by case basis within the precise context of the issue at hand. There is no indication from the panel's ruling as to how the phrase 'whether products are imported or locally produced' should be interpreted. It may require WTO members to apply exceptions in a non-discriminatory manner in order to ensure that governments do not engage in protectionism where intellectual property rights holders tend to be foreign firms. The provision could also be seen to impose a duty on member states not to deny patents on the basis of the field of technology or the location of the firm that develops it.

5.3 Scope of protection

The types of intellectual property covered by TRIPS will now be considered. Protected under section 1 of TRIPS, copyright protects the expression of an idea, not the idea itself. Under most national systems it is extended on a strict liability standard, meaning that liability for failure to uphold another's copyright is not excused by a best effort attempt. Under TRIPS, copyright protection must be granted for at least 50 years after the death of the author, a time period which is viewed as a compromise between the rights of the creator to enjoy the fruits of their work and the right of society to enjoy unhampered access to it. There are various exceptions to copyright, such as fair use, which is of relevance to educators, and free speech.

TRIPS treatment of copyright was examined in a complaint brought by the EC against the United States relating to the playing of music in public places.[37] The EC argued that this practice was a kind of theft – the retail premises were taking advantage of the artists' work for their commercial gain without compensation. Under US domestic copyright law, as in many countries, use of music in stores and restaurants was exempt from the requirement to obtain the rights holder's permission and to pay a royalty fee. This was known as the 'business exemption' category and in order to qualify for this exemption, the size of the premises in which the music was played was limited to a certain area by square footage. The US asserted that this limitation on copyright protection fell within the TRIPS special case exemption which captures the normal exploitation of the work and does not prejudice the legitimate interests of the rights holder. Ruling in favour of the EC, the panel stated that the size specified under the US exemption was quite large, meaning that a substantial majority of premises were covered by it, including those which would have the commercial ability to pay royalty fees to the rights holders of the music.

Trademarks are signs that distinguish goods based on their source and distinctiveness. Under section 2 of TRIPS, trademark protection must be extended for seven years and is renewable indefinitely. Unlike copyright, which applies automatically, trademarks require a commercial use and registration. The TRIPS trademark provisions were challenged in the Australia plain pack-

---

[37] United States – Section 110(5) of the US Copyright Act, Panel Report WT/DS160/R (27 July 2000).

aging case, discussed earlier.[38] The panel ruled that the complainants had not demonstrated that plain packaging laws for cigarette packages formed an obstacle to the registration of trademarks in violation of Article 15.4 of TRIPS. Under the TRIPS Agreement, trademarks that have been registered in any WTO member country grant the owner the exclusive right to prevent all third parties not having the owner's consent from using in the course of business identical or similar signs for goods or services which are identical or similar to those for which the trademark was registered. This guarantee is designed to prevent confusion among consumers in the marketplace, a situation which tends to be presumed when there is a sufficient degree of similarity. Evaluation and determination of similarity is up to the domestic legal system of each member state. Once registered, trademarks can be protected for an unlimited period. This captures the essential commercial purpose of the trademark, as distinct from copyrighted works of art, which have cultural value independent of their economic worth. Members may require that trademark registrations be renewed, but this may not be more than once every seven years. Members are free to determine any conditions attached to the licensing and assigning of trademarks under their national laws, although TRIPS maintains a prohibition on compulsory licensing of trademarks.

Covered by Article 22 of TRIPS, Geographical Indicators are place names that are used to signify that products that originate in particular locations have certain characteristics, such as champagne or Parma ham. The protection of geographical indications (GI) is based on the principle that place names are often used to identify a product. In so doing they convey a certain degree of quality or unique characteristics that might be desirable to consumers. GIs are somewhat analogous to trademarks, except that they always relate to a particular geographical point of origin. Whether or not a certain geographical designation qualifies as a GI and therefore is deserving of special protection under TRIPS (or other international trade agreements) can be very controversial. The scope of GI protections was one of the main stumbling blocks during the negotiations of the CETA between Canada and the EU. The EU is likely exceptionally protective of GIs as a way of shielding its agricultural sector from global competition. Article 22.1 of TRIPS provides that WTO members must ensure that they prevent the misuse of place names by competitors seeking to take unfair advantage of the goodwill associated with products from specific locations by misleading consumers. TRIPS clarifies that in order to qualify for geographical indication status under any member's national laws, it is not necessary to show that the product from that geographical area is in fact better than or different from a similar product that comes from somewhere else. All that must be shown is that a certain reputation or goodwill has been established in that location with respect to that product, suggesting that consumers are choosing to buy that particular variety of good because of its association with that place and its distinctive tradition or culture. To avoid the use of a GI that misleads the public in this respect, producers may use qualifying words such as 'imitation' or 'like', such as 'champagne-style' wine or 'Parma-style' ham. The makers of alcoholic beverages were especially concerned about GIs because this is a vital component of their distinctiveness and therefore their competitive advantage. Article 23 accordingly grants higher levels of protection for GIs for wines and spirits. Competitors may not use the geographical name to link with their product even where there is no danger of the public being misled and there is no provision to qualify the product's origin using 'imitation' or 'like', as mentioned above.

---

[38] Australia – Plain Packaging above n 28.

The most economically significant variety of intellectual property protection under TRIPS is patents. Patents cover new inventions that have industrial application. TRIPS allows requirements on patentability and ensures that protection must be granted for at least 20 years. Exceptions for patentability exist to protect public interest. Article 27 establishes that patent protection must be made available under the national laws of member states for both products and processes in almost all fields of technology. Minimum rights for patent holders are also outlined in the agreement. Patent protection must be made available for inventions for at least 20 years, meaning that after the elapse of this time, the underlying inventions may be reproduced lawfully without any payment or royalties or permission from the original patent holder. As with copyright protection, the 20 year minimum timeframe is intended to balance the incentives needed to encourage innovation and creativity, while ensuring that useful inventions may be widely disseminated to maximize their value to society, once the original inventor has been sufficiently rewarded for their work. TRIPS further requires that patents must confer exclusive rights on the patent holder to sell the relevant product or process and to assign or license it to third parties. Patents must be available under the national laws of member states for both products as well as processes and are extended in almost all fields of technology. Governments may refuse to issue a patent if its commercial exploitation is disallowed for reasons of public order or morality. It is also acceptable under TRIPS for governments to decline to register patents for plants and animals or for surgical or diagnostic methods. The reason behind these latter exceptions is that it is in the public interest for useful medical procedures to be made as widely available as possible because of the broader public benefit which they offer.

5.4 TRIPS and public policy

As noted above, the protection of intellectual property rights either under domestic legal systems or as indicated in TRIPS is constructed with a view to balancing the need to protect the inventor with granting the public sufficient access to the valuable invention. In this regard, Article 8 reiterates some of the principles that were seen in the general exceptions of the GATS and GATT.

1. Members may, in formulating or amending their laws and regulations, adopt measures necessary to protect public health and nutrition, and to promote the public interest in sectors of vital importance to their socio-economic and technological development, provided that such measures are consistent with the provisions of this Agreement.
2. Appropriate measures, provided that they are consistent with the provisions of this Agreement, may be needed to prevent the abuse of intellectual property rights by right holders or the resort to practices which unreasonably restrain trade or adversely affect the international transfer of technology.

The impact of Article 8 is limited by the fact that the measures to which it refers must be consistent with the provisions of TRIPS, meaning that they do not actually operate as exceptions to the agreement's rules. Instead they may be seen to illustrate some of the fundamental principles behind TRIPS – the safeguarding of the social value of intellectual property as well as its commercial potential.

Perhaps the most controversial public policy feature of the TRIPS is compulsory licensing, contained in Article 31. This provision outlines that members may use a patent without the authorization or consent of the rights holder in certain circumstances. Compulsory licensing is available where permission has been sought from the right holder and was not commercially feasible. The scope of the licence is limited to the purpose for which it was authorized and appropriate remuneration will be paid to the rights holder. This mechanism was designed to deal with a national health emergency where developing country members are unable to afford patented drugs in needed quantities. Most of the countries that would need to use the compulsory licensing provision in order to combat the spread of deadly diseases such as AIDS and malaria are the very ones that lack the technological ability to duplicate pharmaceuticals cheaply. In order to address this issue, compulsory licensing allows generic copies of drugs that were made under compulsory licences to be exported to specific countries that lack production capacity. Developed countries may manufacture generic medications on behalf of the listed developing countries that need them in emergency circumstances and provided that some compensation is paid to the patent holder. Norway, Canada, India, the EU and China have indicated their openness to such regimes as exporters of generic medicines to developing countries. So far only Canada has used the compulsory licensing scheme to supply medicine to a developing country, allowing the pharmaceutical company Apotex to export a generic AIDS medication to Rwanda. This provision of TRIPS, while controversial because it effectively takes property belonging to private companies, may be viewed as one of the ways in which the WTO has attempted to rebalance the harmful inequality between the developed and developing worlds in relation to the vital issue of global health.[39] Some have argued that the doctrine of good faith of public international law should prevent the abuse of this provision.[40]

TRIPS further requires WTO members to provide incentives to 'enterprises and institutions' in their territories for the purposes of encouraging technology transfer to less developed countries.[41] This provision is unusual in that at first it does not appear to be a trade-oriented obligation, but rather an investment one. It is unclear how trading with developing countries could itself contribute to technology transfer, unless it can be inferred that importers in foreign states will examine these products and reverse engineer them to gain knowhow regarding their manufacture. It may be that product chains involving inputs from more advanced economies could potentially result in technology transfer to those countries in which other, perhaps less sophisticated, parts of a unified product are added. The reference to institutions in this provision is also curious as it appears to contemplate incentives given to organizations other than private firms which engage in exports, possibly such as universities or non-profit, development-focused organizations. Lastly, the word 'incentives' could be construed as subsidies – governmental assistance to firms to encourage exports to developing countries. Such an understanding of this obligation in the TRIPS would appear to contradict the SCM agreement, which expressly prohibits subsidies which are contingent

---

[39] L Ulrich, 'Trips and Compulsory Licensing: Increasing Participation in the Medicines Patent Pool in the Wake of HIV/AIDS Treatment Timebomb, 30:1 Emory International Law Review 51 (2015).

[40] A Bagchi, 'Compulsory Licensing and the Duty of Good Faith in TRIPS' 55:5 Stanford Law Review 1529 (2003).

[41] Art. 66.2.

on export. Presumably the developmental focus of this section of TRIPS would preclude it being caught by WTO subsidies disciplines without evidence of an adverse effect on the industry in an importing state.

5.5 Intellectual property protection in RTAs

Intellectual property provisions are common to modern RTAs as WTO protections in this regard are often viewed as a baseline or bare minimum. The protection of intellectual property law, along the lines of TRIPS but often exceeding it, is viewed as a vital element of regional economic integration. In some cases intellectual property has also acted as a stumbling block in the negotiation of regional trade agreements, as in the case of GIs under CETA – an issue which has also plagued the ongoing trade negotiations between the EU and China.

The CPTPP contains a chapter on intellectual property which contains many of the elements found in TRIPS. It is worth drawing attention to the key objectives and principles outlined in this chapter of the CPTPP, which indicate the aspirations and expectations of the signatory states:

> The protection and enforcement of intellectual property rights should contribute to the promotion of technological innovation and to the transfer and dissemination of technology, to the mutual advantage of producers and users of technological knowledge and in a manner conducive to social and economic welfare, and to a balance of rights and obligations.[42]

> ...

> Having regard to the underlying public policy objectives of national systems, the Parties recognise the need to: (a) promote innovation and creativity; (b) facilitate the diffusion of information, knowledge, technology, culture and the arts; and (c) foster competition and open and efficient markets, through their respective intellectual property systems, while respecting the principles of transparency and due process, and taking into account the interests of relevant stakeholders, including right holders, service providers, users and the public.[43]

Clearly the protection of intellectual property is but one of the goals of the CPTPP – the emphasis on technology transfer among CPTPP signatories (which comprises both developed and developing countries) is obvious. Disciplines such as these are controversial because they may be seen to support, at least in principle, the so-called forced transfer of technology associated with the activities of many Western companies in China, a major aspect of the ongoing trade tensions between the US and China.

The US–Korea FTA contains an innovative provision regarding the prevention of trademark theft through the internet:

---

[42] Art. 18.2.

[43] Art. 18.4.

1. In order to address the problem of trademark cyber-piracy, each Party shall require that the management of its country-code top-level domain (ccTLD) provide an appropriate procedure for the settlement of disputes, based on the principles established in the Uniform Domain-Name Dispute-Resolution Policy.
2. Each Party shall require that the management of its ccTLD provide online public access to a reliable and accurate database of contact information concerning domain-name registrants.[44]

Such commitments, covering emerging intellectual property issues in relation to digital trade, were beyond the scope of coverage of TRIPS, which was drafted before the internet era. As noted in Chapter 4, the WTO in general has been slow to adapt to the growth in digital trade, leaving developments in this sphere to the bilateral and regional domains.

6. CONCLUSION

The WTO has attempted to strike the correct balance between promoting the liberalization of international trade and the safeguarding of key social interests such as the protection of the environment and human health. This chapter has shown that the WTO has done this chiefly by not intervening in each member's sovereign right to decide what social issues it wishes to pursue or which levels of risk to health and safety it wishes to bear, but by examining the way that this has been done. Where members have applied public interest-style protections in a manner that has adversely affected trade in an arbitrary or discriminatory way, then WTO rules, as enforced through the dispute settlement system, have enabled the finding of violations. This is seen under the General Exceptions of the GATT and in the SPS and TBT Agreements. Likewise, WTO members are free to approach the protection of intellectual property as they see fit under their national laws, so long as they do not fall below the minimum substantive and procedural requirements set by the TRIPS Agreement. Whether the WTO has achieved the appropriate equivalence between trade and nontrade concerns (and by extension between sovereignty and international obligations) is a matter of much debate and will likely remain controversial for some time.

Having finished the book's discussion of international trade, the next chapter will introduce the second major topic of international economic law: international investment law as contained in various treaties and other international instruments.

---

[44] Art. 18.3.

DISCUSSION QUESTIONS

1. Do the general exceptions of the GATT/GATS strike the right balance between trade liberalization and the protection of public policy issues?

2. Should the Essential Security provision in the GATT/GATS be framed in self-judging language – and if not how else might essential security be preserved under the WTO regime?

3. Are WTO members accorded sufficient room to impose sanitary and phytosanitary measures and technical barriers to trade? Are the SPS and TBT Agreements too lenient in this regard?

4. Should the WTO have concerned itself with intellectual property as a barrier to trade and has the TRIPS Agreement done so effectively from the perspective of the WTO's entire membership?

FURTHER READING

T Bollyky, P Mavroidis, 'Trade, Social Preferences and Regulatory Cooperation: The New WTO-Think' 20:1 Journal of International Economic Law 1 (2017).

M Du, 'Re-Conceptualizing the Role of Science in International Trade Disputes' 52:5 Journal of World Trade 697 (2018).

D McDaniels, AC Molina, E Wijkstrom, 'A Closer Look at the WTO's Third Pillar: How WTO Committees Influence Regional Trade Agreements' 21:4 Journal of International Economic Law 815 (2018).

E van der Zee, 'Disciplining Private Standards Under the SPS and TBT Agreement: A Plea for Market-State Procedural Guidelines' 52:3 Journal of World Trade 393 (2018).

PART II
INTERNATIONAL INVESTMENT LAW

6
Bilateral, regional and multilateral investment agreements

1. INTRODUCTION

Having outlined the basic elements of the world trading system as contained primarily in the laws of the WTO, starting with this chapter the book will shift focus to the second major topic in international economic law: international investment law. The focus of the subdiscipline of international investment law is the economic activity of foreign direct investment (FDI). FDI covers the establishment of business operations overseas by multinational firms, meaning companies from one country set up in another country for the purposes of engaging in commercial activities. Unsurprisingly, foreign investors' activities can conflict with host state economic policy in some cases, leading to interventions by the host state government which might, at least in the investor's eyes, be viewed as excessive. Such investors will seek protection against these actions and may wish to resort to international law because they do not trust the legal system of that country, either because it is unfamiliar to them or because it is insufficiently developed or if there are fears of corruption. This chapter will introduce, at a high level of generalization, the main sources of law dealing with these kinds of commercial interactions.

While customary international law still plays a role in international investment law, today treaties are its main source. As discussed in Chapter 1, the modern era of investment treaties began in the 1960s to facilitate European states' recovery from the Second World War, although the regime entered its golden age in the late 1990s and the early years of the twenty-first century, with the rapid conclusion of many hundreds of treaties in a short space of time. Figure 6.1 illustrates that there are now more than 3300 international investment agreements (IIAs) in existence, with the pace of signage having declined significantly in recent years, most likely due to growing aversion to these instruments in terms of their impact on the regulatory freedom of host states as well as their questionable link to actual increases in FDI. IIAs are most commonly bilateral agreements but there are also numerous trade-based regional and multilateral ones, some of which have already been mentioned in this book. Each organization seems to have its own terminology to describe IIAs (for example, Canada calls them Foreign Investment Promotion Agreements or FIPAs, whereas

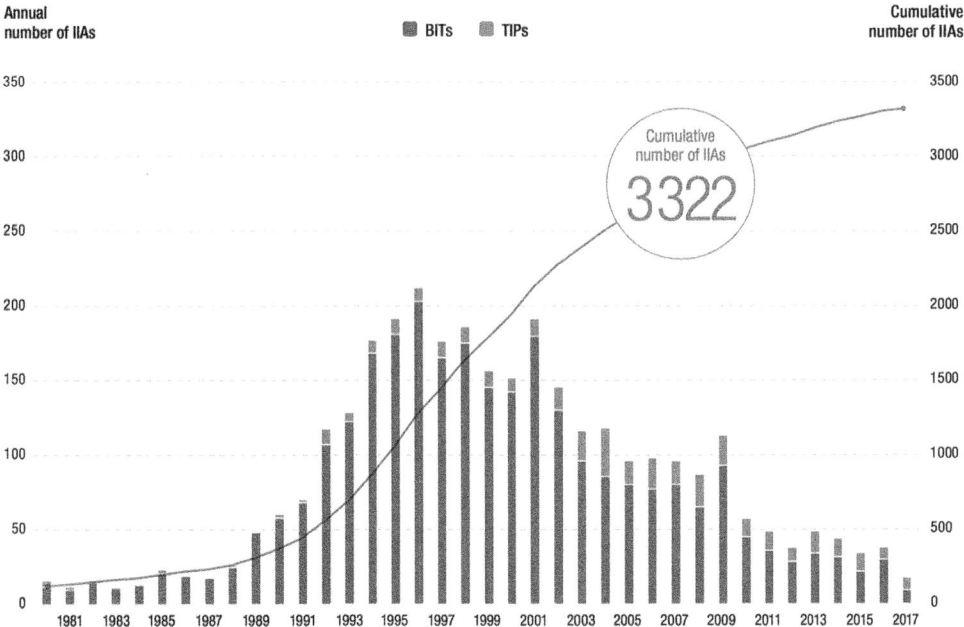

Note: The cumulative number of all signed IIAs, independent of whether they have entered into force, is 3,322. IIAs for which termination has entered into effect are not included.

Source: UNCTAD World Investment Report 2018.

Figure 6.1 Annual number of international investment agreements (bilateral investment treaties and treaties with investment protections) over time

UNCTAD uses the term Treaty with Investment Provisions or TIPs). However termed, they were traditionally concluded between capital exporting (developed) and capital importing (developing) countries, referencing the higher risk and greater investment opportunities in this latter category of economy. In recent years there have been more IIAs signed between developed states and in some cases between developing states, likely reflecting changes in capital flows across the world as well as perceptions of risk. More importantly, the contents of the treaties themselves have changed in recent years, which will be discussed further in the next chapter. Most IIAs are fully searchable by state party on the Investment Policy Hub interactive map maintained online by UNCTAD. It is an exceptionally useful resource.

Clearly, international investment law is much less coherent than world trade law. There is no global regime equivalent to the WTO (which itself is a series of treaties), although some have advocated for it at various times.[1] In addition to binding investment treaties, there are also a number of soft law guidelines issued by international bodies which play a relatively minor but noteworthy role in the global governance of international investment. Many of the legal entitlements available

---

[1] D Collins, *The BRIC States and Outward Foreign Direct Investment* (Oxford University Press, 2013).

to foreign investors, as well as some of the legal obligations which they face, are also enshrined in domestic statutes on foreign investment. Such domestic statutes empower host states to screen foreign investors by subjecting them to various economic or security assessments. Finally, in some instances foreign investors derive rights and obligations from private contracts between themselves and host states. This chapter will consider each of these categories of investment law in turn, beginning with the bilateral investment treaty (BIT).

2. BILATERAL INVESTMENT TREATIES

Like all treaties, BITs are state to state agreements. The original form of IIA, BITs were traditionally concluded between capital importing and capital exporting states to deal with the risks associated with the newfound independence of former colonies and associated impacts on extractive sector projects across the developing world. As with any treaty, including all IIAs, BITs are interpreted according to the rules outlined in the Vienna Convention on the Law of Treaties (VCLT), as noted in Chapter 1. The VCLT also provides default rules regarding the termination of treaties. Notably, under Article 56 b), if a BIT does not specify a termination date a right of denunciation may be implied by the nature of the treaty. In such circumstances, parties must give at least one year's notice of intention to withdraw from the treaty. Termination of a treaty releases the parties from any obligation to perform the treaty, although this does not affect rights and obligations arising prior to the termination of the treaty.[2] Many BITs also specify termination dates.

BITs provide formal safeguards against non-commercial risks and allegedly operate as an incentive to investors seeking opportunities in other countries. It remains unclear whether they actually function to increase FDI and therefore justify the liability they impose upon host states, in contrast to the wide range of rights they accord to investors, although it would seem as though the presence of a BIT in a target country is valued by foreign investors. Something of a subdiscipline within international economics has developed investigating the quantifiable impacts of BIT signage, with some studies indicating that there is no discernible impact on FDI flows just as others show a modest increase in some contexts.[3] There is also debate regarding the capacity of BITs to encourage the development of good governance standards in their domestic legal systems, as some have claimed.[4] While there are many thousands of them, BITs tend to contain the same provisions using similar language, developed from treaty practice throughout the latter part of the twentieth century. The contents of BITs and the protections they afford to investors will be explored in Chapter 7.

---

[2] Art. 70.

[3] 'US–Mexico Canada Trade Agreement: Likely Impact on the US Economy and on Specific Industry Sectors' United States International Trade Commission, April 2019, Publication 4889, chapter 8.

[4] K Vandevelde, *Bilateral Investment Treaties: History, Policy and Interpretation* (Oxford University Press, 2010) cf M Sattorova, *The Impact of Investment Treaty Law on Host States* (Hart, 2018).

3. REGIONAL TRADE AGREEMENTS WITH INVESTMENT CHAPTERS

Much of the modern international law regarding foreign investment is now found in the investment chapters of free trade agreements (FTAs) or regional trade agreements (RTAs). Indeed, such chapters are essentially identical to most BITs. RTAs are concluded with three or more countries, many of which are often in close geographical proximity. The investment chapters of RTAs tend to be somewhat more progressive than the classic BIT, reflecting the fact that such instruments are thought to be emblematic of regional integration across a wide segment of the economy, necessitating inclusion of material which has a social impact, such as exceptions for health and safety. There are several hundred RTAs with investment chapters around the world, some leading examples of which will now be briefly mentioned.

Although closer to a multilateral than a regional treaty, the Energy Charter Treaty (ECT) covers investment protection and promotion as well as trade and transit in the energy sector. It went into force in 1998 and has 53 signatories, including the EU Member States. Like a conventional BIT, it contains provisions for investor–state dispute settlement (ISDS) as well as standard provisions on expropriation, non-discrimination and fair and equitable treatment. The ECT is the most frequently invoked investment treaty in ISDS claims.

The United States Mexico Canada Agreement (USMCA), formerly the North American Free Trade Agreement (NAFTA), is an economic integration agreement between Canada, the US and Mexico covering investment (as well as other matters such as trade), which was signed in October 2018 after months of negotiation regarding the renewal of the old NAFTA. As of the time of writing there is some concern that the USMCA will not be ratified by the US Congress. The investment chapter of the USMCA contains many of the standard elements of a BIT, offering somewhat more detail on a number of matters, some of which will be mentioned in the next chapter. Unlike its predecessor, the USMCA does not include full access to ISDS for all three signatories – a remarkable undercutting of a dispute resolution system which generated many disputes under NAFTA. This omission may indicate a future trend in favour of aggrieved investors using domestic courts to resolve their disputes.

The Association of South East Asian Nations (ASEAN) Comprehensive Investment Agreement of 2009 (ACIA) was adopted to encourage FDI within the ASEAN region (Brunei Darussalam, Cambodia, Indonesia, Laos, Malaysia, Myanmar, Philippines, Singapore, Thailand and Vietnam). This agreement builds on earlier agreements in the region to provide an assortment of protections to foreign investment, as found in a typical BIT. This includes guarantees against expropriation and access to ISDS as an alternative to domestic courts. Less conventionally, ACIA includes special provisions for certain ASEAN members allowing them to bear lesser obligations, reflecting their developmental status.

The MERCOSUR Protocol on Investment Cooperation and Facilitation was signed in 2017 by the MERCOSUR parties Argentina, Brazil, Paraguay and Uruguay. This agreement is the second attempt by the regional trade bloc to agree on a discipline for international investment. The Protocol is dissimilar from a typical BIT in several respects, perhaps most notably due to its lack of an ISDS mechanism. Also lacking are commitments on fair and equitable treatment and full protection and security and guarantees against expropriation, likely reflecting the historic discomfort with these kinds of protections in Latin America. The Protocol does contain numerous provisions on investment promotion and emphasizes sustainable development; it also contains a highly innovative section consisting of obligations imposed on foreign investors. The extent to which this highly progressive IIA is successful for its signatories should indicate how likely it is to be adopted in other parts of the world.

Mentioned earlier in this book, the Comprehensive and Progressive Trans-Pacific Partnership (CPTPP) is an 11-nation regional economic integration agreement containing an investment chapter. The CPTPP (formerly known as the TPP or Trans-Pacific Partnership) would have been the largest regional trading bloc in the world (and therefore deserving of the epithet 'megaregional') had the US not withdrawn from negotiations in 2017. Its current parties are Australia, Brunei, Canada, Chile, Japan, Malaysia, Mexico, New Zealand, Peru, Singapore and Vietnam. Given its geographic scope, the GDP of its members and its progressive elements (including material on data protection and labour rights), the CPTPP is regarded by many as the 'gold standard' RTA going forward. The investment chapter very much resembles a modern IIA, with standard protections for foreign investors coupled with more balanced provisions such as a right to regulate in areas of public health and narrower definitions of indirect expropriation and fair and equitable treatment. The CPTPP retains ISDS, suggesting that there is life in this forum of dispute settlement yet.

4. MULTILATERAL INSTRUMENTS

As noted above, there is no multilateral investment treaty; however, there are a number of multilateral institutions/treaties which have relevance to international investment. They will be considered here in turn.

4.1 World Bank

There are a handful of multilateral instruments which have contributed to the creation of international investment law, such as it exists in its many forms. Perhaps the most significant of these is the World Bank and its varied organs. The World Bank (formal title the International Bank for Reconstruction and Development, or IBRD) is an international development agency that provides loans to developing countries for infrastructure-related projects with a view to improving their economic condition in the long term. As a development agency, it seeks to encourage FDI in developing countries as an alternative to aid. FDI is thought to be more conducive to development than aid, which can create damaging dependency and often leads to corruption. The World Bank's role in international economic law will be explored in more detail in Chapter 10. For now, it can be mentioned briefly that the Bank's Multilateral Investment Guarantee Agency (MIGA) offers political risk insurance (PRI) to offset the risk of excessive interference by host states in developing countries, with a view to incentivizing investment in these places. The Bank's International Finance Corporation (IFC) offers funding in the form of loans to assist investors who pursue investment in developing countries. Lastly, and most importantly, the International Centre for the Settlement of Investment Disputes (ICSID) is the World Bank's dispute settlement forum for investors to bring claims against host states for interference with their investments. It will be examined in much greater detail in Chapter 8.

4.2 The World Trade Organization

Although its focus is trade, some of the WTO agreements are relevant to international investment. The General Agreement on Trade in Services (GATS), which was examined in depth in Chapter 5, attempts to liberalize foreign investment in the services sector through its category Commercial Presence, the third of the four modes of supply of services outlined in Article I. WTO members commit to liberalize services sectors through non-discrimination, market access and transparency. Where commitments have been made, GATS prohibits restrictions on foreign investment, such as maximum capitalization or number of employees. Commercial presence commitments have generally been more comprehensive than some of the other modes of supply of services. Most WTO members maintain significant restrictions in cross-border trade in legal services in the financial services sector, often compelling financial companies to establish overseas in order to enter these foreign markets. GATS further facilitates investment in services through provisions which encourage the mutual recognition of qualifications of service-providing professionals. There is only one multilateral instrument for the recognition of qualifications for a specific profession, encouraging commercial presence establishment (as well as the other modes of investment), and that is for accounting services. Efforts have been made by the International Bar Association to help achieve multilateral recognition for the legal profession but so far this has not been forthcoming.[5]

Another WTO treaty which plays an important role in the safeguarding of foreign investment is the TRIPS Agreement, discussed in the previous chapter. TRIPS sets minimum standards of protection of intellectual property rights for WTO member states. Importantly, these kinds of commercial property are often included in the definition of investment in IIAs and are often highly valued assets held by multinational enterprises. Such firms may only be willing to invest in countries where such rights are safeguarded. It is important to recall that the compulsory licensing rules contained in Article 31 of the TRIPS allow WTO members to take intellectual property belonging to private companies in situations of emergency, typically in relation to pharmaceutical products which may be used to combat epidemics in developing countries. This provision is rightly described as a kind of expropriation, overriding typical protections against expropriation contained in IIAs. In fact, many IIAs specify that obligations contained in the treaty in relation to guarantees against expropriation preclude the compulsory licensing regime contained in the TRIPS. Another crucial aspect of the TRIPS Agreement in relation to international investment is the provision on technology transfer for developing countries. Under Article 66.2, developed country members are instructed to 'provide incentives to enterprises and institutions in their territories for the purpose of promoting and encouraging technology transfer to least-developed country Members in order to enable them to create a sound and viable technological base'. This provision appears to encourage home states to assist companies to engage in foreign investment which is conducive to

---

[5] D Collins, *The Public International Law of Trade in Legal Services* (Cambridge University Press, 2018).

the transmission of skills and knowledge to host states – one of the alleged advantages of foreign investment. Yet many countries resent the notion that technology transfer is forced on their firms, often through joint venture structures in countries such as China. This accusation is central to the ongoing trade war between the US and China, with US firms regularly citing China's technology transfer requirements as an illegitimate taking of hard won expertise without sufficient compensation.[6] Article 66.2 of the TRIPS Agreement suggests, however, that WTO member states bear this obligation as a matter of course. It is debatable that this feature of the TRIPS Agreement was designed to assist economically dominant countries like China.

The WTO's Agreement on Subsidies and Countervailing Measures (SCM) may also be important to the activities of some foreign investors. Despite there being no express reference to FDI or investment incentives in the SCM, the agreement prohibits subsidies which may take the form of investment incentives granted by host states. This kind of investment promotion may be harmful to host states because these can distort the allocation of public resources and suppress legitimate competition. It is also not always clear that foreign investors bring sufficient benefits to host states to compensate for the cost of incentive regimes such as tax breaks.[7] WTO subsidy rules were not designed to address investment incentives. This is why they may be described as something of a blunt instrument for dealing with them. Additionally, the generally weak enforcement of WTO obligations on trade distorting subsidies, including investment incentives, may be the consequence of the political reality that WTO members knew they would eventually be compelled to depart from these obligations because of domestic interest groups.[8]

The WTO agreement most directly relevant to international investment is the Trade Related Investment Measures (TRIMs) Agreement, an aspect of WTO law that was not covered in the first part of this book. The TRIMs, a much narrower agreement than was originally envisioned, prohibits certain types of performance-related measures which may be imposed on foreign investors that have trade distorting effects. Such measures condition the host state's acceptance of the foreign investment on the investor adopting certain trade-oriented actions. The foreign investor is compelled to trade in a way that it otherwise would not, potentially leading to trade inefficiencies – which is why it concerns the WTO.[9] The TRIMs makes the imposition of these types of requirements on investors illegal by reiterating the MFN and national treatment rules of the GATT, ensuring that the measures are not used as instruments of discrimination to favour certain producers.[10]

The precise definition of a trade related investment measure (a TRIM) is unclear but an indicative list of prohibited measures is contained in an Annex to the agreement. They include: local content requirements (meaning rules which require the purchase of local goods in conjunc-

---

[6] G Wildau, 'China Drafts Law to Ban Forced Tech Transfer from Foreign Partners' Financial Times (24 December 2018).

[7] D Collins, *Performance Requirements and Investment Incentives under International Economic Law* (Edward Elgar Publishing, 2015).

[8] A Nov, 'The "Bidding War" to Attract Foreign Investment: The Need for a Global Solution' 25 Virginia Tax Review 835 (2005).

[9] Collins, *Performance Requirements* above n 7.

[10] Art. 2.1.

tion with an investment); trade balancing requirements (rules which require the extent of use of imported products to be linked to value of local products used); foreign exchange requirements (preventing restrictions on access to local currencies to conduct business operations); and lastly export restrictions (rules which restrict the sale of goods for export). Such conditions placed on foreign investors are known as performance requirements and tend to be prohibited in most IIAs. They are forbidden because they make it harder for foreign investors to operate in host states than it is for the equivalent domestic investors, which are uninhibited and therefore very likely in a stronger market position. The provisions of the TRIMs are subject to the dispute settlement procedures of the WTO.[11] This means that there is no possibility of investment arbitration between investors against host states based on TRIMs violations. Instead investors must seek the support of their home state to bring such claims. The TRIMs has been the subject of very little WTO caselaw, primarily because it essentially reaffirms the application of GATT Article III.4 to certain forms of FDI.[12] Most of the disputes citing TRIMs provisions have been related to the automotive industry. The impact of TRIMs in this sector may be expected given the significant role that the automotive manufacturing sector plays in the economy of many leading WTO members. The automotive industry is also known for its use of quantitative restrictions and local content rules, which lie at the heart of the TRIMs' prohibitions. It is worth having a look at some of the TRIMs disputes in more detail, as they illustrate an important link between the two main fields of international economic law – trade and investment.

In 1996, the EC, Japan and the US requested consultations against Indonesia through the WTO dispute settlement procedure, regarding the latter state's allegedly restrictive investment policies towards its automotive sector.[13] Indonesia provided firms (both local and foreign) with import duty exemptions or reductions on required levels of imports on automotive parts based on the percentage of local content that they used in their manufacturing. It also offered tax and import duty exemptions as incentives to firms based on the degree of local content, effectively constituting a breach of national treatment against foreign produced components. The complainants argued that Indonesia's measures were also inconsistent with MFN and the GATT's transparency rules, as well as Article 2 of the TRIMs – the agreement's substantive prohibition on national treatment and quantitative restrictions being used in conjunction with foreign investment laws. The panel agreed with most of these claims, finding that the relevant measures implemented by Indonesia constituted local content requirements that were TRIMs-prohibited trade related investment measures, violating both GATT national treatment and the TRIMs.

The EC and the US brought TRIMS-based proceedings against India in 1999 through the WTO dispute settlement procedure for India's industrial indigenization policies.[14] The EC and the US complained that several regulations instigated by the Indian government in relation to its automobile industry violated GATT (national treatment and prohibition on quantitative restrictions) as well as Article 2 of the TRIMs (the prohibition on trade related investment measures). The

---

[11] Art. 8.

[12] M Trebilcock, *Understanding Trade Law* (Edward Elgar Publishing, 2011).

[13] Indonesia – Certain Measures Affecting the Automobile Industry, Panel Report, WT/DS54/R (23 July 1998).

[14] India – Measures Affecting the Automotive Sector, Panel Report, WT/DS146/R (5 April 2002).

relevant Indian laws required that imports of complete automobiles and of certain parts and components were subjected to a system of nonautomatic import licences. Import licences for these products would be granted only to approved local joint venture manufacturers. This arrangement obliged manufacturers to conform to specified local content as well as export balancing requirements. The panel ruled that India's imposition of these requirements on automotive manufacturers was in breach of its commitments under the GATT and, having reached this conclusion, decided that it was not necessary to consider whether the measures also violated Article 2 of the TRIMs. The panel did not elaborate on the way in which the TRIMs will be interpreted; however, it did note that the TRIMs should not be viewed as a more specific version of the GATT, and as such it was not compelled to consider the TRIMs before the GATT under the principle of the specific agreement illuminating the more general. The panel required the Indian government to eliminate all inconsistent measures.

Canada faced a complaint under the TRIMs from the EU in relation to Canada's feed-in tariff programme through which it imposed restrictions on the sale and distribution of equipment for renewable energy generation (including wind and solar) facilities.[15] The EU (along with Japan) alleged that Canada accorded less favourable treatment to foreign suppliers of the equipment than it did to local ones, in violation of the national treatment obligation of the GATT as well as Article 2.1 of the TRIMs. The measure in question required that the renewable energy equipment had to be supplied with a minimum content (25 per cent for wind and 60 per cent for solar power) from local firms. These were effectively domestic content requirements, affording protection to local producers of such equipment. The Canadian government had maintained that the local content measures were necessary to promote the use of clean energy. The panel upheld the EU's claims under Article 2.1 of the TRIMs, as well as under the GATT, ruling that the measure fell within the type of trade related investment measure described in Article 1 a) of the agreement's illustrative list, namely a local content requirement. The panel considered also whether Canada could rely upon Article III:8 a) of the GATT (which excluded government procurement activities from the scope of the national treatment obligation) to justify breach of Article 2.1 of the TRIMs, ultimately ruling that Canada could not do so because the feed-in tariff programme implemented by the provincial government covered the procurement of electricity that was undertaken with a view to commercial resale, which fell outside the rubric of procurement which contemplated governmental use. The panel's recommendation was appealed to the Appellate Body, which upheld the panel's determination that the local content features of the feed-in tariff measure contravened Article 2.1 of the TRIMs, further confirming that Article III:8 of the GATT was not applicable to the feed-in tariff measures because they involved commercial sales rather than procurement activities.

The last feature of WTO law that should be mentioned in conjunction with FDI is the plurilateral (optional) government procurement agreement (GPA). The GPA has 15 party states plus the EU Member States. Most of these signatories are developed countries and therefore have sizeable government procurement markets. The purpose of the GPA is to ensure that foreign products and

---

[15] Canada – Certain Measures Affecting the Renewable Energy Generation Sector, Canada – Measures Relating to the Feed-in Tariff Program, Panel Report, WT/DS426/R (19 December 2012).

services are treated no less favourably in government procurement than domestic ones. Article IV contains the GPA's MFN and national treatment provisions:

(1) With respect to any measure regarding covered procurement, each Party, including its procuring entities, shall accord immediately and unconditionally to the goods and services of any other Party and to the suppliers of any other Party offering the goods or services of any Party, treatment no less favourable than the treatment the Party, including its procuring entities, accords to: a) domestic goods, services and suppliers; and b) goods, services and suppliers of any other Party.

(2) With respect to any measure regarding covered procurement, a Party, including its procuring entities, shall not: a) treat a locally established supplier less favourably than another locally established supplier on the basis of the degree of foreign affiliation or ownership; or b) discriminate against a locally established supplier on the basis that the goods or services offered by that supplier for a particular procurement are goods or services of any other Party.

The reference to 'degree of foreign affiliation' in Article IV(2) demonstrates that the GPA is an investment-oriented agreement – it directly prohibits discriminatory procurement regulations faced by foreign firms which are established in the relevant party state. Article XVIII:1 of the GPA further requires signatory parties to maintain timely, effective, transparent and non-discriminatory administrative or judicial review procedures for all government procurement bidding regimes. The same tribunal can, and in many cases does, serve multiple functions under both the GPA or procurement rules contained in RTAs. These rules should allow for the clear identification of any prohibited performance requirement/offsets associated with procurement policies, as described above. Although procurement rules are uncommon to IIAs, it should be noted that there are some regional procurement rules contained in economic integration agreements, such as those found in the original NAFTA and the Comprehensive Economic and Trade Agreement between the EU and Canada (CETA).

4.3 International Monetary Fund

Originally introduced in Chapter 1, the IMF, as the international organization in charge of the monetary relations aspect of international economic law, will be explored in closer detail in Chapter 9. For now it is important simply to recognize that the IMF is a multilateral regime which plays a role in fostering foreign investment by allowing foreign investors to access the domestic currency of the countries in which they locate, and also to send profits which they make back to their home state in their own currency. The IMF requires that all member states must not place restrictions on the conversion of currency. Restrictions may include limits on the amount of foreign or local currency that can be purchased, repatriation requirements and ways in which foreign or local currency must be used. Clearly, capital controls limit firms' capacity to globalize by restricting their access to finance. It should be further noted here, as will be examined later, that the IMF does acknowledge that economically vulnerable states may need to impose such controls to prevent capital flight and recessions which may ensue. Additionally and perhaps more obviously, a host state's economic stability will influence its attractiveness to foreign investment. Accordingly, the IMF's assistance with balance of payments equilibrium should assist states in securing external financing through foreign investment.

4.4 New York Convention

Although not an organization in the same sense as the WTO, the World Bank or the IMF, the Convention on the Recognition and Enforcement of Foreign Arbitral Awards (the New York Convention)[16] is a key, binding multilateral instrument that has made much of ISDS possible, increasing the legal security of FDI. The New York Convention requires courts of signatory states to give effect to private agreements to arbitrate and to recognize and enforce arbitration awards made in other contracting states as if they were judgments of the highest domestic courts of signatory states. This enables arbitration awards to enjoy a legal status which exceeds that of many actual courts where there is no treaty in place for the recognition of foreign judgments – as is the case with US courts in many jurisdictions, for example. With 159 signatory parties as of 2019, the New York Convention is widely considered the foundational instrument for international arbitration, including, importantly, that which occurs between investors and host states.[17] Under this treaty, arbitration awards may still be challenged in national courts if there were procedural irregularities in the composition of the arbitral tribunal, or if the tribunal exceeded its jurisdiction. Awards that violate the public policy of the enforcing state may also be disregarded, and in that sense the Convention provides an additional layer of sovereign control that is absent from ICSID, often to the irritation of investors. The New York Convention allows for procedural rules of international arbitration other than those of ICSID to be used, including, most commonly, the United Nations Commission on International Trade Law (UNCITRAL) Arbitration Rules.[18] Like ICSID rules, UNCITRAL rules are often specified as an acceptable procedure for dispute settlement under IIAs and investment contracts. These will be explored further in Chapter 8.

5. INTERNATIONAL INVESTMENT 'SOFT LAW'

There are a handful of other multilateral instruments which should be mentioned in order to give a complete picture with respect to the regulation of foreign investment at the global level. Many of these frameworks or regimes are optional, operating merely as guidelines rather than as a set of binding rules, as in the case of the WTO agreements or IIAs. This does not mean that these instruments have not been influential or will not become more so in the future. Indeed, the growing role of so-called soft law in international economic law has been observed by commentators, and

---

[16] 330 UNTS 38, signed on 10 June 1958, entered into force 7 June 1959.

[17] Most IIAs require signatory states to recognize and enforce arbitral decisions of tribunals taking jurisdiction from the treaty. ICSID awards are self-enforcing and therefore do not require the New York Convention.

[18] UNCITRAL Arbitration Rules (revised 12 July 2010).

has been memorably termed by one as 'minilateralism'.[19] Some of the leading examples will now be considered.

5.1 OECD Guidelines for Multinational Enterprises

The Organization for Economic Cooperation and Development (OECD) is an international organization composed of 36 highly industrialized member countries which has its headquarters in Paris, France. The OECD Guidelines for Multinational Enterprises (the Guidelines) are a set of nonbinding recommendations for multinational enterprises operating in OECD member countries which are the world's most developed economies. The Guidelines provide principles for responsible business conduct in foreign states which are consistent with applicable laws and internationally recognized standards, with a view to ensuring that foreign investment is done in a manner which does not harm the societies of host states. They embody what are normally understood as principles of corporate social responsibility (CSR). In that sense the primary aim of the Guidelines is to promote positive contributions by foreign investors to the economic, environmental and social progress of the states in which they operate. The Guidelines are the only multilaterally agreed and comprehensive code of responsible business behaviour that governments have committed to promoting, expressing the shared values of the governments of some of the major capital exporting countries, which are among the Guidelines' 42 adhering states. The Guidelines are supported by National Contact Points (NCPs), which are agencies established by adhering governments. The NCPs assist enterprises and their stakeholders to take appropriate measures to further the implementation of the Guidelines, also providing mediation and conciliation facilities for resolving disputes which may arise between investors and stakeholders in host states. The Guidelines were most recently updated in 2011, and the new Guidelines were designed to ensure their continued role as a leading international instrument for the promotion of responsible business conduct. It is worth examining the Guidelines' General Policies to get a sense of the types of obligation which they place on foreign investors, as contained in Part II:

> Enterprises should take fully into account established policies in the countries in which they operate, and consider the views of other stakeholders.
> In this regard: A. Enterprises should:
> 1. Contribute to economic, environmental and social progress with a view to achieving sustainable development.
> 2. Respect the internationally recognised human rights of those affected by their activities.
> 3. Encourage local capacity building through close co-operation with the local community, including business interests, as well as developing the enterprise's activities in domestic and foreign markets, consistent with the need for sound commercial practice.
> 4. Encourage human capital formation, in particular by creating employment opportunities and facilitating training opportunities for employees.

---

[19] C Brummer, *Minilateralism: How Trade Alliances, Soft Law and Financial Engineering Are Redefining Economic Statecraft* (Cambridge University Press, 2014).

5. Refrain from seeking or accepting exemptions not contemplated in the statutory or regulatory framework related to human rights, environmental, health, safety, labour, taxation, financial incentives, or other issues.

6. Support and uphold good corporate governance principles and develop and apply good corporate governance practices, including throughout enterprise groups.

7. Develop and apply effective self-regulatory practices and management systems that foster a relationship of confidence and mutual trust between enterprises and the societies in which they operate.

8. Promote awareness of and compliance by workers employed by multinational enterprises with respect to company policies through appropriate dissemination of these policies, including through training programmes.

9. Refrain from discriminatory or disciplinary action against workers who make bona fide reports to management or, as appropriate, to the competent public authorities, on practices that contravene the law, the Guidelines or the enterprise's policies.

10. Carry out risk-based due diligence, for example by incorporating it into their enterprise risk management systems, to identify, prevent and mitigate actual and potential adverse impacts as described in paragraphs 11 and 12, and account for how these impacts are addressed. The nature and extent of due diligence depend on the circumstances of a particular situation.

11. Avoid causing or contributing to adverse impacts on matters covered by the Guidelines, through their own activities, and address such impacts when they occur.

12. Seek to prevent or mitigate an adverse impact where they have not contributed to that impact, when the impact is nevertheless directly linked to their operations, products or services by a business relationship. This is not intended to shift responsibility from the entity causing an adverse impact to the enterprise with which it has a business relationship.

13. In addition to addressing adverse impacts in relation to matters covered by the Guidelines, encourage, where practicable, business partners, including suppliers and sub-contractors, to apply principles of responsible business conduct compatible with the Guidelines.

14. Engage with relevant stakeholders in order to provide meaningful opportunities for their views to be taken into account in relation to planning and decision making for projects or other activities that may significantly impact local communities.

15. Abstain from any improper involvement in local political activities.

The OECD Guidelines have generally been well received by commentators, many of whom note the limits of nonbinding guidelines in effecting change in the behaviours of actors such as international investors.[20] Their actual impact on foreign investors may be difficult to measure and therefore to appreciate.

---

[20] AL Santner, 'A Soft Law Mechanism for Corporate Responsibility: How the Updated OECD Guidelines for Multinational Enterprises Promote Business for the Future' 43:1 George Washington International Law Review 375 (2011).

5.2 OECD Code of Liberalisation of Capital Movements

The Code of Liberalisation of Capital Movements was created by the OECD in 1961, during a period in which many OECD countries were in the process of economic recovery and the international movement of capital faced numerous barriers. All 36 OECD countries, most of which are developed economies, adhere to the Code. Since 2012, the Code has also been open to non-OECD countries. The Code aims to provide a balanced framework for OECD members to progressively remove barriers to the movement of capital, while providing enough flexibility to cope with situations of economic and financial instability. Under the Code, an adhering country is entitled to benefit from the liberalization of other adhering countries regardless of its own degree of openness. This nonreciprocity contrasts with that of the negotiating premise of tariffs at the WTO, for example. OECD members agreed under the Code to established principles such as transparency, non-discrimination, proportionality and accountability to guide their recourse to controls. This can be seen in the following articles:

> Article 1: Members shall, in particular, endeavour: i) to treat all non-resident-owned assets in the same way irrespective of the date of their formation.
>
> ...
>
> Article 3: The provisions of this Code shall not prevent a Member from taking action which it considers necessary for: i) the maintenance of public order or the protection of public health, morals and safety; ii) the protection of its essential security interests; iii) the fulfilment of its obligations relating to international peace and security.

In 2016, adhering countries adopted terms of reference for a review of the Code with a view to improving transparency as well as shared understandings of good practices relating to managing and liberalizing capital flows.

5.3 United Nations Commission on International Trade Law (UNCITRAL)

Part of the UN, UNCITRAL was created to help promote trade and investment around the world through the development of various legal initiatives, including harmonization of domestic legal approaches to these issues. The UNCITRAL Arbitration Rules provide a comprehensive set of procedural rules open to parties in ISDS for the conduct of arbitral proceedings arising out of alleged breaches of IIAs and investment contracts. UNCITRAL rules are widely used in *ad hoc* arbitrations as well as administered arbitrations, although they remain less popular than ICSID rules. UNCITRAL rules cover all aspects of the arbitral process, providing a model arbitration clause, setting out procedural rules regarding the appointment of arbitrators and the conduct of arbitral proceedings, and establishing rules in relation to the form, effect and interpretation of the award. Revised in 2010, UNCITRAL rules include provisions dealing with multiple party arbitration and joinder, as well as liability, and offer a procedure to object to experts appointed by the arbitral tribunal. The revised rules aim to enhance procedural efficiency, containing material on the replacement of an arbitrator, the requirement for reasonableness of costs and a review mechanism regarding the costs of arbitration. They also include more detailed provisions on interim measures.

The 2013 version of the rules incorporates the UNCITRAL Rules on Transparency for Treaty-based Investor–State Arbitration. UNCITRAL's transparency rules, which went into effect on 1 April 2014, are a set of procedural rules that provide for transparency and accessibility to the public of treaty-based investor–state arbitration. They were drafted in response to the many criticisms levied against ISDS (of which more in Chapter 8) due to the confidentiality of its hearings. The transparency rules apply in relation to disputes arising out of treaties concluded prior to 1 April 2014, in circumstances when parties to the relevant IIA who engage in an ISDS dispute agree to their application. The rules further apply in relation to disputes arising out of treaties concluded on or after 1 April 2014, when ISDS is initiated under the UNCITRAL Arbitration Rules, unless the parties otherwise agree. The Rules on Transparency are also available for use in investor–state arbitrations initiated under rules other than the UNCITRAL Arbitration Rules, such as ICSID and in *ad hoc* proceedings.

The United Nations Convention on Transparency in Treaty-based Investor–State Arbitration, also known as the Mauritius Convention on Transparency,[21] is an instrument through which parties to investment treaties concluded before 1 April 2014 express their consent to apply the UNCITRAL Rules on Transparency in Treaty-based Investor–State Arbitration. The Convention supplements existing investment treaties in relation to transparency. The general rule of application is contained in paragraph 1 (bilateral or multilateral application), with paragraph 2 referring to the application of the Rules on Transparency when only the respondent state (and not the state of the investor-claimant) is a party to the Convention. This is known as a unilateral offer of application.

A party to the Convention has the flexibility to establish reservations, excluding from the application of the Convention a specific investment treaty or a specific set of arbitration rules other than the UNCITRAL Arbitration Rules, which would be described as a negative list approach. This gives the Convention a strong degree of flexibility while ensuring that reservations cannot be used to defeat the purpose of the Convention. Along with the Rules on Transparency, the Convention takes into account both the broader public interest and the interest of the parties to resolve investment disputes in a fair and efficient manner.

UNCITRAL also collects and disseminates data about trends in international investment and international investment law. It maintains the very useful Investment Policy Hub database of IIAs, noted above, and its annual World Investment Report provides a comprehensive overview of FDI patterns and investment policy changes at the national and international levels.

5.4 United Nations Convention against Corruption

The United Nations Convention against Corruption (the Convention)[22] is the only legally binding universal anticorruption instrument. In this sense it is not truly appropriate to think of it as

---

[21] 18 October 2017.

[22] Adopted 31 October 2003 by resolution 58/4.

'soft law', although its role in international investment law is an indirect one. The Convention is a crucial instrument by which home states can exert control over the activities of their foreign investors abroad, particularly in countries where corruption is endemic. Most of the UN Member States are parties to the Convention, including the vast majority of the leading capital exporting countries. The Convention covers five main areas: preventive measures, criminalization and law enforcement, international cooperation, asset recovery, and technical assistance and information exchange. It addresses many different forms of corruption, such as bribery, trading in influence, abuse of functions and various acts of corruption in the private sector. With regard to its impact on foreign investment, two articles stand out. First, Article 12 states:

> 1. Each State Party shall take measures, in accordance with the fundamental principles of its domestic law, to prevent corruption involving the private sector, enhance accounting and auditing standards in the private sector and, where appropriate, provide effective, proportionate and dissuasive civil, administrative or criminal penalties for failure to comply with such measures. 2. Measures to achieve these ends may include, inter alia: … (d) Preventing the misuse of procedures regulating private entities, including procedures regarding subsidies and licences granted by public authorities for commercial activities.

Article 16(1) on bribery of foreign public officials and officials of public international organizations provides as follows:

> Each State Party shall adopt such legislative and other measures as may be necessary to establish as a criminal offence, when committed intentionally, the promise, offering or giving to a foreign public official or an official of a public international organization, directly or indirectly, of an undue advantage, for the official himself or herself or another person or entity, in order that the official act or refrain from acting in the exercise of his or her official duties, in order to obtain or retain business or other undue advantage in relation to the conduct of international business.

Where complied with, these international rules should help curtail foreign investors' improper influence over domestic affairs, much as they should enhance market access opportunities for foreign investors who can direct their capital to productive rather than nonproductive expenditures. Domestic foreign anticorruption initiatives will be considered further below.

5.5 UN Global Compact

The UN Global Compact is a voluntary initiative based on the commitments of managers (chief executive officers) of multinational firms to implement universal principles of sustainability and in so doing support UN goals. This means that the relevant firms undertake to operate in a way that meets fundamental responsibilities in the areas of human rights, labour, environment and anticorruption. The Compact consists of ten principles, which together comprise a strategy or policy of ethical behaviour for multinational investors. The ten principles are as follows:

Principle 1: Businesses should support and respect the protection of internationally pro-claimed human rights; and

Principle 2: make sure that they are not complicit in human rights abuses.

Principle 3: Businesses should uphold the freedom of association and the effective recognition of the right to collective bargaining;

Principle 4: the elimination of all forms of forced and compulsory labour;

Principle 5: the effective abolition of child labour; and

Principle 6: the elimination of discrimination in respect of employment and occupation.

Principle 7: Businesses should support a precautionary approach to environmental challenges;

Principle 8: undertake initiatives to promote greater environmental responsibility; and

Principle 9: encourage the development and diffusion of environmentally friendly technologies.

Principle 10: Businesses should work against corruption in all its forms, including extortion and bribery.[23]

These CSR-oriented guidelines, when adhered to by foreign investors, could help resolve some of the imbalance often associated with conventional international investment law as contained in IIAs which do not place any obligations on investors. They should also help achieve some of the benefits said to be associated with FDI for host states.

5.6 Regional development bank lending guidelines

There are a number of regional development banks which complement the work of the World Bank, some of which will be examined in more detail in Chapter 10. For now it is illustrative to consider that many of these agencies, which lend money to sovereign states or in some cases directly to investors, are able to impose conditions on borrowers. A good example of such rules can be found in the Asian Infrastructure Investment Bank's (AIIB) General Conditions for Sovereign-backed Loans of 1 May 2016. This document is effectively a loan contract, much as one would find in the private sector between a conventional bank and a business from which it borrows. From the perspective of informing the behaviour of international businesses, some of the key provisions of the AIIB's General Conditions are as follows:

Section 2.04. The Recipient and the Project Implementing Entity shall use the proceeds of the Loan exclusively to finance expenditures which, except as otherwise provided in the Loan Agreement, satisfy the following requirements ('Eligible Expenditure'):

(a) the payment is for the financing of the reasonable cost of goods, works or services required for the Project, to be financed out of the proceeds of the Loan and procured, all in accordance with the provisions of the Legal Agreements;

(b) the payment is not prohibited by a decision of the United Nations Security Council taken under Chapter VII of the Charter of the United Nations;

---

[23] www.unglobalcompact.org/what-is-gc/mission/principles

...

Section 4.01. The Recipient and the Project Implementing Entity shall carry out their Respective Parts of the Project:

(a) with due diligence and efficiency;

(b) in conformity with appropriate administrative, technical, financial, economic, environmental and social standards and practices, including, without limitation, the Environmental and Social Policy and Standards and the Procurement Policy; and

(c) in accordance with the provisions of the Legal Agreements.

...

Section 5.01. The Member shall periodically furnish to the Bank all such information as the Bank shall reasonably request with respect to financial and economic conditions in its territory, including its balance of payments and its External Debt, as well as that of its political or administrative subdivisions and of any entity owned and controlled by, or operating for the account or benefit of, the Member or any such subdivision, and of any institution performing the functions of a central bank or exchange stabilization fund, or similar functions, for the Member.

The point of these requirements is to ensure that the foreign investor engages in contact in the host state which conforms to the needs of that state from a development capacity and also from the perspective of financial viability. It is in the interest of the host state that the investor's actions are fruitful in terms of both its developmental goals and the investor's own financial health. By placing these obligations on foreign investors which are in conformity with CSR principles, the development bank is able to structure their behaviour in a manner which is not possible under IIAs as they are currently framed. This is important again because IIAs do not do this, as their obligations fall exclusively on the host states.

5.7 Equator Principles

The Equator Principles are a risk management framework which may be adopted on a voluntary basis by financial institutions for the purpose of determining, assessing and managing environmental and social risk in projects to which they lend resources. They are primarily designed to provide a minimum standard for due diligence and monitoring to support responsible risk decision making. In this sense, the Equator Principles are able to exert indirect influence on the activities of international investors seeking project finance. The Equator Principles apply globally to all industry sectors. Currently, 94 institutions across 37 countries have officially accepted the Equator Principles. Collectively these cover the majority of international project finance debt within developed and emerging markets. These financial institutions commit to implementing the Equator Principles in their internal environmental and social policies, procedures and standards for financing projects. They will not provide project finance-based loans to projects where the client will not, or is unable to, comply with the EPs. The Equator Principles have significantly increased the focus on social standards and the important concept of CSR alluded to above in relation to the OECD Guidelines. The Equator Principles attempt to achieve this through robust standards for indigenous peoples, labour standards and mandatory consultation with locally affected communities.

Such principles broadly resemble those adopted by many multilateral and regional development banks. The extent to which they have actually attained these goals is uncertain.

5.8 The International Forum of Sovereign Wealth Funds

Sovereign wealth funds (SWFs) have become influential international investors. Although this form of government controlled entity is not new, the expansion of SWFs' investment has attracted much attention in recent years, perhaps most prominently in the aftermath of the 2008–9 financial crisis. SWFs are special purpose investment vehicles or state owned investment funds created primarily to serve the social and financial interests of home states through the commercial activity of investment in either greenfield or mergers and acquisitions. SWFs invest globally in real estate and financial assets, such as bonds and stocks, as well as alternative investments such as hedge funds.[24] SWFs have been undertaking foreign investment activities of this nature for many decades. It is often thought that they have a positive impact on home states, host states and the global economy. They help to promote economic growth and development, contribute to market stability and influence good corporate governance practices. Still, the public–private nature of SWFs and the large volume of assets they manage have raised fears from recipient countries. SWFs are regarded by some as a threat to the stability of financial markets because of the potential to exit rapidly. Of more concern is the risk they pose to national security as a consequence of their inherent political nature and low transparency, both of which have been widely criticized.

To address some of the concerns associated with the increased foreign investment activities of SWFs, in 2008 a transnational self-regulatory arrangement was created at the behest of the US Treasury, the G7 (Canada, France, Germany, Italy, Japan, the UK and the US) and the IMF.[25] Entitled the Generally Accepted Principles and Practices (GAPP) or Santiago Principles, these standards purportedly subject SWFs to norms of good behaviour on governance, transparency, accountability and risk management, among others. This regime was followed by the creation of a quasi-governance institution called the International Forum of SWFs (IFSWF). Much of the commentary on the Santiago Principles and the IFSWF suggests that governance of SWFs' investment activities remains largely unformalized, and unsophisticated.[26] Others have emphasized the nature of the forum as an incipient actor in global economic governance, along the lines of the WTO or the IMF.[27] There is considerable scepticism about the ability of what is essentially a self-regulatory arrangement to achieve the objective of stronger governance and greater transparency on the part of SWFs.[28]

---

[24] W Yin, 'Corporate Social Responsibility and Sovereign Wealth Funds: Socially Responsible Investing as a Moral Obligation or Legal Liability?' [2018] Journal of Business Law 300.

[25] J Norton, 'The "Santiago Principles" and the International Forum of Sovereign Wealth Funds: Evolving Components of the New Bretton Woods II Post-Global Financial Crisis Architecture and Another Example of Ad Hoc Global Administrative Networking and Related "Soft" Rulemaking?' [2010] 29 Review of Banking & Financial Law 465.

[26] V Barbary, 'Santiago Principles turn 10 Years Old' Top1000Funds (18 September 2018).

[27] Norton above n 25.

[28] F Bassan, The Law of Sovereign Wealth Funds (Edward Elgar Publishing, 2011).

6. A MULTILATERAL AGREEMENT ON INVESTMENT

The OECD attempted to create a multilateral agreement on investment in the late 1990s. It was intended to resolve the patchwork of highly similar IIAs (mostly BITs) that appeared and become quite numerous with the onset of globalization. The Draft MIA had the aim of ensuring the liberalization and protection of foreign investment enforceable through ISDS. The MIA was very much pro-investor and this caused opposition within the developing world, which was concerned that the instrument contained no obligations on investors with respect to contribution to development. Major objections were also made by the developed world in relation to the need to preserve cultural material. The collapse of the MIA was also in part due to the lack of participation in the negotiation process by the developing world, as well as pressure from NGOs to include provisions on environmental and labour protections. Perhaps more fundamentally, traditional capital exporting countries were most concerned with creating a multilateral instrument designed to limit a state's power. In contrast, capital importing states stressed the need to preserve the sovereignty of the government in administering the economy. The positions of most of the wealthy OECD countries in the MIA negotiations reflected their status as FDI exporters, whereas the emerging markets viewed themselves as importers or host states. In addition to the MIA negotiations in the late 90s, investment was dropped from the agenda of the Doha Round of WTO trade negotiations because few of the negotiating parties demonstrated any enthusiasm for exploring the issue. Given the WTO's ongoing troubles and the difficulties in achieving consensus on anything among its 164 members, it seems unlikely that a multilateral investment agreement will be taken up by the WTO any time soon. It may be that as the economic position of nations begins to rebalance between inward and outward FDI among both the developed and developing world, it could be expected that negotiating positions should tend towards equality, making the achievement of a global investment treaty more feasible.[29]

7. MULTILATERAL INVESTMENT COURT

The EU began to negotiate a convention establishing a Multilateral Investment Court (MIC) responsible for the settlement of investment disputes on behalf of the EU, but which could be multilateralized to handle disputes between other parties. The aim of the EU's MIC is to establish a permanent body which would adjudicate disputes under existing and future investment treaties to settle investment disputes and subsequently replace bilateral ISDS involved in investment agreements and EU trade, moving away from traditional arbitration frameworks. In theory, the MIC would help ensure that approaches to resolving international investment disputes are in line with that of the EU to settling international disputes generally – multilateral solutions within a rules-based system designed to bring about a more coherent, transparent and fair system.[30] The MIC is

---

[29] Collins, *The BRIC States* above n 1.

[30] European Commission, 'State of the Union 2017 A Multilateral Investment Court' (European Commission, September 2017).

intended to improve the efficiency of the EU's Investment Court System (ICS) and to address the criticisms of the existing ISDS system, of which more in Chapter 8. In particular, it is believed to be more efficient to have a single multilateral institution to rule on investment disputes incorporating all active bilateral agreements, rather than hundreds of *ad hoc* tribunals.[31] The MIC would establish a permanent body overseeing international investment disputes decisions, which would replace existing bilateral mechanisms of thousands of IIAs, including those in the EU concluded by EU Member States and other interested countries. Achieving consistency is presented as a crucial feature or purpose of the MIC. It is envisioned as a system which promotes awards in which outcomes are similar in similar situations, thus achieving a predictable legal framework and ultimately a coherent body of international investment law. Addressing current problems with ISDS, the MIC would require all parties to provide consent before either is made public according to UNCITRAL rules, and it would have rules ensuring the impartiality of judges.

While the MIC may be regarded as too ambitious to be politically feasible, others hold the creation of some kind of a multilateral dispute settlement system as essential in order to address the perceived failings of the existing system of ISDS, especially in relation to predictability, consistency, transparency, legitimacy and legal correctness.[32] The signatories of the EU's FTAs which have embraced its ICS (such as Canada) may be willing to accept the MIC at some point; however, it is difficult to imagine that it would ever win the approval of the US or China, both of which would be essential to the initiative ever becoming truly multilateral.

8. DOMESTIC FOREIGN INVESTMENT LAWS

Many states proscribe protections for foreign investors under domestic statutes, in some cases consolidating relevant laws contained in a variety of statutory and other legal instruments for the purposes of clarity and convenience. The link between national investment laws and the legal commitments contained in IIAs is captured by the phrase which indicates that the protections contained in the treaty are available only to those investments which are in conformity with the laws of the host state. This is typically labelled 'Admission of Investments'.[33] By requiring that foreign investment must be 'in accordance with its legislation', such provisions effectively incorporate by reference all of the domestic laws which have an effect on the foreign investor. By implication, if the foreign investor breaches the relevant national laws then it is not entitled to be admitted into that state's territory and the protections of the IIA do not operate.

Some countries' governments operate dedicated agencies for the assessment of incoming foreign investment projects. In Australia, for example, this is done by the Foreign Investment Review Board, a body which examines foreign investment proposals and advises the government on any implications for a national interest standpoint. This screening stage allows the host state to control

---

[31] Ibid.

[32] G Ulfstein, 'International Courts and Judges: Independence, Interaction, and Legitimacy' 46 New York University Journal of International Law and Policy 849 (2014).

[33] E.g. Japan–Iran Art. 3 (5 February 2016).

the nature of the FDI which it receives. Canada has the Investment Canada Act which imposes a 'net benefit' test on incoming foreign investors to assess whether it is in the interest of Canada and its citizens.[34] The level of scrutiny accorded to each prospective investment will vary depending on the type of industry and the country from which it originates. Between 1985 and 2017, the Canadian government reviewed and approved approximately 1,740 investments under this system. Only a handful of major proposals have been disallowed, notably in relation to cultural industries and those which may have had an impact on national security, such as those involving telecommunications.[35]

More recently, the EU has considered establishing a screening mechanism for incoming foreign investment on the basis of national security and public order. The European Commission consequently submitted a proposal to the European Parliament for a Regulation on FDI control and the EU institutions reached a political agreement on a revised version of the proposal in late 2018.[36] The new framework to screen FDI entering the EU will create a cooperation mechanism where Member States and the Commission will be able to exchange information and raise concerns related to specific investments. It will allow the Commission to issue opinions regarding whether an investment poses a threat to the security or public order of more than one Member State, or when an investment could undermine a project or programme of interest to the entirety of the EU. It will also encourage international cooperation on investment screening, including sharing experience, best practices and information on issues of common concern. According some discretion to Member States in relation to incoming FDI, the framework will establish requirements for Member States who wish to maintain or adopt a screening mechanism at national level. Prior to this initiative, only 14 EU Member States maintained national screening mechanisms for foreign investment.

Perhaps the most important domestic foreign investment screening system is the Foreign Investment Risk Review Modernization Act (FIRMMA),[37] enacted by the US Senate in 2018, which modifies the legal regime of the Committee on Foreign Investment in the US (CFIUS). FIRMMA expands the jurisdiction of the CFIUS with a view to addressing the increasing national security concerns relating to foreign investment in certain sectors, many of which were not covered by the original CFIUS – notably, real estate and joint ventures into which US technology is transferred. FIRRMA further modernizes CFIUS's processes to better enable timely and effective reviews of covered transactions. The main agenda behind FIRRMA appears to be the control of foreign investment from China in particular. Many more transactions are expected to be covered by FIRRMA, possibly requiring an increased budget for staff to handle the reviews.

The Foreign Investment Law of the People's Republic of China was announced in early 2019 and is to go into effect in 2020. It will be of great interest to international investors in the coming years. As with many domestic foreign investment laws, this new statute contains substantive standards outlining the protections available to foreign investments, and various limits thereto. For example, Article 4 of the Chinese law extends pre-establishment national treatment to foreign

---

[34] Art. 21(1).

[35] Accelero Capital Holdings' proposed acquisition of the Allstream division of Manitoba Telecom Services Inc. in October 2013.

[36] European Parliament, 'Provisional Agreement Resulting from Interinstitutional Negotiations' (6 December 2018).

[37] Title XVII S.2098 (2018).

investors, but indicates that a negative list of derivations from this protection will be published at a later stage. Article 6 states that foreign investments may not endanger China's national security or 'harm the public interests'. The statute contains a number of provisions relating to investment promotion, reserving the state's capacity to extend preferential treatment – presumably meaning investment incentives to foreign firms.[38] Addressing one of the main charges levied against China as a destination of foreign investment in recent years, China's foreign investment law promises that technology transfer will not be forced: 'the State *encourages* technological cooperation to be conducted in the course of foreign investment and on the basis of the principle of *voluntariness* and business rules.'[39] This could assuage much of the concern, especially from the US, that China has illegitimately pressured foreign firms into sharing technology, as noted earlier. It will be interesting to see whether this provision is fulfilled and to what extent Western technology will be willingly transferred to Chinese companies by the firms which invest there.

Turning away from specific national regimes, another key form of domestic law which can affect foreign investors is Environmental Impact Assessments (EIAs), which are routinely imposed by several countries as a condition of entry. EIAs require an evaluation of the effect of a physical investment project's implementation on the natural or cultural environment.[40] They constitute 'a systematic and integrative process' thought to have been developed initially in the US as a consequence of the National Environmental Policy Act.[41] EIAs allow for detailed consideration of the possible repercussions of a project prior to the adoption of a decision or the acceptance of a proposal. In *Pulp Mills on the River of Uruguay*,[42] the ICJ declared that EIAs have 'in recent years has gained so much acceptance among States that it may now be considered a requirement under general international law to undertake an environmental impact assessment where there is a risk that the proposed industrial activity may have a significant adverse impact in transboundary context'. While the specific requirements vary from country to country and in accordance with the type of project, it is common for EIAs to require some form of meaningful public participation with affected communities.[43]

9. HOME STATE CONTROLS OF FOREIGN INVESTMENT

A number of leading home states of foreign investors maintain laws which can operate to control the behaviour of their companies abroad, such as those which would arise in the context of foreign investment. Chief among these are criminal laws relating to bribery and corruption, designed to

---

[38] Art. 14.

[39] Art. 22.

[40] Ibid 1.

[41] National Environmental Policy Act 1969.

[42] Argentina v. Uruguay [2006] ICJ Rep 113 (20 April 2010).

[43] D Collins 'Environmental Impact Statements and Public Participation in International Investment Law' 7:2 Manchester Journal of International Economic Law 4–23 (2010).

prevent undue interference in the proper functioning of the government in host states, especially those in the developing world in which corruption is considered more common. Corruption is thought to undermine the effective contribution of FDI to the development of such countries. A good example of an anticorruption law aimed at foreign investors may be found in Article 3(1) of Canada's Corruption of Foreign Public Officials Act.[44] It states as follows:

> Every person commits an offence who, in order to obtain or retain an advantage in the course of business, directly or indirectly gives, offers or agrees to give or offer a loan, reward, advantage or benefit of any kind to a foreign public official or to any person for the benefit of a foreign public official
> (a) as consideration for an act or omission by the official in connection with the performance of the official's duties or functions; or
> (b) to induce the official to use his or her position to influence any acts or decisions of the foreign state or public international organization for which the official performs duties or functions.

The scope of this law is clearly wide, encompassing a broad range of conduct on the part of Canadian foreign investors.

Among the most influential regimes to combat corruption in foreign investment is the US Foreign Corrupt Practices Act (FCPA).[45] This federal statute was passed in the late 1970s and was designed to prevent US companies and their individual officers from influencing foreign officials with personal payments or rewards. With fines and imprisonment of up to five years as potential penalties, the statute prohibits US companies from securing favourable contracts, incentives or other preferential treatment in foreign countries by paying financial compensation to those who are responsible for issuing official decisions on these matters. The FCPA has been criticized for its detrimental effect on US companies' international commerce. Some believe that it discourages US firms from investing in foreign markets, particularly those in which bribery and other forms of corruption are essential to doing business.[46] It is thought to be already difficult enough for foreign firms to compete with local ones when they play by the same rules – if they are denied the ability to engage in the normal practice of bribery then successful entry and thriving in such markets could become almost impossible.

The UK Bribery Act prohibits bribery of foreign public officials as well as business to business bribery by British companies or their officers.[47] Under the statute, British firms can be convicted in UK courts for acts of corruption committed by employees, agents or subsidiaries anywhere in the world and face fines and imprisonment of a term up to ten years. Unlike the US FCPA, the UK Bribery Act does not distinguish between small and large bribery payments, meaning facilitation

---

[44] S.C. 1998, c. 34.

[45] 5 U.S.C. §§ 78dd-1, et seq.

[46] B Graham and C Stroup, 'Does Anti-Bribery Enforcement Deter Foreign Investment?' Applied Economics Letters (2016).

[47] The Bribery Act 2010, c. 23.

payments designed to expedite official required duties are prohibited. The UK statute incorporates various due diligence defences, precluding liability where the bribing company instigated adequate procedures prior to the commission of a corruption offence.

Some home states recognize civil liability for wrongdoings committed by foreign investors overseas. One of the most important domestic statutes in this regard is the US Alien Tort Statute, also known as the Alien Tort Claims Act (ATCA).[48] This federal statute from 1789 allows foreign citizens to seek remedies in US courts for human rights-oriented violations by US, and potentially non-US, companies which occurred outside the territorial jurisdiction of the US. It reads in its entirety: 'The district courts shall have original jurisdiction of any civil action by an alien for a tort only, committed in violation of the law of nations or a treaty of the United States.' The potential for this short statute to facilitate liability for US multinationals for a range of activities committed abroad has led to extensive criticism. A recent decision of the US Supreme Court (USSC), *Jesner v. Arab Bank*,[49] appears to eliminate the ATCA as a tool for claimants to bring claims against foreign multinational corporations for their employment practices overseas, limiting the much maligned corporate liability aspect of the statute, which had been unresolved in US law. Corporate entities now appear to be immune to lawsuits under the ATCA. The USSC emphasized that claimants can still sue the individual corporate employees responsible for a violation of international law under the statute. Individual corporate officers who commit covered violations could be exposed to liability in US courts if the claims sufficiently 'touch and concern' the US. It should be noted that while the USSC in *Jesner* considered corporate liability under the ATCA in general, its ultimate holding was specific to *foreign* corporations. It remains unclear whether the statute will continue to be a vehicle for claims against US corporations.

Similarly, the English common law has shown that UK corporations may also be held liable for actions committed abroad – a ruling which has considerable bearing on foreign investment of British companies. In *Lubbe v. Cape Plc*,[50] the House of Lords (now the UK Supreme Court) held that in principle it is possible to show that a parent company owes a direct duty of care in tort to anybody injured by a subsidiary company in a group, including those which are located overseas. This case concerned poor health and safety standards for employees in a South African asbestos factory which was a subsidiary of a British company. Taken together, these home state measures go some way to acknowledging the responsibility of the states in which companies are registered with respect to their international activities.

10. INVESTMENT CONTRACTS

In addition to bringing claims through IIAs, international investors may use commercial contracts to protect their assets from undue interference by host states. International economic law tends to focus more on IIA-based rights and disputes but contract-based ones are important, having formed

---

[48] 28 U.S.C. § 1350.

[49] Jesner et al. v. Arab Bank, PLC, No 16-499, 584 USSC (2018).

[50] [2000] UKHL 41.

the basis of several investment claims over the years. Host states dealing directly with foreign firms will often choose to govern their legal relations through concession agreements or other types of contracts, such as Build Operate and Transfer (BOTs) agreements.[51] Such contracts are used frequently where host states seek foreign firms' expertise for the exploitation of natural resources or to build and manage largescale infrastructure projects such as airports, bridges and hydroelectric dams. Since these arrangements are highly individualized, it is necessary to delineate the precise nature of the investor's legal relationship to the host state. Many of these instruments contain standalone rights or obligations in addition to those which are available under IIAs or under customary international law. One example of a contract-based right often granted to foreign investors that is absent from IIAs is that of the stabilization clause. Stabilization clauses promise that host states will not change their legal regimes to disadvantage the investor over the duration of the investment project. Similar to fair and equitable treatment (FET) and, in some respects, full protection and security (FPS) clauses, which will be explored in the next chapter, such provisions ensure that the law of the receiving jurisdiction will remain the same, allowing investors to plan ahead without the fear of being subjected to a sudden reversal in policy that could have severe consequences for their business activities. The breach of a stabilization clause could itself amount to a violation of the FET clause in an IIA, leading to a situation where the investor could bring claims under both the investment contract and the investment treaty – potentially raising jurisdictional issues, especially where a domestic court is willing to hear one aspect of the claim and not the other. This kind of overlap can occur because breach of contractual terms may undermine the investor's legitimate expectations.[52]

Although strictly speaking private in nature because they are essentially commercial contracts between two parties, by definition any contract must be governed by a system of national law. This is often specified in the contract's choice of law provision, typically by reference to the host state's laws or the investor's home state's laws in some cases, where the latter laws are perceived as being more sophisticated. Choice of forum clauses in such contracts enable international arbitration tribunals to take their jurisdiction over associated disputes. Such arrangements also have a clear public dimension because one of the parties is a government or a government agency funded by tax and is at least in theory accountable to its citizens. The distinction between actions undertaken by sovereign states in their capacity as sovereign states rather than as private commercial actors is a blurred one that can cause much confusion when claims are brought by investors against states in international arbitration tribunals on the basis of treaties and contracts.[53]

International investment contracts have been viewed as an effective substitute to treaties due to their capacity to protect foreign investors; however, they have had limited uptake outside of largescale infrastructure projects. This is likely because they present intractable difficulties, including costly negotiation and onerous conditions which may be prohibitive for smaller investors.[54] Only a

---

[51] D Collins, 'Sustainable International Investment Law after the Pax Americana: The BOOT on the Other Foot' 13:2 Journal of World Investment and Trade 325–48 (2012).

[52] AGIP v. Congo, 21 I.L.M. 735 (1982).

[53] I Alvik, *Contracting with Sovereignty: State Contracts and International Arbitration* (Hart, 2011).

[54] D Collins, 'Investment Contracts Are Not a Substitute for Investment Treaties' Columbia FDI Perspectives n 193 (13 February 2017).

minority of ISDS tribunals have taken their jurisdiction through investment contracts. It is worth noting that the CPTPP has further narrowed the scope for investors to make ISDS claims. For a number of signatories, the CPTPP restricts the ability to use ISDS of private companies who enter into an investment contract with the government. One of the advantages of investment contracts over IIAs is that they place obligations on the investors who are one of the parties to the contract. In any legal system, contracts are characterized by an exchange of obligations. This could be one way to compel foreign investors to adhere to environmental, human rights, cultural or other such public interest obligations in the relevant host state. A number of developing countries have indicated that they intend to renegotiate certain investment contracts with foreign investments with precisely this purpose in mind.

11. CONCLUSION

International investment law is the second major topic in international economic law, dealing with the movement of producers (companies) overseas rather than the movement of the products themselves, as in the case of trade. By locating in a foreign state, these international investors may engage in commercial activities which clash with the regulatory actions or objectives of host states. International investment law is the sphere of law which arose to deal with these conflicts. This chapter illustrated that modern international investment law is primarily contained in international treaties which are mostly constituted at the bilateral or regional level, often as specialized chapters within RTAs. There are some multilateral initiatives of moderate relevance to international investment law, including a number of nonbinding guidelines aimed at improving the behaviour of multinational firms. There are also several active proposals to create global instruments covering international investment law.

   This chapter has also drawn attention to the importance of domestic foreign investment laws as methods by which states screen incoming investments. Investment contracts were also mentioned as a source of rights for certain foreign investors. Having now introduced international investment law as a distinct field within international economic law, Chapter 7 will examine the contents of international investment treaties, uncovering the substantive legal protections which are afforded to international investors by host states.

DISCUSSION QUESTIONS

1. Why might a state consider entering into an international investment agreement either bilaterally or regionally? Would this depend on its developmental status?
2. Why is the pace of signage of international investment agreements declining and should this be a cause of concern for internationally mobile firms?
3. Why is there no global investment treaty and should there be one?
4. To what degree has 'soft law' been effective in shaping the extent and nature of foreign direct investment?

FURTHER READING

R Al-Louzi, 'Bilateral Investment Treaties as Tools for Enhancing Foreign Investment Climate and Increasing Competitiveness' 14:1 Manchester Journal of International Economic Law 69 (2017).

RP Lazo, V Desilvestro and A Bazrafkan, 'Missing Investment Treaties' 21:3 Journal of International Economic Law 703 (2018).

MM Mbengue and S Schacherer, 'The "Africanization" of International Investment Law: The Pan-African Investment Code and the Reform of the International Investment Regime' 18:3 Journal of World Investment and Trade 414 (2017).

T Meyer and TJ Park, 'Renegotiating International Investment Law' 21:3 Journal of International Economic Law 655 (2018).

7
International investment agreements: standards of protection, compensation and exceptions

1. INTRODUCTION

The previous chapter explained that the primary source of international investment law is now international investment agreements (IIAs), although customary international law had been more influential in the past and remains operative today. It also noted the role of soft law instruments and domestic foreign investment laws. Refocusing on the core source of modern international investment law, this chapter will explore the contents of IIAs, designed to mitigate political risks in host states. It will do this using various examples from around the world. The chapter will also consider – briefly, given the enormous scope of this topic – some of the investment arbitration cases which have dealt with various provisions. From this material it should become evident why international investment law is so controversial. As alluded to in the previous chapter, while IIAs assign many benefits to foreign investors, they place all of the legal obligations on host states. This chapter will begin with the first part of an IIA, appearing just below the title, which sets off the objectives of the treaty. This is known as the preamble.

2. PREAMBLE

The preamble of an international treaty does not create binding commitments on its signatory parties. However, the Vienna Convention on Law of Treaties (VCLT) Article 31 specifies that treaty provisions must be interpreted in light of the 'object and purpose of the treaty'. The preamble is often a good indicator of this. The preamble can therefore be valuable in terms of providing interpretive insight into some of the rather ambiguous standards of the treaties, as will be discussed further below. In light of this function, the preambles of most IIAs refer to the need to create favourable conditions for investments, or to encourage foreign investment.[1] Vagueness in the meaning of various terms, such as the definition of 'investment', might accordingly be construed

---

[1] UK–Vietnam (1 August 2002).

by an investment tribunal in favour of the investor, which would be needful of encouragement when making investment decisions. On the other hand, some IIAs make reference to the aim of increasing foreign investment for the purpose of advancing economic development.[2] This wording could suggest that ambiguities – again, for example, the definition of 'investment' – could be construed in favour of the state, being the beneficiary of development. Finally, the preambles of some modern IIAs mention parties' right to regulate, especially in relation to health and the environment.[3] This is an important indication of parties' underlying social agendas, possibly suggesting that the obligations incurred by states towards investors should be viewed as secondary to their duties to their citizens.

3. DEFINITIONS OF INVESTMENT AND INVESTOR

One way in which host states control the application of their commitments under IIAs is through the definition of investment and investor. Wide definitions afford protections whereas narrow ones will be restrictive, denying the application of treaty rights to parties who wish to use them. There is no settled definition of either 'investment' or 'investor' in international investment law. States are left to assert their own definitions of these terms in their individual IIAs.

3.1 Investment

The definition of investment requires an assessment of the links between the relevant entity and the host state. A good example of a definition of investment can be found in Article 1(6) of the Energy Charter Treaty (ECT):

'Investment' means every kind of asset, owned or controlled directly or indirectly by an Investor and includes:
(a) tangible and intangible, and movable and immovable, property, and any property rights such as leases, mortgages, liens, and pledges;
(b) a company or business enterprise, or shares, stock, or other forms of equity participation in a company or business enterprise, and bonds and other debt of a company or business enterprise;
(c) claims to money and claims to performance pursuant to contract having an economic value and associated with an Investment;
(d) Intellectual Property;
(e) Returns; [which is defined under Art 7(9) as]: the amounts derived from or associated with an Investment, irrespective of the form in which they are paid, including profits, dividends, interest, capital gains, royalty payments, management, technical assistance or other fees and payments in kind.

---

[2] Australia–Egypt (3 May 2001).

[3] CPTPP (8 March 2018).

This definition is clearly a wide one, encompassing all kinds of commercial activities. Some broad definitions contemplate indirect control over the investment, a departure from the concept of FDI introduced in Chapter 1. This would allow even small shareholders to bring claims under IIAs. The expansion of the definition of investment to include these more tenuous links to the host state has the effect of bringing a much wider range of commercial activities within the scope of protection of the IIA. This enlargement casts doubt on some of the alleged benefits to the receiving states associated with conventional FDI. A number of countries intentionally exclude portfolio investment from the definitions of investment contained in the treaty for this reason.[4] The inclusion of portfolio investment in the definition of investment has the potential to extend the protections available under IIAs to all kinds of entities, including a range of financial products and transactions, such as loan contracts, promissory notes and law firms. For example, in *SD Myers v. Canada*,[5] a tribunal held that a mere sales presence by a US company constituted an investment. It is difficult to see why such transient links to the host state deserve specialized protections under the IIA regime when their contributions are most likely minimal.

The meaning of investment is often established via what is known as the *Salini* Test, taken from the *Salini v. Morocco* dispute.[6] There remains much debate as to whether this test should be followed by investment tribunals, because it is more of a guideline than a set of necessary criteria.[7] The *Salini* Test states that to be an investment, the activity in question must: (1) involve the transfer of funds or the contribution of money or assets; (2) be of a certain duration; (3) include the participation of the individual transferring the funds in the management and risks associated with the project; and (4) bring economic contribution to the host state. Of these, the requirement of certain duration is probably the most difficult to satisfy. To be an investment, one must have a lasting relationship with the host state, although whether that means a few months or a few years is unclear. It probably means that a single transaction, such as a one-off contract, does not count.[8] The final aspect of the test, the obligation to contribute to the host state's development, has been rejected by some tribunals, in part because it is simply too vague to constitute an enforceable legal obligation.[9] Generally speaking, it is highly questionable whether there is an autonomous definition for investment outside that which is specified by the relevant IIA.

3.2 Investor

The definition of 'investor' requires an investigation into the claimant's relationship with the home state, meaning the country from which it originates. If the entity is not sufficiently connected to that

---

[4] Canada–Jordan Art. 1 (28 June 2009).

[5] Award, UNCITRAL (13 November 2000).

[6] Decision on Jurisdiction, ICSID Case No ARB/00/4 (23 July 2001).

[7] See e.g. A Grabowski, 'The Definition of Investment under the ICSID Convention: A Defense of *Salini*' 15:1 Chicago Journal of International Law 287 (2014).

[8] Burimi SRL and Eagle Games SH.A v. Republic of Albania, ICSID Case No ARB/11/18 Decision on Jurisdiction (29 May 2013).

[9] Quiborax v. Bolivia, ICSID Case No ARB/06/2, Decision on Jurisdiction (27 September 2012).

state, then it will not be able to claim the benefits of the IIA. Moreover, as with the definition of invest-ment, if the entity does not satisfy the definition of investor, the arbitration tribunals will not be able to take jurisdiction over the dispute. As with investment, investor is not defined in the ICSID Convention, again leaving it to states to set their own parameters in an IIA. For example, the ECT states:

'Investor' means:
(a) with respect to a Contracting Party:
(i) a natural person having the citizenship or nationality of or who is permanently resid-ing in that Contracting Party in accordance with its applicable law;
(ii) a company or other organization organized in accordance with the law applicable in that Contracting Party;
(b) with respect to a 'third state', a natural person, company or other organization which fulfils, mutatis mutandis, the conditions specified in subparagraph (a) for a Contracting Party.

Clearly only nationals of signatory states can take advantage of the treaty. Unravelling nationality can be quite complex given the elaborate corporate structuring used by many companies with branches around the world.

In addition to what might be viewed as more genuine national investors (companies establishing a genuine commercial presence in the home state), other, somewhat less legitimate investors may also rely on the protection of an IIA. In some cases, subsidiaries owned by foreign companies with limited ties to the home state, sometimes known as 'shell' or 'mailbox' companies, can rely on the protection of another home country's IIA with the host country. Investment tribunals even have permitted national investors to bring claims against their own government through a foreign subsid-iary, as in *Tokios Tokeles v. Ukraine*.[10] This so-called treaty shopping, leveraging tenuous links to the best possible host state, is often considered to be one of the features of international investment law that brings the system into disrepute. Indeed, these connections are often challenged by host states seeking to deny the advantages of their IIAs to companies with weak links to their treaty partners. The appropriate course of action for a tribunal evaluating whether the specific business structure of the alleged investor should be able to benefit from the protections afforded in the IIA is to examine the definition contained in that instrument. In one case, a tribunal found an abuse of process in the corporate reorganization carried out by the claimants (a real estate company), whose sole purpose in this action was to gain access to arbitration against the relevant host state.[11]

In addition to tighter definitions of investor, states can prevent forum shopping and ensure that the protections contained in IIAs are only available to those companies which have genuine links to the home state through Denial of Benefits provisions. These provisions permit signatory states to reserve the right to deny the protection of the IIA to a company incorporated in a party state but with no meaningful economic ties to that state. They do this by requiring that the claimant seeking to rely on the IIA must have a substantial business activity in the home state.[12]

---

[10] Award, ICSID Case No ARB/02/18 (29 April 2004).

[11] Renée Rose Levy and Gremcitel S.A. v. Republic of Peru, Award, ICSID Case No ARB/11/17 (9 January 2015).

[12] Austria–Czech Republic Art 10.13 (15 October 1990).

Twenty-first century IIAs typically include state owned enterprises within the definition of investor.[13] The omission of these business structures in older IIAs reflects the Western origins of international investment law, which lacked a tradition of governments owning a significant stake in firms engaged in international activity. The extension of the benefits of IIAs to state owned enterprises is in part due to the rise of FDI from emerging markets, especially China, where state ownership of commercial entities is more common.[14] Modern definitions of investor likely also encompass sovereign wealth funds (SWFs), which are state owned investment funds rather than companies pursuing commercial activities. These vehicles' importance to international investment law is likely to grow in the coming decades.

4. NON-DISCRIMINATION

International investment law, like international trade law, relies on the concept of non-discrimination as a source of legal protection. Much as in WTO law, there are two non-discrimination standards: national treatment and most favoured nation (MFN).

4.1 National treatment

National treatment, which is contained in most IIAs, requires that signatory states provide a regulatory environment to foreign investors which is the same as that provided to domestic investments, given that the foreign and domestic investors are in the same circumstances. Similar to trade law, the purpose of national treatment is to ensure equality of competitive conditions between equivalent domestic and foreign investors. It also seeks to prevent targeted attacks on foreign investors.[15] For host states, the obligation of national treatment is intrusive because it dictates the nature of the laws and regulations (including statutes as well as judicial and administrative decisions) which the host state is allowed to maintain, heavily interfering with its sovereignty on a wide range of matters.

National treatment tends to be limited to post-establishment investments, meaning those which have already been allowed to enter the host state and have commenced operations. The host state is free to deny entry to foreign firms, in the manner alluded to in the previous chapter, but once they have entered, discrimination is prohibited. This is one of the ways in which IIAs may be seen more as instruments of protection rather than of liberalization, as in the case of trade agreements. Some IIAs extend national treatment to pre entry situations. Pre-establishment national treatment is often limited by a 'negative list' of excluded areas of investment activity to which the treatment does not apply, or a 'positive list' of areas where it is granted. It may be difficult to ascer-

---

[13] Mexico–India (21 May 2007).

[14] Y Shima, 'The Policy Landscape for International Investment by Government-Controlled Investors: A Fact Finding Survey' OECD Working Papers on International Investment (January 2015).

[15] D Collins, 'National Treatment in Emerging Market Investment Treaties' in A Kamperman Sanders ed. *The National Treatment Principle in an EU and International Context* (Edward Elgar Publishing, 2014) 161–82.

tain how compensation would be calibrated for a breach of pre-establishment National Treatment, as no losses may have crystallized which are readily quantifiable for an investment which was never allowed to enter and therefore has not commenced its business activities.

There is much controversy in international investment law regarding the 'likeness' comparator necessary for the concept of non-discrimination to have any meaning, much in the same way as it is a live debate in international trade law relating to goods and services. In international investment law, national treatment requires 'like circumstances', with this phrase often appearing in the text of an IIA. In *SD Myers v. Canada*,[16] the phrase 'like circumstances' in NAFTA was considered, with the tribunal deciding that the foreign investor has to be in the same sector as domestic investors. In *Occidental v. Ecuador*,[17] the phrase 'like situations' found in Article II(2) of the US–Ecuador BIT was examined. Here the tribunal refused to follow *SD Myers'* sector-based test for 'circumstances' as it was too wide. In *Methanex Corporation v. USA*,[18] the tribunal rejected a GATT analysis of national treatment, stating that there must be a comparison between the foreign investor and those most closely comparable in the domestic sphere. In this case, that meant Methanex, as a manufacturer of methanol, had to be compared to other US-based manufacturers of methanol, of which there were several, all in identical circumstances to Methanex. The tribunal did not accept that Methanex should be compared to manufacturers of all or any other gasoline additives as it had sought to do, at least not when more direct and exact comparisons were available. As in the GATT, national treatment in IIAs is understood to cover both *de jure* (expressly nationality-based) and *de facto* (based on some other criteria which may be tied to nationality, even this is not stated overtly) cases.

4.2 Most favoured nation

The most favoured nation standard is found in most if not all IIAs in one form or another. It requires that signatory states must grant equal treatment to investors originating from all foreign states (as provided in other IIAs with the host state) with respect to the laws to which they are subjected. Much as with works in the WTO context, favouritism based on an investor's origin is thereby prohibited. As with national treatment, MFN is designed to ensure equality of competition opportunities among investors of different countries with whom the relevant state has signed IIAs. MFN may be limited to certain sectors or industries, or to investment in the post-establishment stage only. The most significant derogation from MFN treatment relates to preferences granted to certain foreign states under the investment chapters of RTAs which are designed to achieve particularly deep economic integration, beyond that contained in an average BIT.

It is important to understand that granting MFN protection in an IIA may restrict the host country's room for manoeuvre with regard to future investment treaties, much as it requires the state to be cognizant of which protections it has granted in other IIAs in the past. It can create a free rider problem by committing the host country to extend unilaterally to its treaty partners any additional rights that it grants to third countries in future agreements. This problem is exacerbated by the fact

---

[16] UNCITRAL Partial Award (13 November 2000).

[17] ICSID Case No ARB/06/11 (5 October 2012).

[18] 44 ILM 1345 (3 August 2005) (UNCITRAL).

that the globalization of investment has rendered corporate nationality more difficult to establish as a means of distinguishing between companies for the purposes of refining the scope of MFN. The fact that MFN tends to be extended quite broadly under the terms of many IIAs can further complicate this problem. For example, the Energy Charter Treaty guarantees MFN protection for all investment-related activities, 'including management, maintenance, use, enjoyment or disposal'.[19]

An assessment of the scope of an MFN obligation requires an investigation into the contents of treaties other than the one in which the MFN provision appears, making it somewhat more complicated than the WTO equivalent. This is because MFN allows the investor to select features from treaties with third states which may not be present in the treaty at hand. In that sense it acts as a gateway or bridge to protections in a potentially vast array of third agreements concluded by the host state, even if that state did not wish such protections to be offered to the investor in question. An investigation into the effect of MFN therefore necessitates an investigation into a second treaty.

In light of this feature of MFN, one of the main controversies with MFN is whether it was intended only to bring in substantive protections in other treaties (e.g. guarantees against expropriation) or whether it also covers procedural matters, such as dispute settlement. While it is clear that MFN should not be seen to allow the transposition of features from non-investment oriented treaties, it is not clear that it should not cover procedural matters such as dispute settlement – an issue which should only grow in importance as the nature of dispute settlement across the universe of IIAs has become highly variable. In *Maffezini v. Spain*,[20] the tribunal held that the MFN clause expressly allowed the admission of the third treaty's dispute settlement provisions. Subsequent cases, such as *Salini v. Jordan*,[21] as well as *Plama v. Bulgaria*,[22] held that *Maffezini* was wrongly decided and that invocation of the MFN clause was not meant to cover the dispute resolution provisions of a third treaty into the original one. Express statement regarding the coverage of the MFN provision (dispute settlement or not) is thought to be the most advisable course of action for signatory states to resolve this tension.

One of the key challenges arising from MFN is the possibility of treaty arbitrage, or 'treaty shopping' as it is sometimes known, mentioned earlier in relation to the definition of investor. It may be possible for a claimant to use MFN to construct a new and completely favourable treaty composed of the most advantageous features. Tribunals have been split on whether a clause may be applied via MFN in which the favourable elements of the clause are applied while unfavourable elements of the same clause are excluded.[23] Some believe that the wider the interpretation of the MFN clause, the greater the move towards liberalization;[24] of course, this is not necessarily the aim of a state's negotiation in an IIA. Therefore judgments which take a narrow, evidenced-based

---

[19] Art. 10.7.

[20] ICSID Case No ARB/97/7, Decision of the Tribunal on Objections to Jurisdiction (25 January 2000).

[21] ICSID Case No ARB/02/13 (Decision on Jurisdiction) (15 November 2004).

[22] ICSID Case No ARB/03/24 (Decision on Jurisdiction) (8 February 2005).

[23] In Siemens v. Argentina the tribunal decided that the claimant could apply only the favourable elements of a jurisdiction clause, whereas in Hochtief v. Argentina it was decided that all of the clause must be applied, including elements which were not favourable to the claimants.

[24] S Vesel, 'Clearing the Path Through a Tangled Jurisprudence: Most-Favoured Nation in Bilateral Investment Treaties' 32

approach to the interpretation of MFN clauses are likely to produce outcomes more in keeping with the true intentions of the parties to the treaties.

5. FAIR AND EQUITABLE TREATMENT (FET)

Fair and equitable treatment (FET) is a highly indeterminate standard and the one most commonly claimed in IIAs by investors. Essentially, it provides a basic level of procedural protection for foreign investors based on elements of fairness and equity, which may be thought of as an embodiment of the concept of 'due process'. In that sense it addresses more the way in which laws are applied by the host state and its various organs rather than their content. It is often thought of as a 'gap-filling' device, dealing with types of behaviour which are not captured by more specific treaty standards like national treatment. FET is linked to the international minimum standard of protection available under customary international law and in that regard perhaps is merely a restatement of this protection, particularly since it tends to appear in the same form in the many thousands of IIAs.[25]

The inherent vagueness of FET is a characteristic with which the investment tribunals themselves have struggled over the years. For example, the tribunal in *Noble Ventures v. Romania* held that FET was 'particularly difficult to define' and that it is actually a more 'general standard which finds its specific application' in other duties, such as guarantees against discrimination.[26] Still, there appears to be a very high threshold for violation of FET – it requires conduct on the part of the host state that is demonstrably unfair, even outrageous. FET may also be said to embrace some of the concepts of transparency, which is an independent standard in many IIAs that is often itself tied to the concept of good faith. The ambiguousness of FET has led some to consider it as a kind of interpretive aid to the more concrete protections offered by IIAs, rather than a source of protection in its own right.[27]

Given its broad scope and inherent flexibility, the FET standard may offer investors protection against breaches of contract, procedural impropriety and coercion or harassment by the host state. A breached contractual obligation was viewed as an FET violation in *Mondev International LTD v. United States of America*.[28] Procedural propriety and due process element of FET can be seen notably in the case *CMS Gas Transmission Company v. The Republic of Argentina*,[29] and in *ADF Group Inc v. United States*.[30] Freedom from harassment or coercion was viewed as a component of FET in *Saluka v. Czech Republic*.[31] Since there is not one single unified definition of the standard, numerous

---

Yale Journal of International Law 125 (2007).

[25] M Paparinskis, *The International Minimum Standard and Fair and Equitable Treatment* (Oxford University Press, 2013).

[26] ICSID Case No ARB/01/11 (12 October 2005).

[27] K Leite, 'The Fair and Equitable Treatment Standard: A Search for a Better Balance in International Investment Agreements' 32:1 American University International Law Review 363 (2016).

[28] ICSID Case No ARB(AF)/99/2 (Award) (11 October 2002).

[29] ICSID Case No ARB/01/8 (12 May 2005).

[30] ICSID Case No ARB(AF)/00/1, Award (9 January 2003).

[31] UNCITRAL, Partial Award (17 March 2006).

tribunals have emphasized that FET is continuously evolving, which gives investment tribunals considerable leeway in deciding if this standard has been violated in a given situation. The tribunal in *Rumeli v. Kazakhstan* also provided a useful summary of FET, noting that it consisted of the following concrete principles: transparency; good faith; and conduct which is not arbitrary, grossly unfair, unjust, discriminatory or lacking in due process, and is respectful of procedural propriety.[32] More recent tribunals have accorded protection to investors under FET by introducing a 'creeping' component to the analysis of the application of the standard, which is reminiscent of that in the context of expropriation.[33] This suggests that FET is meant to address harm which occurs gradually and which may at first be negligible, only growing to the level of liability over time. The confusion surrounding FET has led some states to include more specific limitations on FET in their IIAs, as in the case of CETA Article 8.10, which reads:

> A Party breaches the obligation of fair and equitable treatment … if a measure or series of measures constitutes:
> (a) denial of justice in criminal, civil or administrative proceedings;
> (b) fundamental breach of due process, including a fundamental breach of transparency, in judicial and administrative proceedings;
> (c) manifest arbitrariness;
> (d) targeted discrimination on manifestly wrongful grounds, such as gender, race or religious belief;
> (e) abusive treatment of investors, such as coercion, duress and harassment.

This approach has been well received by commentators as it is expected to foreclose frivolous claims by investors and provide greater predictability.[34]

Alleged violations of FET have been raised in a number of cases recently brought against Spain for the removal of incentives for investments in the renewable energy sector. For example, in *Masdar Solar & Wind v. Spain*,[35] the tribunal found that Spain was liable for breach of the FET obligation contained in the ECT in part due to the fact that Spain had made specific undertakings to investors regarding the stability of its incentive framework, which it subsequently terminated – surely an expansive understanding of the standard.

6. FULL PROTECTION AND SECURITY

The full protection and security (FPS) standard is found in most IIAs and offers protection for foreign investors against physical harm or damage to their assets which has resulted from civil unrest

---

[32] ICSID Case No ARB/05/16 (29 July 2008).

[33] El Paso v Argentina, ICSID Case No ARB/03/15 (31 October 2011).

[34] DR Amariles and A Van Waeyenberge, 'Fair and Equitable Treatment in Investor-State Dispute Settlement: A New Interpretative Framework' [2017] Journal of Business Law 632.

[35] ICSID Case No ARB/14/1 (23 May 2018).

or other incidents of violence in the host state. FPS has been claimed with much less frequency than FET, although this may change as a result of persistent unrest in parts of the world which are attractive to foreign investors (notably the Middle East with its oil reserves). It obliges the host state to provide protection to the investor in the form of police or military as well as through the enforcement of laws relating to criminal damage. While some tribunals have found otherwise,[36] FPS may be no wider than the general duty in customary international law placed on states regarding protection and security to foreign nationals, which is thought to be premised on a standard of due diligence. Indeed, it would appear as though FPS should be viewed as a standard of due diligence, meaning that it is a relative standard of protection rather than an absolute one. The host state is merely required to provide the protection to the foreign investor that is reasonable under the circumstances. The implication is that the FPS obligation is less burdensome for developing states because they have fewer resources available to devote to the police or military. This feature of FPS seems only fair in that it is likely that the high risk presented by unstable states may be precisely that which renders them attractive as destinations for investment (for example, lower taxes and lower labour costs). The investor should be taken to accept the state as it finds it.

The FPS standard tends to be framed in terms of two obligations, one of which may be described as active and the other as passive. The active part of the obligation is the requirement for the host state to ensure that unruly elements within its territory do not inflict harm on the investor's assets. This may arise in the case of riots or civil unrest where violent mobs or other groupings may engage in destructive actions. This occurred for example in *American Manufacturing & Trading (AMT) v. Zaire*.[37] The passive part of the obligation addresses the investor's entitlement to be free from harm done by the state itself, assessment of which requires evaluation of the connection between the group which has engaged in the injurious behaviour and the government. Under FPS, the host state is under both an *ex ante* and an *ex post* obligation. For *ex ante*, the state must prevent the harm from happening. It is a duty to guard against damage to the foreign investor's assets before it has taken place. The *ex post* aspect of FPS places an obligation on the host state to ensure that the unlawful element within society which has harmed the investor must be brought to justice. The riotous mob must be fully prosecuted under the criminal and potentially also the civil laws of the host state. This facet of FPS is captured by the language 'legal protection' which often comprises the standard in IIAs. While there are relatively few investment cases on FPS, the FPS standard may be poised to become more important due to ongoing civil strife and terrorism in many places where there are extensive foreign investments, where there have already been successful claims brought by investors under this standard.[38] Cybercrime may also fall within the scope of FPS.[39]

---

[36] Noble Ventures v. Romania, ICSID Case No ARB/01/11 (12 October 2005).

[37] American Manufacturing & Trading, Inc. (AMT) (US) v. Republic of Zaire, ICSID Case No ARB/93/1 Award (21 February 1997).

[38] Ampal-American Israel Corporation and others v. Arab Republic of Egypt, ICSID Case No ARB/12/11, Decision on Jurisdiction (1 February 2016).

[39] D Collins, 'Applying the Full Protection and Security Standard of International Investment Law to Digital Assets' 12:2 Journal of World Investment and Trade 225–43 (2011).

7. GUARANTEES AGAINST EXPROPRIATION WITHOUT COMPENSATION

The protection of foreign investors from expropriation is a very old principle of international economic law and in many respects was one of its founding principles, as alluded to in Chapter 1. Lasting economic activity will not be undertaken in foreign territories if there is a risk that all of the effort expended will simply be seized by authorities. Clearly, states are permitted to expropriate property within their territories in accordance with the principle of permanent sovereignty over natural resources (PSNR).[40] Although it is arguably also an aspect of customary international law, most IIAs tend to affirm the state's right of expropriation. Still, in order for the expropriation to be lawful, the state must satisfy four conditions, which are normally stipulated in IIAs. For example, the USMCA states:

1. No Party shall expropriate or nationalize a covered investment either directly or indirectly through measures equivalent to expropriation or nationalization (expropriation), except: (a) for a public purpose; (b) in a non-discriminatory manner; (c) on payment of prompt, adequate, and effective compensation in accordance with paragraphs 2, 3, and 4; and (d) in accordance with due process of law.[41]

Taking each of these requirements in turn, the concept of public purpose is very broad and notoriously difficult to define. It is difficult for a foreign investor to challenge this aspect of the taking, yet tribunals often find themselves evaluating this component of the four-stage test. For example, in *SPP v. Egypt*,[42] the tribunal recognized that the host state's cancellation of the project in order to protect its archaeological and cultural heritage constituted a lawful exercise of the right to expropriate, meaning that it was effectively in the public interest. It may be easiest to think of public interest as being satisfied when the taking is not for the private gain of the ruler but is instead tied to the economic or social needs of the country concerned, as in the case with land expropriations for the purposes of a new railway line.

Second, the measure comprising the expropriation must not be arbitrary and discriminatory within the generally accepted meaning of those terms, echoing national treatment. This implies that the taking by the government must not target property that belongs to a foreign investor. Put more practically, there must be some reason for the taking of that particular property that is not related to the nationality of its owner. For example, in *ADC v. Hungary* the tribunal ascertained that the state had acted in a discriminatory manner because it expropriated the only foreign company, leaving the equivalent domestic firm untouched.[43]

Third, the principle of due process must be observed during the expropriation. Due process is a minimum standard in customary international law and is also contemplated by the FET standard discussed above. It will likely involve observing practices such as reasonable notice before the

---

[40] General Assembly Resolution 1803 (XVII) (14 December 1962).

[41] Art. 14.8.

[42] ICSID Case No ARB/84/3 (20 May 1992).

[43] ICSID Case No ARB/03/16 (2 October 2006).

expropriation takes place, an explanation of the purpose, and a chance to object. If local courts are available to challenge governments' unfair treatment of investors in terms of expropriations, then due process should be satisfied.[44]

Finally, lawful expropriation requires that the taking must be accompanied by some form of monetary compensation. Investors must receive the monetary value of the assets which they have lost or, in the case of indirect expropriation, which reflects the extent to which the assets to which they still retain title have declined in value as a consequence of the host state's actions. This is examined further below, as is the precise measure of compensation.

The four requirements of lawful expropriation must be fulfilled cumulatively, meaning that even if full compensation is paid, if the taking was discriminatory or it failed to follow due process, or if it lacked a public purpose, it will be deemed illegal. If the expropriation is determined to be illegal, then it will carry greater consequences in terms of payments to injured investors, as will be seen later in this chapter.

7.1 Direct expropriation

In addition to the lawful/unlawful dichotomy, there are two other ways of categorizing expropriation: direct and indirect. Direct expropriation covers situations in which the host state takes possession of property held by a foreign investor usually via formal legislation, resulting in the loss of all or almost all useful control of property. This is the most blatant form of expropriation and consequently its definition is more straightforward. Direct expropriation may be further subdivided into nationalization, which is the taking of property as part of a government or social programme. This would fall within the definition of public purpose noted above. On the other hand, confiscation is taking of property for personal gain. Since this does not serve a public purpose, this kind of expropriation is unlawful. Thankfully, direct expropriation is relatively rare in the modern era, although there have been recent incidents in Venezuela and Argentina. Some Western politicians continue to advocate for widescale nationalization of industry, although these policies tend to have limited appeal or economic benefit.

To take one recent example of a direct expropriation, in *Koch Minerals Sàrl and Koch Nitrogen International Sàrl v. Venezuela*,[45] the Chávez government of Venezuela nationalized two fertilizer plants owned by a Swiss investor. The investor brought claims under the Venezuela–Switzerland BIT relating to expropriation and other matters. On the issue of expropriation the tribunal ruled that Venezuela had acted in the public interest and had followed due process of law – therefore the expropriation was lawful. Still, compensation, which had not been paid by the Venezuelan government, was ordered.

7.2 Indirect expropriation

Far more controversially, and much more commonly argued in investment tribunals, indirect expropriation is where there is interference with the ownership of property by the host state without

---

[44] A Newcombe, L Paradell, *The Law and Practice of Investment Treaties: Standards of Treatment* (Kluwer, 2009).

[45] ICSID Case No ARB/11/19 (7 December 2017).

it being covered by a specific, official law or decree. The host state's action has the same impact of taking without actually taking it – title is retained by the investor. Indirect expropriation also encompasses measures 'tantamount to expropriation' in which useful enjoyment of the asset is lost even though some control remains. Another category, 'creeping expropriation', refers to expropriation which takes place incrementally, requiring a determination of the precise point at which the state's measures become actionable. Tribunals have refused to find an expropriation in cases where the investor managed to maintain the necessary control to keep the investment going despite the fact that the company's profitability was diminished.[46] The timeframe is a significant element to be taken into account and permanent deprivations will more clearly demonstrate evidence of expropriation.[47] Tribunals will focus on the effects of the measure upon the investment instead of the intention or the purpose of the government measure.[48]

Given that indirect expropriation does not manifest itself in a formal legal taking, it can be difficult to ascertain whether it has taken place or whether the state is simply engaging in normal regulation. Some home country measures may be a lawful exercise of governmental powers without amounting to an actionable expropriation. Non-discriminatory measures by the host state aiming at improving competition or consumer or environmental protection may be viewed as measures which guarantee the functioning of the state and therefore lie within the decision making power of the state.[49]

The line between indirect expropriation and non-compensable governmental regulation is often blurred, requiring examination on a case by case basis. Expressly including protection from indirect expropriation in an IIA will limit a host state's ability to impose regulations in the interests of its citizens without creating liability to compensate foreign investors. This requires a state to consider the impact of legislation and regulation on foreign investors in a way which it does not have to consider in terms of domestic investors. Some modern IIAs have tightened the definition of expropriation to exclude certain types of regulatory actions, affording them greater policy space. For example, the investment chapter of the CPTPP contains an Annex on Expropriation which states the following:

3. The second situation addressed by Article 9.8.1 (Expropriation and Compensation) is indirect expropriation, in which an action or series of actions by a Party has an effect equivalent to direct expropriation without formal transfer of title or outright seizure.

(a) The determination of whether an action or series of actions by a Party, in a specific fact situation, constitutes an indirect expropriation, requires a case-by-case, fact-based inquiry that considers, among other factors:

(i) the economic impact of the government action, although the fact that an action or series of actions by a Party has an adverse effect on the economic value of an investment, standing alone, does not establish that an indirect expropriation has occurred;

(ii) the extent to which the government action interferes with distinct, reasonable investment-backed expectations; and

---

[46] LG&E v. Argentina, ICSID Case No ARB/02/1 (3 October 2006).

[47] Azurix v. Argentina, ICSID Case No ARB/01/12 (14 July 2006).

[48] Metalclad Corporation v. United Mexican States, ICSID Case No ARB (AF)/97/1 (30 August 2000).

[49] M Sornarajah, *The International Law on Foreign Investment* (Cambridge University Press, 2018).

(iii) the character of the government action.

(b) Non-discriminatory regulatory actions by a Party that are designed and applied to protect legitimate public welfare objectives, such as public health, safety and the environment, do not constitute indirect expropriations, except in rare circumstances.[50]

This more measured approach contrasts sharply with earlier IIAs in which no definition of indirect expropriation was supplied, leaving greater discretion to tribunals. It may be expected that these kinds of annexes will become standard in the coming years. For now, there is a tendency on the part of foreign investors to seek to extend the understanding of the concept of indirect expropriation to cover a broad assortment of governmental actions that have a detrimental impact on business activities.

For example, in the recent case *A11Y LTD. v. Czech Republic*,[51] a UK-based developer of assistive technology solutions for people with sensory disabilities alleged that the respondent state targeted its business and ultimately destroyed its investment through indirect expropriation in the form of the imposition of price caps and other restrictions on the delivery of its service. The tribunal decided that the language contained in various statements issued by the respondent state was neutral and applied uniformly to all companies – they did not target the claimant and were therefore not discriminatory. With regard to other acts of the Czech government, the tribunal found that there had not been an expropriation because much of the loss suffered by the investor was due to the fact that its business model was unsustainable in the longer term and in fact was 'doomed to fail', rather than the result of the state's interference.

8. MEASURE OF COMPENSATION AND DAMAGES

The assessment of compensation for breach of IIAs is one of the most complicated aspects of international investment law, rendered all the more so by the fact that these determinations are made by arbitrators in ISDS tribunals, which are themselves the subject of much criticism for their inconsistencies, as will be explored in Chapter 8. While compensation for breach of international investment treaties is an immense and complex subtopic, a number of key principles stand out. The first of these is that the rules on compensation for breach of international investment law are derived primarily from the law on expropriation. The treaties are silent on compensation for other types of breach and therefore compensation tends to be extrapolated from the principles developed in relation to this kind of injury. Second, and perhaps most importantly, the remedy for breach of international investment law is wholly distinct from that of international trade law. When host states are found liable for violating one of their commitments under an IIA by an investment tribunal the normal obligation is that they compensate the injured investor in the form of cash. The host state is not required to remove or withdraw their illegal or harmful measure as under the WTO dispute settlement system. In that sense, international investment law is less

---

[50] Annex 9-B.

[51] ICSID Case No UNCT/15/1 (26 July 2018).

intrusive than international trade law. Of course, it is not always feasible for countries to pay out compensation awards to injured investors, especially when they are poorly resourced developing countries. This is one of the main criticisms of international investment arbitration – the awards are often seen to be punishingly high, transferring money from taxpaying ordinary citizens to well-financed multinational enterprises. Still, from a sovereignty perspective this may seem like a more appropriate remedy. It may also offer greater satisfaction to the winning party in ISDS, which secures tangible gains that are often elusive to individual traders in the WTO context.

When assessing compensation in international investment law it is useful to think of the matter in terms of two categories, depending on whether the measure which the state enacted was lawful or unlawful, as discussed above. This distinction reflects the expropriation-based origins of compensation. Recall that expropriation is fundamentally lawful if it is done in the public interest and compensation is paid, but it may also be unlawful if there is no public interest, if the measure was disproportionate to the public interest or if it was discriminatory.

8.1 Lawful expropriation: the Hull Formula

The dominant method of compensation in IIAs is the Hull Formula, which specifies that there must be 'prompt, adequate and effective' compensation provided by the host state to the injured investor. 'Prompt' means that the monetary compensation should be paid as soon as possible after the expropriation or other illegal measure has occurred (which may require a determination by the arbitration tribunal), or else interest may be payable. 'Adequate' is normally thought to mean compensation in an amount representing the fair market value of the investment which was expropriated or otherwise harmed – a phrase which sometimes appears in IIAs.[52] Reference to the market may be problematic as there may be no market because the asset is unique, or possibly because the jurisdiction in which it is located does not operate under normal market conditions. Fair market value refers to a normal arm's length unforced sale, rather than one between related companies or in which there is some compulsion, possibly because of knowledge that an expropriation is imminent. 'Effective' simply means that the monetary compensation must be paid in a currency that is fully transferable, meaning one which can be readily converted into US dollars, euros, pounds sterling and so on. It is not much help to an investor to be paid in a currency which is rapidly depreciating, or which is not recognized by the central banks of other countries.

8.2 Lawful expropriation: the Calvo Doctrine

The counterpoint to the Hull Formula in terms of gauging the extent of compensation for a fundamentally lawful measure is the Calvo Doctrine, named after Argentine jurist Carlos Calvo. Its application may be inferred from the absence of a Hull Formula in the IIA because in many respects it acts as a reiteration of the National Treatment rule. It can also be found in investment contracts with Latin American countries. Under the Calvo Doctrine, foreigners operating within the state should receive compensation which is the same as that which is accorded to nationals. This treat-

---

[52] CETA 8.12(2).

ment is enshrined in the constitutions of some Latin American countries.[53] In order to ascertain the degree of compensation owed to the foreign investor under this method, the domestic law on takings – or other kinds of governmental liability, for that matter – needs to be consulted. The state will pay what it would owe if the matter had been purely domestic, brought by a local investor in a local court.[54] This may be dissatisfying to a foreign investor if the normal level of compensation to companies for state actions, such as takings, is something less than fair market value.

8.3 Unlawful expropriation: Chorzow Factory damages

The remedy for an illegal expropriation, and potentially other types of treaty violation, will be determined by the general rules of state responsibility under international law. Compensation for unlawful expropriation is better termed as 'damages' in order to clarify the difference between these awards and those associated with lawful expropriation. The famous *Chorzow Factory* expropriation case of the PCIJ in 1928 (the PCIJ was the forerunner of the modern ICJ) is often cited as the classic statement on compensation for wrongful acts by states under international law.

> Reparation must, as far as possible, wipe out all the consequences of an illegal act re-establish the situation which would, in all probability, have existed if that act had not been committed. Restitution in kind, or if this is not possible, payment of a sum corresponding to the value which a restitution in kid would bear; the award, if need be, of damages for loss sustained which would not be covered by restitution in kind or compensation for an act contrary to international law.[55]

This theory is further expressed in the Articles on State Responsibility, often viewed as a codification of customary international law: 'The responsible State is under an obligation to make full reparation for the injury caused by the internationally wrongful act.'[56] The Articles explain that the state which is responsible for an internationally wrongful act is 'under an obligation to compensate for the damage caused … in so far as damage is not made good by restitution' and, crucially: 'compensation shall cover any financially assessable damage including loss of profits.'[57] It is essential to recognize, however, that the *Chorzow Factory* edict concerned an unlawful expropriation, meaning one which did not satisfy one of the requirements of due process, non-discrimination, public purpose and compensation itself. It was not meant to capture the amount of compensation owing upon a lawful expropriation or whether compensation is specified by reference to the Hull Formula.

The tribunal in the NAFTA dispute *SD Myers* considered the difference between compensation for lawful takings and damages for unlawful ones, noting that the former may not include amounts linked

---

[53] Art. 136 Constitution of Peru (as amended, 1979).

[54] S Montt, *State Liability in Investment Treaty Arbitration* (Hart, 2011) chapter 1.

[55] Factory at Chorzow (Germany v. Poland) PCIJ Rep (1928) Series A, No 13.

[56] Art. 31(1).

[57] Art. 36.

to future profits.[58] In that case, the investor was awarded compensation based on a denial of national treatment, not an expropriation. Including the lost profit stream in an assessment of damages will in most cases result in a higher overall quantum than simply repaying the value of the investment itself. Receiving what the investment would be worth in the market will not cover lost income streams going forward, at least in the case of a successful business over a long period of time. Under this logic, breaches of international investment law as contained in IIAs will tend to be compensated by the host state's payment to the investor of some combination of future profits and the value of the investment project which was either damaged or seized. In most cases damages (or restitution) will amount to more money, possibly because they are intended to redress behaviour that was fundamentally unlawful in a way that taking property is not. Unfortunately this approach is not always reflected in the actual disputes, which tend to treat the issue of compensation, as with most matters in international investment law, on a case by case basis, where compensation based on future projections such as lost profits is not always practical.

9. CAPITAL TRANSFERS

Most IIAs guarantee that investors will be able to transfer the profits they make from their enterprise abroad to their home state. Such provisions prevent situations in which the wealth which foreign investors generate from their business activities is frozen in a foreign bank account and is therefore useless. This is precisely why the IMF requires its members to remove impediments on capital movement where possible, as will be explored in Chapter 9. These provisions in IIAs tend to be phrased with exhaustive language recalling the definition of investment, as in the EU–Singapore Investment Protection Agreement:

1. Each Party shall permit all transfers relating to a covered investment to be made in a freely convertible currency without restriction or delay. Such transfers include:
    (a) contributions to capital such as principal and additional funds to maintain, develop or increase the covered investment;
    (b) profits, dividends, capital gains and other returns, proceeds from the sale of all or any part of the covered investment or from the partial or complete liquidation of the covered investment;
    (c) interest, royalty payments, management fees, and technical assistance and other fees;
    (d) payments made under a contract entered into by the covered investor, or its covered investment, including payments made pursuant to a loan agreement;
    (e) earnings and other remuneration of personnel engaged from abroad and working in connection with a covered investment;
    (f) payments made pursuant to Article 2.6 (Expropriation) and Article 2.5 (Compensation for Losses);
    (g) payments arising under Article 3.18 (Award).[59]

---

[58] UNCITRAL, Second Partial Award (21 October 2002).

[59] Article 2.7(1).

This entitlement is tempered by statements which allow host states to impose reasonable restrictions on transfers of capital where the investor has become bankrupt or must pay a fine in the host state. Very few disputes have been brought under investor–state arbitration involving the breach of transfer clauses.[60] This may be because it is more likely that these types of claims would be framed as expropriations, since in denying repatriation of its assets the investor loses the enjoyment of its investment.

The CPTPP contains additional derogations from the investment chapter's material on transfer obligations in a series of Annexes for each of the signatory parties. For example, Chile reserves the right to maintain or adopt measures to ensure currency stability and the normal operation of domestic and foreign payments. Such measures include the establishment of restrictions or limitations on current payments and transfers (capital movements) to or from Chile, as well as transactions related to them, such as requiring that deposits, investments or credits from or to a foreign country be subject to a reserve requirement.[61] The IMF would most likely support these limitations in line with its objective of ensuring the solvency of its member states.

10. SENIOR MANAGEMENT AND PERSONNEL

Many older IIAs include a commitment regarding the investor's ability to bring personnel with them into the host state for the purpose of the investment activity. These clauses were often entitled 'Entry and Sojourn of Personnel'.[62] In modern IIAs these entitlements tend to appear, in somewhat modified form, in provisions labelled 'Senior Management and Boards of Directors', as in Article 9.11 of the CPTPP:

1. No Party shall require that an enterprise of that Party that is a covered investment appoint to a senior management position a natural person of any particular nationality.
2. A Party may require that a majority of the board of directors, or any committee thereof, of an enterprise of that Party that is a covered investment, be of a particular nationality or resident in the territory of the Party, provided that the requirement does not materially impair the ability of the investor to exercise control over its investment.

The host state will most likely want the foreign investor to bring skilled workers in order to transfer knowledge, as it is understood that technology transfer is one of the advantages of FDI. But it may wish these people to retain some links to the host state, preventing premature departure or exploitation, one of the recognized risks of FDI. Having foreign investors controlled by noncitizens also raises national security risks, which will be discussed further below. There are few, if any, publicly available disputes engaging these types of provisions.

---

[60] OI European Group v. Venezuela ICSID Case No ARB/11/25 (2 March 2015).

[61] Annex 9-E.

[62] India–China Art. 11 (terminated).

11. PROHIBITIONS ON PERFORMANCE REQUIREMENTS

Performance requirements are conditions imposed on foreign investors by host states either in terms of their entry or their ongoing operations. They were explored in the previous chapter in relation to the WTO's TRIMs Agreement. Some believe that prohibitions on performance requirements, such as mandatory technology transfers, are harmful to host states. In other words, developing countries should be allowed to compel foreign companies to share their technology with the host state as a condition of entering their territory and operating within it. It is thought that technology transfer is essential to distribute technological gains from wealthy countries to those which are in the process of developing.[63] It is difficult to make this argument with respect to China, which enjoys almost unparalleled economic dominance worldwide. Prohibitions on performance requirements are common to IIAs because such requirements are considered burdensome for foreign investors. Many treaties simply incorporate the TRIMs' rules and as such do not control measures beyond those which are envisioned by the TRIMs.[64] For example, the ASEAN Comprehensive Agreement on Investment affirms the TRIMs in its provision on performance requirement prohibitions, but adds that member states (of ASEAN) will undertake assessments of performance requirements within two years of the date of the agreement in order to review existing performance requirements and assess whether an expansion beyond merely a reiteration of TRIMs is necessary.[65] Such terms limit a party's capacity to impose performance requirements only to the extent that they were inconsistent with the TRIMs – it would not control a broader range of performance requirements referenced in some IIAs. Broader performance requirement prohibitions in IIAs are sometimes referred to as TRIMs+ obligations because they go beyond the trade-related investment measures indicated in the TRIMs. These include conditions such as mandatory technology transfer.[66] In prohibiting a wider range of performance requirements beyond those which relate to local content in goods, parties to such agreements aim to further liberalize their market for inward FDI, attracting more firms by placing fewer obligations upon them.[67]

The performance requirement prohibitions in the investment chapter of NAFTA were considered by a tribunal in *Mobil Investments and Murphy Oil v. Canada*.[68] The tribunal determined that the provincial government's imposition of a requirement on foreign investors to spend several million dollars per year in research and development as well as education and training was a breach of NAFTA's prohibition on performance requirements, contained in Article 1106(1) c) regarding the mandatory purchase of local goods or services. Canada argued that the research

---

[63] A Kamperman Sanders, 'Incentives and Obstacles for Innovation' in D Prévost, I Alexovicova, JH Pohl eds *Restoring Trust in Trade* (Hart, 2018).

[64] New Zealand–China Art. 140 (7 April 2008).

[65] Art. 7(2).

[66] E.g. Korea–Australia Art 11.9 (17 February 2014) and USMCA Art. 14.10.

[67] United Nations, 'Towards Coherent Policy Frameworks: Understanding Trade and Investment Linkages, Economic and Social Commission for Asia and the Pacific' (United Nations, 2007).

[68] ICSID Case No ARB(AF)/07/4, Decision on Liability (22 May 2012).

and education requirements did not necessarily compel the purchase of or preference for local goods or services and as such did not constitute prohibited performance requirements under the treaty. Canada further attempted to distinguish between prohibited sourcing/local content performance requirements, which would have the purpose of protecting the domestic market, and the research and education requirements, which were aimed at strengthening the country's knowledge capacity and promoting sustainable development. The *Mobil* tribunal found that Canada's measures relating to research and education were performance requirements because they were compulsory, constituting a legal requirement, and also because the meaning of 'services' within that article was held to be sufficiently broad to cover the research and development and education and training obligations. The tribunal's ruling came in spite of the arguably justifiable public policy goal (the improvement of a historically economically disadvantaged region of Canada) behind the requirements.

12. EXCEPTIONS

Exceptions provide nations with a means of addressing policy needs and maintaining autonomy over the domestic economy as well as society in general. As well as moderating expectations and deterring investor behaviour which may be harmful to the host state, they may reduce asymmetry of power for poorer developing nations in certain circumstances and prevent unreasonable compensation arising from attempts to respond to such actions. The extent to which international investment law has accommodated what might be termed public policy or social issues is a matter of extensive debate, especially in academia. The general consensus is that IIAs have performed this role poorly – they have failed to take adequate measures to ensure that FDI is conducted in a manner that does not harm the environment, human rights, culture and other such matters. This accusation forms part of the larger criticism that IIAs are onesided – they do not impose any functional obligations on investors. All of the obligations are borne by the host state, which must use its domestic laws to ensure that investors do not behave in a way which is harmful to its citizens. Rather than imposing obligations on investors, which would be difficult in a treaty between two states to which investors are not a party, public policy issues have been handled as exceptions to the state's obligations. Host states are therefore able, in theory, to violate other parts of the treaty, using these provisions as a justification, potentially precluding or reducing the payment of compensation.

Traditional IIAs, meaning BITs, entirely lacked exceptions for public interest issues. The investment chapters of IIAs began to use language inspired by the General Exceptions to the GATT (Article XX) and the GATS (Article XIV) mentioned earlier in this book. This was a conservative approach in that there was nothing new in this language and it was accompanied by a reasonably significant body of WTO jurisprudence. But, as noted earlier, these standards have become somewhat antiquated, given that they were drafted in the 1940s (the GATS in the 1990s).[69] To date only a small number of ISDS tribunals have actually considered GATT-style general exceptions in an IIA.

---

[69] D Collins, 'The Line of Equilibrium: Improving Investment Arbitration through the Application of the WTO General Exceptions' 32:4 Arbitration International 575–87 (2016).

In *Bear Creek Mining v. Peru*,[70] the tribunal ruled that successful invocation of one of the General Exceptions would not waive the obligation to pay compensation for expropriation, although it could conceivably reduce compensation for other matters. In *Copper Mesa v. Ecuador*,[71] the tribunal found that a General Exception was not applicable because the respondent state's measure was applied in an arbitrary manner, violating the chapeau. There is no indication how tribunals will evaluate the concepts of 'necessary' or 'relating to' contained in GATT-inspired general exceptions, suggesting that further clarification is needed here. Modern IIAs, especially investment chapters in RTAs, often engage with public interest issues by way of dedicated chapters which apply equally to investment as well as trade and other obligations. Some of the key policy issues will now be explored in closer detail.

12.1 Essential security

National security threats from FDI may endanger critical services, increasing the risk of infiltration, sabotage or surveillance. This is why essential security exceptions are common to IIAs. These provisions tend to be similarly worded to the essential security exceptions found in WTO law. For example, Article 22.5 of the China–Hong Kong Closer Economic Partnership Agreement states: 'This Agreement shall not be construed … to prevent one side from taking any measures that it considers necessary to protect its essential security interests.' As in WTO law, the phrase 'that it considers necessary' appears to shelter this provision from the scrutiny of an investment tribunal – it is up to each party to decide whether a matter raises an essential security concern. As suggested in Chapter 5, some believe that there remains some capacity for an international court to evaluate whether an essential security provision has been used in good faith,[72] although it is difficult to imagine that many states would accept an adverse judgment in this regard.

Essential security is linked to the necessity defence found in customary international law enshrined in Article 25 of the Articles on State Responsibility, which was considered by a number of investment tribunals in several claims brought against Argentina.[73] Under this concept the state must establish that there was a situation of grave and imminent peril, that escape from obligation was the only way and that the state did not itself contribute to the situation of necessity. In *CMS v. Argentina*,[74] it was found that the financial crisis was not so severe as to come under the necessity clause, as there was no total economic and social collapse. In *LG&E v. Argentina*,[75] the tribunal formulated a test which considered the necessity provisions of the IIA followed by the extent of

---

[70] ICSID Case No ARB/14/21, Award (30 November 2017).

[71] UNCITRAL, PCA Case No 2012-2, Award (15 March 2016).

[72] S Schill and R Briese, '"If the State Considers": Self-Judging Clauses in International Dispute Settlement' 13 Max Planck Yearbook of United Nations Law 61 (2009).

[73] CMS Gas Transmission Company v. The Republic of Argentina, ICSID Case No ARB/01/8 (12 May 2005); Enron Corporation and Ponderosa Assets, L.P. v. Argentine Republic, ICSID Case No ARB/01/3 (22 May 2007), Sempra Energy International v. The Argentine Republic, ICSID Case No ARB/02/16 (28 September 2007).

[74] Ibid.

[75] LG&E Energy Corp v. Argentina, ICSID Case No ARB/02/1, Decision on Liability (3 October 2006).

the necessity under customary international law. It found that the defence was only applicable in times of war but acknowledged that it can be invoked for a short period of time. Subsequently, in *Enron v. Argentina*,[76] the tribunal ruled that the financial crisis was not sufficiently severe to trigger the necessity defence. This was followed by *Sempra v. Argentina*,[77] as well as *Continental Casualty v. Argentina*,[78] where the tribunals distinguished *CMS* and *Enron*, noting in agreement with *LG&E* that essential security included political, military and economic security. Collectively, the Argentina cases are thought to demonstrate that the necessity defence and the essential security provision in IIAs may be raised for severe economic or financial emergencies, because the adverse impact of such crises can be equivalent to the disastrous impact of war.[79]

12.2 Labour issues

The plight of those who work for multinational enterprises is at the forefront of the criticisms facing international investment, if not economic globalization generally. There is the persistent, but likely untrue, belief that foreign firms seeking to lower labour costs overseas operate 'sweatshops' in which workers are subjected to unsafe conditions and exploitative wages. Many Western firms actually offer higher paying, more rewarding jobs than domestic employers not because they are required to by either domestic or international law, but because this is good business. IIAs have been slow to address labour issues, but some provisions are worth noting.

Many agreements simply reiterate parties' obligations under the International Labour Organization Declaration on Fundamental Principles and Rights at Work.[80] These encapsulate a very basic level of protection, covering such issues as freedom of association and the effective recognition of the right to collective bargaining, the elimination of all forms of forced labour and the abolition of child labour. Another mode of safeguarding labour found in investment agreements are non-lowering provisions, where the parties commit themselves to not lower their labour standards or to derogate from labour law in order to attract investment. For example, the Canada Model BIT, which does not reference labour, does prohibit the relaxing of standards in health and safety for this purpose.[81] The Japan–Vietnam Bilateral Investment Treaty of 2003 achieves this by including a statement in its preamble that the growth of foreign investment can be achieved without weakening health measures. This 'standstill' method, while not as progressive as clear cut improvements in labour protections, represent a step forward in terms of normalizing these objectives in international investment law.

More ambitiously, chapter 23 of USMCA, based on chapter 19 of the CPTPP, set far-reaching labour-oriented goals including the elimination of sex-based discrimination in the workplace (Ar-

---

[76] Enron Corp Ponderosa Asset LP v. Argentina, ibid.

[77] Sempra Energy International v. Argentina, ibid.

[78] Continental Casualty Co v. Argentina, ICSID Case No ARB/03/9 (Award) (5 September 2008).

[79] W Moon, 'Essential Security Interests in International Investment Agreements', 15:2 Journal of International Economic Law' 481 (2012).

[80] CPTPP Art. 19.2.

[81] Art. 11.

ticle 23.9), the protection of migrant workers (Article 23.8), acceptable conditions of work and minimum wages (Article 23.3). The USMCA specifies that parties should endeavour to encourage enterprises to voluntarily adopt corporate social responsibility (CSR) initiatives on labour issues that have been endorsed or are supported by that party.[82] The USMCA also contains provisions on cooperation between parties regarding good practice in labour laws. Parties may request dialogue with each other on labour issues at any time by delivering a written request to a contact point that the other party has designated.[83] In a similarly progressive move, the India Model BIT includes in its General Exceptions measures aimed at 'improving working conditions'.[84] China included a Memorandum of Understanding on Labour Cooperation as part of its free trade agreement with New Zealand, acknowledging the need to maintain a safe working environment for employees. As yet there are no available investment arbitration cases which have addressed labour-based exceptions contained in IIAs, although such claims may be expected in the future given such features are far more common today than they were in the past.

Linked to labour, health-oriented disputes are much more common. For example, the NAFTA disputes *Methanex* and *Metalclad*, mentioned earlier, dealt with chemical substances that posed harm to human health. Several disputes were brought against Canada under NAFTA in relation to its regulation of products which represented various risks to public health.[85] Another high profile dispute which touched on public health issues was *Vattenfall v. Germany*,[86] regarding a Swedish nuclear power plant manufacturer which initiated a claim based on Germany's decision to discontinue the construction of nuclear power plants because of the risk of radiation emission in the event of a catastrophe. The *Philip Morris v. Australia* dispute concerned a tobacco company's allegation that the host state's plain packaging requirement for cigarettes aimed at reducing smoking amounted to an indirect expropriation of the investor's intellectual property rights.[87] Unfortunately, there has been relatively little by way of arbitral reasoning in terms of the precise application of health-based justifications in IIAs. The regulation of public health, as an aspect of worker or consumer safety, is likely to be a source of much tension between investors and host states in the coming years.

12.3 Culture and human rights

As noted in Chapter 5 in relation to international trade, culture is an ambiguous concept which, if safeguarded in an international treaty, could accord signatory states a wide margin of regulatory freedom which could operate against the goal of liberalization. The phrase 'public morals' found

---

[82] Art. 23.7.

[83] Art. 23.11.

[84] Art. 16.1 vi).

[85] Dow Agrosciences v. Canada (UNCITRAL, 2011) (pesticide); Chemtura v. Canada (UNCITRAL, 2010) (food product ban); SD Myers v. Canada (UNCITRAL, 2000) (industrial waste transport prohibition); Ethyl Corp v. Canada (UNCITRAL, 1998) (unleaded gasoline mixture ban).

[86] ICSID Case No ARB/12/12 (2 July 2013).

[87] UNCITRAL, PCA Case No 2012-12 (31 May 2012).

in the General Exceptions of many international economic law instruments, including IIAs, is often thought to encompass culture. For example, the India Model BIT includes in its General Exceptions measures designed to protect 'national treasures or monuments of artistic, cultural, historic or archaeological value'.[88] The Canada Model BIT goes further by specifying that none of the obligations in the agreement apply to investments in cultural industries.[89]

Several investment arbitration disputes have addressed the subject of cultural protection. In one dispute the sanctity of the ancient Giza pyramid site near Cairo was threatened by the construction of a foreign hotel.[90] After the project began, the Egyptian public complained that the project could harm undiscovered archaeological artefacts in the area. The Egyptian government consequently halted all construction on the basis of its need to protect its cultural heritage. The tribunal ruled, however, that the site's archaeological status as a World Heritage Site did not preclude the requirement to compensate the investor. Had there been a cultural exception in the relevant IIA the result might have been different. Similarly, in *Parkerings v. Lithuania*,[91] an investment tribunal assessed whether cultural preservation could operate as a justification for the breach of contract between the local government of the city of Vilnius and the Norwegian investor which had won a concession to operate a car park in the town's historic town centre. Although there was no express cultural exception in the Lithuania–Norway BIT, the tribunal held that the refusal of the project was justified on the basis of historical and archaeological conservation, a finding which was supported by the site's status as a UNESCO culturally protected area. The tribunal in *Lemire v. Ukraine* considered whether cultural protection could justify breach of a host state's commitments to foreign investors with respect to the granting of radio and television licences. The tribunal ruled in favour of the host state, holding that it would not second-guess the regulation of cultural industries by Ukraine. The tribunal stated that the right to regulate 'extends to promulgating regulations which define the State's own cultural policy' and that this right is 'reinforced in cases where the purpose of the legislation affects deeply felt cultural or linguistic traits of the community'.[92]

Indigenous rights may form part of what might be viewed as culture. Such issues are in a sphere of social awareness which has drawn increasing attention from arbitral tribunals as well as IIA negotiators. The tribunal in *Bear Creek v. Peru*, a case dealing with a mine operation against which there had been extensive protests by the indigenous communities, held that it is a host state's purview to establish a legal framework that allows efficient consultation processes with affected indigenous groups.[93] A dissenting arbitrator believed the international law placed obligations to consult with these stakeholders on foreign investors. A similar approach, favouring the establishment of social and human rights obligations on the part of investors, was seen in *Urbaser v. Argentina*.[94] Provisions relating to indigenous rights can be found in the USMCA using language which recalls that

---

[88] Art. 16.1 ix).

[89] Art. 10.6.

[90] SPP v. Egypt, ICSID Case No ARB/84/3 (20 May 1992).

[91] ICSID Case No ARB/05/8 (9 August 2007).

[92] Ibid at [505].

[93] ICSID Case No ARB/14/21, Award (30 November 2017).

[94] ICSID Case No ARB/07/26, Award (8 December 2016).

of the GATT: 'this Agreement does not preclude a Party from adopting or maintaining a measure it deems necessary to fulfil its legal obligations to indigenous peoples.'[95]

Human rights issues may be conceived as an aspect of the cultural norms of a host state or as a component of workers' rights in the context of labour standards. However they are classified, the tension between human rights and the protections due to investors under IIAs is one of the defining controversies of the modern discipline – indeed, of international economic law generally. It is unusual for IIAs to reference 'human rights' expressly by that term. At the same time, human rights law has become increasingly influential in international investment arbitration. The jurisprudence of the European Court of Human Rights (ECtHR) has featured in a number of ISDS awards in relation to matters such as the entitlement to property and due process as guaranteed under the European Convention on Human Rights (ECHR).[96] Under the jurisprudence of the ECtHR, a state's regulatory autonomy is expressed as a 'margin of appreciation' – a doctrine adopted by the ECtHR for assessing whether a state has complied with its obligations under the ECHR. This is tied to debates regarding the judicial technique of 'proportionality' between the regulatory objective and the harm suffered by the investor, an issue which cuts across investment arbitration in many contexts.[97]

12.4 The environment

There is perhaps no social policy issue which has more intensively shaped the debate around international investment law and the entitlement of foreign investors to protections under IIAs than that of the environment. In the twenty-first century, regard for the environment has been all but replaced with the issue of 'climate change', a concept which is so sweeping in its scope that there is scarcely any area of human activity – and, by extension, any kind of governmental action – which it does not have the potential to embrace. Acceptance of environmental protection as a meaningful consideration comes from the belief that environmental issues are not confined by borders but rather generate externalities that make these issues regional or even global. To the extent that older IIAs address these issues at all, it is typically by reference to the 'environment', which was how custody of the earth's natural resources was framed in previous decades. For example, the investment chapter of the US–Korea FTA of 2007 specifies that a party must not be prevented 'from adopting, maintaining, or enforcing any measure … that it considers appropriate to ensure that investment activity in its territory is undertaken in a manner sensitive to environmental concerns'.[98] As with essential security, the self-judging language of this provision is worth noting as it accords signatory parties wide discretion in determining whether or not a measure is linked to environmental matters. The preamble of the India–Singapore Comprehensive Economic Agreement states that 'economic and trade liberalization should allow for the optimal use of natural resources

---

[95] Art. 32.5.

[96] J Alvarez, *The Use (and Misuse) of European Human Rights Law by Investor-State Arbitrators* (Juris, 2018).

[97] V Vadi, *Proportionality, Reasonableness and Standards of Review in International Investment Law and Arbitration* (Edward Elgar Publishing, 2018).

[98] Art. 11.10.

in accordance with the objective of sustainable development, seeking both to protect and preserve the environment'.[99] This statement, which recalls the preamble of the WTO Agreement, should guide interpreting tribunals towards understandings of legal obligations that accord recognition to environmental protection. Commitments not to lower environmental standards in order to attract investment are also found in a number of IIAs, such as the Norway Model BIT.[100] Often presented as the most progressive economic treaty in the world, the CPTPP contains an entire chapter on the environment. Interestingly, this chapter is confined to a more traditional understanding of the environment, focusing on pollution and the protection of wildlife, with no reference to climate change.[101] The chapter consists of general principles regarding the importance of the environment and sustainable development which could be used to interpret other parts of the treaty, including the investment chapter. It also specifies that environmental laws must not be used as a disguised restriction on investment (or trade) between the parties.[102]

Investment tribunals have demonstrated willingness to take into consideration the environmental impact of investment, recognizing that protection of the environment might entitle host states to derogate from the obligations they have incurred in IIAs. Many of these have arisen under NAFTA, the forerunner to the USMCA. Arbitrators have been prepared to find that an environmental purpose can override a host state's commitment to foreign investors. The tribunal in *Methanex v. USA*, mentioned previously, held that a US state ban on the manufacturing and sale of a gasoline additive did not amount to an indirect expropriation, nor was any compensation owed to the foreign investor. This was based in part on the tribunal's findings that the measure had been adopted in order to protect the environment from a hazardous chemical.[103] In another NAFTA-based arbitration, environmental justifications did not excuse the state's regulatory expropriation of an investment relating to a hazardous waste disposal site, although this was due to the uneven manner in which the measure was imposed, rather than its substantive environmental aim.[104] In *Pac Rim v. El Salvador*,[105] the tribunal found that the investor did not comply with the requirement to obtain a mining permit, in part due to the environmental danger to surface land. In *Chevron v. Ecuador*,[106] the tribunal denied allegations of environmental damage brought against an oil company during its extraction activities which the respondent state had argued had a severely detrimental impact upon local populations. In another dispute which raised environmental issues, Costa Rica was able to defend itself against claims of expropriation as well as breach of FET in relation to a series of measures imposed on a tourist resort project situated near an ecological reserve.[107] It can be expected that environmental matters will increasingly feature in investment

---

[99] 26 June 2005.

[100] Arts 11 and 12.

[101] Art. 20.1.

[102] Art. 20.2.3.

[103] Methanex v. United States, UNCITRAL, 44 ILM 1345 (2005).

[104] Metalclad v. Mexico, ICSID Case No ARB(AF)/97/1 (30 August 2000).

[105] ICSID Case No ARB/09/12 (1 June 2012).

[106] UNCITRAL, 2009, Claimant's Notice of Arbitration.

[107] Santa Elena v. Costa Rica, ICSID Case No ARB/12/12 (17 February 2000).

arbitrations, much as their coverage in IIAs will expand in the coming years, as governments and citizen groups remain convinced that these are vital issues of planet-wide concern.

12.5 The 'right to regulate'

The imbalance of power in the drafting and application of IIAs between developed and developing states is thought to be especially stark when considering the protection of social rights. In early stages of development, the fact that a country may prioritize economic matters raises the spectre of a regulatory race to the bottom in order to attract FDI. In recent years a number of states have sought to overcome this challenge by including wording in their IIAs to enshrine their ability to regulate for various social purposes, often at a very general level, encompassing many or all of the specific topics discussed above. The investment chapter of the CPTPP includes the following provision: 'Nothing in this Chapter shall be construed to prevent a Party from adopting, maintaining or enforcing any measure otherwise consistent with this Chapter that it considers appropriate to ensure that investment activity in its territory is undertaken in a manner sensitive to environmental, health or *other regulatory objectives*.'[108] The CPTPP further enshrines states' capacity to enact laws which serve the public interest in a broad sense by tightening the understanding of expropriation. The CPTPP's Annex on Expropriation contains the following limitation: 'Non-discriminatory regulatory actions by a Party that are designed and applied to protect legitimate public welfare objectives, such as public health, safety and the environment, do not constitute indirect expropriations, except in rare circumstances.'[109]

The phrase 'legitimate public welfare objectives' is clearly intended to encompass a broad assortment of host state measures with impacts on society. Some believe that investment tribunals should conduct so-called proportionality analysis in order to balance investors' rights and public interest in an objective, predictable fashion.[110] As suggested earlier, proportionality analysis has very much become a subject of academic interest in recent years, with a number of commentators viewing it as a solution to the tension between the right of a state to regulate in the public interest and the investor's entitlements under IIAs and customary international law.[111]

In addition to enlarged recognition of public interest matters as defences to breach of other treaty obligations, an increasing expectation has been placed on foreign investors to acknowledge certain minimal standards of behaviour when engaging in their commercial activities overseas. These standards are often described as CSR, some of the sources of which were mentioned in the previous chapter. CSR may be seen as shorthand for a whole range of social policy issues, including the environment and human rights. Some IIAs emphasize the need for states to be mindful of these guidelines when enacting their investment laws. For example, the Canada–Peru FTA states:

---

[108] Art. 9.16.

[109] Annex 9-B 3.b). This phrase also appears in the USMCA Annex 14-B.

[110] A Giest, 'Interpreting Public Interest Provisions in International Investment Treaties' 18:1 Chicago Journal of International Law 323 (2017).

[111] Vadi, *Proportionality* above n 97.

Each Party should encourage enterprises operating within its territory or subject to its jurisdiction to voluntarily incorporate internationally recognized standards of corporate social responsibility in their internal policies, such as statements of principle that have been endorsed or are supported by the Parties. These principles address issues such as labour, the environment, human rights, community relations and anti-corruption. The Parties therefore remind those enterprises of the importance of incorporating such corporate social responsibility standards in their internal policies.[112]

Clearly this is only an obligation of 'best efforts', meaning that it would be difficult to initiate a claim on this basis. Adhering to such standards may be both a moral obligation and an indication of good business strategy. The extent to which firms fulfil these guidelines may be reflected in their capacity to satisfy discerning consumers. Still, as noted earlier, IIAs cannot place obligations directly on investors because they are concluded between state parties, and there is limited capacity for international economic law to compel foreign investors to adhere to CSR principles where they do not wish to.

13. CONCLUSION

This chapter has provided an overview of the provisions contained in an average IIA, including both standalone investment treaties and the investment chapters contained in RTAs. Since IIAs accord protections to foreign investors and corresponding obligations to states (the host states which receive the foreign investors), it is perhaps self-evident that these instruments are onesided – they were patently designed to be such. Although foreign investors are subject to the whims of the states in which they locate and are in that sense often highly vulnerable to interference, this does not mean that the international law governing foreign investment does not need to be 'rebalanced' (to use the popular phrase) to some degree. It may be that only by creating such a balance will all the stakeholders involved in FDI, including the citizens of the host state, support the regime in the longer term. As it stands the system is the subject of major criticisms, predominately from academics, but now also from politicians and the wider public. This is no more so than in relation to the one aspect of IIAs that was not discussed in this chapter – the process of dispute settlement. Chapter 8 will devote its attention entirely to this immensely controversial aspect of international investment law: the capacity of investors to bring claims based on the rights outlined in this chapter directly against host states through international arbitration.

---

[112] Art. 810 (21 November 2008).

DISCUSSION QUESTIONS

1. In what way are international investment agreements onesided and how might this be rectified?
2. How are the non-discrimination standards in international investment agreements distinct from those in trade agreements?
3. In what way do international investment agreements protect rather than liberalize foreign investment?
4. Are the protections contained in international investment agreements framed in language that is too vague? What are the consequences of this lack of precision?

FURTHER READING

D Collins, 'Narrative and Lyrical Elements in International Investment Agreements' 24:2 UC Davis Journal of International Law and Policy 179–208 (2018).

T Cottier, R Echandi, R Liechti-McKee, T Payosova and C Sieber, 'The Principle of Proportionality in International Law: Foundations and Variations' 18:4 Journal of World Investment and Trade 628 (2017).

A Davies, 'Investment Treaty Interpretation, Fair and Equitable Treatment and Legitimate Expectations' 15:3 Manchester Journal of International Economic Law 314 (2018).

T Sharmin, 'Application of MFN to the Substantive Standards: Why Should We Re-Investigate the Uncontested?' 15:1 Manchester Journal of International Economic Law 85 (2018).

8

Dispute settlement in international investment law

1. INTRODUCTION

The previous chapter examined the substantive contents of IIAs, the main purpose of which is to safeguard investors against political risks in the foreign states in which they locate. These instruments include protections for investors against discrimination, unfair treatment, physical interference and expropriation at the hands of the host state. Since IIAs do not place any obligations on investors, it was suggested that international investment law, at least as it is contained in IIAs, is unfairly asymmetrical against host states, who bear the burden of liability in the event that they are judged to have overregulated in a manner that adversely affects the rights of foreign firms. As will be shown in this chapter, this assessment is made by private arbitration tribunals appointed by the parties.

Some believe that many developing countries did not appreciate the significance of these obligations which they undertook in IIAs, in particular the reality that under these treaties they could be exposed to arbitration claims in international tribunals for a wide range of measures.[1] While such views tend to minimize the fact that most developing countries received extensive assistance from international bodies such as UNCTAD and the OECD over many decades with regard to the benefits and risks of IIAs, including the dangers of arbitration, there may be some truth in the claims that the full impact of investment treaties on domestic policy may be less beneficial than is often expected. Still, decades of investment arbitration practice and the many hundreds of available decisions have contributed to the honing of these treaties to serve the needs of their signatories, including capital importing states, which in many cases has led to an attenuation of the rights which had traditionally been afforded investors.

It is this highly controversial aspect of IIAs, the dispute settlement mechanism, that is the focus of this chapter. One of the greatest advantages of international investment law generally, and IIAs

---

[1] L Poulsen, *Bounded Rationality and Economic Diplomacy: The Policy of Investment Treaties in Developing Countries* (Cambridge University Press, 2015).

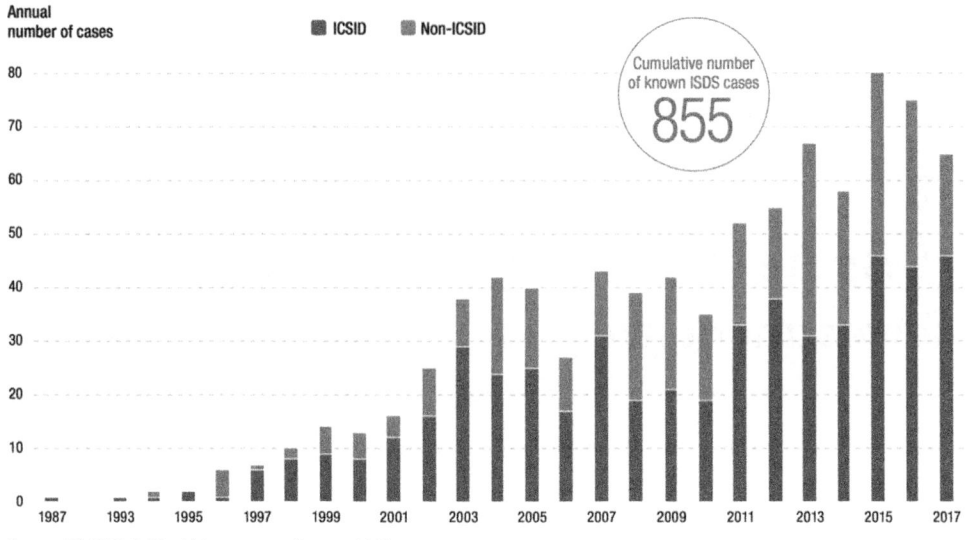

Source: UNCTAD World Investment Report 2018.

Figure 8.1 Annual number of investor–state dispute settlement (ISDS) cases over time

in particular, to investors is that it has traditionally granted them direct access to neutral international dispute settlement, precluding the need to resort to local courts or to use their home state as a representative either in a diplomatic forum or through state to state dispute settlement. Until quite recently, some form of investor–state dispute settlement (ISDS) was provided for in almost every IIA. As of end 2017, there have been more than 850 known (publicly available) ISDS cases since 1987, with a vast increase since the turn of the twenty-first century (see Figure 8.1).

The actual number of cases may be much higher, perhaps more than double this number. The high volume of cases is in large part due to the rise of IIAs during this period, as well as growth in global FDI flows. Most of these cases have been resolved under ICSID rules, which will be discussed in more detail below. While the number of cases per year appears to have declined somewhat in recent years, there is no question that ISDS has become a central pillar of international dispute settlement, issuing more awards than the WTO panels and Appellate Body by far. IIAs also tend to provide for state to state dispute settlement between signatories, but this is rarely used. Today, international adjudication for investment disputes is seen as a major threat to national sovereignty as it often bypasses local courts and gives foreigners greater rights than are available to local investors, who must use these local procedures, even where they are costly or ineffectual.

Given the controversies of ISDS there are many contemporary proposals for reform, ranging from a modernization of the procedural rules (as in the case of ICSID and UNCITRAL rules) to the creation of a standalone multilateral court for investment matters, mentioned in Chapter 6. At the national level, Brazil's Cooperation and Facilitation Agreements (CIFAs) do not contain ISDS at all, reflecting that country's reluctance to embrace the IIA phenomenon. Instead, Brazil's CIFAs establish a system that combines dispute prevention mechanisms, creating institutions to ensure continued communication and foster cooperation.[2] India is focusing on stronger exhaustion of local remedies clauses in its IIAs, allowing resort to ISDS only where local procedures fail. The EU has taken perhaps the most innovative approach to ISDS of all with its new Investment Court System (ICS). Before examining these issues, it is useful to consider the primary purpose behind ISDS – namely, as a safer alternative to domestic courts.

2. THE LACK OF TRUST IN DOMESTIC COURTS

Domestic courts (of either the home or host state) are often undesirable to hear investors' claims because of perceived bias or lack of competence. This may be especially so for those in the developing world, which may be thought to have weaker rule of law or judicial independence, or where there may simply be insufficient resources for courts to issue timely and effective judgements to litigants. Since much foreign investment, and therefore the disputes which arise from it, tends to be focused in the developing world, host state courts are therefore often highly unattractive. Home state courts are also likely to be unsuitable to hear international investment law disputes, even if the foreign investor might wish it. This is primarily because of the Doctrine of State Immunity of customary international law, which prevents courts from hearing claims in which foreign states are defendants. Similarly, the Act of State Doctrine, which is a principle of law common to many countries, establishes that a sovereign state is bound to respect the independence of every other sovereign state, the effect of which is that courts will not sit in judgment of another government's acts done within its own territory. It must be pointed out that the obligations contained in IIAs are not legally enforceable in domestic courts in most countries where international law must be transposed into domestic law by a legislative act for it to have binding effect.

Under international law and in some IIAs, investors may be required to seek a remedy through domestic law first before bringing a claim in international law through international tribunals. This is known as exhaustion of local remedies. Article 26 of the ICSID Convention, of which more below, states expressly that a country may require the exhaustion of local remedies as a condition of consent to international arbitration under the Convention. Some IIAs limit this requirement or specify a timeframe after which international courts must be used. In some states this can be many months long, making recourse to international tribunals difficult. For example, the India Model BIT specifies that the investor must first submit its claim before the relevant domestic courts or administrative bodies of the host state for the purpose of pursuing domestic remedies. Such claim must be submitted within one year of the date on which the investor first acquired, or should have first acquired, knowledge of the measure in question.[3] Languishing a year in the local courts may be viewed as an unfair imposition on foreign investors. However, compelling use of local courts accords greater deference to the sovereignty of host states. It arguably also facilitates the improvement of domestic administrative and judicial procedures by ensuring that such infrastructure is

---

[2] G Vidigal, 'Brazil's New Model of Dispute Settlement for Investment: Return to the Past or Alternative for the Future?' 19:3 Journal of World Investment and Trade (2018).

[3] Art. 14.3.

appealing to international enterprises. If foreign investors get access to international arbitration straight away, there is no incentive for the host state to reform their legal systems with a view to attracting foreign firms. Since this operates as a severe restriction on access to arbitration, many modern IIAs eliminate this requirement entirely, although in recent times some countries have reintroduced the exhaustion of local remedies as a way of safeguarding their judicial sovereignty.[4]

If ISDS is designed to resolve disputes where host state courts are appropriate because of bias or incompetence, there is an obvious question as to the legitimacy of ISDS in situations where two signatory states of an IIA have strong rule of law, independent courts and a good degree of mutual trust. This is typically the case in IIAs concluded between two developed states, such as the CETA between Canada and the EU. Surely a Canadian investor would trust the domestic courts of the EU, just as a European investor would have faith that a Canadian court would be independent and unbiased? Accordingly, it is easier to justify resort to ISDS, perhaps even without exhaustion of local remedies in host states where there is weak rule of law and lack of independence of the judiciary, which may be captured for example in the World Bank's indices of corruption and ease of doing business. It may come as no surprise that countries which score lower on these rankings tend to be more likely to lose ISDS cases,[5] perhaps because lack of properly functioning courts is tied to breaches of IIA standards such as fair and equitable treatment (FET). It may be that ISDS is needed in some treaties, where risk is higher, and not in others. But this is antithetical to the notion of sovereign equality of states and judicial comity, both of which arguably underpin the notion of an integrated global community.

The view that ISDS is superfluous in treaties between two developed countries may be countered by the claim that there are few, if any, countries where all of the courts within that territory are sufficiently independent and competent. It would be disingenuous to argue that the many national and subnational court systems across the EU are equally trustworthy from the perspective of a foreign business. The fact that many EU member states chose to include investor–state arbitration provisions in their pre-Lisbon Treaty BITs with other EU member states suggests that there is some mistrust even within developed states regarding domestic courts' ability to resolve these types of disputes effectively.[6] Many regions in eastern and southern Europe score highly in corruption indices. The same could be said of a number of US state courts, as illustrated in the *Loewen v. United States* case brought under NAFTA in which a Canadian company suffered a clear miscarriage of justice in the hands of a local court in the state of Mississippi.[7] Since it would be arguably discriminatory and arbitrary (not to mention undiplomatic) to select some treaty partners for the inclusion of ISDS clauses and not others, it might make sense simply to keep the mechanism in all IIAs.

---

[4] MD Brauch, 'Exhaustion of Local Remedies in International Investment Law' IISD Best Practice Series, International Institute for Sustainable Development (Winnipeg, MB, Canada, 2017).

[5] D Behn, TL Berge and M Langford, 'Poor States or Poor Governance? Examining Outcomes in Investment Treaty Arbitration' 38:3 Northwestern Journal of International Law and Business (2018).

[6] E.g. Germany–Poland (16 September 1989).

[7] Loewen Group, Inc. and Raymond L. Loewen v. United States of America, ICSID Case No ARB(AF)/98/3, Award (26 June 2003).

Another objection to the inclusion of ISDS in IIAs relates to the unfairness which this engenders for domestic investors, who are compelled to use the domestic legal system when faced with a grievance against the government. With ISDS in place, foreign investors are entitled to a superior system for dispute resolution than that of their domestic competitors. In states where rule of law is weak and courts are incompetent, local investors might suffer, whereas the foreign investor has access to the 'better' international forum.

If the rule of law as enforced by the domestic courts is weak, then surely the foreign investor must be prepared to suffer under this system in order to access the associated benefits – perhaps lower taxes or weaker regulations. The investor must take the host state as they find it, as it were. On the other hand, it must be recalled that one of the drawbacks of domestic courts is the perception that they may exhibit an antiforeign bias. A national investor would not suffer from this mistreatment, unlike in the case of incompetence, which would be problematic for both foreign and local investors.

If the domestic courts are biased, incompetent and lacking independence then it is up to the state to get its own house in order. As suggested above, it is thought by some that the pressure to attract foreign investment serves as a catalyst to improve domestic governance in matters such as rule of law and judicial independence.[8] Fear of claims brought under ISDS may compel the investor to regulate in a manner which is less intrusive and to offer efficient and unbiased judicial and administrative procedures. This claim is strongly doubted, as there is no empirical evidence that ISDS has contributed to 'good governance', as it is often termed,[9] although it is difficult to envision how this might be measured. Rather, it is thought that states must establish their own robust legal institutions, such as effective courts, before foreign investors will come.[10] IIAs with ISDS do not detract from this process but they cannot achieve this on their own. When this takes place it will benefit domestic investors just as well, if not more so. Until it does, then a preferential regime for foreign investors appears to be entirely defensible.

Allegations of anti-state bias in ISDS outcomes, common in much academic criticism of the field, are difficult to sustain. Data on outcomes of ISDS cases suggest that investors and states win a roughly equal number of claims.[11] This is in keeping with theoretically expected outcomes in conventional litigation, sometimes known as the 50:50 rule. This theory suggests that in most litigation systems there should be a roughly 50:50 win rate between claimants and defendants because cases selected for litigation by the parties are likely to be those which are difficult and uncertain. The cases in which the true quality of the claim is close to that which is needed for the claimant to win were the ones likely to be brought to trial, because the clear cut cases will be more likely to settle before trial (or may never evolve into filed cases at all). The difficult and uncertain cases, in turn, are likely to be those that, on average, result in about half the victories going to one party and about half to the other.[12] There is no clear evidence of bias against states in the system, at least in

---

[8] K Vandevelde, *Bilateral Investment Treaties: History, Politics and Interpretation* (Oxford University Press, 2010).

[9] M Sattorova, *The Impact of Investment Treaty Law on Host States: Enabling Good Governance* (Hart, 2018).

[10] J Tobin and S Rose Ackerman, 'When BITs Have Some Bite: The Political Economic Environment for Bilateral Investment Treaties' 6:1 Review of International Organizations 1 (2011).

[11] UNCTAD World Investment Report 2018.

[12] G Priest and B Klein, 'The Selection of Disputes for Litigation', 13 Journal of Legal Studies 1 (1984).

terms of outcomes, unless one believes that the substantive rules of international investment law are themselves biased against states, in which case any time a state loses it can be viewed as a kind of pro investor inherent bias.

The viability of ISDS in terms of its interaction with domestic law had been under threat as a consequence of the Court of Justice of the European Union's (CJEU) far reaching decision in *Slovak Republic v. Achmea*.[13] The judgment concerned a Dutch–Slovak investment treaty which had been invoked by an investor to request a tribunal to pay compensation for the Slovak government's change to its health insurance law. The CJEU ruled that the BIT was in violation of EU law because it created a situation in which an investment tribunal could be called upon to interpret EU law in a dispute between investors and states but its interpretation could not be challenged via the domestic court process, effectively meaning that the CJEU's role as the final arbiter of EU law was undermined. While the decision clearly affects the viability of intra-EU BITs, the decision may have held further implications with respect to EU FTAs which include provision for ISDS. Under EU law, the judicial control of agreements with third countries is based on the assumption found in Article 218(11) TFEU that primary EU law is predominant over international agreements. In late April 2019 the CJEU issued a ruling which confirmed the compatibility of the EU's new ICS (an innovative kind of ISDS which will be discussed further below) with EU treaties.[14]

ISDS requires arbitrators to interpret treaty provisions, yet interpreting legislation is usually a role reserved for national courts. Some believe that investment tribunals have begun to operate very much like domestic courts of law, for example by demonstrating deference to previous tribunal decisions, almost as if a *de facto stare decisis* is in place. This alters the fundamental nature of arbitration, which some assert should be focused on establishing facts as occurred between the parties rather than interpreting the law at a general level.[15] However, as shown in the previous chapter, many IIAs use ambiguous language requiring extensive interpretation. Moreover, states are beginning to revise the wording of their treaties in response to tribunal decisions, much as a national legislature does in response to judicial decisions. Regardless of the misgivings held by many, it would seem as though ISDS remains central to the functioning of the IIA system. Having established some of the controversies associated with ISDS, this chapter will explore some of its main features.

3. INVESTOR–STATE DISPUTE SETTLEMENT CLAUSES

Most IIAs specify that ISDS settlement is available for disputes, often with a choice of various rules such as ICSID or UNCITRAL. Consent to arbitration may be expressly limited by type of claim. For example, China allowed ISDS only in relation to questions of the quantum of compensation for

---

[13] Case C284/16 (6 March 2018).

[14] European Commission Press Release, Brussels (30 April 2019).

[15] C Titi, 'The Arbitrator as Lawmaker: Jurisgenerative Processes in Investment Arbitration' 14:5 Journal of World Trade 829 (2013).

expropriation in some of its early IIAs.[16] There may also be the requirement to exhaust local remedies, as noted above, typically in conjunction with a waiting period. Some IIAs afford investors the option to choose domestic or international procedures to pursue their claims, but not both. Once one route is chosen, the other is foreclosed permanently. Such provisions are sometimes labelled 'fork in the road' clauses. These provisions are designed to prevent the abuse of proceedings through litigation against states in multiple fora, which may in some circumstances unfairly pressure settlement. The fork in the road clause in the Italy–Lebanon BIT was evaluated in *Toto Costruzion v. Lebanon*. Denying the host state's objection to jurisdiction, the tribunal stated that in order for a fork in the road clause to preclude claims from being considered by an international arbitration tribunal, it must be established that the same claim is on a 'different road', meaning that a claim with the same object, parties and cause of action is already brought before a different judicial forum.[17]

Going a step further, the CPTPP has narrowed the scope for investors to make ISDS claims by restricting the ability of private companies who enter into an investment contract to use the IIA's ISDS mechanism. Alongside signing the CPTPP itself, New Zealand also signed side letters to exclude compulsory ISDS with five signatories to the CPTPP – Brunei Darussalam, Malaysia, Peru, Viet Nam and Australia. The Peru and Australia side letters exclude ISDS entirely while the other three side letters take the so-called escalation approach, which provides for dispute resolution on a staged basis, involving consultations, mediation and finally arbitration. This method differs from the traditional one in which a state party provides a standing offer and formal consent to arbitration via the treaty, domestic foreign investment legislation or an investment contract. From there the arbitration agreement is perfected through the commencement of arbitration by an investor. Additionally, New Zealand, Chile and Canada made a Joint Declaration on ISDS under the CPTPP indicating an intention 'to consider evolving international practice and the evolution of ISDS including through the work carried out by multilateral international fora'. It is unclear what the practical consequences of this declaration are, although it would appear that Chile and Canada are unwilling to restrict the availability of ISDS in its entirety.

4. UMBRELLA CLAUSES

Umbrella clauses technically grant substantive protection to investors and as such could have been considered in the previous chapter, but their true power lies in the procedural advantage they offer in terms of their capacity to provide access to international arbitration. Umbrella clauses are often hard to spot in IIAs because they are expressed in deceptively bland language, as in the UK–Bosnia Herzegovina BIT: 'Each Contracting Party shall observe any obligation it may have entered into with regard to investments of nationals or companies of the other Contracting Party.'[18] The effect

---

[16] China–Australia Art. XII 2 b) (11 July 1988).

[17] Toto Costruzioni Generali SpA v. Republic of Lebanon (ICSID Case No ARB/07/12), Decision on Jurisdiction (11 September 2009).

[18] Art. 2.

of committing to observe 'any obligation' is to bind the host state to promises made in various contexts, including, notably, contracts which they have entered into with foreign investors. This is controversial because many if not most breaches of ordinary commercial contracts should rightly be brought in the local courts. It seems unfair to compel the host government to defend itself in the expensive ISDS forum for a simple breach of a contract which it happened to enter into with a foreign firm and which has nothing to do with that state exercising its sovereign rights. Umbrella clauses have begun to disappear in IIAs in recent years, largely as a consequence of the controversy which they have created in terms of their enforceability and the view that their full effects may not have been appreciated by signatory parties.[19]

Traditionally under international law it is understood that a breach of a private contract by a state does not give rise to direct international responsibility on the part of that state.[20] Umbrella clauses change this by elevating an ordinary breach of contract to the level of a treaty violation. Umbrella clauses provide blanket protection for foreign investment, granting them international remedies even in relation to breach of contract. If enforced, they allow contractual undertakings to be recast as international law obligations. An international tribunal rather than a domestic court could be used to settle disputes regarding the breach, even if a domestic court would arguably be a more suitable forum. In that sense, umbrella clauses blur the distinction between private law and public law disputes by elevating private breach of contract to the level of treaty violation. This aspect of the clause was expressed by the tribunal in *Noble Ventures v. Romania*, which stated that an umbrella clause is 'usually seen as transforming domestic law obligations into obligations directly cognizable in international law'.[21]

The enforceability of umbrella clauses is uncertain due to inconsistent arbitral decisions. In *SGS v. Pakistan*,[22] the tribunal held that these provisions do not automatically establish that contract breaches are breaches of international treaty law. It would seem from this decision that only an express inclusion of contract breach would allow for a tribunal to extend an umbrella clause in this manner. Put another way, a tribunal will not 'read in' an enlargement of its jurisdiction unless there is clear intent for it to do so in the text of the relevant IIA. In *Nova Scotia Power v. Venezuela*,[23] the tribunal declined to take jurisdiction over a claim for breach of contract on the basis that the dispute arose out of an ordinary contract, notwithstanding the existence of an umbrella clause. In *SGS v. Philippines*,[24] the tribunal considered that a very similar clause regarding the observation of 'any obligation' which was contained in the Swiss–Philippines BIT did encompass breach of contractual obligations. The tribunal held, on the basis of this umbrella clause, that the BIT had incorporated contractual commitments undertaken by the host state. This was despite the fact that the treaty's language did not specify that 'any obligation' included contract breach. In *Tulip Real*

---

[19] K Yannaca-Small, 'The Umbrella Clause: Is the Umbrella Closing?' in K Yannaca-Small ed. *Arbitration under International Investment Agreements* (Oxford University Press, 2018).

[20] S Subedi, *International Investment Law: Reconciling Policy and Principle* (Hart, 2016).

[21] ICSID Case No ARB/01/11 (12 October 2005).

[22] ICSID Case No ARB/01/13 (8 September 2003).

[23] ICSID Case No ARB(AF)/11/1 (30 April 2014).

[24] ICSID Case No ARB/02/6 (29 January 2004).

Estate and Development v. Turkey,[25] the tribunal concluded that the respondent's actions did not constitute violations of the BIT because the umbrella clause could not cover actions that were not contractual but merely expressions of support for the proposed investment that were contained in a legislative instrument.

One way to resolve the issue of the enforceability of umbrella clauses is to conceptualize different categories of contractual actor. There may be ordinary contractual parties and there may be statelike contractual parties. Where the state is merely acting as an ordinary contractual party, meaning that it has entered into a commercial contract in the same way that any private individual could, then breach of a contract should not be viewed as a treaty violation. Where the host state is acting in the capacity of a state, exercising powers that could only ever belong to a government (perhaps such as a concession contract for a natural resource), then a breach of contract can and should be conceived as a BIT violation, and accordingly deserve resolution through international arbitration.[26] This distinction can be very difficult to establish in practice.

5. INVESTOR–STATE DISPUTE SETTLEMENT

While as a process ISDS is based on and closely resembles commercial arbitration, it is often analogized to administrative law, meaning the system of law which operates in most states through which the courts review decisions of public bodies which affect the rights of private citizens. Through administrative law, one branch of the state (the courts) assesses the actions of another branch (the delegated authority of the legislature). In that sense it is a crucial aspect of the separation of powers so essential to democracy. Administrative law, as a component of the common law, contemplates the review of the decision of the public body, which typically refers to a standard something like reasonableness and often incorporates issues of due process or proportionality, recalling elements of FET, among other standards in IIAs. This aspect of ISDS is often emphasized by academic commentators who decry the transposition of some of the norms of commercial arbitration to this public law-type forum.[27]

5.1 General features

As with any kind of arbitration, ISDS is based on the consent of parties. This may be manifest in an IIA, an investment contract or legislation, such a domestic foreign investment law. As noted above, consent to ISDS can be limited to certain issues or sectors. ISDS concerns legal issues, not political ones. Indeed, it is often stated that ISDS was designed to depoliticize disputes. The extent to which ISDS cases preclude political considerations is a matter of some debate and tends to turn on semantic understandings of 'political' – almost every issue involving a government touches on political issues to some degree.

---

[25] ICSID Case No ARB/11/28 (10 March 2014).

[26] El Paso v. Argentina, Decision on Jurisdiction, ICSID Case No ARB/03/15 (14 April 2006).

[27] S Schill ed., *International Investment Law and Comparative Public Law* (Oxford University Press, 2010).

The arbitrators who decide ISDS cases are experts in international investment law, often also holding expertise in the relevant sector. This is thought to be one of the advantages of ISDS over domestic court procedures presided over by non-generalist jurists. ISDS arbitrators are perhaps somewhat less knowledgeable in public international law generally, often depicted by critics as business people with limited understanding of the public policy debates which underpin so much of the legislation which is challenged by investors. There are now many studies on the demographics of ISDS arbitrators, most of whom are drawn from a small pool of people from developed countries who enjoy regular appointments.[28] As with commercial arbitration, ISDS arbitrators can be challenged by parties for their independence and competence.

While conventional arbitration is often presented as less expensive and faster than domestic court procedures, ISDS is not inexpensive, with average costs of around US$6 million dollars for claimants and US$4 million for respondents.[29] There is currently no rule in any institutional investment arbitration system regarding costs, leaving much discretion to arbitrators. The default option seems to have been to leave the parties to pay their own costs. In some instances, particularly where a party has behaved inappropriately by bringing a frivolous claim or making unfounded assertions, tribunals have been prepared to award costs. This would appear to be a sensible strategy in that it incentivizes conduct which is conducive to fair outcomes – only reasonably strong cases are brought and parties do their best to cooperate and to act in good faith. This may be one reason for the near 50:50 split in terms of outcomes for investors and states, noted above. Some modern IIAs have taken this a step further by enshrining a 'loser pays' principle in the text of the treaty as a default position,[30] meaning that tribunals are allowed to order parties to pay their own costs, but this would be seen as an exceptional outcome. Loser pays rules are common to many civil litigation systems throughout the world and are often thought to act as a counterbalance against frivolous or speculative claims in which well-resourced parties are able to pressure settlement against defendants who cannot afford legal representation. Such unfairness may equally exist in ISDS, where powerful multinationals often launch actions against developing countries.

ISDS is believed to be less adversarial than conventional litigation, which may work towards preserving the relationship between parties with a view to long term compatibility, as characterizes FDI. Also like conventional arbitration, ISDS is premised on confidentiality, aiming to preserve the reputations of parties. In recent years, ISDS has shifted away from classic confidentiality (closed hearings, pleadings and private awards) in favour of greater transparency. This is in part due to heavy criticism from the academic community and greater public awareness of the implications of multinational enterprises challenging the decisions of sovereign states, coupled with the magnitude of awards (in some cases in the billions of US dollars). Much of this derision grew from the public consultations launched by the EU Commission in conjunction with the negotiations of the currently moribund Transatlantic Trade and Investment Partnership (TTIP). Even after transparency reforms initiated through UNCTAD, generally ISDS hearings remain confidential and

---

[28] S Franck, *Arbitration Costs: Myths and Realities in Investment Treaty Arbitration* (Oxford University Press, 2019).

[29] 'Investment Treaty Arbitration: Cost, Duration and Size of Claims All Show Steady Increase' Allen & Overy, London (14 December 2017).

[30] CETA Art. 8.39.5.

there is no right of participation by nonparties. Many awards and other documents are published online, helping contribute to a growing body of what might be termed 'jurisprudence', although there is no doctrine of precedent among investment tribunals. The leading depositories are italaw. com, maintained by the Faculty of Law of University of Victoria in British Columbia, Canada and the PluriCourts Investment Treaty Arbitration Database (PITAD), maintained by the Faculty of Law of the University of Oslo in Norway.

5.2 Remedies

In ISDS compensation aims to make the injured party whole through the provision of money, often termed damages, although 'damages' tend to be associated with illegal expropriation, as illustrated in the previous chapter. One recent study reported that the average size of a claim in ISDS is US$1,204,183,000 (US$719,334,000 excluding the stratospheric *Yukos v. Russia* arbitrations). The average size of an award (where the claimant succeeds) is US$486,135,000 (US$110,872,000 excluding *Yukos*).[31] These are by no means small sums, particularly considering that they represent obligations to be paid by states out of public resources. It is worth emphasizing that the remedy of monetary compensation in international investment law resembles that of private contract law, which prioritizes damages for breach of contractually incurred obligation, rather than public law, which typically mandates a certain form of conduct as remedy. This may be contrasted with WTO law, which adopts a primary remedy of removal of the unlawful measure.[32]

Nonmonetary remedies are referred to as 'specific performance' in the common law of contract because they require the party in breach to follow through with what it said it would do. Foreign investment might be well suited to nonpecuniary remedies such as the cessation of interference or the modification of intrusive regulations; however, these could also be seen as an excessive interference with a state's sovereignty, in line with the objections noted at the beginning of this chapter. They may also require monitoring to ensure compliance in the long term. This may explain why nonmonetary remedies have been granted only on an exceptional basis in international investment law. For example, the tribunal in *Antoine Goetz v. Burundi* was prepared to award a nonmonetary remedy when it offered the losing respondent the option of revoking a measure (its withdrawal of a certificate of tax free exemption which it would therefore have to reinstate) or paying compensation to the investor for their losses associated with the revocation of the certificate, which had been held to amount to an indirect expropriation.[33] In *Enron v. Argentina*,[34] the respondent argued that the tribunal did not have the power to issue a nonmonetary remedy, but the tribunal ruled otherwise. Reviewing the powers accorded to other international tribunals such as the International Court of Justice (ICJ), which had demonstrated its capacity to award nonpecuniary remedies, the tribunal established that it was indeed able to order a remedy of specific performance as an inherent aspect of its jurisdiction. The power of investment tribunals to make nonmonetary awards as

---

[31] Allen & Overy above n 29.

[32] DSU Art. 19(1).

[33] ICSID Case No ARB/01/2 (21 June 2012) at 516.

[34] ICSID Case No ARB/01/3, Decision on Jurisdiction (14 January 2000).

an alternative to monetary compensation can be expressly granted (or restricted) in the text of the IIA which gives the tribunal its jurisdiction over the claim.[35]

Investment tribunals' awards do not aim to punish the wrongdoer, nor are they intended to make an example of them in order to deter future wrongdoing, although that may be a practical consequence for some host states. Deterrence is sometimes cited as an objective of ISDS, but it is far from clear that its remedial structure has this effect in terms of effecting changes to domestic governance.[36] Still, there can be types of behaviour by parties to arbitration that are excessively harmful and are perhaps deserving of additional sanction beyond simple compensation. This can happen in such a way that the mere recovery of the value of the damaged business is insufficient.

Situations like this may be appropriate for an award of moral damages. Although there is no universal definition of moral damages, it is believed to encompass monetary compensation for civil wrongs that are accompanied by torts or other types of harm that are intangible or otherwise difficult to quantify. Moral damages may also be available for breaches of international investment law. Awards of moral damages are often associated with physical injuries or harassment but may also encompass loss of business reputation. Moral damages are also meant to be compensatory; they should not be viewed as punitive, although this motivation can sometimes be inferred from the language of the tribunals which have made such awards. Moral damages are available to legal persons (meaning investing companies) in addition to natural ones (people). Reparation for moral harms is provided for expressly in the Articles on State Responsibility.[37] The first ICSID case to award compensation for moral damages was *Desert Line v. Yemen*.[38] Later, in *Lemire v. Ukraine*,[39] the tribunal established that moral damages should only be awarded when the actions of the host state involve physical duress, have grave effects and result in mental suffering or loss of reputation. In *Al-Karafi v. Libya*,[40] the tribunal granted compensation for moral damages because of damage caused to the investor's worldwide professional reputation. This included harm suffered to the investor's stock market valuation as well as their reputation in global construction markets.

6. INVESTMENT ARBITRATION PROCEDURAL RULES

IIAs contain the substantive rights which investors may assert against host states, and while these are articulated with greater precision in modern IIAs (the investment chapters of RTAs), there is limited material in investment treaties on the actual process through which these rights are actualized. The procedural rules of ISDS are found in the various arbitral systems which may be chosen by the parties.

---

[35] US–Singapore FTA Art. 15.25(1) (6 May 2003).

[36] J Bonnitcha, *Substantive Protection under Investment Treaties: A Legal and Economic Analysis* (Oxford University Press, 2014).

[37] Art. 30.2.

[38] ICSID Case No ARB/05/17 (26 February 2008).

[39] ICSID Case No ARB/06/18 (28 March 2011).

[40] Ad hoc tribunal, Final Award (22 March 2013).

6.1 The International Centre for the Settlement of Investment Disputes

Ratified by 154 states and entering into force in 1966, the ICSID Convention (also known as the Washington Convention) does not provide substantial rules governing the relationship between host states and foreign investors. It is designed to establish a procedural framework for the settlement of investment disputes based on laws found in other agreements, such as IIAs or investment contracts. ICSID is part of the World Bank, referencing that organization's role in administering global economic governance.

Article 25 of the ICSID Convention establishes that the jurisdiction of ICSID extends to any legal dispute arising directly out of an investment between a contracting state (a signatory of the ICSID Convention) and a national of another contracting state. The ICSID's jurisdiction over contracting states and nationals of other contracting states is enlarged by its Additional Facility rules. These permit claims to be brought where only one party has a connection to the ICSID (either the host state has ratified the ICSID Convention or the investor is from a state which has). The Additional Facility rules are less important now, given that ICSID Convention membership is near universal. The subject matter over which the ICSID has jurisdiction is investment. As discussed in Chapter 7, whether an activity constitutes an investment is a highly contentious matter. The ICSID Convention itself does not define investment, leaving it up to parties to set their own definition of this in their IIAs. The ICSID only concerns itself with a genuine legal dispute, not a diplomatic or political one. Disagreements that do not have a bearing on enforceable legal rights are beyond the ICSID's focus. Investors must frame their complaints against host states in concrete terms, referencing clearly identifiable legal entitlements.

Article 25 of the ICSID Convention specifies that the parties to the dispute must consent in writing to submit the dispute to ICSID. Ratification of the Convention does not fulfil this requirement. Once a party has given its consent, it may not withdraw its consent unilaterally. Whether formal consent has actually been tendered is often the subject of dispute, with ICSID tribunals maintaining the power to determine their own jurisdiction in this matter.[41] ICSID tribunals will take jurisdiction only over disputes that are covered by the parameters of the consent which has been tendered by the parties. Furthermore, Article 26 of the Convention establishes that consent to arbitration through the ICSID shall be deemed to be consent to such arbitration to the exclusion of any other remedy, unless otherwise stated. This has the effect of excluding the requirement to exhaust local remedies unless otherwise stated. It will be remembered that some IIAs require that a specific period of time elapse before ICSID arbitration can be pursued, during which time the investor must avail themselves of local administrative and judicial procedures. Once the parties have provided consent to ICSID arbitration, they lose their entitlement to seek relief in another forum, such as a national court. This is the 'self-contained' nature of ICSID proceedings that make it so popular as a forum for dispute settlement. ICSID arbitrations do not require assistance from local courts and all other proceedings are foreclosed, guarding against vexatious litigation on multiple fronts. Article 27 of the Convention provides that the arbitration

---

[41] PNG v. Papua New Guinea ICSID Case No ARB/13/33 (5 May 2015).

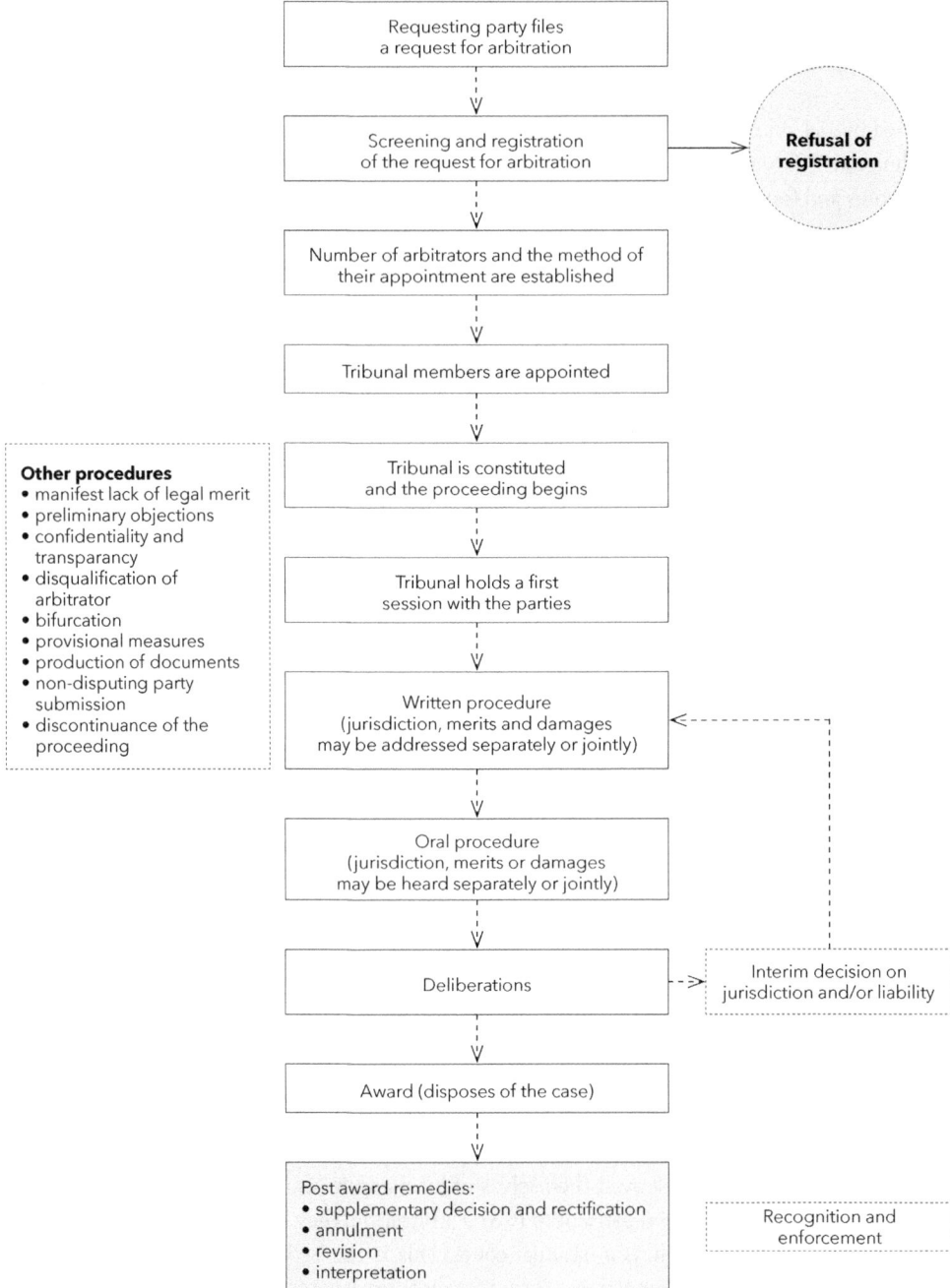

Source: International Centre for the Settlement of Investment Disputes. Reproduced by permission.

Figure 8.2 Stages in an ICSID arbitration

process is protected against interstate claims through the exclusion of diplomatic protection. This means that once the arbitration has begun, investors cannot attempt to use normal diplomatic channels to place pressure on the respondent state. Home states are similarly restricted. This aspect of the Convention is often thought to depoliticize the dispute. In this context it is worth recalling that one of the purposes of international economic law is to maintain peaceful relations between states.

Figure 8.2 illustrates the stages of an ICSID arbitration. The first stage consists of the requesting party (the investor) filing a request for arbitration. This involves an initial screening, which is performed by the Secretary General of ICSID under Article 36(3) of the ICSID Convention and requires an investigation of whether the matter is manifestly outside the jurisdiction of the Centre. Having passed this stage, the number of arbitrators and the method of appointment is established, which in most cases will be done by the parties (one arbitrator each, then agreement on the third), only involving the Secretary General if the parties disagree. Tribunal members are appointed, after which the proceeding begins. Procedural matters may arise at this point including discussions of confidentiality or transparency, disqualification of arbitrators, the production of documents or requests for bifurcation, which mostly refers to the separation of jurisdictional issues from the merits. There is typically a written procedure consisting of a review of documentary evidence followed by an oral procedure, which together may last as much as several months. This will be followed by the tribunal's deliberations, which could lead to an interim decision on jurisdiction or liability on the merits. After this process concludes the tribunal will issue its award, which is the final disposition of the case. Parties may request an interpretation of the award or an annulment, as well as a supplementary decision or rectification of the award under Article 49(2) to correct technical errors or omissions that could affect the award's enforceability. The last stage, which will involve domestic courts, is the recognition and enforcement of the award.

The ICSID maintains a Panel of Conciliators and a Panel of Arbitrators, consisting of lists of persons who may act as conciliators (informal alternative dispute settlement) or arbitrators (the formal binding adjudication procedure). The lists are intended to help the parties to the proceedings identify appropriate individuals who can resolve disputes. An individual does not have to be on the list to be selected as an arbitrator. Parties are free to choose whoever they wish to act as an arbitrator; however, their choices may be challenged by opposing parties.

Article 14 of the Convention outlines certain qualifications that all individuals must possess in order to act as arbitrators. These include high moral character; recognized competence in the fields of law, commerce, industry or finance; and the ability to exercise independent judgement. Curiously, qualification as a lawyer or other legal professional is not necessary. As suggested earlier, there is a small group of individuals who have appeared as ICSID arbitrators over the years.[42] Once chosen by the parties, the tribunal will consist of a sole arbitrator (which is rare) or any uneven number of arbitrators as the parties shall agree. The default option is three people, one appointed by each party and the third appointed by the designated president of the tribunal among the two who have been chosen. The tribunal will decide questions by a majority of the votes. Members of

---

[42] S Puig, 'Social Capital in the Arbitration Market' 25:2 European Journal of International Law 387 (2014).

the tribunal may attach individual opinions to the award, although this is uncommon. Tribunal members now often issue dissent judgments, although this was rare in the past.

Article 42 establishes that the tribunal is empowered to render its decision on the dispute in accordance with the rules of law as may be agreed by the parties. In the absence of such agreement, which may be reflected in the text of the relevant IIA, the tribunal shall apply the law of the contracting state party to the dispute, and such rules of international law as may be applicable. This Article is intended to offer flexibility and certainty to parties. There is flexibility because the parties have the autonomy to choose the legal rules that they want. The certainty comes from the fact that the host state law will otherwise govern. The default reference to the host state's law is appealing because it can be inferred that the legal environment of the host state should govern events which occur within its territory. A state's legal system is also presumably a component of what attracted the investor to it in the first place. There is no formal system of precedent, but later tribunals often rely on earlier tribunals' decisions, as alluded to above, creating a *de facto* system of precedent much as exists in WTO law.

The ICSID tribunal may, unless the parties say otherwise, at any stage of the proceedings call upon the parties to produce documents or other evidence and to visit the scene connected with the dispute, and may conduct such inquiries as it may deem appropriate.[43] It should be mentioned that although ICSID tribunals have broad powers in terms of the production of documents and expert witnesses, they have no power to summon witnesses. Witnesses, especially experts, often do give evidence at the behest of the parties.

Access to ICSID arbitration hearings is limited. The deliberations of ICSID tribunals tend to take place in private and remain confidential. Attendance of nonparties at hearings is subject to both parties' consent. The ICSID Convention itself is silent on confidentiality, which must be requested by parties. Most regularly do so. Many ICSID awards and other procedural decisions are now publicly reported and made available on the ICSID's website, subject to the consent of both parties, which belies some of the assertions made by critics that the ICSID is a secret court. *Amicus curiae* briefs may be permitted by the tribunal regarding a matter within the scope of the dispute. The determination of this issue depends on whether nonparty participation would assist the tribunal in making its decision and whether the relevant participant has a significant interest in the proceeding. The ICSID has empowered tribunals to accept and consider *amicus curiae* submissions if both parties agree and there is a significant interest. In *Bernhard von Pezold v. Zimbabwe*,[44] the tribunal refused *amicus* submissions because the parties withheld consent despite potential relevance of the material.

Article 50 states that where there is a dispute between the parties as to the meaning or scope of an award, either party may request interpretation of the award by an application in writing to the Secretary General of ICSID. This is designed to clarify points which had been settled. It must not address new issues that extend beyond the limits of the award. Article 50 further provides that either party may request revision of an award if some fact of such a nature that would decisively affect the award has become known to them. The new element must be one of fact and not of law

---

[43] Art. 43.

[44] ICSID Case No ARB/10/15 (11 January 2013).

and it must be capable of affecting the award decisively, either on jurisdiction (the tribunal's appropriateness to hear the matter) or merits (the substance of the claim). New facts concerning the quantification of injuries would not count for the purposes of revision.

In keeping with commercial arbitration, on which it is largely based, there is no appeal from the decision of an ICSID tribunal. The lack of an appellate mechanism has been severely criticized as antithetical to procedural fairness.[45] But it is also thought to offer a significant procedural advantage because it achieves finality. This shortens the timeframes and lowers the costs associated with protracted claims going through several layers of adjudication, as in conventional litigation. In addition to concerns regarding legitimacy, the lack of an appellate system was believed to be one of the reasons that some Latin American countries (Bolivia, followed by Ecuador and Venezuela) withdrew from the ICSID Convention. On the other hand, it is difficult to envisage precisely what form an appellate court from which ICSID decisions could be heard would take, were one to be established. Since there are thousands of IIAs, the notion of one tribunal with an authoritative understanding of their content makes little sense. This conundrum belies some of the efforts currently undertaken by the EU for a Multilateral Investment Court (MIC), of which more below.

Although there is no appeal from an ICSID decision, an award may be annulled under the procedure outlined in Article 52. Far from an appeal, the grounds of annulment are very narrow. Either party can request that an award be annulled if the tribunal was not properly constituted, if the tribunal manifestly exceeded its powers, if there was corruption on the part of a member of the tribunal, if there has been a serious departure from a fundamental rule or procedure or if the award failed to state the reasons on which it was based. In these instances, an *ad hoc* committee of arbitrators will be selected to assess the award and annul it (meaning render it void) if the allegation turns out to be accurate. The selection of the annulment committee appears to place much power in the hands of the chairman of the ICSID, who is also the president of the World Bank, taking it away from the parties.[46] The legitimacy of annulment decisions has been criticized, with some asserting that they have regularly exceeded their mandate. Most annulment committees have taken a very conservative approach with respect to their own authority, deferring to the decision of the tribunal. For example, in *El Paso Energy v. Argentina*,[47] an annulment committee denied the application for annulment on the basis that Argentina had been given ample opportunity to present its case and that the tribunal had properly established its jurisdiction under the IIA. Likewise, in *Poštová Banka v. Greece*,[48] the annulment committee explained that there is a high threshold for annulment, which should be viewed as an extraordinary remedy, and that the function of an annulment committee is quite distinct from that of a court of appeal. An annulment committee may stay the enforcement of the award pending its decision and an annulled award can be subsequently submitted to a new tribunal. When compared against the overall number of ICSID cases, there have been a rather small number of requests for annulment.

---

[45] E.g. D Collins, *The BRIC States and Outward Foreign Direct Investment* (Oxford University Press, 2013).

[46] D Collins, 'ICSID Annulment Committee Appointments: Too Much Discretion to the Chairman?' 30:4 Journal of International Arbitration 333–44 (2013).

[47] ICSID Case No ARB/03/15 (31 October 2011).

[48] ICSID Case No ARB/13/8, Annulment Proceeding (29 September 2016).

One of the major advantages of the ICSID as a forum is that there is no power of review of an ICSID award by a domestic court as there is in other types of arbitration, including other dispute settlement systems in international investment law. Article 53 of the Convention provides that the tribunal's award shall be binding on the parties and shall not be subject to any appeal other than the request for revision or annulment discussed above. Additionally, each party must abide by and comply with the terms of the award, except for any stay of enforcement pending revision or annulment. This means that the place of arbitration in ICSID proceedings is irrelevant for the award's validity and enforcement, which is automatic. ICSID arbitration is thereby 'delocalized' – it is independent of judicial interference in the country where the proceedings take place and the award is rendered. A party to ICSID proceedings may not initiate action before a domestic court to seek annulment or other types of review of an ICSID award. ICSID decisions are automatically recognized and enforceable around the world. Under Article 54, courts of all contracting states of the ICSID Convention must treat ICSID awards as the equivalent to final judgments of their highest courts. This should be contrasted with other arbitration systems, which require further domestic procedures to be enforced. Compliance with awards in terms of host states paying out compensation claims to winning investors is another issue. It is thought that the ICSID's status as a branch of the World Bank acts as an incentive to comply with awards. If a state party refuses to pay the compensation to the investor they may not be able to secure a loan from the World Bank in the future, which can be a significant incentive for a developing country. The World Bank's loan facility will be explored further in Chapter 10.

The compliance record of ICSID awards is generally quite good, although data on this matter is limited.[49] One standout is Argentina, the country which has faced the most claims under the ICSID. It has failed to honour some of its compensation obligations pursuant to ICSID decisions and has faced additional litigation on these issues in domestic courts.[50] Compliance is normally achieved on the basis of a host state's reputation to the international business community, as is common under international law, including dispute settlement under the WTO. If a losing state does not fulfil its obligations to make reparation, then future investors will be reluctant to invest within its territory. If a state fails to comply with an award issued by an ICSID tribunal, the investor's right of diplomatic protection is reengaged, meaning that its home state can take action through political pressure to demand the losing state pay the compensation and or damages. This could ultimately lead to geopolitical pressure – precisely the outcomes which international economic law was designed to avoid.

The ICSID Convention also provides for conciliation, which is a less formal process that is useful where the parties are prepared to continue their cooperation in relation to the investment. Article 34 of the Convention provides for the establishment of a Conciliation Commission to clarify the issues in a dispute between the parties, to bring about agreement between them on mutually acceptable terms. Parties are required to cooperate in good faith with the Commission so that it can carry out its functions. Conciliation Commissions have their own system of procedural rules which are more flexible and informal than those relating to arbitration. There is limited publicly

---

[49] 'Survey for ICSID Member States on Compliance with ICSID Awards' ICSID (Washington, DC, US) (1 April 2017).

[50] Blue Ridge Investments, LLC v. Republic of Argentina, No 10 Civ. 153 (S.D.N.Y. 30 September 2012).

available information about the successful application of the ICSID conciliation rules, most prob-ably because parties have chosen not to make their requests for conciliation known.

ICSID is currently in the process of amending its arbitration and conciliation rules through its most comprehensive overhaul to date. The main focus of the amendment is to modernize, simplify and streamline the rules, with a special focus on integrating information technology solutions to matters such as filing and the tendering of evidence.[51] Some of the main proposed amendments include: a new checklist within the rules which sets out that which should be included in a request to commence arbitration or conciliation (this is intended to expedite the registration of a new case and its initial stages); all filing to be done electronically unless special reasons exist to preserve paper; new time limits for various procedural steps; a new set of rules for expedited proceedings which includes additional and shortened timelines; a requirement that parties disclose whether they have third party funding, and the source of that funding, as soon as a claim is commenced; revisions to the process for challenging arbitrators, including a new expedited schedule for parties filing a challenge; publication by the ICSID of legal excerpts of the award subject to an objection by a party; and a new set of rules on mediation in response to calls from states and investors to pro-vide a greater breadth of dispute resolution tools. It should be noted that any amendments to the ICSID rules require the approval of two thirds of ICSID member states. The planned reforms to the ICSID rules have been criticized for focusing on procedural matters rather than broader insti-tutional issues, such as the suitability of party-driven arbitration as a mechanism for the settlement of investment disputes in the first place. One way forward for the ICSID might be to integrate itself into the EU's MIC project,[52] of which more will be discussed below.

6.2 UNCITRAL

UNCITRAL arbitration rules are also used commonly for ISDS and are most likely the second-most popular after ICSID. Mentioned earlier, the organization UNCITRAL was established by the UN in 1964 to harmonize international trade laws with a view to promoting economic development. UNCITRAL established a model system of procedural rules for international arbitration which were originally drafted in 1985 but were revised most recently in 2013. Reference to UNCITRAL rules can be found in a number of IIAs, typically in conjunction with the ICSID as the chief alternative.

UNCITRAL arbitration rules, which were originally designed for normal commercial arbitra-tion, are comprehensive, covering all aspects of an arbitration from the appointment of arbitrators to jurisdiction, interim measures and awards and enforcement. Unlike the ICSID, UNCITRAL does not establish an institutional setting for an arbitration, nor is there a roster of suitable ar-bitrators. One of the distinctive features of UNCITRAL rules is that they require very specific statements of claim as well as a clear indication of the relief that is sought. Unlike the ICSID, under UNCITRAL rules the parties have the option of seeking provisional measures, such as injunctions, directly from domestic courts. This can result in considerable time saving.

---

[51] 'Proposals for Amendment of ICSID Rules – Synopsis', ICSID Secretariat (Washington, DC) (2 August 2018).

[52] N Butler, 'Treating the Symptoms Rather than the Cause: A Critique of ICSID's 2018 Rules Amendment Proposals' International Trade Law and Regulation 2 (2019).

Perhaps the most crucial difference between ICSID and UNCITRAL rules is that arbitrations constituted under UNCITRAL rules are not automatically enforceable in domestic courts. Unless the relevant IIA itself provides that the arbitration decisions issued under the terms of the treaty will be enforceable (which many do), enforcement will rely on the New York Convention, mentioned in Chapter 6. The New York Convention, while assisting with recognition and enforcement, also provides that arbitration decisions may be reviewed for procedural irregularity on various grounds by domestic courts, potentially lengthening the whole process and making the outcome less certain.

UNCITRAL established its Rules on Transparency in Treaty-Based Investor–State Arbitration in an effort to address some of the concerns about the openness of its procedures. Discussed in Chapter 6, these rules apply automatically to all UNCITRAL arbitrations, unless the state parties to the relevant IIA agree otherwise.[53] UNCITRAL's transparency rules were designed to address some of the misgivings expressed by the public regarding the lack of openness in investor–state arbitration. They aim to enhance public accessibility as well as participation in dispute settlement, including a default rule that hearings will be publicly held.[54] UNCITRAL's transparency rules have proved popular and have even been adopted by some ICSID tribunals.

As an institution, UNCITRAL undertakes significant reform initiatives concerning ISDS through various working group summits. These tend to involve the participation of high level representatives of a number of countries with expertise in international investment law. In that sense UNCITRAL's very laudable efforts in improving ISDS end up being highly political processes. To its credit, UNCITRAL has tended to embrace transparency in these meetings, publicly disseminating recordings of discussions and written summaries. UNCITRAL has attempted to set a framework for a multilateral investment court since 2017. As noted in Chapter 6, the primary objective of this initiative is to address the concerns under the current systems with respect to the duration of arbitration, costs, third party funding, the arbitrators' independence and expertise and transparency, among other matters.

6.3 Iran–US Claims Tribunal

The Iran–US Claims Tribunal was one of the foundational dispute settlement mechanisms under international investment law, if not international economic law. It contributed enormously to the corpus of decisions from which a significant portion of contemporary international investment law was derived. Although it no longer operates, the jurisprudence, if that word can be used, of the Iran–US Claims Tribunal was highly influential in establishing the modern understanding of concepts such as expropriation and compensation. Located in The Hague, the Netherlands, the Iran–US Claims Tribunal was created in the aftermath of the Islamic Revolution in 1979 when a number of expropriations of US firms, particularly in the petroleum sector, were instigated by the new Iranian government. While the Iran–US Claims Tribunal did resolve some state to state claims between the US and Iran, its primary function was in relation to disputes between investors and the Iranian state. When the tribunal was first constituted, US$1 billion of Iranian money held by Iranian banks in the US was placed in an account in the Netherlands out of which claims against

---

[53] Art. 1.

[54] Art. 6(1).

Iran recognized by the tribunal would be satisfied. The tribunal consisted of nine members: three appointed by the US, three by Iran and three by agreement of the two parties. UNCITRAL rules were applied to the proceedings, although the tribunal modified these rules to some extent. Extensive case law was generated by the tribunal and although there was no principle of precedent, there was an effort by the tribunal to achieve consistency. More than four thousand private claims from US investors against Iran (and from Iranian investors against the US) have been heard by the tribunal since it was created in 1981. It was closed to new claims after 1982 and issued its final judgment (on investor–state matters) in the early 2000s. The value of jurisprudence from the Iran–US Claims Tribunal in terms of establishing broadly applicable rules of international investment law is questionable because of the tribunal's distinct historic context. Still, it is widely considered to be a vital contributor to development of international investment law, for example by establishing key aspects of the principles of expropriation and compensation.

7. THE INVESTMENT COURT SYSTEM (ICS) AND THE MULTILATERAL INVESTMENT COURT (MIC)

The European Commission of the EU adopted a new methodology to settle investment disputes, which involves the ICS. First instigated in 2015, this procedural system features in a number of bilateral economic agreements concluded by the EU in recent years, such as the CETA and the EU–Singapore FTA. It was established in response to some of the problems recognized within traditional *ad hoc* mechanisms for arbitrating investment disputes with the ISDS, including, variously, weaknesses in consistency, transparency and legitimacy.[55]

The ICS consists of a first tier roster of 15 home and host state-appointed arbitrators from which parties may select tribunal members. Since these individuals are appointed by states, rather than by the investors as in conventional ISDS and commercial arbitration, they resemble judges rather than conventional arbitrators, as under ICSID, for example. This aspect of the process is thought to provide a degree of legitimacy that many believed was lacking in normal investor–state dispute settlement arbitration, as noted earlier. The ICS procedure also creates a code of conduct specified for the adjudicators, which was missing in other systems. This reflects the concern that previous processes lacked sufficient integrity.

The most striking feature of the new system is the establishment of an appeal process from tribunal decisions to a standing body of full time judges who are also designated by state parties. This is another departure from the principle of party autonomy which characterizes conventional arbitration. The individuals on the appellate court, who have not yet been selected for the CETA or the EU–Vietnam FTA, are even more judgelike in that this role is their full time job – they do not simply render decisions and then go back to their normal work as counsel or academics. The top tier court is intended to achieve a degree of consistency in decisions, which many feel is lacking in normal ISDS. It is a groundbreaking feature because ISDS decisions under all other systems had

---

[55] European Commission, 'Commission Welcomes Adoption of Negotiating Directives for a Multilateral Investment Court' (European Council – News Archive, 10 March 2018).

been final, other than the limited ICSID annulment process and the UNCITRAL review for procedural errors by domestic courts. The ICS has default rules on transparency and contains rules restricting third party funding, as seen in the investment chapter of the CETA, where the procedural rules are laid out. At a general level, the ICS may be seen as something of a compromise between those who advocated for the elimination of investor–state dispute settlement from IIAs and those who wished it to remain untouched. So far it has been criticized for failing to achieve the goal of legitimacy and for slowing down the normal process.[56]

The ICS system contained in the CETA, the EU–Vietnam FTA and (in a slightly different form) the EU–Singapore EPA appears to be part of a transition stage towards the EU's ultimate goal of establishing a MIC, mentioned in Chapter 6 and earlier in this chapter. The MIC would be based on the ICS model, with a first tier tribunal and a second tier appeal court. A world court of appeal for ISDS would be very difficult while there are thousands of treaties from which it draws its jurisdiction. There would be a range of different meanings for various terms, such as national treatment, MFN and expropriation. This would render definitive interpretations by such a court unrealistic and potentially problematic and would eliminate the flexibility of adapting the concepts to suit each country's needs. There is also the question of whether the court would adopt an approach of collegiality, as currently practised by the WTO Appellate Body, where one decision is issued from the entire division which heard the case, or whether there would be dissents, as is the case for modern ISDS. If there were dissents, this could lead to the impression that the decision was not wholly valid, perhaps undermining the purpose of finality. Last, for an appellate court to work for ISDS, it would be essential to establish the standard of review over the decisions of the lower tribunal, meaning the normal *ad hoc* arbitration panels which are used today. Given the significant volume of cases generated by ISDS tribunals each year it might be expected that the appellate court would take a more deferential approach, such as that characterized by the WTO's Appellate Body, otherwise it might be inundated with cases. An interventionist stance could lead to a situation where appeals become normal, effectively relegating the first tier tribunal to a perfunctory role. The establishment of the MIC might also create friction with arbitration pursued under ICSID because ICSID prohibits appeals and any other remedies against arbitral awards. ICSID also allows parties to appoint arbitrators to the tribunal, which is not envisaged under the MIC, where arbitrators are chosen by the relevant states (home and host states). Finally, the MIC could pose potential problems with respect to the recognition and enforcement of its awards, which are automatic under ICSID.[57]

8. STATE TO STATE DISPUTE SETTLEMENT

Most IIAs provide mechanisms for the resolution of disputes between the two (or more) contracting parties. In the case of FTAs with investment chapters, such features may cover commitments made in the investment chapters as well as the trade chapters. Much as the state to state dispute

---

[56] C Lévesque, 'The European Commission Proposal for an Investment Court System: Out with the Old in with the New?' CIGI, Investor-State Arbitration Series Paper No 10 (September 2016).

[57] R Howse, 'Designing a Multilateral Investment Court: Issues and Options' 36 Yearbook of European Law 209 (2017).

settlement systems in FTAs have been poorly used, as suggested in Chapter 3, these mechanisms have so far been of limited relevance in international investment law, which has been driven by claims brought by investors directly. The importance of state to state dispute settlement may grow given that some modern IIAs are eliminating ISDS, as in Brazilian CIFAs, or restricting it severely, as in the USMCA and the CPTPP, where it is only available for certain kinds of disputes or in certain designated sectors.

The state to state dispute settlement mechanisms within IIAs tend to refer to the establishment of an arbitration tribunal, often following a period of attempted settlement through negotiations or other alternative dispute settlement methods. For example, Article 8 of the China–Korea BIT of 2007 provides:

1. The Contracting Parties shall consult promptly through diplomatic channel, upon request by either Contracting Party, to resolve any dispute in connection with this Agreement, or to discuss any matter relating to the interpretation or application of this Agreement or to the realisation of the objectives of this Agreement.
2. If a dispute cannot thus be settled within six months, it shall, upon the request of either Contracting Party, be submitted to an ad hoc arbitral tribunal.

This Article proceeds to specify how the arbitral tribunal will be appointed, that the law of the treaty itself (supplemented by the rules of international law) will govern the dispute, that the decision shall be binding on both parties and that the tribunal shall select its own procedure.[58]

It should be acknowledged that the ICJ, a state to state dispute settlement forum for many aspects of public international law and often described as the World Court, has played a limited role in international investment law. This is despite its long history and the potential for the treatment of foreign investment to be a source of tension among states. IIAs tend not to reference the ICJ as a forum for the resolution of state to state claims, although the president of the ICJ can be used to help select an ISDS arbitrator if the parties cannot agree.

Last, it is worth recalling from Chapter 6 that there are several investment-oriented agreements managed by the WTO and for which WTO dispute settlement, outlined in Chapter 3, can be used. The WTO dispute settlement system is, of course, a state to state dispute settlement mechanism. Through this process, complaints regarding failure to fulfil commitments made under the GATS, the TRIMs and TRIPS may be enforced by states on behalf of their investors. Recall that remedies for breach of WTO law do not yield monetary damages, so this recourse may offer limited utility to an aggrieved investor.

9. ALTERNATIVE DISPUTE SETTLEMENT

Formal binding arbitration is a last resort in international investment law, much as it is in the law of the WTO, in RTAs and in conventional domestic civil litigation. Formal procedures are inevita-

---

[58] Art. 8 (3)–(6).

bly expensive, are time consuming and do not lend themselves to long term commercial relationships. This is why alternatives regularly feature in international investment law.

9.1 Mandatory conciliation

Alternative dispute settlement methods, such as conciliation (discussions with a view to reaching a compromise) and mediation (similar to arbitration but nonbinding), are believed to save time and cost. They may also preserve the integrity of the relationship between the parties, which is thought to be conducive to long term business. They are a kind of structured diplomacy designed to deescalate conflict. Most IIAs include material on alternative dispute settlement before formal arbitration proceedings can be brought, whether state to state or investor–state. Informal resolution of conflict is seen as less expensive and conducive to conserving amity between parties. It may prevent formal dispute settlement in the form of arbitration.

Alternative dispute settlement through nonbinding mediation and conciliation is often framed in best efforts language. For example, Article 20 of the India–ASEAN Investment Agreement states:

> 5. In the event of an investment dispute referred to in paragraph 1 of this Article, the disputing parties shall as far as possible resolve the dispute through consultations and negotiations, with a view towards reaching an amicable settlement. Such consultations and negotiations, which may include the use of non-binding, third party procedures, shall be initiated by a written request for consultations and negotiations by the disputing investor to the disputing Party.
> 6. With the objective of resolving an investment dispute through consultations and negotiations, a disputing investor shall provide the disputing Party, prior to the commencement of consultations and negotiations, with information regarding the legal and factual basis for the dispute.

Other treaties present arbitration and conciliation/mediation as options which are equally available to parties. This approach can be seen, for example, in the 2003 Israel Model BIT:

> If a dispute under paragraph 1 of this Article cannot be settled within six (6) months of a written notification of this dispute, it shall be on the request of the investor settled as follows:
> (a) by a competent court of the Host Contracting Party; or
> (b) by conciliation; or
> (c) by arbitration by the International Center for the Settlement of Investment Disputes (ICSID).[59]

As with arbitration itself, informal dispute settlement procedures are confidential and it is difficult to establish the degree to which informal procedures have played a role in settlements. The ICSID

---

[59] Art. 8.1.

reports that 36 per cent of the total disputes brought before its tribunals since its inception were settled.[60] ISDS tribunals take a strict approach to the obligation to pursue conciliation. In *Murphy Exploration v. Ecuador*,[61] the tribunal emphasized that reference to consultation in the IIA was not a mere formality but an essential mechanism to reduce costs and delays in the resolution of disputes between parties who were in a long term commercial relationship.

9.2 Informal home state dispute resolution

Although home state courts are undesirable as fora for the resolution of disputes relating to foreign investment for the reasons noted earlier, this does not mean that the governments of foreign investors' places of origin do not have a role to play in the maintenance of peaceful relations between investors and the places in which they operate. Some home states maintain informal dispute resolution mechanisms to address problems that may arise when their own companies engage in investment activities abroad. These are often associated with OECD members' obligation to maintain contact national contact points regarding each state's fulfilment of its obligations under the Guidelines on Multinational Enterprises, mentioned in Chapter 6.

At the national level, Canada maintains an informal dispute settlement mechanism addressing the activities of Canadian companies overseas. Created in 2018, the Canadian Ombudsman for Responsible Enterprise (CORE) replaces an earlier initiative which was aimed exclusively at Canada's extractive sector.[62] Among the first mechanisms of its kind in the world, the CORE investigates allegations of human rights and other social harms linked to Canadian investors' activity abroad. It seeks to resolve disputes or conflicts between impacted communities and Canadian companies, with an emphasis on collaboration. It is empowered to independently investigate, report, recommend, remedy and monitor its implementation. It is unclear at this time whether the CORE will publish its investigations or interventions with a view to providing greater transparency into its activities and those of Canadian companies, in turn fulfilling their CSR obligations. It is often thought that public disclosure of investigations of this nature may act as an incentive to pressure investors to behave in a manner which is more supportive of the needs of the constituents of the states in which they operate.

10. CONCLUSION

The debate regarding the legitimacy of dispute settlement in international investment law through international arbitration tribunals shows no sign of abating. If anything the disdain appears to be intensifying, to the point that the traditional system of ISDS is on the verge of collapsing due to the weight of opposition, especially from the academic community but also from citizen groups,

---

[60] 'ICSID Case Load Statistics 2018' ICSID (Washington, DC) (2018).

[61] ICSID Case No ARB/08/4 (15 December 2010).

[62] D Collins, 'Alternative Dispute Settlement for Stakeholders in International Investment Law' 15:2 Journal of International Economic Law 673–700 (2012).

including many of those who resist economic liberalization in any form which it assumes. Notwithstanding the vulnerability of foreign firms who enter unstable countries lacking rule of law, IIAs are by their nature onesided in favour of investors in terms of their substance. With regard to the process by which they are enforced, which was the focus of this chapter, the bypassing of local court procedures in favour of the international tribunals does appear suspect in places where rule of law and independent courts are strong.

ISDS reform initiatives can be found in all regions and countries at different levels of development. Individual states have been the driving forces behind certain approaches, including Brazil, India and the EU. Modifications to ISDS have also appeared in megaregional initiatives such as the CPTPP and the USMCA. Multilateral engagement on ISDS reform is also gaining pace, seen in UNCITRAL Working Group discussions on the possible reform of the ICSID and the ICSID's own work on the amendment of its rules. While eliminating or restricting access to international arbitration may be addressing the wrong problem – perhaps it is the IIAs themselves which need to be reformed rather than the procedural mechanisms to enforce them – ultimately ISDS should be designed to produce fair outcomes that capture societal values, at least as these are perceived by the system's users.

Mindful that the economic gains to be achieved from FDI for investors and states relies heavily on the ability of multinational enterprises to access foreign currency and on the economic stability of host states, the next chapter will consider another important aspect of international economic law: monetary relations, as supervised by the International Monetary Fund (IMF).

DISCUSSION QUESTIONS

1. To what extent does ISDS undermine national judicial sovereignty and should this be viewed as an unacceptable compromise for states seeking FDI?
2. How does ISDS differ from dispute settlement under the WTO and are the reasons for these differences justified?
3. What are the major problems with dispute settlement under ICSID and how might these issues be resolved?
4. Is a world investment court feasible or desirable?

FURTHER READING

C Ajibo and N Nwafor, 'Jurisdictional Competence and Deferential Standard of Review in Investor-State Dispute Settlement: A Case for Balance of Prerogatives' 14:2 Manchester Journal of International Economic Law 199 (2017).

R Howse, 'Designing a Multilateral Investment Court: Issues and Options' 36 Yearbook of European Law 209 (2017).

JM Hunter and JG Olmedo, 'Enforcement/Execution of ICSID Awards against Reluctant States' 12:3 Journal of World Investment and Trade 307 (2018).

J Paine, 'On Investment Law and Questions of Change' 19:2 Journal of World Investment and Trade 173 (2018).

PART III
INTERNATIONAL MONETARY LAW AND DEVELOPMENT

9
International monetary relations and the International Monetary Fund

1. INTRODUCTION

The previous two chapters dealt with international investment law, specifically the contents of IIAs and the dispute settlement mechanism enabling investors to enforce these rights. It will be remembered that in Chapter 7 it was noted that in order for multinational enterprises to secure profits from their activities overseas they should be permitted to transfer the proceeds of their investment, denominated in the local currency, to that of their home state. Equally, foreign investors should be able to access sufficient local currency to finance their operations in the host state. From the perspective of host states incurring the obligations outlined in Chapter 7 and seeking to avoid defending themselves in the dispute arena explained in Chapter 8, host states should accordingly seek to remain economically stable, meaning that their monetary system is able to facilitate such transactions. Economic stability is, of course, a condition that a state should want in its own right, not simply because it makes it attractive to foreign investment. Economic stability tends to be reflected in the value of a country's currency, with stable exchange rates being conducive not only to political and social equilibrium but also to healthy levels of international trade (domestic companies and consumers can buy foreign goods and services) as well as international investment, as noted above. Furthermore, a state's refusal to honour its debts by paying out sovereign bonds may amount to a breach of the state's obligations under investment treaties, raising the spectre of additional liability in investment tribunals.[1]

All financial transactions between states (including those related to trade and investment) require an international legal framework for payment. There are three major impediments to this system. The first is currency rate fluctuation, meaning uncertainties in the value of a currency over time. The second is restrictions on convertibility of currency, meaning the ability of private parties and governments to access currency of a particular jurisdiction. Finally, there is the problem of

---

[1] Abaclat and Others v. Argentine Republic, ICSID Case No ARB/07/5 (formerly Giovanna a Beccara and Others v. The Argentine Republic) Decision on Jurisdiction (4 August 2011).

balance of payments disequilibrium, which means that the state becomes insolvent because it is spending more than it is earning, often because it imports more than it exports and has a public sector which is too large relative to the resources generated by income tax. All of these can result in economic instability. In a highly integrated world, such instability has the propensity to spread from one country to another, often as a virus spreads from person to person through contact. This is why the term 'contagion' is often used to describe an international economic crisis. The way in which international economic law manages these issues is the focus of this chapter, which is concerned primarily with the work of the International Monetary Fund (IMF), one of the three Bretton Woods institutions created in the 1940s to save the world from war and economic ruin by identifying and treating economic crises before they escalate.

Unlike the first two topics in this book, the monetary relations aspect of international economic law is perhaps somewhat harder to grasp as a concept. Trade and investment are concrete, tangible elements of the global economy. The goods, and even the services, supplied across international borders or by internationally mobile firms can be seen and felt. In contrast, money is by its nature an abstraction. Indeed, it was a key point in human civilization when money was 'invented' as a symbolic store of value to simplify trade, arguably the second most important abstraction after language (or third if you include God). Gold has intrinsic value because it is beautiful to behold and has industrial applications, but paper dollars are worthless. Electronic payments are even less valuable, composed of subatomic particles which can barely be measured, let alone bought and sold. Like paper dollars, their worth is purely representational. This is why it is sometimes hard to come to terms with 'the supply of money', much as it is not always easy to appreciate that a state, which has the authority to print its own currency, can run out of money to pay for things like public services or that it would need to ask for loan on which interest will be charged. Yet these very real phenomena are vital aspects of global commerce, and therefore within the sphere of interest of international economic law.

A second difficulty with international monetary relations as a subject within international economic law is that international monetary law as supervised by the IMF is not truly 'law' at all – this is another reason why it can be more challenging to come to terms with than international trade or investment. Although it is an international organization of unquestionable importance, with global reach, the IMF does not truly impose legally binding obligations on its members which create enforceable legal rights. In that sense the work of the IMF and the monetary discipline within international economic law is more accurately described as a kind of global governance. This chapter will begin with a brief commentary on payment methods in international trade in order to highlight the importance of money in the global economy.

2. TRADE TERMS AND INTERNATIONAL PAYMENT METHODS

Firms which engage in trade have a number of options regarding the format of payment for foreign goods and services. The method chosen will depend on the risk they are prepared to accept, which in turn is linked to the relationship they have with their international trading partner. The first option is open account, which is probably the least secure payment method for exporters.

The buyer receives the goods and then pays for them, usually with a credit period attached which can be up to three months long. This payment method extends the period before which the exporter receives cash, potentially undermining their liquidity if a period of credit applies. Open account may be appropriate if the exporter has an established business relationship with the importer or if the importer is a multinational business with strong buying power and a strong credit rating. It may also be suitable for smaller value exports. The second option is bank collection, which is a more secure option than an open account. Under this system the exporter's bank collects the money on the exporter's behalf. An instruction document is forwarded by the exporter's bank to the importer's bank for release against either payment or acceptance. Bank collection can be a good way of sharing risk between exporters and importers. The third method is via a letter of credit. This involves a bank's promise to another bank that they are familiar with the exporter and will act as a guarantor for their transaction. Both the exporter and the importer's banks must agree to act in this way. Once it is agreed, if the importer is unable to make payment, its bank will cover and pay the outstanding amount, provided that certain delivery conditions have been met. Finally, there is the option of advance payment, which is the most advantageous method for the exporter because the buyer must pay for the goods before they receive them, much as consumers do when they purchase goods online. Advance payment is the best system for payment when the relationship between the exporter and importer is new and therefore there is a lack of trust between the parties. It can also be useful where the importer does not have a strong credit rating or where the goods being sold are of high value.[2] As to the payment system itself, this will tend to be done via electronic transfer between financial institutions, each of which will have its own procedures and protocols. Standardization has facilitated the internationalization of these systems, although there are country specific networks. Having outlined in simple terms how money is exchanged in the context of trade, this chapter will now turn to its main focus, the work of the IMF.

3. THE INTERNATIONAL MONETARY FUND

3.1 History

The IMF is an international organization composed of 188 member countries. As noted in Chapter 1, it was established alongside the World Bank and the GATT to prevent economic recession and the escalation of armed conflicts. The IMF commenced financial operations on 1 March 1947, though it came into official existence on 27 December 1945, when 29 countries signed its Articles of Agreement. The IMF was originally created as part of the Bretton Woods agreement to encourage international financial cooperation and stability by introducing a system of convertible currencies at fixed exchange rates, with the US dollar redeemable for gold at the set amount of US$35 per ounce. The IMF supervised this system, ensuring that a country was free to readjust its exchange rate by up to 10 per cent in either direction, with larger changes requiring the IMF's

---

[2] Institute of Export and International Trade, 'Methods of Payment' (2018).

permission. The US abandoned the fixed system of exchange rates based on the gold standard in the 1970s because it no longer held enough physical gold to back all of its dollars in circulation (due to the rapid expansion of the US economy). From that point onward the IMF promoted a system of floating exchange rates, meaning that market forces determine the value of currencies relative to one another. This system remains in place today.

The 1970s saw massive borrowing by the developing countries, approaching US$1 trillion by the mid-1980s. The rise in interest rates in the US and the appreciation of the dollar led to major difficulties in the developing world in servicing their debts. The switch from a fixed to floating exchange rate system is thought to have contributed to deteriorating economic conditions in industrialized countries, including the US itself. At this point the IMF played a crucial role in imposing order on the global financial system, as several countries announced their inability to pay their debts – they had spent more than they could afford on public services and on imports from other countries. The IMF sought to mobilize additional financial resources, essentially increasing lending, to reduce the debt burden, especially that which was faced by the developing world. As a result of this and other measures, many countries regained access to international banks and creditors, allowing their economies to stabilize. The severity of the debt problem moderated considerably, especially in Latin America in the early 1990s. Following the breakup of the Soviet Union in 1989, a new category of country, in particular the former communist states, joined the IMF. The IMF aimed to assist these states which were undergoing transition from a centrally planned economy to a market-oriented economy. It did this in part by encouraging privatization, which is often viewed as an essential element of the transition process. Indeed, the IMF continues to provide financial assistance and technical support for the privatization and sound management of state enterprises. For example, in 1997, the East Asian financial crisis began when the currencies of the 'Asian Tiger' economies (South Korea, Singapore, Hong Kong, Taiwan) plummeted and their stock markets crashed. Rescue packages were launched by the IMF aimed at cutting public spending. The features of these types of initiatives will be examined further below.

While currency problems were the dominant challenge to which the IMF turned its attention during its earlier decades, banking crises and sovereign defaults became the key focus after the 1980s and into the twenty-first century. Indeed, these are the issues with which the IMF is most closely associated today. In the early part of this century, the IMF moved from providing relatively brief and comparatively modest balance of payments support in the era of fixed exchange rates to coping with more chronic debt sustainability problems that emerged in the developing economies and later transferred to advanced economies. This latter aspect of its work is associated with the global financial crisis of 2008–9 and its aftermath. The IMF has engaged in what might be described as 'serial lending' to deal with these kinds of chronic problems, with programmes in some cases spanning decades. More recently the IMF has faced the real risk of lending into insolvency, most obviously in the case of Greece and a handful of other countries in the eurozone since 2010.[3]

---

[3] C Reinhart, C Trebesch, 'The International Monetary Fund: 70 Years of Reinvention' 30:1 Journal of Economic Perspectives (Winter 2016).

3.2 Policy overview

Today, the purview of the IMF covers the monetary relations component of international economic law. It is charged with maintaining free transfer of currencies, ensuring that transnational commercial transactions can take place and that foreign investors can have access to domestic capital to fund their operations. The IMF also has the perhaps more widely recognized role of preventing member states' balance of payment problems through short term loans, known as 'bailouts' – many of which have been taken by developed countries – on condition that they implement certain pro market economic reforms, sometimes referred to as 'haircuts'. As suggested above, the IMF's objective of liberalizing currency transfers in order to promote capital movement is a pivotal component of home state policies towards outward FDI as well as their capacity to attract inward FDI. The liberalization of currency is vitally important to trade. This is because in a highly globalized world suppliers will often need access to foreign finance to purchase inputs, just as consumers will sometimes draw upon foreign capital to purchase the goods and services.

While most developed countries maintain a fully convertible currency, many developing countries do not – including some of the large emerging markets, such as India – in part because it is concerned that if it does not impose restrictions, much of its capital could be taken out abruptly, leading to economic instability. Limitations on currency transfer can be problematic for foreign companies buying assets in these countries and which must repay investors from profits earned abroad. The IMF's critical emphasis on sovereign liquidity and the maintenance of balance of payments equilibrium underlines a key exception to the guarantee of free movement of investors' capital of which international investors must be aware. This is crucial given the increasing incidence and severity of sovereign debt problems worldwide.

Exploring the work of the IMF today reveals what some might view as a curious interest, on the part of the organization, in matters which appear to stray well beyond its core focus on monetary relations and sovereign debt. Issues such as climate change and gender appear prominently on the IMF's website and feature in a number of the institution's policy research papers. Progressivism of this nature is very much in fashion and in one sense it is difficult to criticize the IMF for drawing attention to these important issues through its highly visible global platform. Still, as the IMF is neither a development agency nor an environmental agency, it is hard to resist the conclusion that in so doing the IMF may be suffering from what is often referred to as mission creep. The climate change movement, for example, is a good example of a policy agenda which, due to its sweeping impact across so many aspects of commercial activity, carries with it the danger of drawing the IMF away from what should be its central mandate – the stability of the world's exchange system and the liquidity of sovereign states. The relevance of various progressive issues to this central objective is tenuous to the point that one cannot help but wonder if the IMF's ostensible interest in such fields is designed primarily to improve its public image.

The IMF's stated objectives, found in Article I of its Articles of Agreement, bear a striking resemblance to those of the WTO. This article states that the IMF seeks to ensure growth in international trade to ensure full employment, an increased standard of living and productive use of the world's resources. Most importantly, the IMF aims to promote stability in the global economic system by shortening the duration and lessening the degree of disequilibrium in the international balance of payments of its members. It does this by encouraging currency exchange stability and the promotion of currency convertibility, and by acting as a lender of last resort to states to create liquidity in the supply of money. In keeping with the modern emphasis on transparency in international governance, the IMF engages in information collection and dissemination.

While the goals and methods of the IMF are less characteristic of international 'law' than the rules of the WTO and IIAs, its policies nevertheless constitute obligations on the part of its constituent members, which are also found in the IMF's Articles of Agreement. As a source of international governance (as distinct from black letter law) the principal function of the IMF is to supervise the international monetary system. Several associated functions may be derived from this. These are: granting of credit to member countries in the midst of temporary balance of payments deficits; surveillance over the monetary and exchange rate policy of member countries; and issuing policy recommendations. The main principles by which it achieves these aims are: first, the application of the principles of market economy; second, opening up of the economy by removing all barriers of trade (through which it cooperates with the WTO); and third, the prevention of deflation, meaning a decrease in the general level of prices of goods and services, which tends to be associated with economic recession.

3.3 Institutional issues

As with many international organizations, the IMF is managed by a Board of Governors and an Executive Board and employs an international staff of more than 2000 employees, three times as many as the WTO. Every member country appoints a representative (usually heads of central banks or ministers of finance) to the Board of Governors, which is the highest decision making body in the IMF. It meets once a year and takes decisions on fundamental matters such as electing new members or changing quotas. The Executive Board is entrusted with the management of day to day policy decisions. The Executive Board comprises 24 Executive Directors who supervise the implementation of policies set by the member governments through the Board of Governors. The IMF is headed by the Managing Director, who is elected by the Executive Board for a 5 year term of office. The current Managing Director is Christine Lagarde, a lawyer and former French politician. At the time of writing she is due to be replaced by Kristalina Georgieva, a Bulgarian national and former interim president of the World Bank. By convention, the director of the IMF is normally a European.

The rights and obligations of IMF members are determined by a system of quotas, outlined in Article III of the Articles of Agreement. Quotas are decided by a vote of the Board of Governors. A member's quota determines its payment obligations, access to credit facilities (loans) and voting rights. Quotas are based on a state's economic size, essentially its GDP. This is a departure from the principle of sovereign equality of states which characterizes the voting of the WTO. Different voting majorities are required for different types of decisions. Some believe that the weighted voting system used by the IMF's Board of Governors and Executive Board creates problems of democratic legitimacy.[4] The IMF's quotas were recently reallocated to reflect changes in the global economy,

---

[4] D Leetch, 'Transparency and Democracy in the Governance of the International Monetary Fund and Reforms in Progress: A Voting Power Analysis' in E Sciso ed. Accountability, Transparency and Democracy in the Functioning of Bretton Woods Institutions (Springer, 2017).

notably the rise of emerging markets such as China and India, although China's lack of power in IMF governance may be one of the reasons why it sought to pursue its own multilateral monetary project through the Asian Infrastructure Investment Bank (AIIB) – although this organization does not yet appear to have delved into monetary matters in the manner of the IMF.

The capital or the resources of the IMF come from two sources: subscription or quota of the member nations (effectively annual membership fees) and the IMF's own borrowings. Each member state is required to subscribe an amount equivalent to its quota. As soon as a state joins the IMF it is assigned a quota, which is expressed in the IMF's own currency, known as special drawing rights (SDRs), of which more below. The size of the IMF's holdings equals the sum of the subscriptions of members. The IMF is authorized to borrow from other international capital markets in special circumstances if its own resources prove to be insufficient, although there is no record of this having ever taken place. The IMF also sells gold to member countries to replenish currency holdings. Currently the IMF holds US$1 trillion of reserves which it is able to lend to its member states, with an additional US$300 million available for technical advice and training.

4. OBJECTIVES OF THE IMF

The IMF's main objectives, and by extension the obligations of its members, may be found in its Articles of Agreement. The Articles of Agreement of the IMF are the legal basis of the international monetary system. They have the force of an international treaty, although, as noted below, there is limited enforcement capacity. Each of the IMF's key objectives, some of which are framed in terms of its members' obligations, will now be considered in turn.

4.1 Objective 1: maintain stable exchange rates

Under Article IV, IMF members are obligated to collaborate with the IMF itself and with other members to assure a stable system of exchange rates. Members must follow exchange policies which are conducive to economic stability, orderly growth and reasonable price stability. Additionally, members cannot manipulate the value of their own currency in order to gain competitive advantage, prohibiting the so-called currency wars in which a state attempts to devalue its currency to gain an advantage in export trade. This strategy is based on the fact that as the exchange value of a given country's currency declines, its goods become relatively cheaper to foreign purchasers, raising the volume of exports and typically boosting the economy. The IMF will oversee every member's fulfilment of these obligations.

Strategically undervalued exchange rates not only operate as subsidies to exports, they also effectively raise import tariffs above the levels negotiated at the WTO, in clear violation of GATT Article VI and Article II. It is thought that undervalued currencies can undermine all trade defence instruments, including antidumping, antisubsidy countervailing duties and safeguards, discussed in Chapter 4. This rule was designed to avoid the exchange rate policies 'anarchy' of the 1930s and the balance of payment crisis experienced by many states after the end of the Second World War.

The founders of the IMF believed that protectionist measures such as currency manipulation were one of the main causes of economic collapse in the period. If no country was allowed to devalue its currency to gain a commercial advantage over its neighbour under international law, the balance of payments of all countries would be protected and there would not be a damaging 'race to the bottom' as occurred during the Great Depression.[5] On the other hand, studies have suggested that currency manipulation, achieved via methods such as quantitative easing (printing more money), is not actually effective in stimulating exports, as is often believed. In fact, downward currency manipulation can lead to a decline in exports and ultimately inflict harm on the states which use it.[6]

It is the IMF which arguably bears the burden of preventing aggressive currency manipulation for the purposes of gaining the upper hand in international trade. When states accuse others of engaging in this practice, this is often a veiled accusation that the IMF has failed to discharge its duty in this regard by policing the bad behaviour of its members. In a recent prominent incident, the US accused China of engaging in currency depreciation to advantage its exports and also as a tool to combat US tariffs on China, although it fell short of formally declaring China a currency manipulator under US domestic law.[7] This was presented by the US as an explanation for China's significant trade surplus with respect to the US (it exports far more to the US than vice versa). It is unlikely that China is engaging in currency manipulation. There have always been fluctuations in the value of the renminbi versus the US dollar, with the latter being substantially stronger because of the US' pre-eminent role as the world's only global superpower and still the largest economy, at times by a wide margin depending on the numbers used. Chinese manufacturers need to purchase their inputs from other countries using their own currency and this would become dangerously expensive if China were to suppress the renminbi's value artificially. Moreover, China must use its own currency to buy US government bonds, which it has done in abundance. Since these instruments are denominated in US dollars, a weak renminbi would undermine China's purchasing power. If China or other countries are indeed manipulating their currency strategically in response to tariffs which have been imposed by countries like the US on the basis of thinly justifiable essential security accusations (as mentioned in Chapter 5), then perhaps this is an appropriate kind of retaliation – an illegal response to an illegal action. Such retaliation is sanctioned by neither the WTO nor the IMF. Indeed, it is often observed that international economic law has failed to police currency manipulation adequately and that a major change is needed to address this important obstacle to global economic liberalization.[8] Regional attempts to deal with this issue will be explored further below.

---

[5] V Thorstensen, D Ramos, C Muller, 'The "Missing Link" Between the WTO and the IMF' 16:2 Journal of International Economic Law 353 (2013).

[6] A Rose, 'Currency Wars? Unconventional Monetary Policy Does Not Stimulate Exports' NBER Working Paper No 24817 issued in July 2018.

[7] S Fleming and C Smith, 'US Declines to Label China a Currency Manipulator' Financial Times (17 October 2018).

[8] C Wong, 'Regulating Currency Manipulation: Political, Legal and Economic Barriers to Reform' 51:4 Journal of World Trade 691 (2017).

4.2 Objective 2: no restrictions on currency conversion

Under Article VIII there must be a system of unhindered transfers of payment between residents and non-residents of each member state. This means that currencies must be freely convertible into one another and there should be no restrictions on how a currency may be used or where it may be held. Discrimination in currency convertibility, meaning allowing conversion of one IMF member's currency but not another's, is also prohibited. As discussed earlier, unrestricted transfer of currency is critical to international investment law because it enables foreign investors to send the profits they earn from their operations back home to their shareholders. It should be noted that members may be entitled to break this rule where their currency is scarce and the economy is at risk, for example in situations of 'capital flight'.

The IMF's jurisdiction over the financial flows associated with the current account (a country's investment and trade transactions with the rest of the world) primarily involves an emphasis on best efforts mutual self-restraint, with the IMF acting as an intergovernmental referee. This is because the IMF has limited hard legal powers to enforce compliance with its Articles of Agreement, of which more will be said below. Similarly, the IMF has limited formal power to influence its members' capital flow measures. A state's capital account consists of cross-border investments in financial instruments as well as changes in central bank reserves, essentially incorporating a state's assets as well as its income. The IMF may neither prohibit a member state to restrict capital in or outflows nor require it to impose capital account restrictions, except in very special circumstances, most notably in the context of an IMF programme. In recognition of the limits of global governance in monetary matters (as in other aspects of economic law) the IMF has never been able to convince a sufficient proportion of its members to surrender sovereignty over capital flows in a formal manner.[9]

4.3 Objective 3: sovereign debt relief

Article V specifies that the IMF will provide financial assistance to its members which experience serious financial and economic difficulties. These are the so-called bailouts which featured prominently in the global media during the financial crisis of the late 2000s. Money for this purpose will be drawn from the reserve contributed to by all of the IMF member states. Loans are short term and intended to redress members' balance of payment problems, which occur when a state spends more than it earns. This must be contrasted with the type of loans offered by the World Bank, which will be examined in the next chapter. Seeking an IMF loan is viewed as a last resort and the loan is often obtained in conjunction with loans from other sources, such as the European Central Bank in the case of EU member states. It may also be perceived as an act of humiliation because the borrowing state is admitting that it cannot manage its own economy and needs help from the global community.

---

[9] M Broos and S Grund, 'The IMF's Jurisdiction Over the Capital Account – Reviewing the Role of Surveillance in Managing Cross-Border Capital Flows' 21:3 Journal of International Economic Law 489 (2018).

If a state calls on the IMF for assistance, that state buys foreign currencies from the IMF in return for the equivalent in the domestic currency. This is called a 'drawing' on the Fund. Structuring the transaction in this way suggests that the IMF does not actually lend, but rather sells the required currency to the members on certain terms. The IMF's unique financial structure does not allow any member to obtain financial assistance over a long time period because the total amount that a country is entitled to draw is determined by the amount of its quota. A member is entitled to draw an amount not exceeding 25 per cent of its quota. The first 25 per cent is called the 'gold tranche' ('tranche' is French for 'slice') or 'reserve tranche' and it can easily be drawn by countries with balance of payment problems. This amount of the quota represents the members' owned reserves and therefore no conditions are attached to such drawings. Essentially a pre-existing entitlement to money which the IMF holds on the member's behalf, this may be called 'ordinary, drawing rights' and even the Fund cannot deny its use. No interest is required to be paid on the first credit tranche; however, such drawings are subject to repayment within a period of three to five years. This kind of borrowing is also known as a stand-by arrangement. This method of borrowing has become the most normal form of assistance by the IMF. Standby arrangements can be extended for up to three years, while repayments are required to be made within 3–5 years of each drawing. Additional drawings, each equalling 25 per cent of a member's quota, are also available subject to IMF approval, and therefore they are 'conditional'. Originally it was possible to borrow amounts equal to 125 per cent of a member's quota. At present, the borrowing limit is 450 per cent of a member's quota, which must be redeemed within five years.

Loans may also be done via the IMF's Extended Fund Facility (EFF). This kind of borrowing is suitable for member states which suffer from chronic balance of payments difficulties, meaning those which last longer than a few years, often caused by structural imbalances in production and trade rather than one-off shocks or recessions. Created in 1974, the EFF is designed to provide assistance to members to meet their balance of payments deficits for a longer period (3–4 years) and in larger amounts than are available under their allocated quotas. Repayment provisions of EFF cover a period of 4–10 years. Unlike standby arrangements, conditions for granting EFF loans are stringent and will be explored further below.

Distinct from the ordinary drawing rights, there are some special finance options available to assist states to handle their balance of payments difficulties. Introduced by the IMF in 1964, the Compensatory Financing Facility (CFF) now allows members to draw up to 45 per cent of their quota. In 1986 a new mechanism, the Structural Adjustment Facility (SAF), was introduced for the benefit of low income countries. This was due to the realization that the existing, rather stringent and inflexible, credit arrangements were inadequate to cope with the growing debt problems of the IMF's poorest members. Under the SAF, credit facilities for economic reform programmes are available at a low interest rate of 0.5 per cent, compared to 6 per cent for most of the Fund's loans. SAF loans are for 10 years with a grace period of 5.5 years. Least developed countries facing protracted balance of payment problems may receive assistance under SAF provided they agree to undertake medium term structural adjustment programmes to foster economic growth and improve balance of payments conditions, of which more will be said below. The Poverty Reduction and Growth Facility (PRGF), introduced in 1999, provides concessional lending to help the poorest member countries, with the aim of poverty reduction and economic growth. Under the

PRGF, low income member countries are eligible to borrow up to 140 per cent of their quota for a three-year period. Only 0.5 per cent interest is charged and the repayment period covers 5.5–10 years. Financial assistance under this facility is subject to the IMF's standard suite of conditions. Finally, there is the Supplemental Reserve Facility (SRF). This option provides additional short term financing to member countries facing exceptional balance of payment difficulties because of a sudden and disruptive loss of market confidence reflected in capital outflows. The SRF was introduced in 1997 following the East Asian financial crisis.

5. LOAN CONDITIONALITY

It was mentioned several times above that IMF loans are made available subject to certain conditions. These typically involve the borrowing state instituting reforms to redress the economic problems which led to it asking for a loan. These are linked to Arts I, IV and V of the Articles of Agreement, which require that the IMF maintain adequate 'safeguards' regarding the use of its resources, essentially ensuring that the loans will be repaid. Conditions on the loans are individually negotiated and will vary according to each member's circumstances, although they are often accused of being too standardized. Conditions are usually concerned with revenue generation and administrative streamlining with a view to reducing government expenditures. Such conditions could include preventing tax avoidance, lowering pension age and decreasing the size of government generally. They are also focused on enhancing international trade and attracting foreign investment.

The main conditionality requirement in IMF loans is the introduction of structural reforms. As noted earlier, low income countries drew from the IMF in the early 1980s, when many of them faced severe balance of payment difficulties along with serious debt repayment problems. The Fund consequently initiated economic stabilization programmes and structural adjustment programmes. A stabilization programme involves addressing demand management. This means that the borrowing state is required to take steps to influence aggregate demand (more people buying things) in an economy through looser fiscal policy – such as cutting income tax, which gives consumers more income to spend – or through monetary policy – such as lowering interest rates, making it cheaper to borrow and therefore stimulating consumer spending. Structural programmes concentrate on supply management. This involves cost control strategies, such as lowering public spending, perhaps in relation to pensions, education or healthcare.

The IMF's loan conditionality guidelines specify that the responsibility for the design and implementation of a state's conditionality policies is on the state itself, seemingly emphasizing the sovereignty that a state should have over its own economy even though it is a member of a multilateral organization. Policies must consider the domestic and social policy objectives of the individual member, with the overriding purpose being balance of payments equilibrium. Conditions prescribed by the IMF are macroeconomic, meaning that they are not directed at reforming a specific underperforming company, industry or sector. Perhaps most crucially, conditionality must not intrude into the political affairs of the member. This last requirement again reflects the understanding that the IMF's agenda is one of economic health, not political reform.

The IMF's conditionality requirements are controversial for several reasons. Generally speaking, they tend to reflect a free market-oriented ideology associated with the foreign policy of the US, which has the largest share of voting quotas. Tied to this, the Fund's conditionality policies are thought by some to cast the organization in the role of a 'neo-colonist' in that they are designed to put foreign countries in a better position to receive trade and investment from the West. Structural adjustment programs are sometimes thought to exacerbate poverty, leaving countries beholden to the demands of the IMF and by extension the US. IMF conditionality is often criticized because it is rigidly applied and therefore not adaptable to the interests of a given member, including its social needs – for example, in relation to healthcare or education – which many would argue are more important than a state's financial solvency. Last, conditionality is controversial because it represents a surrender of economic sovereignty which can be embarrassing for certain countries, especially those which are at a higher developmental status. This has led to a deep seated resentment towards it in countries such as Greece.

In light of some of these concerns, it has been questioned whether the IMF's lending policies could be challenged under general international law as an intrusion into state sovereignty, representing a kind of coercion. The problem with this view is that debtor states have accepted loan conditions voluntarily. Moreover, since there is a lack of a functional definition of coercion in international law, as long as the IMF's conditionality requirements fit the broadly framed objectives of Articles I (v) and V.3 of the Articles of Agreement, a state's right to restructure its sovereign debt should be construed as having been accordingly limited.[10]

The IMF continues to assist states experiencing economic crises. Recently it has extended loans to Venezuela. In addition to the collapse of its government, following years of extreme socialist policies, including nationalization and trade barriers, Venezuela suffers from hyperinflation and a destabilized exchange rate with crippled human capital and physical productive capacity. It also has a severe and highly complicated debt situation.[11] The IMF extended a loan programme to Sri Lanka, begun in 2018, by an additional year to give the state more time to complete economic and structural reforms following political turmoil. The conditionality attached to this loan involves prudent public spending and a greater buildup of foreign exchange reserves to protect against market shocks. It also includes competitive reforms to Sri Lanka's state owned enterprises.[12] Ecuador has recently received a billion US dollar loan package from the IMF and other lenders (including the World Bank), representing a break from the socialist policies of that state's recent past. Most of the money is intended for social investment, with an average 5 per cent interest rate and loan periods of up to 30 years. Ecuador's willingness to request IMF assistance is seen as a demonstration that the government intends to stabilize its finances and embrace marked-oriented economic reforms. The loan is designed to support the government's plans to create a more dynamic, competitive economy.[13]

---

[10] V Paliouras, 'The Right to Restructure Sovereign Debt' 20:1 Journal of International Economic Law 115 (2017).

[11] 'US Considers Emergency Economic Aid for Venezuela' Financial Times (3 March 2019).

[12] 'IMF Extends Sri Lanka Loans Programme in Respite for Colombo' Financial Times (1 March 2019).

[13] 'IMF Agrees to $4.2bn Fund for Ecuador' Financial Times (21 February 2019).

6. INTERNATIONAL LIQUIDITY AND THE SPECIAL DRAWING RIGHT

Article XV of the IMF Articles of Agreement establishes the special drawing right (SDR), which exists as a reserve asset that objectively regulates international liquidity – essentially the IMF's own currency. Members may exchange their SDRs for the real currency belonging to another nation. Exchanges may be done through the IMF or through direct agreement with another member. An amount of SDRs is allocated to each member each year based on the member's quota, which itself is tied to the IMF's assessment of its economic strength in the global economy. SDRs were established in 1969 with the objective of alleviating the problem of international liquidity, meaning access to money. Sometimes described as 'paper gold', SDRs are just a book entry in the special drawing account of the IMF. Whenever they are allocated, it gets a credit entry in the name of the participating countries in the relevant account. Once allocated to a member, SDRs are owned by it to be used to overcome balance of payment deficits. The SDR's exchange value is defined as a composite of five currencies. As of 2018, the SDR valuation basket is as follows: US dollar: 41.73 per cent; euro: 30.93 per cent; Chinese yuan: 10.92 per cent; Japanese yen: 8.33 per cent and UK pound sterling: 8.09 per cent. The inclusion of the Chinese yuan is a new development reflecting the maturity and importance of the Chinese economy. The SDR facility has not been popular, partly due to problems in initial SDR allocation levels.

7. SURVEILLANCE AND CAPACITY BUILDING

Under Article IV the IMF engages in official visits to its member countries on a periodic basis. The IMF uses these visits to collect data on national economies, international trade and the global economy in general. It also provides regularly updated economic forecasts at the national and international level. These forecasts are published in the highly regarded World Economic Outlook, and are accompanied by lengthy discussions of the effect of various economic policies on growth prospects and financial stability. This aspect of the IMF's agenda reflects the emphasis on transparency seen in international economic law generally discussed several times throughout this book.

Part of the IMF's surveillance and reporting activities consists of official visits to its member states. A few examples are illustrative. In 2018 the IMF performed an official visit to Uruguay, after which it delivered a report on the state of its economy which has been published on the IMF website. The report issued following the visit made the following observations. Uruguay's economy is resilient because of strong institutions, prudence, ample reserves and moderate growth with high inflation, but there are low levels of investment. More structural reforms are advocated, including more deficit reduction and reductions in public spending. The country demonstrates good uncoupling from the region (avoiding overreliance on Argentina and Brazil) through trade ties with China as well as trade diversification. The IMF suggested that Uruguay decrease its public debt, commit to fiscal sustainability and pursue more efficient 'social spending'. In particular, there has been too much spending on pensions and inflation-linked wages. Public enterprises also need to be managed more effectively. The adjustability of the peso (Uruguay's currency) will cushion shocks of global downturn. The IMF also recommended improved use of technology for financial transactions and various other matters aimed at improving competitiveness.[14]

After its official visit to Finland in 2018, the IMF made the following observations in its report. Finland is recovering well from the fallout of the global recession of the early 2000s but unemployment is still high. Inflation is low due to a wage freeze. Finland's shrinking working age population will constrain long term growth. The Finnish economy is highly sensitive to economies of other Nordic countries, suggesting needed diversification. Wages may be too high relative to productivity, which could lead to further unemployment. Interestingly, the IMF reported that employees tend to change their jobs less frequently in Finland than in other countries leading to inefficiencies and low productivity. Unemployment insurance is too generous and therefore benefits should be tapered over time. Strangely for a Nordic country, the IMF also observed low participation of women in the workforce. The retirement age is too low and household debt is too high. Zoning problems have made housing unaffordable. At a general level the IMF suggested that the government should spend less and save more.[15]

In addition to its regular visits such as these, the IMF provides technical assistance, training and policy advice to member countries through its capacity building programmes. These programmes include training in data collection and analysis, which are linked to the IMF's project of monitoring national and global economies.

8. IMF DISPUTE SETTLEMENT

The IMF attracts somewhat less attention from international lawyers than it does from economists, in large part because the obligations contained in its Articles of Agreement suffer from a lack of enforceability and there is no formal system for the settlement of dispute regarding adherence to or breach of IMF obligations, as there is in the WTO. Likewise, limited facility exists for the interpretation of IMF obligations, which, as noted above, may be better understood as guidelines. Questions of interpretation may be raised with the Executive Board. Appeals from this decision may be made to the Committee of Interpretation of the Board of Governors. In theory, recourse to the ICJ is available regarding IMF obligations, although this has never been sought. A teleological (purposeful) approach will be taken to interpretation, meaning that the Executive Board must be mindful of the overarching pragmatic, geopolitical dimension of its role, rather than taking a dry, technocratically legalistic view.[16]

The IMF's By-Laws outline rules regarding the settlement of disputes between its Members:

---

[14] 'Uruguay: Staff Concluding Statement of the 2018 Article IV Mission' International Monetary Fund (Washington, DC) (12 December 2018).

[15] 'Finland: Staff Concluding Statement of the 2018 Article IV Mission' International Monetary Fund (Washington, DC) (6 November 2018).

[16] A Qureshi and A Ziegler, *International Economic Law* (Sweet and Maxwell, 2011).

H-2.   If a member complains to the Executive Board that another member is not complying with its obligations concerning exchange controls, discriminatory currency arrangements, or multiple currency practices, the complaint shall give all facts pertinent to an examination.

H-3.   Upon receipt of a complaint from a member, the Executive Board shall make arrangements promptly for consultation with the members directly involved.

Records of these consultations, which appear to be considerably less formal than binding arbitration, are not available in a publicly accessible format. As such there is no indication that this system will ever approach anything near to the caselaw or jurisprudential nature that has arisen in relation to WTO dispute settlement or even ISDS. Perhaps the reason for this deficiency in rule of law within the IMF may be that issues of fiscal and monetary autonomy are viewed as being too sovereign in nature, in contrast to those relating to trade and investment. Or it may reflect the reality that IMF obligations, at least as between members, were never intended to be legally binding – they are merely recommendations.

9. ENFORCEMENT OF OBLIGATIONS

When the par value system collapsed in the 1970s, there was limited willingness among members to reshape the IMF's Articles of Agreement to convey stronger enforcement powers to the IMF Executive Board. Yet non-fulfilment of IMF obligations would obviously undermine the effectiveness of the system. As with much of international law, one of the most effective methods for achieving compliance is through reputational sanctions, and the IMF appears to rely on this method heavily to fulfil its objectives. It does this by publishing reports about members' noncompliance on its website, which are then sometimes picked up by the financial media.

Formal sanctions, of which there are a handful, are found in Article XXVI. First, there is a Declaration of Ineligibility. Such a declaration means the IMF can declare that a member cannot use its loan resources. Second, there is Suspension of Voting Rights. If this sanction is levied against a member by the IMF the member can no longer vote in IMF decisions. Finally, there is Expulsion – the member is forced to withdraw from the IMF. Czechoslovakia was expelled from the IMF in 1954 for failing to provide data on time and Zimbabwe was expelled in 2003 because of overdue financial obligations to the fund, having previously lost its eligibility to secure IMF loans. More recently, both Venezuela and Argentina were threatened with expulsion due to nonrepayment of loans and the persistent provision of inaccurate financial information, respectively. Of course, members are free to withdraw of their own accord, as Cuba did in 1964.

The IMF bylaws outline the procedures which must be pursued in conjunction with any sanction brought against a Member:

K-1.   The Managing Director shall report to the Executive Board any case in which it appears to him that a member is not fulfilling obligations under the Articles.

K-3. Before any member is declared ineligible to use the general resources of the Fund, the matter shall be considered by the Executive Board, which shall inform the member in reasonable time of the complaint against it and allow the member an adequate opportunity for stating its case both orally and in writing.

K-6. Before any member's voting rights are suspended the matter shall be considered by the Executive Board, which shall inform the member in reasonable time of the complaint against it and allow the member an adequate opportunity for stating its case both orally and in writing.

This process appears to satisfy what would be understood by most lawyers as due process, as would be expected of a multilateral organization. There are no publicly available records of any decisions or judgments issued under these rules.

Although its members have been reluctant to empower the Fund in terms of its legal authority for enforcing rules, they have endorsed a gradual expansion of its bilateral and multilateral surveillance mandate. In this sense IMF members have implicitly favoured 'soft' law over 'hard' law solutions. It is uncertain whether the IMF's surveillance functions and the associated mechanisms of peer pressure and moral suasion are adequate means for the organization to fulfil its mandate. The absence of legally binding enforcement powers or a formal dispute settlement system does not appear to have severely compromised the Fund's role in overseeing monetary relations between states. It would seem as though the IMF has cultivated an effective informal enforcement mechanism that encourages compliance by virtue of adverse market reactions – if it is reported that members have misbehaved they are likely to suffer from a lack of investment as well as difficulty in raising funds. If the IMF were to label certain policies illegal or noncompliant, in so doing publicly undermining the efficacy of some members' policies, the IMF could further exert considerable pressure on its members to abandon measures which violate the Articles of Agreement. Resort to these soft sanctions was not needed in the past, primarily because the Fund's regular interactions with its members offered less overt ways to modify a contested policy without having to prove an actual breach of the Articles of Agreement in a formal judicial setting.[17]

10. COORDINATION BETWEEN THE IMF AND THE WTO

The lack of an enforcement mechanism or a dispute settlement system within the IMF is mitigated somewhat by the coordination envisioned between the IMF and the WTO. This creates obligations enforceable through the WTO dispute settlement system outlined in Chapter 3. This interaction is found in the GATT, Article VII of which states that the valuation of goods for customs purposes must adopt currency conversions which are consistent with IMF rules. More importantly, GATT Article XV provides that WTO members should cooperate with the IMF regarding exchange rate issues. This includes consultations with the IMF regarding exchange rates and the acceptance of

---

[17] Broos and Grund above n 9.

IMF decisions regarding exchange rates. The obligation not to apply restrictions on international transfers and payments for current transactions relating to GATS specific commitments on services in conjunction with IMF obligations is further contained in the text of the GATS.[18]

Given its importance in international economic relations, it may be worthwhile to create a mechanism inside the WTO to offset the effects of exchange rate misalignments on existing trade arrangements. This could be done as a correction of tariffs to reflect accurate values or through the introduction of an exchange rate misalignments clause in antidumping, anti-subsidy countervailing duties or safeguards measures. This mechanism could include mandatory investigation to be available on a short-term basis. It might also be limited to certain sectors, since the effects of misalignments are different among sectors.[19] Clearly monetary issues are very politically sensitive. Given its focus on legalism, the WTO may be an unsuitable forum for such disputes, although its diplomatic function could operate as a forum for de-escalating currency wars before they lead to retaliation.

Apart from the WTO, the IMF could also play a more active role in promoting international responsiveness to issues relating to capital flows. Through deeper cooperation with various national governments and international bodies such as the G20 and the OECD, the IMF could transform itself into a more formal standard setting body. The IMF already takes part in G20 Finance Ministry meetings and is part of the Advisory Task Force on the OECD Code of Liberalisation of Capital Movements, which monitors its implementation and advances work on the trends of capital account measures. There appears to be limited willingness among policymakers to align the OECD Code, which promotes full liberalization, with the IMF's institutional view, which adopts a more cautious approach. The current consensus in the OECD favours a noncompulsory role for the IMF in which it offers nonbinding guidance to the OECD and its members. Enhancing this function for the IMF could grant additional soft powers to the IMF concerning the oversight of capital account policies.[20] Noting the shortcomings of the IMF's multilateral management of international monetary matters, some discussion of efforts at the regional level is instructive.

11. MONETARY RELATIONS AND REGIONALISM

Regional efforts to address the monetary relations component of international economic law have been limited and so far unsuccessful. Still, a few examples are worth discussing.

11.1 Asia and the Chiang Mai Initiative

Following the 1997–8 Asian financial crisis, during which massive amounts of capital left the region, the Association of Southeast Asian Nations (ASEAN) and three other states embarked on several new initiatives to increase financial cooperation with a view to preventing further catastro-

---

[18] GATS Art. XI.

[19] Thorstensen, Ramos and Muller above n 5.

[20] Broos and Grund above n 9.

phes and providing emergency liquidity. These included regional economic surveillance led by the Economic Review and Policy Dialogue (ERPD), local currency bond market development and a regional liquidity support facility, called the Chiang Mai Initiative (CMI), named after the location in Thailand where the meetings took place. The Chiang Mai Initiative Multilateralisation Agreement took effect in 2010 and still operates, although its impact on the region is thought to have been minimal. It establishes a pool of foreign exchange reserves accessible by participating central banks in order to combat currency manipulation. The CMI essentially functions as a network of bilateral currency swap arrangements. This means that in the event of a balance of payments or liquidity crisis, a member state can exchange its local currency for US dollars drawn from the CMI's pool. Although the CMI is a common liquidity pool, there is actually no common or centralized fund, as in the case of the IMF. The contributions remain in the central banks of member countries. In that sense, the CMI is more accurately described as a series of promises to provide funds. Each state's borrowing quota is based on its contribution multiplied by a borrowing multiplier, which is set at a different level for each member state. The conditions for securing a swap include undergoing a completed review of the state's economic and financial situation, compliance with conditions imposed by the CMI (such as submission of a periodic surveillance report) and participation in the ERPD, which essentially involves further surveillance and transparency. Although not complicated, these are seen as exhaustive and time consuming conditions.[21] An independent surveillance unit, the ASEAN+3 Macroeconomic Research Office, was established in 2011 to enhance transparency and monitoring of member states' monetary policies. Additionally, in 2012, the CMI's total resources were doubled in size to US$240 billion. A crisis prevention facility, now called the CMI Stability Fund, was also introduced to provide short term liquidity support to address sudden but temporary liquidity shortages. As with the IMF, reforms to the CMI have been suggested. In particular, commentators have recommended that a secretariat should be established in charge of all aspects of the CMI and that it should be delinked from IMF programmes by upgrading their capacity to conduct regional surveillance, formulate independent conditionality associated with crisis lending and monitor policy and economic performance.[22]

11.2 North America and the USMCA

Control of currency manipulation has not featured prominently in RTAs, nor have such instruments contemplated loan functions along the lines of the IMF. An earlier version of the CPTPP (when it was called the TPP and included the US) was supposed to contain material on currency manipulation as a form of trade protectionism in a Joint Declaration of the Macroeconomic Policy Authorities of Trans-Pacific Partnership Countries. Similar material can be found in Chapter 33 of the USMCA, entitled Macroeconomic Policies and Exchange Rate Matters, which appears to have been inspired by this earlier feature of the TPP. This chapter affirms the three countries' commitment to market determined exchange rates as well as adherence to the IMF rules regarding the avoidance of exchange rate manipulation in order to gain an unfair competitive advantage in trade and to ensure balance of

---

[21] 'Chiang Mai Initiative: An Asian IMF?' The Asian Century Institute (5 April 2017).

[22] M Kawai, 'From the Chiang Mai Initiative to an Asian Monetary Fund' ADBI Working Paper 527 (19 June 2015).

payments equilibrium. The USMCA contains transparency and reporting requirements which require public disclosure of monthly data on international reserve balances and intervention in foreign exchange markets, including quarterly balance of payments data and other public reporting, via the IMF. The USMCA further establishes a Macroeconomic Committee among its three party countries that will meet at least annually to monitor implementation. If one party believes that the measures or policies of another violate reporting commitments, it can initiate a bilateral consultation process. The IMF can be invited to engage in this process if parties in the dispute fail to agree. Additionally, the USMCA specifies that parties have recourse to the treaty's state to state dispute resolution mechanism for any alleged failure to meet Chapter 33's transparency and reporting obligations, although this does not cover substantive matters such as market intervention or alleged manipulation of foreign exchange rates. Omission of these more serious matters from the formal dispute settlement is somewhat disappointing but hardly surprising given that monetary policy matters encroach very deeply into regulatory sovereignty, as suggested earlier. Some believe that currency manipulation is an intractable problem which requires diplomatic rather than legal solutions.[23]

The United States, Mexico and Canada each have floating exchange rate regimes which currently meet the transparency and reporting requirements of the USMCA's Chapter 33. In that sense the significance of the USMCA in terms of the three countries' monetary policy is limited. Still, the agreement is groundbreaking because it explicitly covers macroeconomic and exchange rate policies, for the first time in an RTA. As noted above, monetary matters have normally been left out of trade agreements because they are often viewed as a threat to macroeconomic and exchange rate policy independence. Crucially, the agreement 'does not apply with respect to the regulatory or supervisory activities or monetary and related credit policy and related conduct of an exchange rate or fiscal or monetary authority of a Party'.[24] Similar commitments may be expected in future US trade agreements, particularly since the US is disposed to accusing other states of engaging in currency manipulation as an unfair trade practice, notably China and Korea. Given the policy sensitivity of this sphere of international economic relations, it can be expected that many states are likely to resist binding currency commitments in future trade agreements.[25]

12. CONCLUSION

This chapter sought to present an overview of international monetary policy from the perspective of the management of the IMF, touching upon some developments at the regional level to combat currency manipulation and sovereign liquidity crises. International monetary relations is a complex field of study which, despite a lack of robust legal framework, plays a role in the global economy that must not be underestimated.

---

[23] C Wong, 'Regulating Currency Manipulation: Political, Legal and Economic Barriers to Reform' 51:4 Journal of World Trade 691 (2017).

[24] Art. 33.3.

[25] S Segal, 'USMCA Currency Provisions Set a New Precedent', Centre for International and Strategic Studies (5 October 2018).

For its part, the IMF has arguably been successful in relation to its own expanded resources, provision of credit for the developing countries, attaining exchange stability, helping the expansion of world trade, ensuring international liquidity, establishing the multilateral trade and payment system, eliminating short-term disequilibrium of balance of payments in many states and controlling competitive currency devaluation. It has also set up the machinery for consultation among its members to provide guidance to member countries in formulating their fiscal and financial policies.

The IMF may also be charged with numerous failures. Some would argue that it has failed to achieve the basic objectives of international exchange stability. It has been powerless to prevent competitive devaluation of currencies by its members. In that sense the Fund has also failed to persuade the member countries to eliminate exchange controls and other restrictions on foreign trade. It could also be argued that the IMF did not establish a stable and sound international monetary system, as demonstrated by the serious monetary crises which have arisen in part due to rapidly fluctuating exchange rates. Today the IMF considers exchange rates as one of the many macroeconomic variables it monitors in order to support global economic stability.[26] Furthermore, some believe that the IMF has discriminated in favour of some developed states, neglecting the genuine interests of underdeveloped ones. Developing countries still have inadequate representation in IMF governance and decision making. It has also been argued that the IMF has harmfully interfered in the economic policies of developing countries by placing ill-devised conditionality restrictions that were not in their best interests in the long term. Some might even go as far as labelling the IMF an 'antidevelopment' institution because of the punishing conditions it inflicts on borrowing states. In this regard, when put into perspective, the IMF's loan conditionality policies are considerably more intrusive into states' sovereignty than WTO rules or even the protections afforded to investors in IIAs. Finally, the IMF's economic forecasts are often wildly wrong. A good example of this is in relation to the UK's decision to leave the EU in 2016, which the IMF predicted would lead to recession and a loss of employment in the hundreds of thousands, neither of which occurred. This prediction arguably also constituted inappropriate political interference.

Given the IMF's possible inadequacies, reform of the IMF as well as the global rules on monetary relations remains a popular topic of discussion. In 2017 the G20 Finance Ministers and Central Bank Governors established the G20 Eminent Persons Group on Global Financial Governance (EPG). This body is mandated to review current and possible future challenges and opportunities facing the international financial and monetary systems and to consider the optimal role of international financial institutions, including the IMF (and the World Bank, of which more in the next chapter). The EPG was also designed to recommend practical reforms to improve the functioning of the global financial architecture and governance with a view to promoting economic stability and sustainable growth. In future the IMF could play a more central role in determining what policies support or undermine the stability of its members and the global financial system as a whole. It is well placed for this task because its current oversight of capital flows already injects a degree of order into the international monetary system, much as its surveillance mandate is the only sys-

---

[26] Thorstensen, Ramos and Muller above n 5.

tematic effort to track global capital flows.[27] In terms of its broader influence, some believe that the IMF's sustainability policies (encompassing issues such as the environment) should be made by standing expert panels, drawn from agreed lists including the market, civil society and the public sector. While these determinations will not be binding, they could be incorporated by reference into its sovereign loan packages.[28]

The IMF's function in maintaining the stability of the global monetary system is complemented by the work of another one of the Bretton Woods institutions. While the IMF's role is to prevent the escalation of economic crises due to problems with the supply of money, it is the World Bank which is charged with promoting economic development in the world's less economically advanced countries. This issue will be examined in the final chapter.

DISCUSSION QUESTIONS

1. Why is it important for states to remain solvent and what role does the IMF play in this regard?
2. Is currency manipulation adequately controlled under international law? How might this be improved?
3. To what extent do the IMF's loan conditionality policies unfairly intrude on borrowing states' sovereignty?
4. How might the IMF be reformed to better deliver its mandate?

FURTHER READING

L Boggio, 'Investors and Sovereign Debt Restructurings: The Protection of Financial Property before International Courts and Arbitrators' 15:2 Manchester Journal of International Economic Law 143 (2018).

M Broos, S Grund, 'The IMF's Jurisdiction over Capital Account – Reviewing the Role of Surveillance in Managing Cross-Border Capital Flows' 21:3 Journal of International Economic Law 489 (2018).

A Feibelman, 'The IMF and Regulation of Cross-Border Capital Flows' 15:2 Chicago Journal of International Law 409 (2015).

C Wong, 'Regulating Currency Manipulation: Political, Legal and Economic Barriers to Reform' 51:4 Journal of World Trade 691 (2017).

---

[27] A Feibelman, 'The IMF and Regulation of Cross-Border Capital Flows' 15:2 Chicago Journal of International Law 409 (2015).

[28] A Gelpern, 'Sovereign Debt: Now What?' 41 Yale Journal of International Law 45 (2016).

10
International development and the World Bank

1. INTRODUCTION

From time to time even the most economically advanced countries experience financial difficulties, rendering them incapable of paying their debts, engaging in trade or attracting investment. Chapter 9 explained that when this occurs, the IMF is available to help contain the crisis by providing liquidity in the form of short term loans designed to get the country back on its feet. This final chapter will explore how another Bretton Woods institution, the World Bank, assists countries suffering chronic economic difficulties as the consequence of underdevelopment which would not be addressed by a one off cash injection to improve liquidity. The World Bank, along with regional development banks, helps achieve this assistance by extending long term loans aimed at securing future economic progress through the establishment of infrastructure, sometimes in conjunction with private sector investment and typically incorporating principles of CSR principles. This chapter will also consider how development has been adopted as an agenda of the WTO.

The inclusion of the material on development in this book (as in the agenda of the Bretton Woods Conference) is based on the idea that improving the economic condition of poorer states arguably is or at least should be an objective of international economic law. This is premised on the link between poverty reduction in poor states and the overall welfare of all states, which, due to the interlinked nature of the global economy, is of interest to the entire world. It is important to recognize also that some of the causes of poverty in the developing world are thought to have foreign origins, notably the exploitation of natural resources associated with the colonial period. Furthermore, the rule of law, including fair, independent and efficient courts, is a highly important component of, if not essential to, economic and social development. As mentioned already, it is often suggested, although not quite empirically proven, that foreign investment at least contributes to the establishment of 'good governance' in places where these institutions may be deficient.[1]

---

[1] M Sattorova, *The Impact of Investment Treaty Law on Host States: Enabling Good Governance?* (Hart, 2018).

As with monetary relations, much international economic law for development purposes is nonbinding or 'soft', distinct from the main rules on internal trade and investment contained in the law of the WTO and IIAs, respectively.

2. THE CONCEPT OF DEVELOPMENT

The objective of development – or, more specifically in modern times, 'sustainable development' – falls within the express mandate of several global institutions. Other than the World Bank itself, the most important of these is probably the UN. The UN General Assembly Declaration on the Right to Development of 1986 illustrates the obligations it places on its member states concerning development:

Article 3
1. States have the primary responsibility for the creation of national and international conditions favourable to the realization of the right to development.
2. The realization of the right to development requires full respect for the principles of international law concerning friendly relations and co-operation among States in accordance with the Charter of the United Nations.
3. States have the duty to co-operate with each other in ensuring development and eliminating obstacles to development. States should realize their rights and fulfil their duties in such a manner as to promote a new international economic order based on sovereign equality, interdependence, mutual interest and co-operation among all States, as well as to encourage the observance and realization of human rights.

Article 4
1. States have the duty to take steps, individually and collectively, to formulate international development policies with a view to facilitating the full realization of the right to development.
2. Sustained action is required to promote more rapid development of developing countries. As a complement to the efforts of developing countries, effective international co-operation is essential in providing these countries with appropriate means and facilities to foster their comprehensive development.

...

Article 10
Steps should be taken to ensure the full exercise and progressive enhancement of the right to development, including the formulation, adoption and implementation of policy, legislative and other measures at the national and international levels.

Article 3.3 is noteworthy because it speaks of the 'New International Economic Order' which is based on the equality of states. This principle is often associated with the recognition of a state's right to expropriation, as discussed in Chapter 7.

For the purposes of fulfilling these obligations, establishing the definition of 'development' under international economic law is problematic. Indeed, the categorization of a state as 'developing' rather than 'developed' is among the most controversial aspects of international economic law, in part because the status of 'developing' accords these states special treatment, including less onerous obligations than those borne by developed states. Some of the trade aspects of this privilege will be explored below. There is no settled definition of developing country. Most international organizations consider a developing country to be one with weak industrialization, low income per person and a deficient infrastructure both physically (such as hospitals and roads) and institutionally (such as courts and legislatures). The status 'developing' is also associated with lower standards of living in terms of health and length of life, as well as low levels of literacy and high infant mortality rates. Least developed countries tend to suffer these conditions most severely. They are characterized by having a gross domestic product (GDP) per capita of less than US$1000. Used as a benchmark for development, or lack thereof, the UN's Human Development Index (HDI) is a compound indicator involving variables such as life expectancy, literacy, GDP and education.

In the WTO, developing country status is by self-election, meaning that each state is able to declare whether it considers itself to be developing. The self-selection process itself continues to attract criticism, especially in relation to the large emerging markets like China and India, which have vast GDPs (although somewhat less impressive GDPs per capita) and major influence as world powers in terms of their capacity to negotiate trade concessions, effect changes in the global economy and participate in the exploration of space. Proposals have been made by the US and other states for a WTO General Council Decision towards changing the rules related to self-declared development status. The delegation of the US made the following request to the WTO General Council in February 2019:

> The General Council, Agrees as follows: To facilitate the full implementation of future WTO agreements and to ensure that the maximum benefits of trade accrue to those Members with the greatest difficulty integrating into the multilateral trading system, the following categories of Members will not avail themselves of special and differential treatment in current and future WTO negotiations: i. A WTO Member that is a Member of the Organization for Economic Cooperation and Development (OECD), or a WTO Member that has begun the accession process to the OECD; ii. A WTO Member that is a member of the Group of 20 (G20); iii. A WTO Member that is classified as a 'high income' country by the World Bank, or iv. A WTO Member that accounts for no less than 0.5 per cent of global merchandise trade (imports and exports).[2]

It should be noted that a nation's status as a developing country carries different implications than the designation as a nonmarket economy, issues which were explored in more depth in Chapter 4.

In modern times, the achievement of development as a goal has been modified in favour of the related concept of sustainable development. This principle reflects the understanding that devel-

---

[2] Draft General Council Decision, Procedures to Strengthen the Negotiating Function of the WTO, WT/GC/W/764 (15 February 2019).

opment goals can conflict with environmental standards regarding the preservation of ecosystems. Sustainable development contemplates economic advancement through the use of natural resources while preserving the environment for future generations, meaning that the resources will not be exhausted in the service of the current population or that any externalities from their exploitation will be minimal relative to their beneficial output. Sustainable development as an objective is seen most notably in the WTO preamble as well as in some IIAs, such as the CPTPP. It is further reflected in the lending guidelines in many of the development banks, discussed further below.

Sustainable development is sometimes associated with the principle of Common but Differentiated Responsibility, which acknowledges that developed countries may have engaged in practices in the past which by today's standards would be considered non-sustainable – indeed, this was how they achieved high levels of industrialization.[3] Consequently, poorer countries should be allowed to pollute in order to catch up, meaning that they should be held to lesser obligations in certain areas under international law. The moral equivocation in this concept is missed by many – either sustainability is a goal, or it is not. If environmental harm is understood as unacceptable, surely the source should not matter.

3. INTERNATIONAL ECONOMIC LAW AND DEVELOPMENT

Before embarking on a discussion of the developmental policies of the World Bank, it is important to highlight the developmental aspect of the two major topics of international economic law: trade and investment.

3.1 The WTO

As mentioned in Chapter 2, the preamble to the WTO Agreement clarifies the organization's development objective: 'there is need for positive efforts designed to ensure that developing countries, and especially the least developed among them, secure a share in the growth in international trade commensurate with the needs of their economic development.'

More practically in terms of constituting legal obligations on its members, the GATT contains terms according leniency or 'special and differential treatment' for developing states. This is contained in the so-called Enabling Clause, officially called the Decision on Differential and More Favourable Treatment, Reciprocity and Fuller Participation of Developing Countries, which was adopted under the GATT in 1979. It enables developed members to give differential and more favourable treatment to developing countries.

Special and differential treatment encourages but does not force developed countries to grant tariff concessions to developing countries on a nonreciprocal basis.[4] In other words, developed WTO members should give concessions in favour of exports from developing members without the

---

[3] Principle 7, Rio Declaration (1992).

[4] Art. XXXVI.

expectation of anything in return. This is contrary to the WTO's main premise of reciprocity in trade negotiations. Special and differential treatment is primarily designed to increase developing countries' trading opportunities through greater market access to other countries. It also takes the form of leniency. For example, the prohibition on export-oriented subsidies that we looked at does not apply to least developing countries under the Agreement on Subsidies and Countervailing Measures. Moreover, the standards of proof required to substantiate a claim of subsidization brought against a developing country are more onerous, avoiding costly harassment of the governments of developing countries. Subsidies which would normally be actionable are not regarded as so when they are granted by developing country members in the context of privatization programmes where there has been debt forgiveness of the commercial enterprise.[5] Under the Anti-Dumping Agreement, developed country members are instructed to take special care in exploring constructive remedies instead of imposing antidumping duties on developing countries.[6] Under TRIPS, developing countries may wait a year before implementing their obligations under the agreement. A further five-year delay applies where a particular area of technology is currently not protectable under the domestic law of the particular developing country.[7] There are longer phase-in periods for developing countries to comply with health and safety regulations imposed by other members under Article 10 of the SPS and Article 12 of the TBT agreements respectively. Lastly, developing countries get additional time to respond to any complaints brought against them through the WTO dispute settlement procedure, as well as longer timeframes to comply with rulings of the WTO court. Developing countries are entitled to longer timeframes to fulfil their obligations.[8]

WTO rules also allow for the use of a generalized system of preferences (GSPs), under which developing country members can be treated more favourably for the purposes of MFN without an MFN violation. Preferences extended by rich countries to poor ones through GSPs can be additionally problematic for developing countries because they may come with conditions. The US and the EU GSPs in particular tend to impose a wide range of conditions on beneficiary countries, often relating to specific, sensitive goods, as in the case of cotton, which has traditionally enjoyed subsidies within the US in part due to influential lobbies. GSPs are also often subject to conditions that are unrelated to trade, such as the beneficiary country's efforts to assist in the war on terrorism or combating drug crime. The legality of these types of nontrade conditions was confirmed by the WTO Panel and Appellate Body in a dispute brought by India against the EU.[9] The EU had granted India some preferential trade concessions but only on condition that India cooperated in the prevention of drug trafficking. In order to qualify for the reduced tariffs available under GSPs, exported products must fulfil requirements relating to the identification of where they originate. Rules of origin (ROO) of traded goods, mentioned in Chapter 2, are therefore a key component of all GSPs. Clear notification of origin counters the potential for abuse of the preferential scheme by preventing a

---

[5] Part VIII.

[6] Art. 15.

[7] Art. 65.

[8] Art. 12.10.

[9] European Communities – Conditions for the Granting of Tariff Preferences to Developing Countries, Appellate Body Report, WT/DS246/AB/R (20 April 2004).

product from being exported from a country outside the scheme to a country within the scheme before being reexported to the donor country. ROO normally require that there is a minimum level of value added in the beneficiary country. The complexity of these rules tends to increase the more components there are in a given product, so in practice the more difficult rules are usually associated with highly manufactured goods rather than agricultural products. Complying with these rules may on its own impose a significant financial burden on some developing countries.

GATT Article XVIII contains an 'infant industry' protection for developing country members, allowing them to impose protective measures to assist in the establishment of an industry which would otherwise be unable to withstand global competition. In addition to the nonexpectation of reciprocity in negotiations, GATT outlines further that, in the course of WTO trade negotiations, developing countries should not be required to make concessions that are inconsistent with their developmental, financial and trade needs. This clause is circumscribed by the so-called 'graduation clause' which provides that as a developing country's capacity to make contributions or trade concessions increases along with their economic development, they are expected to participate more fully in the framework of rights and obligations under the GATT. Under Article XXXVII, developing country members should be the top priority for trade barrier reductions.

Technical assistance is available through the WTO Committee on Trade and Development. The WTO holds regular training sessions on trade policy in Geneva and organizes several hundred technical cooperation meetings annually, including various seminars and workshops of interest to trade representatives, trade lawyers and diplomats from developing countries. The WTO also engages in an integrated programme with other major international organizations, such as the IMF and the World Bank, for a joint technical assistance programme exclusively for least developed countries.

Another significant achievement on the part of the WTO in terms of development is its work in relation to trade facilitation, meaning rules aimed at simplifying border formalities to make it easier for goods to pass from one state to another. Such transaction costs can be high and delays at borders can be long for developing countries – it can take days for goods to cross borders between African countries and there is often harassment and solicitation of bribery by customs officials. The WTO's Trade Facilitation Agreement entered into force in 2017, requiring all WTO members to implement streamlined procedures for traded goods at borders. It is expected that compliance with these rules could lower trade costs by more than 14 per cent, with the greatest gains to be secured by the world's poorest countries.

Despite these features of WTO law, the organization is often criticized for failing to address the needs of its developing country members (which comprise two thirds of its membership).[10] Perhaps the most glaring of these is its failure to curtail widespread agricultural subsidies by developed countries which have undermined the comparative advantage of much of the developing world. Still, it must be emphasized that the WTO is not a development agency. Its core mission is not the advancement of peoples or governments in the developing world, although these things are normally thought to result from the elimination of unnecessary barriers to trade. Indeed, the WTO often takes credit for bringing millions of people out of poverty around the world. Free trade on its own is insufficient if it only exacerbates inequalities and does not lead to raised standards

---

[10] S Rolland, *Development at the WTO* (Oxford University Press, 2012).

of living and a growing volume of real income in all of the WTO's member states, not just the rich industrialized ones.

3.2 International investment law

It is worth recalling that many IIAs were concluded between industrialized and developing states, especially in the early years of this practice. It was noted in Chapter 7 that the preambles of many IIAs refer to the objective of achieving the economic development of party states,[11] seen also in the preamble of the ICSID Convention. Some commentators suggest that there is a duty on the part of the foreign firm to contribute to the development of the host state.[12] The UN's development goals lend some weight to the suggestion than the principle of development is part of customary international law. Under this logic, the obligation to contribute to the host state's economic development may be viewed as the corresponding duty to the assortment of rights enjoyed by the investor under the IIA. The existence of a right to development is reflected in comments made by arbitrators, some of whom appear to be willing to infer that the contribution to development is part of the definition of investment.[13] This chapter will now turn to its main focus, the work of the World Bank.

4. THE WORLD BANK GROUP

The World Bank Group (collectively known as the World Bank, the term which has been used throughout this book) is the principal international organization for the purpose of development assistance. It consists of five organizations: the International Bank for Reconstruction and Development (IBRD), confusingly also the original name of the World Bank; the International Development Association (IDA); the International Finance Corporation (IFC); the International Centre for the Settlement of Investment Disputes (ICSID); and the Multilateral Investment Guarantee Agency (MIGA).

Across its various constituent organizations, the World Bank provides monetary loans directly to states and to private companies for the purposes of investment, insurance and dispute settlement rules for investing companies. In contrast to the IMF, discussed in the previous chapter, the World Bank's loans comprise long term assistance for development projects. Like the IMF, the World Bank also engages in data collection and dissemination regarding the economic health of developing countries. Among the most famous of these activities is the World Bank's highly regarded annual Doing Business Report, which ranks 190 countries according to their receptiveness to business. New Zealand is the current champion, with Singapore and Denmark in second and third place respectively.[14] Moving up the list is often viewed as a way of attracting foreign investment.

---

[11] France–Ethiopia (25 June 2003).

[12] D Desierto, 'Development as an International Right: Investment in the New Trade-Based IIAs' 3:2 Trade Law and Development 267 (2011).

[13] Malaysia Historical Salvors Sdn Bhd v. Malaysia, ICSID Case No ARB/05/10, Decision on the Application for Annulment (16 April 2009) Dissenting Opinion of M Shahabuddeen.

[14] Doing Business 2019: Training for Reform, World Bank Group (Washington, DC, 2019).

Membership in the World Bank is limited to states and is almost universal, with 189 members as of 2019. Four of the five World Bank organizations noted above have a three-tier membership structure consisting of a Board of Governors, an Executive Board and a president. David Malpass was nominated as president of the World Bank (the umbrella organization) in March 2019 by US President Donald Trump and confirmed by the Bank's Board the following month. An American, Malpass was previously a senior economist in the US Treasury as well as chief economist at the investment bank Bear Stearns. He is expected to refocus the Bank's lending towards the poorest countries and to emphasize private lending over that which is directed primarily to sovereign states, in contrast to his predecessor's interest in broader issues such as climate change.[15] Although the choice of a World Bank president formally lies with the World Bank's Board of Directors, it has been practice since Bretton Woods for the president of the World Bank to be an American, just as the managing director of the IMF is normally a European. Like the IMF but in contrast with the WTO, the World Bank has a system of weighted voting reflecting each member's economic size. This also determines financial contribution. As of 2019, the US held 15.98 per cent of the voting shares in the World Bank. Other leading voting members include Japan, at 6.89 per cent; China, at 4.45 per cent; Germany, at 4.03 per cent; and the UK and France, each at 3.78 per cent. The World Bank is sometimes criticized for being controlled by a small number of economically powerful countries, chiefly the US. It is thought that the organization's policies tend to be reflective of their interests.

4.1 The International Bank for Reconstruction and Development

Under Article I of the IBRD Articles of Agreement, which were drawn up in 1944 and amended three times since (most recently in 2012), the purpose of the IBRD is to assist in the development of members' territories, promote balanced growth of international trade and raise living standards. It does this by extending loans extended to middle income countries (meaning developing but not least developed) which are unable to obtain them elsewhere. The IBRD is therefore the chief lending branch of the World Bank. This is why it is often referred to simply as 'the World Bank', and indeed many people are referring to the work of the IBRD when they use the phrase World Bank.

There are a number of conditions placed on loans granted by the IBRD which are set out in Article III. First, financing must be for development purposes and must promote foreign investment. The total loans must not exceed IBRD reserves and the IBRD must act prudently, which will be determined in part by an assessment of whether the borrower can repay. Article IV further specifies that the terms of loan must be reasonable. Financing requires the permission of the loan committee; however, there must be no interference from the IBRD regarding which members receive loans.[16] The IBRD does not require any security from its borrowers as a matter of policy. This act of good faith must be balanced by the need of the IBRD to protect its own interests, especially the priority of its debt claims over those of third party creditors. This is reflected in the 'negative pledge' clause of the General Conditions, section 6.02 a) of which reads:

---

[15] J Politi, 'David Malpass Defies Doubts to Secure World Bank Presidency' Financial Times (5 April 2019).

[16] Art. III.

It is the policy of the Bank, in making loans to, or with the guarantee of its member countries not to seek, in normal circumstances, special security from the member country concerned but to ensure that no other Covered Debt shall have priority over its loans in the allocation, realization or distribution of foreign exchange held under the control or for the benefit of such member country. To that end, if any Lien is created on any Public Assets as security for any Covered Debt, which will or might result in a priority for the benefit of the creditor of such Covered Debt in the allocation, realization or distribution of foreign exchange, such Lien shall, unless the Bank shall otherwise agree, ipso facto and at no cost to the Bank, equally and ratably secure all Loan Payments, and the Member Country, in creating or permitting the creation of such Lien, shall make express provision to that effect; provided, however, that if for any constitutional or other legal reason such provision cannot be made with respect to any Lien created on assets of any of its political or administrative subdivisions, the Member Country shall promptly and at no cost to the Bank secure all Loan Payments by an equivalent Lien on other Public Assets satisfactory to the Bank.

The negative pledge, evincing legal language resembling that of a commercial loan, seeks to prevent other foreign currency creditors of a World Bank member state from receiving security from the relevant borrower or guarantor in priority to the IBRD, meaning that such creditor would be entitled to be repaid before the IBRD. The IBRD does this by providing that any lien (essentially a right to keep property) against an external debt by a member state which might result in their having priority in terms of repayment must be secured to the IBRD, effectively allowing the IBRD to supersede that other creditor in priority. In other words, the borrower must ensure that the IBRD gets paid first among all of its creditors. The negative pledge extends not only to security that may be granted in respect of assets owned directly by the relevant member state government, but also to assets of any entity that is owned or controlled by or operating for the benefit of that member state. Since it is framed so broadly, the negative pledge presents a potential challenge to any foreign investor that wishes to lend on a secured basis to a project that is owned or controlled by a member state with IBRD debt. The IBRD's General Conditions do not include a definition of 'ownership' or 'control' for purposes of determining whether the assets of an entity may fall within the scope of the negative pledge. The lack of certainty as to whether a particular project or project assets may be subject to the negative pledge could affect the decision by a potential investor to invest in a project financing or affect the manner in which such an investment is made. While the IBRD is able to waive the application of the negative pledge in respect of particular transactions, it has only done so on rare occasions. Since its introduction, there have been a number of calls for reform of the IBRD's negative pledge. These include clarification as to the entities to whom the pledge would apply and the adoption of a formal, narrow interpretation of control and ownership, providing for easier identification of assets subject to the negative pledge.[17]

There is some capacity for dispute settlement for the IBRD's loan agreements. Section 8.04 of the General Conditions specifies as follows:

---

[17] U Kirklar, 'World Bank Negative Pledge and Project Financings' Latham and Watkins (14 December 2016).

(a) Any controversy between the parties to the Loan Agreement or the parties to the Guarantee Agreement, and any claim by any such party against any other such party arising under the Loan Agreement or the Guarantee Agreement which has not been settled by agreement of the parties, shall be submitted to arbitration by an arbitral tribunal as hereinafter provided ('Arbitral Tribunal').

(b) The parties to such arbitration shall be the Bank on the one side and the Loan Parties on the other side.

(c) The Arbitral Tribunal shall consist of three arbitrators appointed as follows: (i) one arbitrator shall be appointed by the Bank; (ii) a second arbitrator shall be appointed by the Loan Parties or, if they do not agree, by the Guarantor; and (iii) the third arbitrator ('Umpire') shall be appointed by agreement of the parties or, if they do not agree, by the President of the International Court of Justice or, failing appointment by said President, by the Secretary-General of the United Nations. If either side fails to appoint an arbitrator, such arbitrator shall be appointed by the Umpire. In case any arbitrator appointed in accordance with this Section resigns, dies or becomes unable to act, a successor arbitrator shall be appointed in the same manner as prescribed in this Section for the appointment of the original arbitrator and such successor shall have all the powers and duties of such original arbitrator.[18]

Conventional international commercial arbitration facilities, such as the Stockholm Chamber of Commerce or the International Chamber of Commerce, are available to resolve disputes between the IBRD and its borrowers in line with the above parameters. The IBRD does not maintain a publicly accessible record of these disputes.

Much like the IMF, the IBRD has been criticized because of the market-oriented reform policies which are tied to its loan packages, as they are focused on making the borrowing state more attractive to foreign investors – essentially, foreign market entrants. These adjustment programmes, especially those related to privatization, are seen by some as harmful to economic development if they are implemented without sensitivity with regard to context, and too quickly. Although IBRD reforms were designed to promote development, market-based reforms have been disparaged for ignoring the needs of these countries' citizens. Some believe that the IBRD placed too much emphasis on the growth of GDP, with insufficient attention to stability and the practical implications of growth on better living standards.[19] By the late twenty-first century the IBRD had responded to some of these criticisms by changing its loans conditions, allowing for social spending to be maintained and encouraging a more gradual adaptation to various market-oriented policies. Its policies remain committed to established CSR principles, such as those mentioned in Chapter 6.

4.2 International Development Association

Known as the World Bank's 'soft' lender, the IDA provides long term, low interest loans and grants to the world's poorest countries. There are currently 81 countries eligible to use its resources,

---

[18] IBRD PolicyGeneral Conditions for IBRD Financing: Development Policy Financing, 2017 (17 July 2017).

[19] J Stiglitz, *Globalization and Its Discontents* (WW Norton & Company, 2003).

measured by per capita GDP and by the inability to raise capital from other sources. The IDA was created in 1960 because IBRD lending was inadequate for the needs of the poorest countries. Under Article I of the IDA's Articles, the purpose of the IDA is to promote economic development and increase productivity in the poorest countries. IDA projects include clean water, sanitation, education, electrification and agricultural innovation. Funded largely by regular contributions from the World Bank's developed country members, IDA loans are offered on more flexible, less onerous terms (interest rates of 0 or 1 per cent) and for very long periods (up to 40 years), often with no expectation of repayment. Several of the countries which had been eligible for IDA loans have 'graduated' to a higher level of development, precluding them from accessing the IDA's resources, becoming eligible for conventional IBRD loans. Examples of such countries include Egypt, India and Thailand. The remaining eligible countries are predominately in Africa and are experiencing long term population declines, suggesting that the IDA itself has an uncertain future.

4.3 International Finance Corporation

Established in 1956 as the 'private sector arm of the World Bank', the IFC provides funding for commercial enterprises operating in developing countries engaging in development-oriented activities. Accordingly it can be seen as a driver of FDI into the developing world, fulfilling one of the World Bank's primary goals. Funds are issued at market or near market rates for periods of around ten years and are exclusively available for projects that are profit seeking but which have a developmental agenda, especially in relation to the generation of employment and economic self-sufficiency. The IFC's resources come from borrowing from and investing in international capital markets and its total investments are in the tens of billions of US dollars. Article I of the IFC Articles of Agreement specifies that the loans which it extends must be on sound commercial grounds, meaning that the borrower is a viable business. The investment must benefit the local economy, including the natural environment. The activities for which the loan was extended must not have been able to receive financing from commercial banks and the host member country must consent to the financing. Lastly, and perhaps most crucially, the IFC cannot become involved in the management of the investment project or dictate where proceeds of investment are to be invested. In recent years the IFC has focused on a set of development goals including sustainable agriculture, improved healthcare and education, increasing access to financing for microfinance and business clients, advancing infrastructure, and help to small businesses.

4.4 The Multilateral Investment Guarantee Agency and political risk insurance

Before explaining the role of the MIGA, it is necessary to provide some background on political risk insurance (PRI). In addition to relying on the protections contained in an IIA, investors can obtain insurance to cover any losses they may suffer from political, meaning non-commercial, risks they may face abroad. PRI is a financial product like any other kind of insurance. In exchange for the payment of regular premiums based on the level of perceived danger in the host state, the insured party will be covered by the insurer for losses suffered in the event that something goes wrong in relation to excessive governmental interference. There may also be a deductible or excess payable by the insured in order to spread the risk between the investor and the PRI provider. By paying out the amount of an investor's loss resulting from various kinds of regulatory interference by host states (not due to commercial problems such as poor sales), PRI can lessen the likelihood that the investor will suffer from injuries which are beyond their control. It can also be helpful in situations where host states are insolvent and therefore cannot pay out awards against them issued by ISDS tribunals. In addition to paying premiums and any deductibles/excess, the investor will have to satisfy the conditions specified in the various PRI package's terms and conditions. Private insurance packages can offer PRI products. PRI may be offered by national or bilateral guarantee programmes from home states, with the US OPIC being the best known example. One of the chief providers of PRI is the World Bank's MIGA.

MIGA was created by convention in 1988 to provide guarantees against non-commercial risks faced by investors operating in developing states as a way of raising investment levels in the world's poorest countries. As outlined in the MIGA Convention, the PRI offered by MIGA covers four main categories of behaviour by host states. These are host country restrictions of currency transfers, expropriation, breach of contract and war or civil disturbance.[20] Only investments that contribute to the host country's development and are in conformity with its national laws are eligible for MIGA protection, as ascertained by MIGA itself.[21] It is believed that MIGA prefers to extend PRI insurance to investments which are covered by an IIA, presumably because IIAs are thought to mitigate risk and also because the subrogation provisions in these instruments would allow MIGA to recover its losses via claims against the host state through the ISDS provisions in such instruments. MIGA (and the IFC) have policies of CSR for investors that use them, including requirements of environmental impact statements and public consultations for citizen groups that may be adversely affected by investment projects.

4.5 International Centre for the Settlement of Investment Disputes

ICSID's arbitration procedures were discussed at length in Chapter 8. It is important to emphasize that as part of the World Bank, ICSID's original (and arguably continuing) purpose was to foster FDI into the developing world as an aid to development. This is despite the fact that ICSID arbitration rules have been used for disputes involving investors in advanced economies. There is also the ongoing debate as to whether access to neutral arbitration has acted as an impetus for FDI in high risk countries. In this chapter it is useful to mention some of the governance aspects of ICSID in terms of its position within the World Bank.

The Chair of ICSID's Administrative Council is the World Bank president sitting in another capacity.[22] The Chair is a nonvoting member of the Administrative Council. Among the Chair's specified duties under the ICSID Convention is the resolution of certain disputes about asserted disqualifications of ICSID arbitrators. The duties of the Chair of the Administrative Council in-

---

[20] Art. 11.

[21] Art. 12.

[22] Art. 5 ICSID Convention.

clude: designating ten individuals to each of the ICSID Panels of Arbitrators and of Conciliators;[23] constituting conciliation commissions and arbitral tribunals in certain circumstances;[24] appointing *ad hoc* Committees for annulment proceedings;[25] deciding proposals to disqualify a sole arbitrator, a majority of a tribunal or a single member of a tribunal or commission where the other members are equally divided.[26] These are clearly highly significant functions for the president of the World Bank. Thankfully, such actions have often been guided by advice from the ICSID Secretary-General and the Secretariat.

5. WORLD BANK PANDEMIC BONDS

The World Bank's Pandemic Emergency Financing Facility (PEF) was created in 2016 to channel funding to developing countries facing the risk of a pandemic, meaning the outbreak of a serious disease across a large region. The PEF facility represents the first time that World Bank bonds have been used to finance efforts against infectious diseases. It is also the first time that the economic risks associated with pandemics in low income countries have been transferred to financial markets. The PEF is able to provide more than US$500 million to cover developing countries against the risk of pandemic outbreaks over a five-year period. It is funded through a combination of bonds and derivatives and future commitments from donor countries. Due to high demand for this kind of funding, the World Bank was able to price the bonds well below their original expected price. This enabled the facility to attract a wider, more diverse set of investors. The PEF covers six viruses that are most likely to cause a pandemic, among which are a new pandemic influenza virus, SARS and Ebola. PEF financing to eligible countries is instigated when an outbreak reaches predetermined levels of contagion, including number of deaths, the speed of the spread of the disease and when the disease crosses international borders. These determinations are made based on publicly available data as reported by the World Health Organization (WHO).[27] The PEF facility was tested recently when a severe attack of Ebola hit the Democratic Republic of Congo in 2017, becoming the second largest outbreak ever recorded. Despite its mandate, the PEF bonds have yet to pay out any money to investors. This is because of the requirement that in order for a country to achieve support from the PEF facility the disease must spread across an international border, which has so far not been the case.[28]

---

[23] Art. 14.

[24] Art. 30 and Art. 38 ICSID Convention, Art. 6 Arbitration (Additional Facility) Rules and Article 10 Conciliation (Additional Facility) Rules).

[25] Art. 52 ICSID Convention.

[26] Art. 58 ICSID Convention, Art. 15 Arbitration (Additional Facility) Rules and Art. 15 Conciliation (Additional Facility) Rules.

[27] 'World Bank Launches First-Ever Pandemic Bonds to Support $500 Million Pandemic Emergency Financing Facility', The World Bank (Washington, DC) (28 June 2017).

[28] K Allen, 'World Bank's "Pandemic Bonds" under Scrutiny after Failing to Pay Out on Ebola' Financial Times (21 February 2019).

6. WORLD BANK DISPUTE SETTLEMENT

There are two complaints systems available for third parties to challenge the manner in which World Bank funds have been dispersed in target states. These are the Inspection Panel for projects funded by the IBRD and the IDA, and the Office of the Compliance Advisor Ombudsman (CAO) for MIGA and the IFC. There is also an internal dispute settlement mechanism for disputes arising between the World Bank and its members. Each will be discussed briefly.

6.1 The Inspection Panel

Established in 1993, the Inspection Panel is an independent complaints mechanism for two or more people who believe that they have been, or are likely to be, adversely affected by a World Bank-funded project in a material way because of the Bank's failure to fulfil its own operational procedures. It covers the activities of the IBRD and the IDA. As such, the Inspection Panel is the World Bank's independent complaints mechanism. Its mandate is to ensure that stakeholders who may be adversely affected by Bank-financed projects are able to make their grievances known so as to ensure compliance with the Bank's policies concerning community engagement and account-ability. The types of complaint brought to the Inspection Panel includes issues such as adverse effects on people and livelihoods as a consequence of displacement and resettlement related to infrastructure projects, such as dams, roads, pipelines, mines and landfills. It may also evaluate risks to people and the environment related to dam safety, use of pesticides and other indirect effects of investments. The Panel is further responsive to the concerns faced by indigenous peoples, their culture, traditions, lands tenure and development rights. This could include adverse effects on physical cultural heritage, including sacred places as well as harm to natural habitats, including protected areas, such as wetlands, forests, and water bodies.

Although the Inspection Panel can issue decisions which carry legal consequences in terms of the Bank's behaviour, it is a nonjudicial body – its work is more accurately described as an administrative review which acts independently, impartially and objectively. In this respect, the Panel has the power to review Bank-funded projects and determine whether they comply with the World Bank's operational policies established to provide social and economic benefits and to avoid harm to people or to the environment. The Panel does not investigate or engage in fact finding unless it receives a formal, written request by an affected party.

The requesters need to show in writing that they live in the project area, or represent people who do, and have been or are likely to be adversely affected by project activities. Requesters must demonstrate that they believe that they may suffer actual or future harm resulting from a failure by the Bank to comply with its policies and procedures. Their concerns must have been brought to the attention of Bank management, and they are not satisfied with the outcome. Requests may be submitted in writing in any language with no specific form or format required. The request should be dated and signed by the requesters or their representative. It may be submitted via mail or electronically along with any supporting documentation. Requesters may ask for confidentiality in the handling of the request.

The Inspection Panel consists of three members appointed by the director of the World Bank for a term of five years. The biographies of the Panel members are available on the World Bank website, along with a list of former Panel members. Individuals have experience in development, however not all have legal qualifications. The Inspection Panel maintains a database of publicly available cases (130+), which are redacted to protect sensitive information. The Panel's deliberations, which are heavily fact-based rather than jurisprudential in nature, result in recommendations to the World Bank's Board of Directors. In the interests of transparency, the Panel also issues Annual Reports outlining some of the key cases during the year. Since Inspection Panel 'cases' are nonlegal in nature, it is unclear whether there is a specific standard of review which they implement when reviewing the actions of the World Bank or of its borrowers. For example, in a 2014 claim brought against the Bank for its funding of an education project in Armenian schools, the panel appeared to be working on a standard of 'material harm'. In that case the Panel was unable to find sufficient evidence that this standard had been breached and accordingly it did not recommend further investigation.[29]

6.2 Office of the Compliance Advisor Ombudsman

Complaints related to the projects supported by the IFC and MIGA are dealt with by the Office of the Compliance Advisor Ombudsman (CAO). Like the Inspection Panel, the CAO responds to complaints from project-affected communities with the objective of enhancing social and environmental outcomes in project-affected communities. The dispute resolution function of the CAO seeks to resolve grievances brought against private sector operators of projects which have received IFC or MIGA support. Dispute resolution processes typically involve alternative dispute resolution oriented methods, including mediation, joint fact finding, information sharing and facilitated dialogue. In the interests of transparency, the CAO maintains a database of all of its cases which are fully available on the internet, redacted to protect sensitive information.

The CAO does not make judgements about the merits of a complaint, nor does it impose solutions or find fault. Its objective is to help the parties play a lead role in identifying and implementing their own solutions. It also does not assess cases involving fraud, corruption or procurement irregularities, as these are directed to a specialist agency. There is a strict timeframe for the resolution of CAO complaints. The CAO inform complainants of the eligibility of their case within 15 working days. When a complaint is accepted for further assessment, the CAO has approximately 120 working days to conduct an assessment of the conflict and the stakeholders' alternatives for resolving the issues. This process is designed to clarify issues raised by the complainant, to gather information on how other stakeholders view the situation and to help the parties determine whether and how they may be able to resolve the complaint. CAO partners with neutral third party facilitators who are independent of the CAO and IFC/MIGA. CAO Dispute Resolution is confidentiality at the request of stakeholders. Based on the results of the assessment, the CAO specialists will work with the stakeholders to develop a jointly agreed process of assisted negotiation, mediation or other collaborative strategy for addressing issues raised in the complaint, or determine that a collaborative solution is not possible and transfer the case to CAO Compliance for appraisal of IFC's/MIGA's environmental and social performance. The World Bank's internal review mech-

---

[29] Report Number 89836 (1 August 2014).

anisms have been praised by commentators as embodying the rule of law in development finance. This has helped legitimize the organization as an instrument of global economic governance.[30]

6.3 Disputes against members by the Bank

The World Bank has some capacity to enforce the obligations of its members with respect to various obligations, including the use of loan funds. Along with this there is limited facility for dispute resolution between member states and the Bank (not among member states). These procedures are outlined in the IBRD Articles of Agreement, included here in relevant part:

Article VI (2) Suspension of Membership
If a member fails to fulfil any of its obligations to the Bank, the Bank may suspend its membership by decision of a majority of the Governors, exercising a majority of the total voting power. The member so suspended shall automatically cease to be a member one year from the date of its suspension unless a decision is taken by the same majority to restore the member to good standing. While under suspension, a member shall not be entitled to exercise any rights under this Agreement, except the right of withdrawal, but shall remain subject to all obligations.

Article IX: Interpretation
(a) Any question of interpretation of the provisions of this Agreement arising between any member and the Bank or between any members of the Bank shall be submitted to the Executive Directors for their decision. If the question particularly affects any member not entitled to appoint an Executive Director, it shall be entitled to representation in accordance with Article V, Section 4 (h).
(b) In any case where the Executive Directors have given a decision under (a) above, any member may require that the question be referred to the Board of Governors, whose decision shall be final. Pending the result of the reference to the Board, the Bank may, so far as it deems necessary, act on the basis of the decision of the Executive Directors.
(c) Whenever a disagreement arises between the Bank and a country which has ceased to be a member, or between the Bank and any member during the permanent suspension of the Bank, such disagreement shall be submitted to arbitration by a tribunal of three arbitrators, one appointed by the Bank, another by the country involved and an umpire who, unless the parties otherwise agree, shall be appointed by the President of the Permanent Court of International Justice or such other authority as may have been prescribed by regulation adopted by the Bank. The umpire shall have full power to settle questions of procedure in any case where the parties are in disagreement with respect thereto.

There are no records kept of the outcomes of such arbitrations which are available for public viewing on the World Bank website, nor does the World Bank list countries which have faced suspension. It

---

[30] C Yifeng, 'International Organizations and Strategies of Self-Legitimization: The Example of the World Bank Anti-Corruption Sanctions Regime' 13:3 Manchester Journal of International Economic Law 314 (2016).

might be expected that arbitration facilities such as the Stockholm Chamber of Commerce or the International Chamber of Commerce could be used in conjunction with this arbitration procedure.

7. REGIONAL DEVELOPMENT BANKS

There are several regional development banks which perform a similar function to that of the World Bank and are therefore relevant to the developmental component of international economic law. The leading ones will now be considered.

7.1 Asian Development Bank

The ADB was created in the early 1960s as a regional financial institution designed to foster economic growth and cooperation in one of the poorest regions in the world. The ADB assists its members by providing loans, equity investments, grants and technical assistance advisory services to promote social and economic development. With its head office in Manila, Philippines, the ADB is composed of 68 members, 49 of which are from the Asia and Pacific region. In partnership with its member governments and other financial institutions, the ADB is focused on supporting projects in developing member countries that create lasting economic and development impact. The ADB also provides direct assistance to private enterprises of developing member countries through equity investments and loans. The operational priorities of the ADB are addressing remaining poverty and reducing inequality, gender equality, climate change and environmental sustainability, improving quality of life in cities, promoting rural development and food security, strengthening governance and institutional capacity and fostering regional cooperation and integration. The ADB's funding is derived from bond issues on the world's capital markets as well as members' contributions, retained earnings from its lending operations and the repayment of loans. As of 2017, the ADB's total operations amounted to US$32.2 billion, consisting of US$20.1 billion in loans, grants and investments from its own resources, including nonsovereign operations of US$2.3 billion; US$11.9 billion in co-financing from bilateral and multilateral agencies and other financing partners; and US$201 million in technical assistance.

There are two levels of evaluation of ADB supported projects. The first is self-evaluation, which is conducted by those responsible for designing and implementing a country strategy, programme or project. The second is independent evaluation undertaken by the Independent Evaluation Department (IED). The IED independently evaluates the implementation of ADB policies, strategies, operations and special concerns that relate to organizational and operational effectiveness.

Additionally, the ADB's Accountability Mechanism provides a forum where people adversely affected by ADB-assisted projects can voice and seek solutions to their problems and report alleged noncompliance with ADB's operational policies and procedures. It consists of two separate but complementary functions: a problem solving function and a compliance review function. The objective of this mechanism is to ensure that the ADB is accountable to people for the projects which it assists. The Accountability Mechanism has two separate offices: the Office of the Special Project Facilitator (SPF) and the Office of the Compliance Review Panel (CRP). The SPF and CRP work jointly in conducting outreach activities aimed at making the mechanism better known and understood both within and outside ADB. They support the SPF and CRP in carrying out the separate functions of problem solving and compliance review. The CRP focuses on ADB's accountability as to whether it has or has not complied with its operational policies and procedures that affect or may affect local people directly, materially and adversely.

Compliance review begins with the CRP determining the eligibility of a request for compliance review and recommending that the ADB Board of Directors authorize a compliance review. If approved, the CRP conducts an independent investigation and makes recommendations to the ADB's Board of Directors to ensure project compliance, including remedial changes in the scope or implementation of the project. The CRP then monitors the implementation of its recommendations and any remedial actions approved by the Board of Directors. The CRP consists of three members – a full-time Chair and two part-time members. Two CRP members are from regional member countries, with one of them from a developing member country, and the third member is from a nonregional country. The CRP reports directly to the Board on all activities except two specific ones, where it reports to the Board Compliance Review Committee.

7.2 European Bank for Reconstruction and Development

Founded in 1991 and headquartered in London, UK, the European Bank for Reconstruction and Development (EBRD) was established to herald a post-Cold War era in central and eastern Europe, furthering progress towards market-oriented economies and the promotion of private and entrepreneurial initiative. As a development bank, the EBRD provides financing for investment projects and business advisory services including economic forecasting. The EBRD is active in 38 countries across three continents and in operations across a range of industries, including infrastructure, agriculture and climate finance. Prospective clients must demonstrate that their proposed project or business meets the minimum requirements to be eligible to be considered for EBRD involvement. The EBRD also regularly works on policy reform with governments, business leaders and regional officials with a view to implementing policies which improve economic conditions.

EBRD financing for private sector projects ranges from US$5 million to US$250 million and consists of loans or equity. Smaller projects may be financed through financial intermediaries or through special programmes for smaller direct investments in less advanced countries. Small and medium sized enterprises can receive EBRD assistance through financial intermediaries. The EBRD's Policy and Partnerships department is responsible for leading the coordination of strategies, policies and related initiatives supporting the Bank's developmental mandate. It is also charged with the mobilization and management of donor funds and for the oversight of the EBRD's engagement with key external stakeholders and organizations.

The EBRD maintains an independent Evaluation Department to assess the performance of the Bank's completed projects and programmes relative to objectives. The central objective of evaluation is to contribute to the Bank's legitimacy and relevance and to its superior institutional performance. To achieve its core objective, the Evaluation Department fulfils two primary functions. First, it provides a critical instrument of accountability through objective, evidence-based performance assessment of outputs and outcomes relative to targets. Second, it contributes to institutional learning for future operations by presenting operationally useful findings. Reports produced by the Evaluation Department aim to identify objectives and results relating to project outputs (the products, capital goods and services which result from an operation), outcomes (the short and medium term effects directly attributable to outputs) and impacts (the positive or negative long term effects to which an operation contributes, directly or indirectly, intended or unintended). Evaluation reports are publicly available on the EBRD website.

The EBRD established the Office of the Chief Compliance which is responsible for reviewing procedures governing the ethical behaviour of Bank officials, employees and consultants. This office conducts investigations on alleged staff misconduct. It also sets the standards of integrity that the Bank expects of its business partners. This body appears to have a rather narrow, corruption-oriented focus. Results of these investigations are not readily available on the EBRD website.

7.3 Inter-American Development Bank

The IADB provides developmental finance with a view to reducing poverty and improving living standards in Latin America and the Caribbean. It consists of 48 member countries and is headquartered in Washington, DC. The IADB has operations in 26 borrowing member countries, with regional and regional offices in Asia and Europe. The main aims of the IADB are to improve health, education and infrastructure through financial and technical support for sovereign countries. Created in 1959, the IADB is the leading source of development finance for the region, providing loans, grants and technical assistance. Like most development banks, the IADB seeks to achieve measurable results with high standards of integrity, transparency and accountability. The Bank's current focus areas include social inclusion and equality, productivity and innovation and economic integration. There are also aims relating to gender equality and diversity, climate change and environmental sustainability, institutional capacity and the rule of law. IADB clients include central governments, provinces, municipalities and NGOs. Its approved lending totalled US$11.4 billion in 2017.

The evaluation of projects undertaken by the IADB is a shared responsibility between management, through the Board of Directors, and the Office of Evaluation and Oversight (OVE). Management focuses on project evaluations and monitoring portfolio performance. Independent of management, the OVE's activities include ensuring that strategies, policies and programmes comply with the IADB's objectives and mandates. The OVE oversees the Bank's internal monitoring mechanisms and conducts *ex post* project evaluations.

Additionally, the Independent Consultation and Investigation Mechanism (MICI) is a grievance mechanism available to groups of individuals or communities who may be adversely impacted by IADB-financed operations due to the Bank's potential noncompliance with its own operational policies. The goal of the MICI is to ensure that the operations financed by the IADB meet the high standards of social and environmental sustainability. The MICI process includes two phases: a consultation phase that provides parties the opportunity to address requesters' concerns in a voluntary, flexible and collaborative manner; and a compliance review phase that enables requesters to ask for an investigation of a Bank-financed operation. This latter stage has the objective of establishing whether the Bank has failed to comply with any of its relevant operational policies and whether that has caused harm to requesters. Complaints may be submitted directly to the organization through the website, which contains a database of cases.

7.4 African Development Bank

Founded in 1964, the AfDB is a regional development bank comprising 80 member countries, with its head office in Tunis, Tunisia. The primary objective of the AfDB Group is to support sustainable economic development and social progress in its regional member countries, contributing to poverty reduction. This is achieved by mobilizing and allocating resources for investment in member countries and providing policy advice and technical assistance to support development efforts. The AfDB adheres to its Sustainable Development Goals, which include ending hunger, promoting gender equality and reducing inequality generally, sustainable management of resources (especially water), responsible agriculture, the expansion of infrastructure, access to energy, the promotion of health, combating climate change and the preservation of ecosystems.

Recognizing the deficiency of infrastructure in Africa, the Bank has made significant contributions in this policy area and remains a key priority. The Bank also seeks to play a leading role in fostering Africa's economic integration to create larger, more attractive markets, to link landlocked countries, including fragile states, to international markets and to support intra-African trade. Working both directly and indirectly with governments, the Bank aims to facilitate private investment in Africa. It seeks to support private sector investment in Africa by delivering finance and providing advice and technical assistance. The Bank further aims to foster African entrepreneurship by supporting micro, small and medium enterprises. The promotion of better governance and risk management of financial institutions is also key to the AfDB's strategy. The Bank assists in the establishment of institutions that support inclusion and promote accountability, such as through strengthening the capacities of parliamentarians, the media and civil society organizations. To address unemployment and increase the supply of skilled workers, the Bank supports technical and vocational training linked to specific needs in the labour market.

The AfDB's Development Effectiveness Reviews, designed to monitor project outcomes, consist of a series of publications which assesses the AfDB's contribution to the fulfilment of development goals. It is considered to be a management tool designed to help the organization improve in the delivery of its mandate and to provide full transparency and accountability to member countries. There is also an Independent Review Mechanism (IRM) within the AfDB which was established in 2004 for the purpose of providing people adversely affected by a project financed by the Bank with an independent mechanism through which they can request that the Bank complies with its own policies and procedures. The mechanism is available when two or more affected persons believe that the Bank has failed to comply with any of its policies and procedures and that this failure has adversely affected them, or threatens to. Recommendations from the IRM are distributed to the Bank's staff, its members and the general public with a view to achieving full transparency and accountability.

7.5 The New Development Bank

The New Development Bank, or NDB – also known as the BRICS Bank – was created in 2015 by the BRICS consortium (Brazil, Russia, India, China and South Africa). Since it lacks a distinct regional focus, the NDB might be more properly termed a multilateral development bank. The aim of the NDB is to provide development assistance in member countries through support to public and private projects. The NDB is positioned as an alternative to both the World Bank and the IMF. The NDB operates with a one vote, one share system of governance (unlike the IMF/WB). Despite having operated for a few years now, it is still unclear how the NDB will be different from the IMF/WB in terms of the types of loans which it extends and the conditions it places on them. In 2016–17, the Board of Directors of the NDB approved loans involving financial assistance of more than US$3.4 billion for projects in the areas of green and renewable energy, transportation, water sanitation, irrigation and other areas. In 2019 the NDB instigated a bond programme denominated in Chinese yuan, the so-called Panda Bonds. Under the programme, the NDB is able to issue yuan bonds in an aggregate amount of 10 billion yuan issued within two years of the programme registration date.

In efforts to combat corruption, the NDM operates 'whistleblower' procedures based on the International Financial Institutions Anti-Corruption Task Force. The requirement for reporting instances of noncompliance with the Bank's policies and procedures to its Compliance Division is part of its Anti-Corruption, Anti-Fraud and Anti-Money Laundering policies and its Code of Business Conduct and Ethics. The policies provide that any Bank staff who observe an act of misconduct in the Bank's operation have an obligation to report such information to the Compliance Division immediately. The Compliance Division receives complaints from the public regarding corruption of fraudulent practices including money laundering in relation to NDB-financed projects or against NDB staff.

8. THE ASIAN INFRASTRUCTURE INVESTMENT BANK

Analogous to the NDB in that it is intended to function as a complement to the Western-dominated IMF/WB regime, the Asian Infrastructure Investment Bank (AIIB) is a multilateral development bank with a regional focus created in 2016 to improve social and economic outcomes in its member countries. The AIIB is often associated with funding for China's ambitious and controversial One Belt One Road initiative, through which it aims to expand its connectivity with Asia and Europe through road, rail and sea infrastructure as well as improved telecommunications over a period of several decades.[31] In fact, most of the financing for this project has come from China itself. Headquartered in Beijing, the AIIB began operations in January 2016 and has grown to 93 approved members worldwide. The UK was a founding member of the AIIB, despite US misgivings. Membership now includes Russia and India as well as developed countries such as Australia, New Zealand and Canada. The US and Japan have not joined, remaining suspicious of the AIIB's role in China's geopolitical ambitions. The current president of the AIIB is Jin Liqun, a Chinese national and former high-ranking World Bank manager.

AIIB has a single funding stream for both sovereign and private projects, providing it with greater flexibility to assist projects by sovereign states, state owned enterprises and private entities.[32]

---

[31] J Chaisse and M Matsushita, 'China's "Belt and Road" Initiative: Mapping the World Trade Normative and Strategic Implications' 52:1 Journal of World Trade 163 (2018).

[32] G Sanders, 'Financing of Investment Projects at the AIIB: Institutional Set-up and First Experiences' 14:2 Manchester Journal of International Economic Law 262 (2017).

The AIIB has three thematic priorities: sustainable infrastructure, cross-country connectivity and private capital mobilization. The AIIB has expressed its approach to development as 'lean, clean and green', meaning that it will have a tight budget, focus on openness, transparency and accountability and pursue environmental sustainability. It has also heavily emphasized combating corruption. It anticipates significant engagement with other institutions (IMF, OECD) as well as academia, sponsoring an annual conference and journal. The AIIB seeks to finance infrastructure in a broad sense including internet-based information infrastructure as this is seen as vital to the modern digital economy.[33] It expects to facilitate international production capacity cooperation while meeting Asian infrastructure investment demands in conjunction with the highly anticipated One Belt One Road, which contemplates land-based transportation links to western Asia. The AIIB aims to finance a Belt and Road project only if commitments for high standards are made, especially those regarding environmental sustainability.

The AIIB generally operates by consensus decision making. However, where consensus has not been achieved, a 75 per cent affirmative vote has been applied. It is thought that such qualification to full consensus decision making has contributed to the rapid responsiveness of the AIIB, in contrast to some of the other development banks. Still, China possesses 26.06 per cent of the Bank's total voting power, which means that it has *de facto* veto power over important issues, such as decisions on the size of the Board of Directors, the election of the president, and the amendment of the Articles of Agreement, all of which require a supermajority vote. The AIIB has a nonresident director system which means that the Bank's 12 directors need not reside in the headquarters in Beijing, allowing them to participate in decision making remotely. It is thought that this will also encourage the delegation of some decision making functions, improving the efficiency in the Bank's overall management.

In terms of dispute settlement and the enforcement of its members' obligations, Article 38 of the AIIB Articles of Agreement specifies the disciplinary actions which may be taken against members.

1. If a member fails to fulfil any of its obligations to the Bank, the Board of Governors may suspend such member by a Super Majority vote as provided in Article 28.
2. The member so suspended shall automatically cease to be a member one (1) year from the date of its suspension, unless the Board of Governors decides by a Super Majority vote as provided in Article 28 to restore the member to good standing.
3. While under suspension, a member shall not be entitled to exercise any rights under this Agreement, except the right of withdrawal, but shall remain subject to all its obligations.

Article 54 on interpretation of the Articles of Agreement is taken word for word from that of the World Bank's Articles of Agreement. Questions regarding interpretation of the Articles of Agreement arising from disputes between members of the Bank will be submitted to the Board of Directors. Disagreements resulting from decisions of the Board of Directors between a member and a country which has ceased to be a member may be submitted to arbitration. The AIIB has a fraud and corruption reporting facility but does not have a complaint mechanism/ombudsman regarding the implementation of its policies in specific projects, as is common in other development banks.

---

[33] B Gu, 'Chinese Multilateralism in the AIIB' 20:1 Journal of International Economic Law 137 (2017).

A complaints handling mechanism, perhaps along the lines of the World Bank's Inspection Panel, has been proposed for the AIIB but has not yet been forthcoming.

9. CONCLUSION

This chapter illustrated how the World Bank seeks to advance the goal of economic development among the poorer countries in the world through the provision of long term loans designed to enhance infrastructure with a view to attracting private sector investment. This is also fostered by World Bank loans to companies and through the provision of PRI, as well as dispute settlement through ICSID. Much like the IMF, the work of the World Bank has been the subject of criticism, with some arguing that it has done more harm than good and that its loan conditionality is often poorly designed. This chapter also noted how these activities are complemented by the work of regional development banks and the new, still largely unknown AIIB. This chapter began by returning to the WTO, which, although not strictly speaking a development organization, has instigated a number of vital policies intended to ensure that the benefits of free trade are more widely shared across the global community.

DISCUSSION QUESTIONS

1. Does the WTO pay sufficient regard to the interests of its developing country members? How might it do so more effectively?
2. To what extent do the World Bank's loan conditionality requirements reflect the dominance of a market-oriented ideology and is this problematic?
3. Is political risk insurance an effective alternative to ISDS, and, if so, under what circumstances?
4. To what extent do the regional development banks and the new Asian Infrastructure Investment Bank complement the work of the World Bank?

FURTHER READING

K Crow, 'The Concept of "Development" in International Economic Law Three Definitions and an Inquiry into Origin' 14:2 Manchester Journal of International Economic Law 169 (2017).

B Gu, 'Chinese Multilateralism in the AIIB' 20:1 Journal of International Economic Law 137 (2017).

T Karagöz, 'The Influence of Investor-Centered Values in the Operation of Political Risk Insurance' 19:1 Journal of World Investment and Trade 118 (2018).

Z Xiangchen, X Qingjun, W Jinyong, 'Capacity Constraint: A Fundamental Perspective for the Development Issue at WTO' 53:1 Journal of World Trade 1 (2019).

Index